THIS ALMOST CHOSEN PEOPLE

THIS
ALMOST CHOSEN
PEOPLE

Essays in

The History of American Ideas

by

RUSSEL B. *Blaine* NYE

MICHIGAN STATE UNIVERSITY PRESS

For
John A. Hannah
In recognition of his twenty-fifth year as
President of Michigan State University

Acknowledgments

I<small>T IS</small> manifestly impossible to acknowledge indebtedness to all those whose specialized scholarship has made this survey of these broad conceptual categories possible. As part payment of the debt, and as a guide to the reader who wishes to go behind generalizations, I have listed the majority of these studies at the close of each essay. Like any one who ploughs in these fields, I have particular indebtedness to Merle Curti, Denis Brogan, Henry Steele Commager, Stow Persons, Harry Hayden Clark, and the late Carl Becker. I am also particularly beholden to my colleague Walter Adams for his comments on portions of the manuscript, and to Lyle Blair for useful suggestions. This is also the place to express my appreciation to the Humanities, Social Science, and Reference divisional staffs of the Michigan State University Library for their invaluable help in gathering materials.

Russel B. Nye

East Lansing, Michigan

Contents

I shall be most happy indeed if I shall be an humble instrument in the hands of the Almighty, and of this, his almost chosen people.

—ABRAHAM LINCOLN, Speech to the New Jersey Senate, February 21, 1861

On my first arrival. . . , I found that there was a great deal to reflect upon and to investigate, and that America and the American people were an enigma.

—CAPTAIN FREDERICK MARRYAT
Diary in America, (1839)

A Prefatory Note
to the Reader

A NATION is, in many ways, a product of its ideology. Ideas provide necessary forces in the making of civilizations and express that complex of motives within which a people live, think, and move. To search out and describe some of these ideas which have informed the American style is the aim of the collection of essays which follows. The point is not to determine, first or last, simply the validity of these ideas alone. It is rather to show how they have given an ideological backbone to American thought and activity and to sketch out some of the changes these basic cultural presuppositions have undergone from their beginnings to the present. Gunnar Myrdal, a most perceptive analyst of American life, has put it well in *The American Dilemma*:

America, compared to every other country in Western civilization, has the most explicitly expressed system of general ideals in reference to human interrelationships. This body of ideals is more widely understood and appreciated than similar ideals are anywhere else. The American Creed is not merely—as in some other countries—the implicit background of the nation's political and judicial order as it functions. . . . It is the cement in the structure of this great and disparate nation.

There is no attempt here to be definitive. The configurations of the American character have been shaped and its course of action determined by more ideas—some more acts of faith, perhaps than ideas—than any single attempt to delineate them could possibly include. Arthur O. Lovejoy, for example, once identified sixty-five different meanings for the word *nature* alone, so that no historian of ideas need ever suffer from the illusion of conclusiveness.

These essays touch no more than a small segment of the perimeter of a great uncharted expanse of American intellectual history. The present aim has been, rather, to choose a few of those concepts which have influenced—and which have been influenced by—the American experience, and to show how they have begun, developed, matured, and changed, suggesting in the process something as to the place of these ideas in the total pattern of the American mind.

I

The American Idea
of Progress

Americans still believe that somehow and sometime
something better will happen to good Americans
than has happened to men in any other country.

—HERBERT CROLY

J. B. BURY'S DEFINITION of the theory of progress has become
classic; that is, the belief that "civilization has moved, is
moving, and will move in a desirable direction." This belief
in progress derives from the conviction that man, through his
natural faculties and merits, can always achieve conditions of
existence more satisfying to him, and can always subdue nature
and himself to serve his ends. The doctrine of progress has
taken two historical forms. One is based on the assumption
that if the obstacles to man's advancement are removed, and
the flaws in his institutions corrected, progress will be swift
and sure; otherwise it is slow, even uncertain. Thus the
eighteenth century, in abolishing political and ecclesiastical
authoritarianism, predicted a great leap ahead for mankind,
while the nineteenth saw the key to progress in science and its
applications to human problems. The other form assumes
progress to be inevitable, slowed perhaps by man's follies and
the defects of his institutions, but so deeply imbedded in the
nature of things that it will continue to operate regardless of

man's efforts. The one belief is purposive, active; the other passive, dependent on natural law. Americans have, at different times, accepted both.

The belief that man moves always toward a better world is no doubt as old as man and certainly, in the Western world, as old as the Greeks. It received its modern articulation during the seventeenth and eighteenth centuries, growing out of the Enlightenment's belief in rationalism and its faith in man's perfectibility. Before the theory of progress could take this modern form, however, the view of the theologians that this world was merely a transition to another, was replaced by the view that man's happiness was available here and now as well as hereafter. If, as Locke said, evil and error came from institutions, and ignorance was the great foe of progress, it seemed likely that man could better himself and his state by educating his reason and repairing his institutions so that they aided rather than impeded his progress. If social problems originated from an imperfect society, then their solution lay in eradicating that society and substituting a better one for it.

The doctrine of progress in this fashion took on revolutionary connotations in the eighteenth century; it represented a clean, distinct break with the past and the status quo. It also attained a kind of theological status, representing God's plan for mankind, and evidence of His reason and beneficence. The continental philosophers, especially, seized upon the idea with enthusiasm. Herder, in 1774, believed that "genuine progress, constant development, even if no individual gain anything thereby, this is the purpose of God in History." Condorcet, in his *History of the Progress of the Human Spirit* (1794) hoped to show, he said,

by reasoning and by facts, that there is no limit set to the perfecting of the powers of man; that human perfectibility is in reality indefinite; that the progress of this perfectibility, henceforth independent of any power that might wish to stop it, has no other limit than the duration of the globe upon which nature has placed us.

This concept of progress, as it took shape in the eighteenth century, found ardent supporters in America. America was a new country, a blank tablet on which men could write what they wished, with none of the prejudices and faults of the old world to cloud their minds. The American colonists were building a new society from which all the flaws and inequalities of Europe could be erased; none of the old institutions of feudalism—primogeniture, entail, monarchy, the church-state, hereditary aristocracy, and so on—were successfully transplanted to the New World. There, Thomas Paine felt, men could take a fresh start in a new setting where education might vanquish ignorance, science disease, and government injustice. The idea that men could shape their world for the best was especially appealing to Americans, who believed that they already had done a good deal toward accomplishing exactly that.

The Revolution marked a great step forward in the acceptance of the doctrine of progress in America, for it seemed to those who led it that it meant the creation of a new kind of government, unique in the history of the world, based on natural law. The rapid growth of the new nation and its apparently limitless resources for further growth encouraged even greater optimism. The frontier and the relatively open society of the new country allowed each man to believe that he could improve his condition and make his fortune by his own efforts; the promise of reward if he did so was neither remote nor small. The prospect of abounding opportunity that characterized the America of the latter decades of the eighteenth century stimulated the trend toward making the idea of progress a national principle. Americans believed implicitly what Condorcet's book explained: that mankind had passed through nine epochs of civilization, each better than the last, and that the tenth, soon to come, would be by far the best of all. The conditions under which they lived tended to support this view, and to indicate that their epoch might be that fortunate tenth.

The eighteenth century's belief in progress was founded first of all upon a powerful conviction of human worth and perfectibility. Condorcet, for example, believed that the human species can be improved, firstly, by new discoveries in the arts and sciences, and, consequently, in the means of well-being and common property; secondly, by progress in the principles of conduct and moral practice; and thirdly by the improvement of human faculty.

The agent in each case was human reason, the power which provided both the instrument and substance of improvement. If there was unanimity among American commentators on human nature, it was on the concept of man's perfectibility through reason. In this they resembled the French, rather than the British philosophers. To the majority of British thinkers of the Enlightenment, the terms *progress* and *perfectibility* had a much more tentative and limited meaning than they had in France or in America. Excellence, in the British interpretation, consisted of conforming to a universal norm, the same for all rational beings. Progress—if it could be called such—was possible only in the sense of restoring men and corrupt institutions to agreement with that norm. The vision of a steady inexorable upward march toward perfection occurred chiefly to Frenchmen such as Turgot, Helvetius, and Condorcet, and to only a few self-assured Englishmen, such as William Godwin, who wrote in 1793, "The vices and moral weaknesses of man are not invincible; man is perfectible, or in other words, susceptible of perpetual improvement."

American thinkers tended to agree with Godwin. Jefferson felt that "no definite limits can be assigned to the improveability of the human race," whereas Joel Barlow's "Columbiad" (1806) was a rimed paean to progress. "All things in the physical world," Barlow once wrote, "as well as the moral and intellectual world, are progressive in nature." John Adams, though less sanguine about the potentials of human nature, agreed that there was "hope for splendid improvements in human society, and vast amelioration in the condition of mankind." Franklin, impressed by "the growing felicity of mankind, the improvement in philosophy, morals, politics, and even the conveniences of common living," wished it had been his destiny "to be born two or three centuries hence." "It is impossible to imagine," he wrote to his scientist friend Joseph Priestley, "the Height to which may be carried, in a thousand years, the Power of Man over Matter." Priestley, the English refugee scientist who came to America in 1791 to stay, believed that "the human species itself is capable of a similar and unbounded improvement; whereby mankind in a later age are greatly superior to mankind in a former age." George Washington admitted to a "fond, perhaps an enthusiastic idea, that the world is much less barbarous than it has been, its melioration must still be progressive," and James Wilson of Pennsylvania concluded that "We have more and better things before us, than all that we have yet acquired or enjoyed."

Surveying the past, observing man's steady advance from savagery to civilization and his expanding mastery over nature, the men of the later eighteenth century found ample—though sometimes qualified—proof that there really did exist in man and the universe an inherent drive toward betterment. They thought that they possessed, through their reason, the beginnings of a method to improve humanity more swiftly and effectively than ever before. The Enlightenment believed it knew a great deal about man and nature; because of this its philosophers hoped to discover an orderly way of directing man's progress, and of making use of the forces of nature and human nature to do it. They felt that every human problem was answerable to human intelligence and amenable to a rational solution. Whatever the frailties of humanity, the Enlightenment believed that men were educable. "Many people lead bad lives," remarked Franklin, "that would gladly lead good ones, but know not *how* to make the change." This *how* was the key to progress. The rate of advancement, as men gradually solved their problems, could be measured by reference to his degree of control over nature; advances in his social relations; and improvements in his own moral and intellectual makeup.

At this point, however, the philosophers of progress met two stumbling blocks—the Calvinistic doctrine of a stable universe and fixed human nature, controlled only by God; and the Chain-of-Being design of an orderly hierarchical universe in which any major change was unthinkable. The Calvinist's belief in the essential depravity of human nature failed to support any faith in progress—except by virtue of God's explicit Providence, which was certainly not within man's control. If men were wholly subject to God's power, there was no reason to suppose that they could direct or control their affairs in any meaningful way. Even Franklin wondered if progress were possible at all until "men would cease to be wolves to one another," a state of affairs he doubted would soon arrive. The Chain-of-Being concept, an integral part of the seventeenth- and eighteenth-century view of the universe, conceived human nature to be constant and the universe a closed system of order and law. This view carried with it the corollary of staticism, for if, as Pope said,

> Order is Heavn's first law, and this confest,
> Some are and must be greater than the rest,

all things had stations within the hierarchy and presumably should remain in them. The principle of stability, inherent in the Calvinistic-Newtonian scheme, pointed in one direction. The principle of change, inherent in the idea of progress and inspired by the conviction that man, by use of his reason, could make himself and his world better pointed in another.

Here the American experience itself helped to provide an answer. It was not easy to persuade Americans who had wrested a civilization out of the wilderness and who were at the moment building a nation where none had existed, that progress was impossible—at least in the United States. They had accomplished a great deal toward improving their world, and they had the evidence around them to prove it, for they had no doubts whatever but that the United States was better than anything that had ever gone before, quite possibly the best that would ever be as it continued to improve. Jefferson, in his later years, saw the great march of progress "passing over us like a cloud of light," and so did many others of his generation. If it were possible to create better institutions (as Americans had) it must be equally possible to make better men. The majority of Americans could simply not agree with Pope's "Whatever is, is right," since they were making "what is" better—nor did they feel that Pope and the Enlightenment had ever properly considered the potential of American society.

Timothy Dwight of Yale, who was certainly no radical and who hated French philosophy like poison, illustrated this basic contradiction in American thought. Dwight considered human nature thoroughly untrustworthy; yet a deep faith in progress, *American* progress, threaded through his whole intellectual life. In the first flush of enthusiasm over Cornwallis' surrender he expressed a firm belief in "the tendency of human affairs, unless interrupted by extraordinary events, to be constantly progressive toward what may be termed natural perfection." Thirty years of American history may have tempered his enthusiasm but did not change his mind. Late in life he wrote, "The melioration of our character will undoubtedly make a slow progress, yet I believe it is really progressive."

Certainly Dwight, like many others, was aware of the difficulty of holding two contradictory views at the same time, but like the others he was little bothered by it. Belief in progress ran through the early years of the United States as a consistent theme. William Ellery Channing, who belonged to the next generation, echoed it in 1824 in words that might as easily have been written in 1774 or 1794: "If there be one striking feature in human nature, it is the susceptibleness of improvement."

The United States took shape at a particular moment in history when Americans shared certain portions of the common heritage of British and European culture and ideas. But the fact that American culture and thought developed within an *American* environment influenced that heritage even as the new nation derived from it. American conditions were different, sometimes in kind, sometimes in degree. What happened in America happened in a new, comparatively isolated, frontier nation with a brief history and shallow roots. The new country had no hereditary monarchy or aristocracy, no feudal past, no entrenched state church, no absolute caste system, and after 1776 not even a "tyrant." The country began with an achieved liberation and a firm belief in progress.

The eighteenth-century American's belief in progress presupposed a world improved by reason and the grace of God. This forward movement was a slow, inevitable, divinely-ordained perfection. Men could hasten it by revising their ideas and institutions, but not by much. The drive for betterment, the philosophers of the period thought, was inherent in the nature of life. The universal perfection of which the eighteenth century dreamed, however, was the ultimate substance of things hoped for, to be approached a step at a time as divinity willed it. The "Melioration" of man's problems, to use a favorite contemporary term, *would* come. Men should do nothing to impede it, of course, but whether or not, progress was part of a huge cyclic change, a wave in the tide of affairs that could neither be stopped nor diverted.

After the turn of the nineteenth century, the American idea of progress became much more kinetic and positive. The nineteenth century believed that men could so manipulate their society that progress could be materially hastened. They concluded that social change was not simply a series of events, arranged by chronology, that shifted the direction of some institutions, but they believed that they could also change the character and quality of those institutions to make them new and different in kind and result. It was a rule of nature, wrote Emerson, that it "slept no moment of an old past, but every hour repaired itself and improvement was its law." Man was also equally improveable, for he was endowed with reason, will, and conscience, inwardly impelled by God's decree to seek betterment. "We learn that the highest is present in the soul of man," Emerson noted. "Who can set bounds to the possibilities of man?"

There were good reasons, American thinkers of the opening decades of the nineteenth century assumed, for believing that the rate of man's advancement could be spectacularly accelerated, and they saw evidence, as they looked around them, that this was exactly what was happening. Conditions of life had improved visibly over the preceding century; economic standards were higher, scientific discoveries more numerous, technological advances easily noticeable. Advances in machinery had transformed the physical aspects of living and had reduced much of its drudgery and danger. Education and social improvements were on the way to reducing poverty, ignorance, and crime—or so it seemed. The peace that followed the War of 1812, and the obvious success of the great American political experiments of 1776 and 1787 lent further proof to progress far beyond what the eighteenth century had dreamed of. The philosophers were certain that men had discovered new ways of perceiving truth, by way of the inward intuition—that faculty identified by Emerson and the transcendentalists as the great primal reason that made God's truth available immediately to man.

During the first half of the nineteenth century the doctrine of progress took on a new kind of emotional validity for American thinkers that it had not had before. "No word in the English language," said a writer in *The Southern Quarterly Review* in 1854, "is so much used as the disyllable progress. In America we use it so much, that we have made a verb of it." Progress, it was assumed, was an inexorable law of history; mankind advanced always toward perfection, sometimes stumbling and sometimes losing his way for the moment, but he always moved ahead, improving himself and his world. The impediments he encountered were surmountable; he contained within himself the elements of his ultimate success. He was by no means a helpless sinner in the hands of a Calvinist God, but a self-reliant, free-standing individual, capable of making choices to his own benefit. John O'Sullivan summarized it superbly in an editorial for *The United States Magazine and Democratic Review* in 1840:

In all history . . ., the reflecting mind can observe the operation of one mighty principle. On all is written the great Law of Progress. This is indeed the distinguishing mark of our species, obviously dividing it from the beasts that perish. One after another the generations may pass from the stage of action . . ., empires may sink in ruin, and whole nations be swept from the face of the earth, but the course of the whole race is onward. Every age takes some one step in advance of its predecessors.

Emerson, quite typically, wrote in his essay on *Fate* that the "indwelling necessity" and "central intention" of all creation was nothing less than "universal harmony and joy." His friend William Ellery Channing felt that a man need only "to trust, dare, and be" to have "infinite good ready for your asking." Their fellow-minister Theodore Parker believed that progress was inherent in God's plan for mankind, since "from the infinite perfection of God there follows unavoidably the relative perfection of all that He creates." The whole force of history, these men believed, pointed toward the United States as the climax of a divinely-ordained march toward human betterment. As John O'Sullivan explained in 1839,

The last order of civilization, which is the democratic, received its first permanent existence in this country. Many events, it is true, in the remote history of the world, prepared it for the reception of this principle, yet the peculiar duty of this country has been to exemplify and embody a civilization in which the rights, freedom and mental and moral growth of individual man should be made the highest end of all social restrictions and laws. To this result the discipline of Providence has tended from the earliest history of the Anglo-American race.

The thinkers of the early nineteenth century thus made the principle of progress into a rule of life; theirs was no tentative acceptance, but a fervent, clear belief. There were a number of reasons for this. Some of the responsibility for improving the world had shifted from God to man, who was held much more accountable for determining his future, and much more capable of it than before. Progress was conceived not simply to be part of a remote, ageless cycle, but something accessible, responsive to manipulation. As Albert Brisbane wrote, men could find ways of "*hastening* this progress, and of anticipating results, which if left to the gradual movement of society would require centuries to effect." By using government as one of the instruments of change, many Americans believed that in the United States, at least, one might obtain "progress by legislation," a kind of self-willed bootstrap-lifting by statute.

Nowhere was the impact of this newly-affirmed belief in progress more visible than in the growth of American reform, which swelled over the early nineteenth century like a wave. "Perhaps there has been no age," the *North American Review* editorialized in January of 1827,

since the world was established as the abode of man, so generally confident of progress, and so full of anticipation of further advancement, as our own. It looks back at the ages that are past, and asserts it is wiser and better than they. It looks forward on the ages to come, and acknowledges they will far surpass it.

The American of the period faced the future with magnificent assurance. "There is at hand," wrote William Ellery Channing in 1830, "a tendency and a power to exalt the people" founded on "a devotion to the progress of the whole human race;" so too the Shaker seeress Paulina Bates welcomed "the present age as commencing the most extraordinary and momentous era that ever took place on earth." Convinced of both the possibility and the availability of progress, the men of Emerson's and Jackson's time looked ahead toward an improved society, a perfected democracy, an inspiring future. "No reform is now deemed impossible," said the Reverend Orville Dewey of Massachusetts in 1844, "no enterprise for human betterment impracticable. Everything may be made better; the veriest conservative admits that. All the mental activity of the world converges on that point." The Southern novelist and critic, William Gilmore Simms, even wrote a sonnet-sequence of twelve poems, titled "Progress in America," and published in *The United States Magazine and Democratic Review*. J. A. Saxton, writing in the transcendentalist *Dial* that same year, saw progress as an accumulative process, with each successive social advance accelerating the next one:

Every step of progress makes each succeeding one easier, every improvement in the social institutions of a nation prepares the way for another, that is to follow it, brings it nearer, and gives assurance that it shall be accomplished with less expense of human happiness.

In this spirit of confidence, American reformers sought for ways to reform, repair, and redirect their society. The conviction that progress was attainable, here and now, sent hardheaded Yankee workmen into utopian communities; it sent cultured gentlewomen poking into jails and madhouses; it sent ministers and politicians into the hurly-burly of abolitionism. They all labored hard to remove impediments from the path of improvement—a good digestion, a ten-hour working day, rights for women, better jails, labor unions, extended suffrage, temperance, utopian economics, and a state of spiritual communion with God were each of them steps which might advance humanity a step nearer the ideal society. Harriet Martineau, the English reformer, on completing her tour of the United States in 1836 remarked that she found there "a remarkable set of people living and acting vigorously . . ., with a well-grounded faith, directed toward a noble object"—that of creating a better world.

In science and technology, especially, Americans of Emerson's and Jackson's time believed they had powerful allies for the improvement, not only of material life, but of the intellect and the spirit as well. Through science, which liberated man from bondage to matter and enlarged his control over the world, he could channel his energies toward bettering his condition. Samuel Knapp, writing in the preface to his *Lectures in American Literature* (1829) put into enthusiastic terms the feeling of the American that the future was his, and that it was his through the great advantage he held in starting afresh in the great fields of knowledge opened up by the science of his era. "Everything, in America," he wrote, "was to be begun,"

and everything seemed to depend upon themselves; with this happy difference, however, between us and those in paradise, for our safety and happiness were to depend upon eating freely of the tree of knowledge, which was forbidden to him who first sprang from the dust of the earth.

Americans, like Adam but without his fated rejection, held Eden in their hands.

Edward Everett, soon to become president of Harvard, thought "the mechanician, not the magician, is now the master of life," whereas James K. Paulding believed that "the inventors of machinery . . . have caused a greater revolution in the habits, opinions, and morals of mankind, than all the efforts of legislation. Machinery and steam engines have had more influence on the Christian world than Locke's metaphysics, Napoleon's code, or Jeremy Bentham's codification." Salmon P. Chase, writing in 1832, believed that machinery represented "a new and almost infinite power, brought to bear on the action of the social system. What we claim for machinery," he continued,

is, that it is in modern times by far the most efficient physical cause of human improvement . . ., taking from none, yet giving to all, producing almost unmingled benefit, to an amount and extent, of which we have as yet, probably, but a very faint conception. . . . Not only has machinery set free from the necessity of labor, many to teach, but a far greater number to be taught. . . . [It has] freed the inherent energy of moral ideas, removed obstructions out of the way of their action, and has brought them into contact with the objects on which they are to act.

The steam engine, the printing press, the telegraph, the railroad, the reaper, and other inventions were hailed as machines of progress. Jacob Bigelow, writing of *The Elements of Technology* in 1829, predicted that though "the strides of the past" have seemed rapid indeed, "we have scarcely crossed the threshhold of the temple of human knowledge" in the application of machines to the tasks of life. The steam engine alone, wrote a correspondent for *The Scientific American*, "has revolutionized the age and has done more to exalt humanity and benefit the human race than all the victories of Caesar or the triumphs of Napoleon." J. A. Etzler's *New*

World, or Mechanical System (1840), predicted a future of machines

that are much stronger than all the men and beasts together that you are able to muster, and as strong as you wish them, most obedient to your will, imperishable, working for you day and night, without food or wages, and which, with a few simple tools, cultivate all your land, build your houses . . . and ultimately change your country—your unproductive woods and prairies, your dismal swamps and ponds, your mountains and vallies, and your poorly cultivated farms—into a general paradise.

John C. Calhoun thought that "the subjugation of electricity to the mechanical necessities of man would mark the last era in human civilization," whereas the potentialities of the telegraph *De Bow's Review* found almost unimaginable in 1846: "Scarcely anything now will appear to be impossible. . . . We limit not what man may achieve, nor determine what is beyond his reach." Walt Whitman, for his part, wrote that a "passing glance at the fat volumes of the Patent Office Reports" made him "bless his fate for being born in 1857."

In addition, the early nineteenth century believed it had found another effective aid to progress in the principle of association. If men joined together in societies to multiply their strengths, they could by concerted effort do in decades, or less, what otherwise might take centuries to accomplish. William Ellery Channing explained in *The Christian Examiner* in 1829,

In truth, one of the most remarkable circumstances or features of our age, is the energy with which the principle of combination, or of action by joint forces, by associated numbers, is manifesting itself. It may be said, without much exaggeration, that everything is done now by Societies. Men have learned that wonders can be accomplished in certain cases by union. . . . Men, it is justly said, can do jointly, what they cannot do singly. The union of minds and hands, works wonders. Men grow efficient by concentrating their powers. . . . Nor is this all. Men not only accumulate power by union, but gain warmth, and earnestness. . . . Union not only brings to a point forces which before existed, and which were ineffectual through separation, but, by the feeling and interest which it rouses, it becomes a creative principle, calls forth new forces, and gives the mind a consciousness of powers, which would otherwise have been unknown.

Education, too, was accounted a powerful force for social and moral advancement. The American common school, said the great educator Horace Mann, was "the greatest discovery ever made by man" as an instrument of social progress; the greater the spread of education, which encouraged men "to have just views of the nature, value, and relations of things," remarked a writer in *The North American Review* in 1821, "the greater the prospects of a virtuous and happy community." In a democratic, progressive nation it was deemed vitally important to create and maintain an educated electorate capable of intelligent, progressive action, capable of recognizing its mistakes and planning its future. As Congressman Robert Dale Owen of Indiana (son of the famous English reformer) remarked in 1846, "They who decide mighty questions should be enlightened. As we would have the destinies of our kind shaped by an enlightened tribunal, let the schools of our people . . . be our peculiar care."

Between 1810 and 1870 (except in the South) free public education was made increasingly available to all who could profit by it. Local, county, and state-supported schools grew swiftly in number, broadened their curricula, and spread their influence ever wider through American society. Academies and colleges multiplied, wrote President Philip Lindsley of Nashville in 1829, "like mushrooms in our luxuriant soil." Beginning in 1827 Massachusetts led the way toward mass public education by requiring every sizeable town to maintain a free high school; later in 1842 Massachusetts again set a precedent by requiring that each child attend school for a minimum number of months each year for a minimum number of years.

By 1860 the principle of state-supported and -supervised schools for children for all ranks, and the principle of required attendance, had been accepted in all the Northern and Western states. To the underprivileged the public school meant an opportunity to improve one's station and earning capacity; to the reformer and philanthropist it meant that at least one ancient obstacle to social improvement—ignorance— might ultimately be eliminated. "The great call of the age still continues to be for the wider dissemination of existing knowledge," a reviewer concluded in *The North American Review* in 1827, for only in education lay the hope of eradicating those barriers to progress,

prejudice, which acts like a law of moral entail, and brings down error from one generation to another . . .; diversity of intellect, and opposition of opinion, which keep truth in perpetual balance . . .; interest, which sways man downward . . .; and pride, the champion who, with visor down, is always ready to do battle for self.

In the decades after 1820 the concept of universal education was consistently regarded as the nation's best guarantee and evidence of its progress, for, as President Francis Wayland of Brown University concluded, "The progress of a nation in wealth, happiness, and refinement, is measured by the universality of its knowledge of the laws of nature, and its skill in adapting these laws to the purposes of man."

Americans of the early nineteenth century, then, believed deeply in a kind of progress which could be hastened by science, government, education, technology, and by the efforts of individuals and groups in combination. This progress was a real thing, visible in the life of their own times. To the contemporary European intellectual, the idea of progress was a philosophical abstraction to be defined and explored, an intellectual principle by which one's interpretation of history could be manipulated. In the United States, however, the idea had much more dynamic reality. The achievements of the American people, illustrated by their successful revolution, their establishment of a new kind of government that seemed to work, their conquest of a great, untapped continent, all helped substantially to make the concept of progress a real and demonstrable fact in America, rather than simply a philosophical theory. The American could look around him and see its results. "The former wild prairie, now a cultivated farm," wrote N. H. Parker of the frontier lands in 1857,

the floating palaces upon the bosom of the river which but a little while ago rolled on undisturbed in its lonely beauty; the churches and schoolhouses where stood a few summers ago the Indian's wigwam

were positive evidences of the Americans' progress in settling and peopling this new empire.

Since it was assumed that all men, not merely a chosen class, profited from this upward trend, the idea of progress was integrated into American democratic idealism, built into its social and intellectual framework. The consideration of almost every issue of general importance to the early nineteenth century was formulated and in some way influenced by the era's assumption of unlimited, available progress, and almost every leader of contemporary thought affirmed his faith in it. "The law of man's nature," wrote Salmon P. Chase, "impressed on him by God, is onward progress." "The law of progress" meant, said Charles Sumner in an oration of the same name, that

Man, as an individual, is capable of indefinite improvement. Societies and nations, which are but aggregations of men, and finally the Human Family, or collective Humanity, are capable of indefinite improvement. And this is the destiny of man, of societies, of nations, and of the human family.

Quotations to this effect could be multiplied by the dozens from the writings of the period. William Henry Channing found confidence in progress so pervasive that "doubt of enlarging Good is virtual atheism, and Fear of Progress the unpardonable sin," while scientist George Perkins Marsh agreed that advances in scientific knowledge

open a prospect of vast addition to the powers hitherto wielded by man. It is too soon even to conjecture by what limits these powers are conditioned, but it would seem that there is every reason to expect that man's most splendid achievements hitherto, in the conquest of Nature, will soon be eclipsed by new and more brilliant victories of mind over matter.

Senator William H. Seward, when he reviewed the course of American history, saw in it proof of "a law of progress and development impressed on us by nature herself;" by all the laws of reason "this progressive march was destined to indefinite continuance." Even John C. Calhoun, not the most sanguine of political philosophers, found the present age "but the breaking of the dawn of the world's great jubilee," heralding "a day of more refinement, more intellectual brightness, more moral elevation, and consequently of more human felicity, than the world has ever seen from its creation." Walt Whitman believed the near future promised "such unparalleled happiness and national freedom, such unnumbered myriads," that "the heart of a true man leaps with a mighty joy to think of it."

George Bancroft, the era's reigning historian, in an 1854 oration titled "The Necessity, the Reality, and the Promise of the Progress of the Human Race," gave the idea of progress its most eloquent contemporary exposition. "The course of civilization," he concluded,

flows on like a mighty river through a boundless valley, calling to the streams from every side to swell its current, which is always growing wider, and deeper, and clearer, as it rolls along. Let us trust ourselves upon its bosom without fear; nay, rather with confidence and joy. Since the progress of the race appears to be the great purpose of Providence, it becomes us all to venerate the future. . . . Everything is in movement, and for the better, except only the fixed eternal law by which the necessity of change is established.

Of this there was no doubt, he wrote in his essay *The Office of the People in Art, Government, and Religion* (1835) for it is certain that "The irresistible tendency of the human race is therefore to advancement. . . . The movement of the species is upward, irresistibly upward." Judged by this standard,

Jacksonian America, as Bancroft observed it, represented the highest point yet reached in the species' upward march. The poet Longfellow, more succinctly, heard the same message in the sound of the Bells of San Blas:

> Out of the shadows of night
> The world rolls into light;
> It is daybreak everywhere.

Through the first half of the nineteenth century, then, Americans believed that their progress was inevitable and assured. They expected, as Arthur Ekirch has shown in his study of the idea from 1815 to 1860, a continual unfolding of benefits to be attained by taking best advantage of all the available scientific, technological, and intellectual advances. The United States had progressed mightily since 1776, was continuing to do so, and would maintain the same rate of improvement if it continued to pursue the same path. Even James Fenimore Cooper, a man not overly sanguine about society's ability to improve itself, felt that in America things might be different; in the United States, he admitted grudgingly, "all that reason allows may be hoped in behalf of man."

This fervent, deep-rooted belief in what George Bancroft called "the necessity, the reality, and the promise of progress" was the result of a re-evaluation, in terms of the American experience, of the Enlightenment's doctrines and of four decades of territorial expansion, nationalistic confidence, and growing wealth. The nation was proud of its position and power, conscious of its development from thirteen weak and divided colonies to a powerful, united nation. What had happened in America since Yorktown furnished it with convincing proof that there was such a thing as progress, as the Enlightenment promised, and that it was especially swift and decisive in its American manifestations. If any portion of the world had the right to assume the reality of progress, Americans believed, they did.

Believers in the idea of progress, however, faced two hard facts during the latter half of the nineteenth century—war and science. It was difficult to place the Civil War within an optimistic context, but many decided that it did, after all, accomplish two important objectives which struck observers as progressive indeed—the war abolished slavery and preserved the Union, both of which marked great forward steps in the advancement of American civilization. Science, in the form of the Darwinian hypothesis, presented a more complicated problem of alignments. The principle of "survival of the fittest" was hard to evaluate in terms of the law of progress, since it seemed more like retrogression, away from humanity toward animalism, away from Christianity toward naturalistic chaos. But after speculating about its implications, the thinkers of the later nineteenth century found that, after all, the evoluionary thesis fitted rather neatly with the theory of progress. In fact it could be shown that evolution was progressive and progress evolutionary. Darwin provided a mechanism, or so it seemed, which rendered progress inevitable, suggesting the presence in the world of a grand design which brought everything into order and completeness. Herbert Spencer, Darwin's chief interpreter, held that not only was evolution a fixed natural principle, but that it moved always toward perfection, "towards a complete development and a more unmixed good."

By the closing decades of the nineteenth century American intellectual life was marked by a belief in progress that amounted almost to cocksureness. The average man lived with assurance and a sense of adequacy, quite certain that the future would be better. The triumphs of applied science, the advances of communications and transportation, and the proliferation of the good things of life made progress visible to him, as he contrasted his life with his grandfather's. Charles Eliot Norton, writing not long after the Civil War, expresses this optimism vividly:

I believe that we have really made an advance in civilization, that the principles on which our political and social order rest are in harmony with the laws of the universe, that we have set up an ideal which may never be perfectly attained but which is of such a nature that the mere effort to attain it makes progress in genuine happiness more certain. . . . We are getting rid of old world things and becoming accustomed to the new. We are forming new creeds, new judgments, new manners; we are becoming a new race of men.

This confidence in their ability to handle whatever history threw their way had much to do with the positive achievements of Americans in the latter portions of the nineteenth century and the early twentieth. Without this faith in their future they might have found it impossible, or at least more difficult, to adjust to the shocks and travails of moving from a simpler to a complex society, of exchanging isolation for world leadership, of living through two tremendous world wars and a suddenly changed world after each. Without this sense of affirmation and optimism in itself the United States might have reacted quite differently to the twentieth century.

The nation's mood as it approached the turn of the twentieth century, in 1901, could hardly have been more confident. Taking stock of the century just past, and looking into the future, the journalist Charles E. Russell thought that "the last hundred years saw more accomplished for the well-being of mankind than was done in all the centuries before," and he predicted that the next hundred would be even more spectacularly progressive. The New York *Evening Post,* in January, 1901, devoted a full section to thirty-eight articles, assessing the past century's accomplishments and prophesying the future's. Charles Sanders Peirce, Andrew Carnegie, Arthur T. Hadley, Simon Newcomb, W. P. Trent, Alfred Wallace, and other American leaders all joined to look ahead to "a material and intellectual advance wholly unprecedented in the history of human progress." The nation's future seemed assured. "O days of the future I believe in you," wrote Walt Whitman, "I isolate myself for your sake, O America, because you build for mankind I build for you."

Two men, Charles Darwin and Auguste Comte, provided the intellectual underpinnings of the late nineteenth-century belief in progress. Darwinist evolutionary theory, interpreted by numerous commentators, equated evolution with progress. As Darwinian-Spencerian social theorists explained it, the aim of social evolution was the survival of the fittest, which caused the improvement of both individual and society. While the failure of the fit to survive might seem cruel, their loss meant social gain; as evolution proceeded and the unfit disappeared, the perfect society approached closer to reality. Herbert Spencer wrote, "Progress is not an accident, but a necessity. What we call evil and immorality must disappear. It is certain that man must become perfect."

Nor did the Darwinian hypothesis necessarily deny Christianity, as some seemed to think, for there were ways of making the two compatible. The man who did most to fit Darwinism into the patterns of Christian orthodoxy and of progress, and who could find no inconsistencies among them that could not be explained away, was John Fiske, the Harvard historian and lecturer who devoted much of his life to joining the new biology to Christian ethic. In his *Cosmic Philosophy* (1874), and dozens of essays, Fiske explained that Darwin and Spencer had shown the "irreconcilably upward path" of human development by establishing evolution as a law of nature. "From man's origins," he wrote, "we gather hints to his destiny, and the study of evolution leads our thoughts through Nature to God." Because the theory of evolution implied a plan, behind which lay the "unseen and incalculable Power of God," thought Fiske, it proved the validity of progress and held out the prospect of "a future lighted for us with radiant colors of hope."

The same confidence which Darwin aroused in religious thinkers such as Fiske, the social thought of the French philosopher Auguste Comte produced in social thinkers of the period. Comte's study of the past convinced him that the path of social progress followed natural laws. Since these were discoverable, it was possible to evolve a "social science" by which men could improve and perfect their society. With the laws of social science at hand, men could then identify and accelerate desirable trends and eliminate undesirable ones. What needed to be done, therefore, to insure social progress, was to formulate these laws and apply them. Comte's influence was pervasive in American social thought, both directly and indirectly, and the new discipline of sociology (to which Comte gave a name) was developed swiftly in the United States. His "positive" (or scientific) philosophy of society proved the possibility of progress and suggested ways to promote it; it assumed a faith in science, in man's reason, and in his ability to use both for his advancement. Comte convinced social philosophers that progress could be planned, even guaranteed, and he furnished reformers an effective way of attacking social problems by showing how to identify their components.

The new approach to social progress was most clearly seen in the work of anthropologist Lewis Henry Morgan and sociologist Lester Ward. Morgan, in his *Ancient Society* (1878) set out to analyze the history of society by determining its laws of development. Man advanced, he concluded, through three social stages—savagery, barbarism, and civilization—each of which could be observed and authenticated by a study of the past. There was always "a higher plane of society to which experience, intelligence, and knowledge are steadily tending." Since the present stage was the highest form of civilized life yet attained, Morgan predicted that "democracy in government, brotherhood in society, equality in rights and privileges, and universal education, foreshadow the next higher plane in society." Morgan thus not only provided anthropological evidence for the theory of progress, but gave it specifically American coloration and tied it directly to the American social experiment.

Lester F. Ward's *Dynamic Sociology* (1883) joined the nineteenth century's confidence in man's rationality to Comtean social dynamics. Man, since he is a rational creature, said Ward, can improve his society by making better use of his energies and resources. *Planning* was Ward's key word; men should be "social engineers," approaching their social problems exactly as the scientist approached his. Through his intelligence and skill man was capable, Ward believed, of "organizing human happiness." Man could, Ward wrote, control and direct his progress; to use his phrase, he could "improve his society by cold calculation."

Comte's ideas, adapted to American uses by Morgan, Ward,

and others of the new school of sociologists, were optimistic and positive; he furnished the times with new ways of discovering and relating social knowledge. Within the Comtean frame of reference John Dewey wrote that social progress lay in "the application of intelligence to the construction of proper social devices," and that its guarantee "lies in the perfectibility of social mechanisms corresponding to specific needs." In the same mood Walter Lippmann wrote in 1914 that to achieve control of the forward direction of society, one needed to "devise its social organizations, alter its tools, formulate its method." The Comtean point of view filtered into and through American social thinking over the next half-century, giving it a pervasive and dynamic optimism.

The closing decades of the nineteenth century, and the opening years of the twentieth, rang with convictions of progress. Andrew Carnegie, the apotheosis of capitalistic conservatism, and B. O. Flower, one of the most ardent of socialist reformers, both agreed on the reality of American progress and the prospect of more. Carnegie, in the 1893 edition of his *Triumphant Democracy,* believed that the United States was in the midst of the greatest wave of progress in history. "The old nations of the earth," he wrote,

creep on at a snail's pace; the Republic thunders past with the rush of the express. The United States, in the growth of a single century, has already reached the foremost rank among the nations, and is destined soon to out-distance all the others in the race.

Flower, writing at the same time, hailed the "onward march of progress, the dawn of an era for larger truth . . . the inevitable triumph of the new over the old," and saw evidence of it everywhere about him. There was no reason to doubt the reality of progress, or its promise. The course of events, judged from the past, pointed all the other way.

The Philadelphia Centennial of 1876, marking one hundred years of national independence, furnished the nation with its first great opportunity to assess and to celebrate its convictions of progress. "What an age! What a land! Where

24

elsewhere, one so great?" wrote Walt Whitman, and he
prophesied that another hundred years would produce "a
race of perfect men, women, and children, grandly developed
in body, emotions, heroism, and intellect." Dozens of books
and thousands of sermons and orations played variations on
this theme. E. O. Haven's *American Progress*, B. J. Lossing's
*American Centenary: A History of the Progress of the Re-
public*; Thomas Woolsey's *First Century: A Review of American Progress*; Charles Sumner's *Prophetic Voices Concerning
America*; H. W. Warren's *Past Successes: Future Responsibilities*—all published in 1876—were but a few of the volumes
which surveyed American progress over the previous century
and projected its continuance into the next. Ministers everywhere that year gave centennial sermons; there were thousands
like the Reverend T. G. Cotton, of Hudson, Michigan, who
titled his Sunday sermon in July "Progress, the Lesson of the
Century," asking his congregation to be "thankful that we
live in a land where God is always making all things new, and
where the new is always better than the old." Economist David
A. Wells, surveying recent economic changes in a book of the
same name in 1891, believed that a review of the period from
1860 to 1890 "seemed to warrant the following conclusions:"

that the material progress that these changes have entailed has
been, for mankind in general, movement upward and not downward;
for the better and not the worse; and that the epoch of time under
consideration will hereafter rank in history as one that has no
parallel . . .; when the whole plane of civilization and humanity
rose to a higher level . . .; and what the watchman standing on this
higher eminence can now see is, that the time has come when the
population of the world commands the means of a comfortable
subsistence in a greater degree and with less of an effort than ever
before.

Even those who were critical of American society and its
imperfections were convinced that it would move ahead swiftly
once certain hindrances were removed. Edward Bellamy, who
believed that the greatest single obstacle to social advancement was the competitive principle, advocated in his tractarian

novel *Looking Backward* (1888) that it be replaced by Christian cooperation, since the "Brotherhood of Humanity is one of the eternal truths that govern the world's progress." The co-existence of material wealth and social degradation, which Henry George treated in *Progress and Poverty* (1880), demonstrated to him that what the age called "progress" merely served, he said, to give poverty "a darker hue." To him the primary obstacle to progress lay in monopolistic ownership of land, and the remedy "a single tax" that would free the energies of the individual and the resources of the nation.

The politics of the period had an optimistic and progressive cast, and the word itself—explicitly and implicitly—appeared consistently in the era's political dialogue. The Grangers, Greenbackers, and third-party dissidents fought the "monopolists" and the "interests" so that well-being and power might flow unimpeded, they hoped, to the laborer and farmer. The nation was not moving ahead fast enough, the Populists thought—how did it happen, asked Ignatius Donnelly, the Minnesota radical, that the "two great classes" of the day were "tramps and millionaires"? In brave words the Populists wrote into their platform of 1892 their belief that American political life could be reorganized "to the end that oppression, injustice, and poverty shall eventually cease in the land." William Jennings Bryan, the Populist's messiah, visualized the America of the future "increasing in population, in wealth, in strength, and in influence, solving the problems of civilization." The chief point of political activity, it seemed, was to locate and remove whatever held the nation back from the progress that was its birthright and its destiny.

The theologians of the Social Gospel, a reform movement which swept Protestant theology after 1880, were equally convinced of the reality of progress and the necessity of removing impediments from its path. Washington Gladden, the Ohio minister who became a leader in the movement, composed the words to a hymn which began "In hope that sends a shining ray/Far down the future's broadening way," while the Reverend Samuel Batten wrote with typical confidence, "There are no necessary evils. There are no insoluble problems. Whatever is wrong cannot be eternal, and whatever is right cannot be impossible." The Reverend Josiah Strong predicted that the United States, "with all the majesty of numbers and the might of wealth behind it," could by perfecting its society represent "the largest liberty, the purest Christianity, the highest civilization yet known." The key to progress lay in "Christianizing the social order," thought Walter Rauschenbusch, the chief theologian of the Social Gospel group, and "bringing it into harmony with the ethical convictions which we identify with Christ." The "social hope" of the future, Rauschenbusch wrote in *Christianity and the Social Crisis* (1907) derived from the possibility of turning "life on earth into the harmony of the heavens."

The "progressive" strain in post-1900 politics carried the concept in its name. More sophisticated and much more ideologically mature than their Populist and Greenbacker predecessors, the progressives sought much the same ends, assuming that the people could solve their own political problems if given the machinery and the opportunity. Since "the divine spark is in every soul," wrote William Allen White of Kansas in a re-statement of Emersonian faith, progress "to some upward ideal of living among men is the surest fact of history." A new civilization was on the way, and those who called themselves political Progressives looked for ways to hasten it. The direct primary, the reformed ballot, the apparatus of clean elections, a corrupt practices Act, city home-rule, and a host of similar reforms, gathered under the general heading of "progressive," threaded through the political activity of the period.

Charles E. Merriam, the Chicago political scientist who served as academic spokesman for the movement, expressed the heart of the progressive political philosophy thus:

This is a world of experiment and change, a world in which constant readjustments are being made in the future even more rapidly than in the past, as man's control over the forces of nature, including human nature, expands and develops and reaches points hitherto unattained.

The energy of Theodore Roosevelt and the idealism of Woodrow Wilson, a combination intended to transform the age, represented the Progressive belief that progress toward a higher democracy was possible here and now, if only the system were modified and employed to realize it. "The modern idea is to leave the past and to press on to something new," wrote Wilson, and in pre-war 1913 he gave the progressive concept perhaps its most eloquent expression. "We are going to climb the slow road," he said,

until it reaches some upland where the air is fresher, where the whole talk of politicians is stilled, where men can look in each other's faces and see that there is nothing to conceal; and whence, looking back over the road, we shall see at last that we have fulfilled our promise to mankind.

The men who helped to provide much of the intellectual background for the political progressivism of the period— such as historian Carl Becker, reformer Henry Demarest Lloyd, Herbert Croly the political analyst, social psychologist James Mark Baldwin—agreed in principle that progress was not only possible in twentieth-century America, but practically accessible. They believed, in essence, that the present could escape its past, that by attaining freedom from history society could create a new milieu for its own advancement. "Man is free to create a future that will fit his needs," wrote Becker in 1913, "because he is less a product of his past than of his environment." Because he is free of his past, not trapped by it, man can search the past for usable experience which can help him to control his present and partially, at least, to direct his future. He may "appropriate out of the past," Becker believed, "something which may serve that ideal of social progress which is the aim and substance of our modern faith." Croly's *Progressive Democracy* (1914) not only accepted the possibility of an ideal democratic society (which showed many of the marks of Rooseveltian progressivism) but outlined the ways of attaining it. All of these men believed, in one way or another, that human nature was educable and correctible, that its potential for progress could be released by the mechanisms of an advanced industrial civilization. Industrialism offered the gift of plenty; the democratic process offered the tools of social justice. They felt sure that man, with God's assistance, could remake the institutions of scarcity and put in their places the means for plenty and the good life.

There were nay-sayers, of course, who did not fully believe with the progressives that advancement was so sure nor so complete as the era believed, nor that the future held any such optimistic guarantees. At the same time that Charles Russell was hailing the new century in *Munsey's,* William Merriam in *The North American Review,* examining the census reports of 1900, was not certain that they added up to progress. "There are further inquiries to be made, when the figures are finally tabulated," he wrote cautiously, "as to whether we are not losing rather than gaining in our national life." Mark Twain, in his oft-misunderstood *Connecticut Yankee in King Arthur's Court* (1889) displayed a curious ambivalence toward his society that later, in *The Mysterious Stranger* and other stories, turned into a savage denial of man's ability to improve himself and a bitter attack on his moral sense, his reason, and his conscience. There were two different versions of humanity in Twain, and the one that judged the "damned human race" as not worth saving finally won out. Among other literary men, Stephen Crane, Frank Norris, and Theodore Dreiser, to name the most explicit, were hardly more optimistic than Twain in their readings of human progress. William Graham Sumner, the great Yale sociologist, gradually lost hope for the future as he observed the political and economic issues of the period closing in on society, finally prophesying that the twentieth century would lose itself in "a frightful effusion of blood in revolution and war."

The most decisive negative of the period was that registered by Henry Adams, the brilliant, erratic historian who gradually lost faith in the world as his "education," as he called it, continued after 1865 to his death in 1918. At first a believer in progress, Adams gradually found fewer and fewer reasons to believe it. He could not find proper proof in the study of history, which showed him as it did Twain "the persistently fiendish treatment of man by man; the perpetual effort of society to establish law, and the perpetual revolt of society against the law it had established." Instead of forward movement in the universe, he saw it instead in his *Letter to American Teachers of History* (1910) as a clock running down, swiftly, to end in cosmic silence. Chaos, he concluded in his *Education* (1907) was the law of nature—not progress, or order, or hope.

The nay-sayers, however, were a minority. By 1890 the concept of progress was firmly embedded in American thought, so much so that it was virtually an intellectual cliché. The Western world, and especially the United States, seemed to be working toward a general state of well-being and happiness, and the flood of mass production and affluence drowned the few dissenting voices that doubted. As the present was superior to the past, so the future would improve upon the present. The general attitude of Americans was never better expressed than by the Reverend R. S. Storrs, who, when asked to speak in 1890 at a college honorary society, chose as his topic "Sources and Guarantees of National Progress." "It is a fact of encouraging significance," he began, "that almost uniformly the lines of change have been in the direction of better things." He then proceeded to list eight guarantees of America's future progress—wealth of material resources, a supply of great men, a "strong native stock," a "readiness for labor," a "disciplined community life," a democratic form of government, a deep religious faith, and so on. Thus, he concluded,

The feeble communities of two and one-half centuries ago have been steadily, at last victoriously changed, into the magnificent national organism which now faces mankind upon these shores. The Lord hath hastened it in his time; and the imagination fails to prefigure what hereafter is to follow. We need no sign in the sky to assure us that a power greater, and a plan more far-reaching than any of man have been concerned in the progress, and it does not seem presumptious to expect that consummations are still to be reached yet more delightful and more stupendous.

This was the new century's faith. The distinguishing belief which held American society together as a tightly organized unit, and which gave it esprit and morale, wrote the German observer Hugo Munsterberg in 1911 was "neither race nor tradition, nor the actual past," but the conviction of progress, of "the future for which together they are building." Then the war came. To some, the experience of World War I completely destroyed the idea of progress; to others, it so modified and changed their attitude toward it that it no longer resembled the confident doctrine that Storrs and his generation so confidently affirmed. "The generation which lived through the War could no longer believe anything," Will Durant wrote later. "The idea of progress seemed now to be one of the shallowest delusions that ever mocked man's misery, or lifted him up to a vain idealism and a monstrous futility." The war convinced many Americans that man might not be fully rational after all, or, if he were, that he could not be trusted to use wisely the knowledge that reason gave him. The machine, hailed by an earlier era as man's liberator, seemed to have turned into nothing more than an instrument of anger. The faith that men could manipulate the apparatus of power in a moral way gave place to great intellectual disillusion. Ezra Pound's "Hugh Selwyn Mauberly" concluded that in the war

> There died a myriad,
> And the best, among them,
> For an old bitch gone in the teeth,
> For a botched civilization,

and one of John Dos Passos *Three Soldiers*, reflecting the mood of much of postwar fiction, found "civilization nothing but a vast edifice of sham." Robert L. Duffus, in a bitter essay called "Progress—1917," felt the conflict meant only that

Ten million men have perished to prove that progress is not automatic, nor comfortable, and not in any way a law of nature; even more, that there are dark forces that tear at the fabric of civilization as fast as it is woven.

The idea of progress, in his judgment, belonged to those "dead Victorian Galahads with mufflers and cough drops" who believed that "the path of progress was so well engineered . . . that humanity could stroll along it, day by day, without consciousness of effort."

Even the most optimistic could not make much out of the Great War. In 1915, before American entry into it, a symposium of ministers and educators in Chicago wrestled with the riddle of progress in a war-torn world and ended only with questions, not answers. "Can we seriously claim," the summary of the conference read,

in view of the terrible and horrible things that have been taking place in Europe . . . that there is such a thing as Progress? And if there be such a thing, has it any significance, any moral value? If Progress is not only real, but good and admirable, why this awful war? How can we escape discouragement and disillusionment; where are we to find balm and comfort—an explanation that shall give us new courage and faith and hope?

John Dewey, writing in 1916, took as positive a view as circumstances seemed to warrant, suggesting that since the war had at least revealed man's essential "stupidity and carelessness" it might at least bring after it "a more responsible faith in progress than that in which we have indulged in the past."

Dewey's position represented the most confident view of progress that the wartime generation dared to take. *The Nation*, debating the question "Does the War Disprove Progress?" concluded that it did not—quite—although the wartime experience showed clearly that "with the great resources at the disposal of the modern world . . ., progress is not so rapid as might be wished." But for the most part the nineteenth-century's dream of movement ever-onward toward perfection disappeared in the gunfire of 1917. Mankind was apparently going nowhere; all those problems which once seemed on the way to solution now needed solving again "We blunder on," wrote a correspondent for *Living Age* in 1916,

mystified yet hopeful, trembling yet trustful. We discovered machinery, and we believed it would save our labor and give us ease from toil; yet everybody seems to work harder than before. We mastered the sea, the mountains, and the air; yet we are the slaves of destruction. We go on making bigger ships, bigger factories, bigger empires, bigger guns, and how have we profited? Man must ask himself finally and irrepressibly whether happiness can be the end of so terrible, so insupportable a journey.

The war was, in the opinion of the thoughtful, merely a manifestation of much deeper faults that might well crack contemporary civilization. War brought out the worst in man and his institutions, the worst that had always been there and would remain. The conflict had at last destroyed, in the opinion of Professor Harry F. Ward of Union Theological Seminary, "the false security which emanates from the idea of automatic progress" that left the American people "so unprepared and helpless when the World War hit them." One could only begin all over again. "The chaotic stuff of the old nations, governments, and societies," wrote Robert Duffus, "must pass again through the brains and fingers of mankind, and those straining shuttles must give it form again."

The legacy of the World War, as it affected the doctrine of progress, created a double strain in American thought, a basic ambivalence—reinforced by subsequent events and ideas —that persists to this day. The American intellectual, wrote Charles A. Beard wryly in 1928, could not decide whether "the curve of contemporary civilization now rises majestically toward a distant zenith, or in reality had begun to sink rapidly toward a nadir near at hand." There were those who believed that the worst was over, that better was yet to be, that there was hope for man's advancement as each generation learned a bit more about his problems. There were also those who believed that worse might come, that there was no guarantee it would not, that one could only look ahead without much more hope than chance might offer. Will Durant, answering the question "Is Progress a Delusion?" in 1926, replied that it was not, that despite the waste of war one might live in confidence that "what is finally fair and noble" in the world "will escape mortality, to illuminate and gladden generations

33

to come." But Frederic C. Howe, a disillusioned Wilsonian reformer writing in the same year, concluded that "facts were of little value, morality did not guide men," and that in America, as in Europe there was only "conquest, plunder." "The illusions I had spent a lifetime in hoarding," he found, "were of no use in this world."

The nineteen-twenties, that era so neatly bracketed by the peace negotiations of World War I and the crash of 1929, displayed both sides of this double view of progress. On the one hand, the decade contained a strong strain of optimism, a feeling of progress so strong that it conceived of itself as a new era, on the verge of a great forward step in civilization. Charles and Mary Beard's synthesis of history, *The Rise of American Civilization,* which appeared in 1927, mirrored this perfectly. The Beards' work found the nexus of American progress in the new technology, and expressed with sincere conviction the belief that, with war done with and the machine under control, progress was assured. In writing a new introduction for a re-edition of J. B. Bury's *The Idea of Progress* in 1932, Beard expressed the view that "by immense efforts of will and intelligence, employing natural science as the supreme instrumentality of power, mankind may rise above necessity into a kingdom of freedom." There were many who agreed with him.

There were also many who did not, who found contemporary civilization mirrored most accurately in T. S. Eliot's poetic picture of a barren wasteland, populated by hollow men stuffed with straw; or at best in the crass, valueless society of Sinclair Lewis' *Babbit* and *Main Street,* or of John Dos Passos, *U.S.A.* Two strikingly perceptive novels, both published in 1926, reflected the prevailing temperament among the young intellectuals. Ernest Hemingway's *The Sun Also Rises,* a novel of the postwar's "lost generation," ended in dispair and nihilism. William Faulkner's *Soldier's Pay* grimly symbolized the wreckage of the postwar world by building its plot about a doomed, dying veteran. At the same time that the Beards were publishing their study of an advancing American civiliztion, young Philip Richards was writing that the old American faith in a progressive future

has all faded like a beautiful dream. Apparently it needed the Great War to persuade some people that we are as far as ever from perfection—nay, that we are quite possibly on the wrong road together. . . . If progress means—as it surely must, if it means anything—a continuous advance in one direction, it must be obvious to every reader of the daily press that, even in Europe, mankind is not progressive.

The debate persisted throughout the decade and into the thirties, centering for the most part about the function of science and technology in the progressive process. Did the machine endanger, or accelerate, the creation of a better life? Joseph Wood Krutch, writing in *The Modern Temper* (1929), thought that science, originally hailed by the previous century as a "liberating force," had already "begun to reveal its limitations." Science, wrote Krutch, destroyed or attenuated man's positive beliefs, progress among them, and failed to enrich life as it had promised. "There impends for the human spirit," he said, "either extinction or a readjustment more stupendous than any made before." John Dewey, though he agreed that machinery meant "an undreamed-of-reservoir of power" for human use, also warned that "we have harnessed this power to the dollar rather than to the liberation and enrichment of human life." Beard, for his part, was convinced otherwise. "Modern civilization founded in science and the machine will not decline," he wrote; rather, "according to signs on every hand technology promises to extend in area and intensify its characteristics" in a "long and highly dynamic future."

Ralph E. Flanders, writing in Beard's collection, *Toward Civilization* (1930) believed that science was about to create "a new age and a new man;" Gerald Wendt, writing in Harold Stearn's symposium, *America Now* (1938), concluded that because of science the United States "stood at the threshhold of a great new epoch." In 1927 Dr. J. P. Simonds of Northwestern University summarized the prevailing attitude of scientists in addressing himself to the question, "Has man progressed socially as well as biologically?" "Has anything happened to man as a unit in organized society," he asked, "that is at all comparable to what has occurred to him as a biologic unit. . . ." The evidence was all affirmative; "man has made social progress . . . as great in its way, as the less readily disputed biologic progress of which man himself forms the capstone."

Two factors, the one economic and the other intellectual, influenced the course of discussion of the idea of progress during the nineteen-thirties: the depression and the rise of Protestant neo-orthodoxy. The stock crash of 1929 shook the faith of Americans in the workability of their economic system and served to underline the warnings of those who suspected that progress was at bottom only an illusion of prosperity. In the midst of want, fear, and idleness, and seventeen million unemployed, how could one proclaim the progressive achievements of modern society? Observers were struck by the anomaly of Chicago's 1933 Century of Progress Exposition, or "World's Fair," which opened during the depths of the nation's unemployment. "The middle class paradise which we built on this continent . . . will be in decay before the half-century is rounded," Reinhold Niebuhr commented at the time. "We may offer an example on a rather grand historical scale of the fate of a house that is built upon sand." The comparison which came most quickly to mind, he noted, was that of "Louis XVI and his court, in a period of history which may be regarded as roughly analogous to ours."

Against this point of view Franklin D. Roosevelt arrayed the whole apparatus of the "New Deal," based on the conviction—adapted from Ward, the Progressives, and the social philosophers of the nineteenth century—that by planning and social engineering the nation could not only survive the depression but carve a new and better kind of society out of the remnants of the old. A strong believer in progress, supported by faith in a guiding Providence and the essential rationality of man, Roosevelt thought that what bound men together was their "hope of a common future" that improved on the present. "Out of every crisis, every tribulation, every disaster," he once wrote, "mankind rises with some share of greater knowledge of higher decency, of purer purpose."

Roosevelt set his administration, therefore, against the drift of contemporary uncertainty. Much of his political effectiveness derived from his ability to give new impetus to the doctrine of progress in an era that had a right to seriously doubt it, and to restore faith to a tradition of liberalism that seemed to be losing it. Democracy and science, Roosevelt believed, would "provide an ever-richer life and ever-larger satisfaction to the individual." "With this change in our moral climate," he said in his Second Inaugural, "and our rediscovered ability to improve our economic order, we have set our foot upon the road of enduring progress." His last words struck the same note of optimism; the speech in preparation at the time of his death concluded, "The only limit to our realization of tomorrow will be our doubts today. Let us move forward with a strong and active faith."

Through the twenties and thirties, wrote Walter M. Horton in *Christianity Today* (1947) "a mood of frustrated idealism and general disillusionment" swept American Protestantism. The churches tried to keep "up-to-date," squaring theology with the latest advances of science, adapting it to prosperity and depression and the threat of war, little realizing that the basic Christian assumption of progress was being undercut by the turn of events. The neo-orthodox movement in Protestant theology struck the churches precisely at their weakest point— their apparent failure to reconcile the doctrine of progress with the actual facts of war, depression, and disillusion. Karl Barth in Europe, and both Paul Tillich and Reinhold Niebuhr in America revived the concept, historically Calvinist in character, that since human nature was essentially weak, imperfect and untrustworthy, progress therefore was likely to be halting and uncertain, if it came at all. The neo-Calvinists suggested that advances in man's condition were dependent on factors not always under his direction, and that there might never be final answers to some of his problems. The "Tragic irony" of American history, as Niebuhr pointed out, was that the study of it destroyed one's belief in progress. "History does not move forward without catastrophe," Niebuhr wrote in 1940 on the eve of another war,

happiness is not guaranteed by the multiplication of physical comforts; social harmony is not easily created by more intelligence; and human nature is not as good or as harmless as had been supposed.

The trouble lay with man himself, who was not—as Emerson and Carnegie had maintained—fully capable of controlling himself or his destiny. "More and more we are weighed down by a tyrannous sense of the inevitable," wrote theologian Ross Hoffman, "by the discouraging feeling that nothing much can be done against the trend of forces and events." The carefully constructed structure of progress, built on the rationalism of the eighteenth century and buttressed by the science of the nineteenth, was in danger of falling down. Neo-orthodox theology, with reinforcement from the trend of events, set about to dispel romantic illusions about the nature of life and to set the doctrine of progress within a realistic context, where if to function at all it must do so within strict limitations. The neo-Calvinist point of view did not completely cancel hope. Instead, it suggested that while progress is neither automatic or inevitable, man's capacity for error need not prevent him from making advances—but he must not take them for granted, nor expect too much, nor be disappointed at his failure.

Neo-orthodoxy placed progress in a shadow already lengthened by German historian Oswald Spengler's popular study, *The Decline of the West* (1918-22) which attracted a wide American audience. Spengler's prediction that a new age of barbarism was at hand, and that the super state of Caesarism would soon displace the democracies, fitted the mood of the pessimist. Sigmund Freud's *Civilization and its Discontents* (1930) reinforced Spengler's message. Freud, already a powerful force in American psychology, saw life as an insoluble, dark conflict of love and aggression which ended in defeat and unhappiness. All that Spengler, Freud, and others had to say seemed to be borne out by what happened in Europe in the late thirties and by the Second World War. There was a strong feeling that progress, wrote sociologist Horace Kallen, was "a lie that modern man tells himself, an illusion that he has whistled up to comfort his soul."

No one could satisfactorily explain the ironic paradox of the twentieth century, as Henry Luce noted in 1941, that "No other century has been so big with promise for human progress and happiness. And in no one century have so many men and women and children suffered so much pain and anguish and bitter death." Vannevar Bush, president of the Carnegie Institute put it bluntly: "The first World War shook our optimism, the depression shook it further, and the second World War nearly destroyed it. Now, though we may still hope that our race will go forward in progress, we are confronted with facts that take all the former exuberance out of hope." Even the great breakthrough in science that created atomic energy also produced the atomic bomb. Theologian Walter Horton commented on "the strange paradox that modern science should so recently have been used to prove that . . . the progress of mankind onward and upward was assured," and that it should not bring mankind "several steps nearer the final holocaust."

The recent attitude toward the idea of progress in America has remained much the same as it existed in the years following World War I, displaying the same double tradition of conditional belief and modified doubt. Two world wars, depression, and an uncertain peace have left their marks on the traditions. It would be unthinkable, in the sixties, for another Bancroft to assume the necessity, or the reality, or the promise of progress, yet the idea itself still exhibits remarkable tenacity in modern intellectual life. Whatever evidence recent history and philosophy may have produced against belief in progress, Americans at large have consistently refused to give it up, however they may have modified it from its eighteenth- and nineteenth-century versions.

The prevailing modern approach to the idea of progress is one of thoughtful acceptance, accompanied by the realization that whatever progress there may be is limited and most certainly not to be taken for granted. No one can assume that progress is constant or automatic, explained Professor Sidney Fay to the American Historical Association in 1947, but we can assume it is "possible and even probable as a result of man's conscious and purposeful efforts."

Anthropologist Margaret Mead thinks that the contemporary world is still a place "in which too many of the wrong things happen somewhere, but this is a world in which we now have the means to make a great many more of the right things happen everywhere." Adlai Stevenson has explained that the twentieth century must face the fact "that our wisdom is imperfect, and that our capacities are limited," but must also recognize that "progress is a basic law of life." Dwight Eisenhower, speaking in 1950, believed that "we must not be discouraged by the inescapable slowness of world progress. However disappointing may be the lack of speed, every new evidence of advance brings immediate hope of a brighter tomorrow." Scientist Vannevar Bush agreed that while "there is no certainty in either science or progress . . ., we may reasonably expect to learn more and accomplish something each successive day" in the hope that "our sorry old world may yet become a happy place to live in."

Whatever proofs to the contrary, contemporary America has a deep and emotional attachment to the concept of progress, and still retains belief in it as an integral part of the American tradition. This has been most aptly expressed by Bernard Baruch, who, looking back over more than a half-century of history, wrote in 1954,

When I was a younger man, I believed that progress was inevitable—that the world would be better tomorrow and better still the day after. The thunder of war, the stench of concentration camps, the mushroom cloud of the atomic bomb are, however, not conducive to optimism. . . . Yet my faith in the future, though somewhat shaken, is not destroyed. I still believe in it. If I sometimes doubt that man *will* achieve his moral potentialities, I never doubt that he can. I still believe that with courage and intelligence we can make the future bright with fulfillment.

The American Idea of Progress

BIBLIOGRAPHICAL ACKNOWLEDGEMENTS

There are a number of general treatments of the idea of progress, the earliest of which is J. B. Bury's classic *The Idea of Progress* (London, 1928). Others are Charles A. Beard's essay, "The Idea of Progress," in his *Century of Progress* (Chicago, 1932); Bruce Mazlish, "The Idea of Progress," *Daedalus* XCII (Summer, 1963) 447-61; Morris Ginsberg, *The Idea of Progress* (Boston, 1953); Carl Becker, *Progress and Power* (New York, 1949); and Sidney Fay, "The Idea of Progress," *American Historical Review* LII (January, 1947) 231-46. A good brief general treatment of the doctrine in America occurs in Stow Persons', *American Minds* (New York, 1958). Ralph H. Gabriel, *The Course of American Democratic Thought* (New York, 1940) is especially useful for studying the concept from 1830 to 1920. Valuable specific studies, which have furnished material for this chapter, are Arthur Ekirch, *The Idea of Progress in America 1815-1860* (New York, 1944); David A. Noble, *The Paradox of Progressive Thought* (Minneapolis, 1958); Boyd C. Shafer, "The American Heritage of Hope," *Mississippi Valley Historical Review* XXXVII (December, 1950); Clarke A. Chambers, "The Belief in Progress in Twentieth Century America," *Journal of the History of Ideas* XIX (1958) 197-224; Rush Welter, "The Idea of Progress in America," *ibid.,* XVI (1955) 401-15; and Paul A. Carter, "The Idea of Progress in American Protestant Thought 1930-1960," *Church History* XXXII (March, 1963) 75-89. The oration by R. S. Storrs referred to herein appears in *The Magazine of American History* XXIV (October, 1890) 241-68. John Dewey's essay, "Progress," appeared in *The International Journal of Ethics* II (April, 1916) 310-22. Other references in this chapter are to be found in "Symposium on Progress," *The Nation,* June 17, 1915, 1 and in the same issue, "Does the War Disprove Progress?"; Robert L. Duffus, "Progress: 1917," *New Republic,* July 14, 1917; "Have We Advanced?" *Scientific American,* February 19, 1916; Frederic C. Howe, *Confessions of a Reformer* (New York, 1926); Will C. Durant, "Is Progress a Delusion?" *Harper's* CLIII (November, 1926) 742-51; Harry F. Ward, "Progress or Decadence?" in Kirby Page, ed., *Recent Gains in American Civilization* (New York, 1928); J. P. Simonds, "Progress," *Scientific Monthly* XXIV (June, 1927) 537-47; Reinhold Niebuhr, "Catastrophe and Social Control," *Harper's* CLXV (June, 1932) 115-18; Vannevar Bush, "Science and Progress," *American Scientist* XLIII (April, 1955) 241-58; David Sarnoff, "The Fabulous Future," *Fortune* LI (January, 1955) 82, 114-19; Margaret Mead, "One Vote for This Age of Anxiety," *New York Times,* May 20, 1956. For a brief treatment of the Neo-orthodox movement in theology, see Walter M. Horton, "The New Orthodoxy," *American Scholar* VIII (Winter, 1938) 3-11, and for a survey of contemporary American churches, his essay "American Christianity" in H. S. Leiper, *Christianity Today* (New York, 1947). Reinhold Niebuhr, *Christianity and Power Politics* (New York, 1940), his *Irony of American History* (New York, 1952) are representative of his thought; also quoted is Ross Hoffman, *Tradition and Progress* (Milwaukee, 1938). Horace M. Kallen, *Patterns of Progress* (New York, 1950) provides a social philosopher's view; Adlai Stevenson, *A Call to Greatness* (New York, 1954) a political thinker's. Henry Wriston's essay, "The Individual," appears in *Goals for Americans* (New York, 1960).

II

The American as Nationalist

My country right; my country wrong; but right or
wrong, my country.
—OLD NAVY TOAST

THE TERM *nationalism*, as it is used in the study of American
ideas, contains within it at least three major meanings.
First, it connotes (in the usual and general interpretation)
that sense of national identity, that quality of national character of which patriotism is the most important characteristic.
Second, it is used in a peculiarly American meaning to desig-
nate the doctrine that the political authority of the federal
government is superior to that of its subordinate units—in
contrast to states' rights or localism. In this sense, nationalism
and federalism are allied political terms. Third, as opposed to
internationalism, it describes the belief that national interests
take precedence over international considerations, that the
national advantage has priority in any issue which involves
other nations. "Manifest destiny," imperialism, and isolationism have all been characteristically nationalistic in this sense.

Depending upon the pressures of internal and external
circumstances, nationalism in one or more of these three manifestations has been evident in every era of American history.
To create an American nationality in the first, broad sense
was the primary objective of the first half-century following

independence. By Jackson's time this had been successfully accomplished; the average American knew with some certainty who he was, and what he was, in relation to the rest of the world. The Civil War, of course, provided another set of answers to the contest between state and national sovereignties, though conflicts between federal and local political, social, and emotional allegiances still occur. The continuous dialogue in American life between nationalism and internationalism, initiated in Washington's Farewell Address, has continued undiminished into the twentieth century, where changes in society, communications, and the sources of world conflict have forced the United States to reconsider its traditional nationalism within the context of new problems of global war and human survival.

The concept of nationalism is itself of comparatively recent origins, perhaps less than two hundred years old. Consciousness of one's nationality of course has deep historical roots, but modern nationalism is primarily an eighteenth-century (or at most a late seventeenth-century) phenomenon. Loyalty to one's king, awareness of group differences, pride in one's origins, and other elements of national feeling had existed for centuries, but the fusion of intellectual, emotional, and psychological components into that web of common culture, language, sentiments, aims, manners, and ideals called *nationalism* did not begin in western Europe at the earliest until the fifteenth century. Medieval loyalties were so easily transferable as to be almost interchangeable; attachments tended to be regional and limited; local customs and privileges were strong and jealously guarded; political, social, and economic life were organized in small units.

It is significant that as late as the American Revolution, professional soldiers, whose nationality mattered not at all, were still used in war. The gradual change of the older feudal concept of loyalty to one's lord into a broader, more generalized concept of loyalty to one's country and society occurred somewhere between the seventeenth and nineteenth centuries. Actually, modern nationalism may be said to have its origins in the rise of three powerful national states—England, France, and Spain—and to have grown to maturity in the revolutions of the eighteenth and early nineteenth centuries which spread across Europe, Latin America, into Asia in the later nineteenth and into Africa in the twentieth.

While the history of American nationalism has much in common with that of western Europe, it cannot be traced or construed in the same terms. American nationalism has developed in its own unique fashion; the product of a process somewhat different from Europe's, it is not to be interpreted within the same pattern.

First, American nationalism developed extremely swiftly, and from a virtual vacuum. The United States had only a brief colonial history at the time of its formation, and no national history at all before that. Unlike European nations, the United States has no past which stretches infinitely backwards into history, but rather a specific, measurable, and recent one. European and Asian nationalisms grew out of centuries of customs, traditions, wars, successions of rulers, and ancient tribal pasts. The United States appeared suddenly, made out of a mixture of racial stocks, a variety of religions, diverse climatic and geographical conditions, and dissimilar sets of economic interests. Historians have usually agreed that the essential elements of an operative nationalism include a cohesive body of traditions, an established historical continuity, a common language, and a common territory. Of these the United States possessed in 1776 only a language. Its boundaries were vague, its past non-existent, its traditions completely English and not American at all. Yet, as John Adams observed, somehow it all made a nation:

The complete accomplishment of it, in so short a time, and by such simple means, was perhaps a singular example in the history of mankind. Thirteen clocks were made to strike together—a perfection of mechanism which no artist had ever before effected.

Second, the United States was the result of a willed, creative act, by an identifiable set of people who deliberately set out to make a nation. The Founding Fathers, completely reversing the European experience, constructed the political machinery of a nation—in the Declaration, the Articles, the state constitutions, and the Constitution—without any of the traditional cultural, psychological, economic, and social foundations to support it which in Europe took centuries to build.

As Lincoln phrased it, Americans quite literally brought forth upon this continent a new nation by a series of decisions which had no parallels in previous history. Instead of developing over generations that common body of traditions, laws, myths, symbols, heroes, customs, literature, and dialects out of which nationalism eventually crystallizes, the American nation came first and others after. Noah Webster, for example, pointed out that the United States existed before it was really a nation—five years after the close of the war that made it a political unit, Webster told his fellow Americans that they still had "an empire to raise and support by your exertions, and a national character to establish and extend by your wisdom and virtue."

Third, American nationalism developed without reference either to a church or a monarchy. The United States was the first to break the church-state relationship common to all Europe. It had no place in its political system for an established church—unlike England, Spain, or Italy, for example, whose nationalisms were powerfully affected by ecclesiastical influences. Nor was the nation, from the beginnings of its independence, at any time associated with a monarchy. Its existence originated in a rejection of monarchy. Never since, unlike most of the states of central and eastern Europe or of Asia, has it been associated with an authoritarian government. The United States never possessed either a church or a ruler whose interests were identified with those of the nation.

Fourth, the United States evolved without the presence of a military or an aristocratic caste. The army which won American independence was a civilian army, dissolved immediately after the peace, and its first great military leader set the precedent that the military must always be subordinate to the civilian authority. American nationalism never displayed a military character—as say France under Napoleon, or Ger-

46

many under Bismarck. Neither was American nationalism influenced at any point by an aristocratic, ruling class, since it emerged from a society which had no European-style elite but rather one whose interests were spread over a relatively wide social spectrum.

Fifth, American nationalism was never deeply rooted in race or place. Much (though not all) of European nationalism sprang from racial consciousness, from the idea of a *Volk* or People (with a capital letter). The English awareness of ancient Anglo-Saxon roots, the Nordic myth, German Teutonism, Gallic assumptions of absolute superiority, even the Irish use of Catholicism as a kind of racial rallying point—these have no duplicates in American nationalism. The most racially diverse of nations could hardly be expected to be otherwise; despite its traditional Protestantism, America's commitment to religious pluralism prevents any ardent religious nationalism.

Since they all came originally from somewhere else, the first Americans had none of the provincial European attachment to geography. Since the first citizens of the country were *politically* conscious of their nationality before anything else, American nationalism has always been connected not to places but to principles. "Give the American his institutions," the Scots traveller Charles Mackay remarked in 1857, "and he cares little where you place him." The sheer fluidity of American society (a legacy of its frontier past) constantly mitigates against the development of a European sense of "homeland." The European first becomes conscious of his nationality because he lives in a place where his father, and no doubt his father in turn, lived before him. The mobile American may be equally aware of his land, but it is a generalized attachment, often in terms of the abstract landscape of "America the Beautiful."

Sixth, American nationalism developed not from a state, but from an idea—the idea of popular liberty as it took shape out of the Cromwellian revolution, out of Locke and 1688, out of the English-Continental natural-rights debates of the eighteenth century. No nationalism has ever been so clearly based on an ideology. Possessing no fixed political tradition of the state, the American colonists merged the English revolutionary heritage and the theory of natural rights into one and took it as their own. The Declaration of Independence shows how thoroughly they appropriated the prevailing British and French traditions, naturalized them, and made the result into that peculiarly American combination of liberty and equality which holds American nationalism together and creates its distinctive ambiance.

Seventh, American nationalism did not emerge out of a long, persistent contest against powerful rivals and national enmities. Americans did not have to establish a national identity or a distinctive culture by struggle against older cultures to which it was tributary, such as the Norwegians against the Danes, or the Russians against the French and Germans, or the Germans against the French, or the Scots against the English. The United States never possessed traditional antagonists to feed its nationalistic fervor—as the conflict between Ireland and England fed the Irish and the Wars between France and Germany fed both, or as Arab countries today draw their patriotic sustenance from enmity toward Israel and Latin American nations toward *Yanquis*. Great Britain, of course, at first came close to filling the role of national enemy, but two wars within the first generation settled that.

Instead of identifying England and Europe as adversaries, the United States has instead made them reverse images of what it should be, using them for nationalistic purposes in a different way. In developing their own sense of nationality, Americans have consistently conceived of the United States and Europe in polar terms. British and European society has served as a model of what the United States should *not* be, bringing America's concept of itself into focus and providing a foil against which American achievements may be measured. Thus Franklin, who spent fifteen years in London, contrasted the "extreme corruption prevalent . . . in this old, rotten state" with the freshness of America. Jefferson, advising a young friend against a European education, thought that an American in Europe "loses in his knowledge, in his morals, in his health, and in his happiness." Washington Irving wrote pityingly that British observers could never really comprehend America, since "the themes it offers for contemplation are too vast and elevated for their capacities." Rejection of Europe was, and is, a major theme in the formation of American nationalism, stemming from the singular sense of difference, of novelty, that is characteristically American.

This strong American sense of new beginnings was clearly a part of the atmosphere of the post-Yorktown years. With only the briefest history of their own, Americans felt little responsibility to the past and sanguine about the future, for they had no record of failure to disillusion them. They were impatient of "established" institutions, for they had just established some of their own and disestablished a good many English ones. The nation was imbued with a sense of *newness*, of experiment and hope. As Washington Irving remarked later, the United States, since it had "sprung into national existence in an enlightened and philosophical age," was free of many of "the inveterate diseases of the old countries, contracted in rude and ignorant ages." Thomas Pownall, who served as royal governor of both Massachusetts and North Carolina, shrewdly observed this quality in his society; America was founded, he said, "totally and entirely on a New System of Things and Men."

Americans realized their national singularity only gradually; the Constitutional Convention, no doubt, marked the final American rejection of Europe. The delegates at Philadelphia were former British subjects who recognized that the British political tradition had many virtues, and who felt that the stability, expertise, and economy of the British system provided an alluring model for their own. But during the discussions Charles C. Pinckney rose to make a comment which penetrated directly to the heart of the matter. Americans, said Pinckney, were neither English, nor European, nor Roman, nor Greek.

We have universally considered ourselves as the inhabitants of an old instead of a new country. The people of this country are not only very different from the inhabitants of any state we are acquainted with in the modern world, but I assert that their situation is distinct from that of either Greece or Rome, or of any state we are acquainted with among the ancients.

Therefore, he concluded, the convention must think and plan in terms of "a new country . . ., where there is more equality of rank and fortune than in any other country in the world."

Few of the men at Philadelphia, and probably not Pinckney himself, fully comprehended the implications of his speech. They went on to erect precautions against European-style mob rule that could not happen in the United States because it had no European mobs; they created protection for property and position in a nation where property was more available than anywhere else in the world and position (in the European sense) practically non-existent. But they did perceive, bit by bit, that the United States was something new and singular in the world. The Americans of Washington's time knew very well that they were not merely Europe projected, but a new civilization with a separate future.

English and European commentators and travellers, of course, never let them forget it; for the most part, they treated the new nation with either curiosity or contempt, forcing Americans constantly to study, analyze, and explain themselves. As Franklin had noted in 1775, an American "was understood to be a kind of Yahoo," an attitude maintained by later travellers such as Tom Moore, who found the United States of 1814 "one dull chaos, one unfertile strife," or the English visitor who in the early nineteenth century spoke of American democracy in these terms:

It is impossible not to discuss the futility of this form of government. It was weak and wicked in Athens. It was bad in Sparta, and worse in Rome. It has been tried in France, and terminated in despotism. It was tried in England, and rejected with utmost loathing and abhorrence.

Americans, in defending themselves against such unusually vicious attacks by English and European critics, were well aware of their relative youth and of their differences with the older transatlantic civilization. No other nation has ever been expected so often to defend its right to exist, and Americans have had to answer many times the question posed by Crève-coeur, "What is an American, this new man?" Each time the answer has tended to reaffirm their sense of separate, indi-vidual, national identity.

It is impossible to point to a particular year in American history and say "Here American nationalism began." The development of an American identity was a long, subtle process which began with the first settlers who landed at Virginia or Massachusetts. The plain fact that they were Englishmen who were not in England and who intended— for the most part—not to return to England, must have planted in their colonies the seeds of some kind of national-istic feeling. Some colonists, of course, ranging from the cut-purse fleeing justice to the Puritan bent on founding a new Jerusalem, came specifically to escape from Europe, expecting America to be different and, hopefully, better. The New England settlers came with the conviction that they were a chosen people designated for a special destiny, producing (as historian Max Savelle has pointed out) a quasi-patriotic feel-ing which was no doubt the closest thing to an American nationalism that existed prior to the eighteenth century.

Yet to use the word "nationalism" to describe the colonial state of mind would be inaccurate. Those who lived in the British-American colonies were Englishmen, purely and sin-cerely, albeit they might occasionally, as Cotton Mather did in 1691, use the term "American" to indicate the kind of Englishmen they were. The atmosphere of the Enlightenment militated against nationalism, since the Age of Reason prided itself on its cosmopolitan spirit, its avoidance of the insular and provincial. Believing in the common rationality of intel-ligent men everywhere, and in the universal consistency of human nature, the seventeenth and early eighteenth-century intellectual stressed the resemblances among people rather than their differences. The ideal of the enlightened man was to be "a citizen of the world," like Voltaire, who refused to be bound to any country but mankind.

The formation of an American spirit, however, coincided with the introduction into Western thought of that body of ideas loosely called Romanticism, which in the later eighteenth century began to sweep across Europe. Romanticism impinged on American thought at precisely that critical point when the American sense of self-awareness was most ready to respond. The Romantic movement emphasized particularity, individuality, and difference, as against the Enlightenment's respect for universalism, cosmopolitanism, and likeness. The Romantic not only created an atmosphere favorable to nationalism, but encouraged it; he regarded a nation as an organism with a life of its own, a "national spirit," a "national destiny."

Franklin, Paine, Jefferson, and their fellows were children of the Enlightenment; they were urbane and cosmopolitan gentlemen at home anywhere in the civilized world. But they were also fervent Americans (like John Adams, who called himself "John Yankee" in deliberate distinction from "John Bull") who were aggressively conscious of their differences with Englishmen and Europeans. For this reason Philip Freneau and Joel Barlow could call for "a parliament of man" to rule the world in good eighteenth-century fashion, but also place America as the leading power within it. As Romanticism grew in America it furnished not only a set of conditions favorable to the development of a native nationalistic feeling, but a compulsive bond among Americans who held different points of view about their position and rights within the Empire.

Early in the eighteenth century there existed a feeling of nationality, a common sense of relationship, dim yet perceptible, among the American colonies. By mid-century, certainly, the term "American" had taken on a meaning distinct from "British," "English," or "West Indian." There were, for example, already identifiable differences in vocabulary, and possibly in pronunciation, which stamped certain kinds of colonial English as American. New words were entering the colonial language from French, Dutch, German, and Indian; new terms (such as "back country" and "lightning bug") were coined to describe new phenomena; English terms such as "navigable stream" took on specifically American meanings. By 1756 linguistic divergences were clear enough that the English lexicographer Samuel Johnson thought that there might well be an American brand of English.

At the same time, the American colonies were gradually finding out that they possessed a history, and that it was worth recalling. One of Franklin's chores as colonial agent in London, for example, was to purchase American historical materials for the Philadelphia Library Society. Whereas the aim of seventeenth-century colonial chroniclers had been religious, the eighteenth-century historian's interest was clearly secular. Where had this American society come from, and how had it come to be? Thomas Prince's *Annals,* Hutchinson's *History of the Colony of Massachusetts,* Robert Beverly's *History of Virginia,* William Stith's *Virginia,* William Douglass' *Summary . . . of the British Settlements,* and other histories were written in part, at least, to call attention to the colonial past, a sure indication of cultural self-consciousness. William Smith wrote his *History of New York* (1757), he said, to give "an accurate history of the British empire in this quarter of the world, and the prospect of doing some small service to my country by laying before the publick a summary of its first rise and present state," certainly an expression of something close to nationalism.

These were small signs, but significant ones. While it is difficult to define exactly what the colonies meant by certain terms, it is clear from context that by the opening of the eighteenth century, the word "American" was ordinarily used to describe a particular kind of British colonist. Its use as a separate name for English residents of North America (commonly employed by English officers as a term of contempt) was observed in the war against Spain in 1739, wherein colonial militia served with English troops. Eliza Pinckney of South Carolina made sure she was introduced as "American" when she was presented at Court in 1750, and Franklin's "Poor Richard" called his fellow-colonials "American patriots" in 1752 without the least thought of disloyalty to his King. Colonial students attending Edinburgh in the 1760's were known as "Americans," to be distinguished from other colonials, and both English and colonial newspapers of the period habitually used the term in a similar sense. "Country," on the other hand, in the eighteenth century apparently meant *region* or *province* (as a sergeant in Washington's militia spoke of "our country, New England") or less often (as William Smith apparently used it) the colonies as a whole.

After 1750, however, the term *American* had universally recognized connotations of nationality. When Christopher Gadsden of South Carolina, at the Stamp Act Congress of 1765, said that "There ought to be no New England man, no New Yorker, known on the Continent, but all of us Americans," he spoke with patriotic inclusiveness. From Gadsden it was but a short step to Patrick Henry's premature but nonetheless fervent outburst of 1774 in Continental Congress, "The distinctions between Virginians, Pennsylvanians, New Yorkers, and New Englanders are no more. I am not a Virginian, but an American!" What Henry said was not yet true, nor even typical of all colonists, nor would it be for another generation; but when Edmund Burke in England spoke of "conciliation with America" the next year, he used the word as Henry meant it, tacitly including the residents of all thirteen colonies as one people.

There were divisive factors at work in eighteenth-century colonial life, of course, which tended to reduce the trend toward unity and self-awareness. Each colony had its own history; each had been settled at different times by persons of different religious heritages, commercial aims, and social relationships. The differences between Massachusetts and Maryland, or Rhode Island and South Carolina, were very real. Since each colony for many years had tried to operate with as much autonomy as possible, each had an instinctive suspicion of centralized or distant authority. Portions of several colonies were sparsely settled frontier, whose inhabitants felt at home only in an unformed society. Distances were great, communication unreliable—one could not blame Jonathan Boucher when he confessed himself unable to see how these thirteen disparate colonies could ever discover national unity of their own. To expect "Virginians to form a cordial union with the saints of New England," he thought, would be to expect "the wolf and the lamb to feed together."

Yet there were powerful factors at work to unite the colonies. The simple fact of distance from England tended to generate a society which gradually changed into something different and ultimately American. Placing a number of Englishmen in a new and widely different geographical, economic, social, and political environment produced, generation by generation, a people whose habits and minds diverged more and more from those who remained at home. By the opening of the century the colonists were a relatively homogeneous people, the majority of them born on American soil. It was not always possible—or desirable—to continue to do or believe the same things or to live in the same way in the New World as in the old.

As they created their own society more than a thousand miles removed from the mother country, American colonists were bound in time to display notable variations from the home population. In 1750, English customs, law, church, politics, manners, and language in the Americas had been separated from the homeland for more than a hundred years. The colonies were British, of course. English life and institutions always provided a common central point for colonial culture, yet American habits of thought and patterns of action were not merely imitations of the original. As English and European travellers rarely failed to observe, American life by mid-century displayed a style of its own.

During the early eighteenth century the colonies made tremendous advances in intercolonial communications. New England ships sailed to southern ports, New York and Pennsylvania merchants traded with Boston, Southern produce sold in New York and New Jersey. Northern boys married Southern girls and vice versa; Southern families often sent their sons North for an education, while it was common for Northern college graduates to serve in the South as tutors and teachers. By 1750 there were newspapers in every colony and several in each major city; these circulated freely throughout the colonies and with unusual dispatch after Franklin, who was made Deputy Postmaster General in 1753, reorganized the mail services. Magazines (though many were short-lived) appeared in profusion in the 1740's and after, many of them self-consciously American, dedicated to encouraging a native culture. By mid-century travellers in the colonies remarked that there seemed to be more similarities among the colonies than differences, and correspondingly greater contrasts between the colonies and the rest of the Empire. America was not a microcosm of England.

St. Jean de Crèvecoeur, who became a citizen of New York under the Americanized name of John Hector St. John in 1765, put his finger on another important element in the nationalizing process—that is, the assimilation of diverse European stocks to produce a new American nationality. The colonies in the eighteenth century attracted increasing numbers of non-English colonists whose attachments to the Empire were nil, and whose interests were wholly American. As Crèvecoeur noted, these immigrants quickly developed loyalty to their new home, not to England, and severed just as quickly their allegiances to whatever their country had been. "Here," he wrote in his *Letters of an American Farmer* (1782), "individuals of all nations are melted into a new race of men."

The surrender of loyalty to one country, and its swift transfer to another—as Crèvecoeur perceptively observed it in himself and his contemporaries—was a uniquely American phenomenon. A Dutchman in England or a German in France could never have been so completely accepted and absorbed, as in the case Crèvecoeur cited of the family "whose grandfather was an Englishman, whose wife was Dutch, whose son married a French woman, and whose present four sons have now four wives of our different nations." The product of all this received a new nationality by natural right, for he "becomes an American by being received in the broad lap of our great Alma Mater." This assimilative process, peculiar to the American situation and central to the American colonial experience, produced, Crèvecoeur believed, "new laws, a new mode of living, a new social system . . ., a new man, who acts upon new principles" and who could be nothing else but American.

The struggle between France and England during the first half of the eighteenth century did much to encourage the nascent nationalism of the American colonies. Beginning with the War of Jenkins' Ear against Spain in 1739, Britain began to demand military assistance from the colonies. Serving with British troops, American militiamen discovered significant differences in how they felt and talked and acted, which their contact with Englishmen accentuated rather than diminished. There was little affection lost between the two during the affair, and subsequent military cooperation during the French and Indian wars did not improve the situation. English arrogance infuriated American troops, whose insouciance and independence in turn irritated their commanders. Not all Americans were grieved at Braddock's debacle in the Pennsylvania forest, and Franklin among others took a bit of grim satisfaction at seeing the English learn a lesson.

In another fashion, the service of Americans in the wars against the French helped to solidify and encourage American feeling, since they felt that they were contributing valuable assistance against a common imperial enemy. For the first time, all colonies cooperated in a massive military effort against the "Gallic peril" of Catholic France and felt that they had acquitted themselves well—so well, in fact, that many were convinced that they had tipped the scales for the British cause and had very probably saved Britain herself from French conquest. As Daniel Dulany pointed out in his *Considerations* (1765), since American arms had been "indispensably requisite to the success" of the British cause, the colonial role furnished "an inexhaustible subject" for future praise.

The aggressive British-American patriotism of the war years swiftly gave way to disillusion when England showed few signs of rewarding what the colonies believed were their invaluable services. Franklin spoke for many colonists in 1767, when after having helped Britain win victory, he found that every Englishman "seems to consider himself a piece of a sovereign over America; seems to jostle himself into the throne with the King and talks of *our subjects* in the colonies." The French and Indian wars exposed deep-seated antagonisms between colonies and mother country. With the French threat removed from North America, England no longer needed to make concessions to American sensitivities to gain cooperation. London's policy of "salutary neglect" and leniency was finished.

As the American participation in the wars against the French tended to isolate the colonial identity, so the postwar disappointments of British colonial policy tended to harden colonial feelings against England. Ironically, with the French gone, England took over priority as the common American adversary. It required a certain kind of genius to turn patriotic colonists into rebels within the short space of twenty years, but the British imperial policy succeeded in doing so. A century spent in either evading or protesting governmental restrictions had already shown the colonies some of the advantages of presenting a common front against authority from London. After 1763 the constant, never-settled question of taxation, the suppression of the westward movement, the quartering of soldiers in American homes, the use of admiralty courts and the restrictions placed on jury trials, the clumsiness and stupidities of an inept administration, and all the other grievances detailed so precisely by Franklin in his savage *Rules By Which a Great Empire May be Reduced to a Small One* (1773) unified the colonies as nothing else could have done. "Come join hand in hand, brave Americans all," ran a popular broadside against the Stamp Act,

> And raise your bold hearts to fair Liberty's call!
> Then join hand in hand, brave Americans all,
> By uniting we stand, by dividing we fall.

By 1776 Americans were united in a common national purpose, of which the Declaration of Independence was the ultimate proof.

The relationship between the colonies and England during the eighteenth century was curiously ambivalent. First of all, and especially in the flush of patriotism that followed the victorious wars with France and Spain, the colonists were loyally British. Francis Hopkinson (who ten years later signed the Declaration of Independence) wrote in 1766 that "We in America are in all respects Englishmen, notwithstanding that the Atlantic rolls her waves between us and the throne to which we all owe allegiance." A majority of American colonists at the time probably thought of England as "home" (whether they had ever been there or not) and looked to it as their source of ideas, manners, culture, liberties, and everything that made American society meaningful.

Much of this genuine loyalty to the Empire lasted to the verge of revolution. The Virginia Convention of 1774, rebellious as it was, nevertheless vowed "inviolable and unshaken fidelity and attachment to our most gracious Sovereign," and Continental Congress itself, in July, 1775, assured George III of its continued allegiance. Even Jefferson, two months after Bunker Hill, wrote that he looked "with fondness towards a reconciliation with Great Britain," and President Ezra Stiles of Yale, in the midst of the war, nostalgically recalled "the antient national affection we once had for the present state, which we gloried in being part of the Empire."

The American colonist was proud to be English; he considered England superior to the rest of Europe, its Protestant society (as opposed to Papist France) based on the rule of law, reason, and liberty. Yet he thought of himself as a particular—and special—kind of Briton. He was quite conscious that he was *American* English, and he used the label "American" with greater frequency to indicate the kind of Englishman he was, as distinct from those who lived in England or in another colony. This was perfectly clear from the accounts of American travellers in England. Some, of course, liked it so much they returned at every opportunity or stayed permanently if they could. Others, however, who came back with "St. James' customs" or "London tricks" were lampooned as well as envied. Americans tended to stick together in London, where English ignorance and arrogance helped to solidify their feelings of identity. There were many reports of colonials who had to answer queries as to "whether Boston was the capital of Philadelphia" or if New England were in the West Indies. The English tradition of contempt for colonials helped to reinforce American solidarity; Franklin remarked bitterly in 1775, on "the base reflections on American courage, religion, and understanding" common in English society.

As tensions increased between the colonies and the mother country in the 1750's and 1760's, Americans began to find London society less admirable, less pleasant, and even inferior to the colonial model. Disillusioned American travellers noted the corruption of British politics, the vicious inequalities of the social system, the empty pretentiousness of the aristocracy—which, as one American said, "placed multitudes below the Savage state so that a few may be rais'd above it." What the observant American saw in England sometimes shocked him; William Samuel Johnson found the government shot through with "Intrigue, Party, Interest, and Money," and strait-laced Josiah Quincy went back to Boston disgusted with "this rotten old State." There was a growing conviction in the colonies that England was a decadent nation, that America very likely held out the only real hope for the English future; John Penn in 1771 compared England to "an old man . . ., tottering upon the brink of the grave, whereas America is growing daily toward perfection." It was this America, not England, wrote young Philip Freneau, that would become

> The seat of empire, the abode of Kings,
> The final state wherein time shall introduce
> Renowned characters and glorious works,
> Of high invention and of wondrous art,
> Which not the ravages of time shall waste
> Till he himself has run his long career.

By 1760 an American thought of himself as an Englishman with a difference. He might be as faithfully loyal as any man living in England, but he had a distinct and separate regard for his native colonies and how they fitted into the imperial frame. There were two English societies—his own and that one centered in London—and by insisting that both be recognized he widened the internal rift in the Empire already opened by the French wars. The colonists were always careful to emphasize the dual nature of their imperial allegiance. Franklin did not call himself a British subject, but "an American subject of the King." Young Alexander Hamilton, when he engaged in debate with Loyalist Samuel Seabury, agreed that "we are a part of the British Empire, but in this sense only, as being the freeborn subjects of his Britannic Majesty," thus separating himself from the English Briton with whom he had in common only his fealty to the King. American colonists after 1765 were caught in a conflict of divided loyalties, between their genuinely patriotic attachment to Empire and Crown and their own growing sense of national identity.

This conflict can be most clearly observed in Benjamin Franklin, who in 1765 was a loyal Briton and in 1776 a rebel leader. He believed that America had evolved a society of its own, with its own rights and its own character, which Crown and Parliament were bound to respect. This identification with America did not conflict with his loyalty to King and country but complemented it; as he told Lord Kames in 1767, he believed the American colonies were destined to "become a great country, populous and mighty" and that a sensible government would make a place for it within the Empire. Had this been done, he and many like him perhaps would not have felt forced to choose between their imperial loyalties and their sense of Americanness—but as Franklin also told Kames, he could not find in London "a sufficient quantity of the wisdom necessary to produce such a conduct." Jonathan Boucher, on the other hand, torn between his Americanism and his British loyalty, finally stayed with his King, trying to explain that he was English, yet also American:

It is folly to imagine that, as an Englishman, interested in the welfare of England, I am not equally interested in the welfare of
America. . . . With respect to America, it has been the country of
my choice. I am married in America; and settled in it, if I may
leave, most probably for life. . . . My connexions and friends, whom
I love as I do my own soul, are all of this country.

What Americans wanted and needed after 1765 was recognition by England of their right to exist as a separate, special
kind of Englishman, and the right of the American colonies
to exist as a self-conscious unit within the imperial system.
Franklin spent years in London vainly attempting to explain
this to the English. No American in his right mind considered
leaving the Empire; few, indeed, would have received the
suggestion with anything but horror. But the need for recognition pervaded American thinking, colored American emotions, and influenced American political decisions after 1765.
If Britain had been able to accommodate this need for native
identity within the framework of British nationalism, many
of the problems that plagued American-English relations after
1765 might well have been avoided.

The colonists over the years developed the belief that
because of their special attributes as Americans and their
particular position in the Empire, they were entitled to special
consideration, and that they should be allowed to control
their own destiny with a minimum of interference. Instead,
London retaliated with the well-known series of acts and
orders culminating in the Prohibitory Act of 1775, which
declared the thirteen colonies enemies and to be treated as
such. If American identity could not be maintained within
the Empire, if the newly-formed, aggressive nationalism that
had grown up since 1750 could not be fitted into the imperial
pattern, then it seemed inevitable to the colonial leaders that
it would have to be accomplished outside it.

The Revolution was the decisive act of colonial nationalism.
The term "British Americans," formerly used by the colonists
to describe themselves, disappeared at once. "Our great title
is Americans," wrote Thomas Paine. Granted that the Declara-

tion of Independence did not create a nation full-born, it did join the "United Colonies," and while the Articles of Confederation carefully placed "all sovereign power" in "the States separately" it did at least establish a unified approach to problems of war and self-government. As Charles Beard once wrote, the Declaration made clear that there were *thirteen* colonies, but also that they were *united*. The fact that these colonies combined to declare independence, if it did not create a nation, most certainly created a commonality of purpose in which the seeds of nationality lay. The issues raised by independence and war could be confronted and solved only in nationalistic terms.

Obviously the *victorious* revolution was the most powerful nationalizing force of all—a war in which, historian David Ramsay wrote in 1789, "A continental army, and Congress, composed of men from all the States, by freely mixing together, were assimilated into one mass." During the war the new country gained a set of heroes, a rudimentary government, a charter of liberties, and a list of victories on land and sea, all of which it needed to reinforce its convictions of nationality. The Revolution provided the country with an instant national past. Americans forgot the desertions, the "sunshine patriots" and the unseemly wranglings and remembered Patrick Henry's "Give me liberty or give me death!," the martyrdom of Nathan Hale, Washington's prayers at Valley Forge, and fifers playing "The World Turned Upside Down" at Yorktown. All the necessary materials of a nationalistic tradition came directly out of the war experience.

American leaders after the war agreed that a strong sense of nationalism was especially important for the country's survival. What seemed to Washington a postwar slackening of patriotism troubled him; he hoped most, he wrote John Adams in 1786, "to see the people of America become *one* nation in every respect." Jefferson agreed that it was needful "to cultivate the idea of being one people;" Hamilton told Rufus King that "We are laboring hard to establish in this country principles more and more *national*." Nationalism, properly conceived and channeled, produced responsible, involved citizens. Thus the Creator, Nathaniel Chipman wrote, "incorporated this passion deep and strong in the very nature of man" in order to "fit man for society and civil government." Cultivation of the patriotic impulse was widely acknowledged to be essential to the creation of a national character. "No people," wrote Samuel Knapp, "who do not love themselves better than all others, can ever be prosperous or great. . . . If 'know thyself' be a sound maxim for individual consideration, 'think well of thyself' should be a national one." Therefore, thought Noah Webster, "Every engine should be employed to render the people of this country *national* . . ., and to inspire them with the pride of national character."

For this reason the postwar years rang with demands for a national literature, a national culture, a national system of education, a national history, even a national language (a few enthusiasts suggested Greek or Choctaw) to help to create a nation where none had before existed. Constant watering of the tree of patriotism sometimes led to strange growths—to spread-eagle oratory, flatulent "epics," flag-waving provincialism. But it could also inspire, as it did in Jefferson, a deep, dignified, and dedicated nationalism of the highest order: "The first object of my heart is my own country. In that is embarked my family, my fortune, and my own existence. I have not one farthing of interest, nor one fibre of attachment, out of it."

The Revolutionary War settled the matter of whether or not an American nation would exist, but it did not specify what kind of nation it would be, nor guarantee that it would survive. Nor did the Constitution, second only to the war itself as a nationalizing force, precisely do either. The Convention voted narrowly in May, 1787, that "a national government ought to be established" and then struck out the word *national*; nowhere does it appear in the final document. Similarly, the Constitution did not define citizenship except in dual terms, making each qualified American a citizen of both state and nation. While it furnished some answers to the question of whether the national government or the states were the more powerful, the Constitution did not supply them all, or for that matter enough of them to prevent the first great crisis of nationalism during the War of 1812. The conflict seemed to New England to be a war waged for the benefit of other sections and detrimental to its own; the vote for it, in June, 1812, was perilously close in the Senate and hardly overwhelming in the House. During the war the Federalists toyed with the idea of secession, and demanded a revision of the state-federal relationship that, as Matthew Carey wrote, nearly ran "the national vessel on the rocks and quicksand." The nationalists won the issue and the war, but not by much. Victory did not decide the contest of national and states' rights, which was soon to reappear.

Yet the War of 1812 did, in other ways, hasten the completion of American nationalism. It was a war that the American people were glad to see end; it cost huge sums of money, dislocated business and trade, and exposed huge cracks in the national political structure. But the war seemed to be a victory. American forces met and defeated (or at least had not been defeated by) the world's greatest military and naval power, albeit England's attention had been elsewhere engaged at the time. The war might have been avoided by better statesmanship, and might even have been fought more logically with France, yet from the American viewpoint it gave notice to the world that the United States had arrived as a power. The bumbling and bickering, the charred remnants of the White House, the success of the British blockade, the captured merchantmen and impressed seamen could all be forgotten if one chose to remember the *Constitution* and the *Guerrière,* Perry's gallant "We have met the enemy and they are ours!" or Jackson's victory at New Orleans. "The war has given strength and splendor to the chain of the Union," wrote a South Carolinian. "Every link exhibits the lustre of the diamond. Local feelings are absorbed in the proud feelings of being an American."

The close of the war marked the end of America's lingering colonial complex. It was not really a "second war of Independence," though in a subtle sense there is reason for so calling it, for as Woodrow Wilson once wrote, the war gave the United States "spirit and full consciousness and pride of station as a nation." Out of the clash between the old sense of dependence on Europe and the growing self-consciousness of the new republic, there came a new spirit of self-confidence. The war knit the nation together and matured it. "It has renewed," said Albert Gallatin, who served in Jefferson's cabinet, "and reinstated the national feeling and character which the Revolution had given, and which were daily lessening. The people now have more general objects of attachments. . . . They are more American, they feel and act as a nation."

The eagle never screamed more loudly and proudly than in Jacksonian America. Thomas Low Nichols, writing of those years, remembered that

We were taught every day and in every way that ours was the freest, the happiest, and soon to be the greatest and most powerful country in the world. . . . Our education was adapted to intensify our self-esteem. Ours was the model government of the world; our institutions were model institutions, our country the model Republic. I do not in the least exaggerate. We read it in our books and newspapers, heard it in sermons, speeches, and orations, thanked God for it, in our prayers, and devoutly believed it always.

American holidays were given over to sky-rocketing oratory, parades, pageants, and other evidences of patriotic enthusiasm, especially on the Fourth of July and Washington's birthday. Monuments and statues dedicated to national events and heroes appeared in profusion (exceeded only by the post-Civil War decades) while biographies of American heroes by Parson Weems and dozens of authors like him sold by hundreds of thousands.

Few European visitors failed to note such manifestations of the national pride. One English traveller, in 1834, found the country filled with "presumption, conceit, and gross national vanity." Americans, he complained, "like the Tartar conquerors of China . . ., consider all but themselves barbarous. They are fanatically proud of their own wild country, and love to disparage the rest of the world." But such opinions failed to bother the American who, as Nichols wrote, thought his "the best country in the world":

For all other countries he entertains sentiments varying from pity to hatred; they are the downtrodden despotisms of the old world. There is a certain administration for France, and that respect for Russia which one great and growing power gives to another. But a genuine American does not think much of Europe anyway.

Nationalist fervor was equally visible in the contemporary recognition of the use of history as example and guide for patriotic Americans. Emphasis on the study of American history in the schools produced a flood of texts. Laws requiring the teaching of American history appeared in a number of states, beginning with Massachusetts in 1827. Meanwhile the great Romantic historians—Sparks, Irving, Prescott, Motley, Parkman, Hildreth, Bancroft—wrote history for the public from a national point of view. George Bancroft, in particular, dedicated his life to the discovery of the American character in the past, believing that the United States had been designed by a Divine Providence "to organize social union through the establishment of personal freedom." In his *History of the United States,* begun in 1834, he intended, he said, "to follow the steps by which a favoring Providence, calling our institutions into being, has conducted the country to its present happiness and glory . . ., molded by the creative forces of reason, sentiment, and nature."

As John Trumbull's grandly-conceived paintings in the Capitol dome aroused and expressed the nationalistic pride that swelled Jacksonian America's breast, so did Bancroft's history say what all Americans felt, but few could phrase in such mellifluous prose. This aggressive, self-confident national-ism, of course, produced much of the energy behind the great blooming of nineteenth-century art and literature, which was as avowedly nationalistic as it was culturally creative. A great nation produced great art; America was soon to produce the greatest. Architect Robert Mills (designer of the Washington Monument) wrote:

The nature of our public institutions, the independent character of our people, and the wide field for successful enterprise opened in the various pursuits of life, all tend to enlarge the mind and give the most exalted views on every subject of art and science. Taken in the aggregate, there is not a more liberal or enlightened people on the face of the globe than the people of the United States.

Because of the "vast advantages attached to freedom . . ., and the spirit of energy with which a free people pursue whatever they perceive to be for their interest," said William M'Clure, the geologist, in 1821, America was destined to pre-eminence in all the arts and sciences.

The early decades of the nineteenth century were also much concerned with developing symbols to express this bursting pride and confidence. The United States began its existence with none of the symbolic equipment—heroes, songs, legends, flags, monuments, and so on—needed to express and demonstrate national feeling. Since it had rejected England, the new nation could not use any of the traditional emblems connected with the King, Magna Carta, the long military and naval tradition, and other elements of British nationalism.

Denied the Anglo-Saxon and Anglo-Norman heritage, the nation turned to Greece and Rome (particularly to Rome, the most powerful republic in history) for symbols it might adapt to its own uses. The eagle, both a Roman and an American bird, furnished an equivalent for the British lion. The Great Seal of the United States, adopted in 1776, with its slogan of "E Pluribus Unum" and related devices, was directly derived from similar Roman apparatus. Roman architecture furnished patterns for American public buildings; the upper house of the Congress became a Senate; even Horatio Greenough's statue of Washington, done in 1841, clothed him in a Roman toga. Without a nationalistic tradition of its own, the United States drew heavily on classicism for the forms and symbols it needed to affirm its sense of nationality.

For their heroes Americans turned naturally enough to the recent war, to Marion the Swamp Fox, Ethan Allen's sturdy mountaineers, the defenders of Bunker Hill, the martyred

Nathan Hale, the ragged veterans of Valley Forge, and most of all to Washington, who even before the war closed had almost attained the status of a national deity. Parson Weems' biography (c. 1800) and John Marshall's *Life* (1805-07) fixed the Father-of-His-Country image in the American nationalist tradition. His place was subsequently more firmly secured by his likeness on coins, Gilbert Stuart's portrait in thousands of homes, his name on hundreds of towns and streets, Emanuel Leutze's "Crossing the Delaware" in uncounted reproductions, and of course the Washington Monument (1848-1884). Washington served as the major symbol of American unity.

For their national holidays, Americans during their first half-century or so chose Washington's birthday and the Fourth of July—the day on which Congress finally adopted the amended Declaration. The Fourth of July celebration soon became the most important American national ceremonial; anniversaries of the adoption of the Constitution never aroused so much interest. No token of nationalism became more important than the American flag, which curiously enough at first played a relatively small part in the development of nationalist psychology. Created in 1777 by substituting thirteen stars for the crosses of St. Andrew and St. George in the "Great Union" flag flown by Washington's army, the familiar stars and stripes remained chiefly a naval flag until 1834, when the Army adopted it. Although Francis Scott Key's "Star Spangled Banner" emerged from the War of 1812, neither the song nor the flag attained great importance as national symbols until the Civil War. "My Country 'Tis of Thee," rather lamely put to the tune of "God Save the King" in 1832, never really provided a satisfactory national anthem, nor did the much later "America the Beautiful." "Brother Jonathan" and "Yankee Doodle," at first conceived simply as comic Downeast rustics, were transformed into national prototypes in the late 18th century, but "Uncle Sam," a creation of the War of 1812, soon displaced them.

Certainly by 1830 (to choose a date somewhat arbitrarily) the United States possessed a clear understanding of its identity. Hugh Swinton Legaré found evidence of this in the fact that in America Providence had apparently decided to grant humanity a fresh start. Only in this *new* land, he wrote, did men have the opportunity to control and direct their society "by such principles as philosophy and experience had shown to be best, although they had no where else been fully admitted in practice." In America, far removed from Europe, the Founders

had no inveterate prejudices to encounter here—there was no inheritance of abuses . . ., no grievances established by custom, no corruptions sanctified by their antiquity. . . . The fortunes of the species, are thus, in some degree, identified with those of the REPUBLIC—and if our experiment fail, there is no hope for man this side of the grave.

Francis Grund, the Austrian intellectual who toured the United States in the eighteen-thirties, commented in *The Americans* (1837) on the differences between American patriotism and the European brand. American nationalism was based, he believed, on three things. First, on equality of expectations—each American could legitimately hope for personal and material security. Second, on religious sentiment, for Grund found the churches to be perhaps the most powerfully cohesive factors in American civilization. Third, on the American conviction that the nation had a moral commitment to lead the world toward a better future. These things, Grund felt, largely motivated the vigorous, distinctive nationalism he observed in Jacksonian America.

There was no need, then, in the period following the War of 1812, to encourage nationalism in the broadly patriotic sense, for there was plenty of that. The United States possessed, in more than sufficient measure, that national spirit and self-awareness that Washington, Webster, and Hamilton had hoped it would obtain. Because of the nature of the American political system, the term *Nationalism* instead began to take on a narrower and more specialized meaning, prescribed both by the unique nation-state relationship inherent in the federal political structure, and by the double set of allegiances which the Constitution recognized and perpetuated.

Nationalism, and its antonym *states' rights,* meant that national authority should take precedence over that of the states when the two sets of interests did not coincide. This concept of federal nationality, expressed by the word *union* (later to become the magic talisman of the North) meant nothing to a Briton or European, for it existed only within the American framework of experience. After 1820 the issue of political nationalism appeared more frequently and with greater urgency as the conflict between federal and state loyalties sharpened. The necessity arose to evolve a workable balance between the antagonistic forces of nationalism and sectionalism, those "two opposite tendencies" in American life, Tocqueville called them in 1835, "like two distinct currents flowing in contrary directions in the same channel."

The problem grew partly from national expansion and national diversity. In the seventy years between 1790 and 1860 the national population rose from four million to thirty-one million, while the United States doubled and tripled and quadrupled in size to include areas with highly diverse climate, topography, resources, and population. It needed to be held together. Europe, crammed into a much smaller area, was divided into ten nations; it was freely prophesied (with some logic) that the United States might well go the same way. When California and Oregon joined the Union, for example, the best way to reach them was by a 20,000 mile journey around Cape Horn. It seemed, Henry Adams later remarked, that "Nature had decided that the experiment of a single republican government must meet extreme difficulties," yet no American seriously considered it possible for the nation to disintegrate.

There were a number of reasons why the United States did not dissolve as Europeans frequently predicted it would. Internal migration settled new states from old, while the old states renewed themselves by immigration from abroad. Half the people in Illinois, Missouri, and Texas, according to the census of 1850, came from established communities in the East and South, and almost two-thirds of those in Michigan, Wisconsin, and California. While these new states had family ties with the East and South, they were also closely bound to them by internal commerce. As John C. Calhoun pointed out in 1847, trade held the nation together: "The more enlarged the sphere of our commercial circulation—the more extended that of social intercourse—the more strongly we are bound together—the more inseparable are our destinies." These new states, despite their distance from Washington, historically were children of the Federal government, which distributed their land, protected them from Indians, governed them as territories, and supervised their admission to the Union. Their orientation was always national. Fanny Wright, who travelled through the back country in 1818 and 1819, noted even then that "Bred up under the eye, and fostered by the care of the federal government, they have attached themselves to the national institutions with a devotion of feeling unknown in older parts of the Republic."

Providentially for the United States, it participated in the world-wide major revolution in transportation and communication which furnished the country with effective new ways of unifying its vast expanses. Turnpikes and canals supplied swifter and more economical means of moving people and goods; steamboats and railroads changed the whole pattern of industrial development. By 1860 the United States had 4000 miles of canals, 1000 steamboats on the Mississippi alone, and 30,000 miles of track. The first long-distance telegraph message (1844), the high speed press, and an improved postal system changed continental communications. The United States, during the years between Jefferson and Lincoln, developed a highly-integrated economic system and a complex network of internal communication which bound the nation together more closely than ever before, "throwing new bonds around the union," wrote Asa Child, "which will grow stronger as we pursue our forward march."

While nationalism grew, so did sectionalism, at an equally swift rate. Whatever the commitments of the American public to the national purpose, there were regions within the nation which were so geographically and socially unified as to possess a sense of distinction from the rest of the country. The United

States had a traditional resistance to nationalization, too—a belief in provincial individuality that had deep historical roots. As Frederick Jackson Turner later characterized it, the United States was "a union of potential nations, a federation of sections." Throughout the first half of the nineteenth century there was a constant exploration of the issue of national versus sectional interests; the controversy over states' rights attempted to establish what a reasonable and acceptable definition of *nationalism,* in this peculiarly American situation, really was.

The issue was most clearly brought into focus by the argument over state and national sovereignty that ran through the period between the close of the War of 1812 and Lincoln's election in 1860. It divided the North and South, the Charleston *Mercury* thought (somewhat extravagantly) into "two nations, as distinct as the English and French." During the 1830's lines of division on the matter were beginning to appear, soon to grow sharper. On the one side, sentiment in the Northeast and Northwest polarized about the concept of nationalized union: on the other, sentiment in the South, strongly influenced by the economic and social conditions of slavery, crystallized about the diffused, particularized concept of states' rights. It was not a question of patriotism—the Southern point of view was as thoroughly American as the Northern—but one of fixing the boundaries of national authority. The North called for the recognition of a centralized, nationalized power that represented the majority will and was responsive to it; the South demanded a re-definition of *Union* that recognized sectional and minority rights.

The case for state sovereignty was ably argued by John Taylor of Caroline, among others, in *Constructions Construed and Constitutions Vindicated* (1820). The ultimate sovereignty, wrote Taylor, rested in the people of the states, each separately considered. The people made the states, and the states, acting through the Constitution, made the Union; the federal union was therefore a creation of the state, and the state a creation of the people. The great architect of states' rights, however, was John C. Calhoun of South Carolina, who developed the concept that the nation was built out of a compact among co-equal elements, each of which retained its sovereignty. "Ours is a system of governments," he wrote,

> compounded out of the separate governments of the several States composing the Union and of one common government of all its members, called the Government of the United States. The former preceded the latter, which was created by their agency.

Questions of the nature and scope of political authority raised by the Southern argument had a crucial bearing on the nature and coloration of American nationalism. The position of slaves and the institution of slavery within the Southern social and political system, of course, further complicated the issue of relationships between the states and the Federal union. The South maintained that the Union was chiefly an abstract convenience, the North that it was palpable and indivisible. What was the national unit—a state, or a union of states? To which of these did the national allegiance belong?

While Southern political thinkers developed their concept of divided nationalism and state sovereignty, Northerners became increasingly committed to the belief that sovereignty was located in the people—nationally considered—and that the federal union of the states was a perpetual, undivided entity which expressed that sovereignty. The idea of a supra-political union of the American states, arising out of a common human fraternity, had been popular since the eighteenth century, when James Wilson in 1790 called for "a Union of hearts and affections" derived from "the patriotic emanations of the soul" which would be "diffused over the whole Union" and bind it together by "an expansion of mind, of talent, and of temper."

To men of the generation of Washington, Jefferson and Madison (who himself hoped for "one paramount Empire of reason, benevolence, and brotherly affection") the word *union* carried connotations that lay beyond legal or political definition. A pervasive belief in unionism was even more fundamental to the national feeling, Josiah Quincy thought in 1812, than "that paper contract called the Constitution," for it secured national unity through a "moral sentiment which pervades all, and is precious to all."

To the post-Revolutionary generation, the concept of a strong federal union seemed an essential device for preserving national unity, security, and liberty, but not as an end in itself. So long as this feeling held true, the majority of Americans, North and South, believed the exact nature of this union not irrevocably fixed, but subject to change and modification according to need. Within the next generation, however, the feeling arose that the idea of the Union was itself so valuable, so exalted, so crucial to the pursuit of American ideals, that it represented something much more than a means. William Ellery Channing, speaking in 1835, expressed the change precisely. "Most men value the Union as a means," he wrote, "to me it is an end. Most would preserve it for the prosperity of which it is the instrument; I love and would preserve it for its own sake." "So dear to me is Union," he added, "next to liberty, it is our highest national interest." Alexis de Tocqueville, writing his impressions of America that same year, noted that to Americans "the Union is an ideal nation that exists, so to speak only in the mind," and that it served as a powerful factor in conditioning American nationalism.

This belief in the United States as the ideal Union, gathering greater emotional charge as the years passed, came into direct conflict with the concept of state sovereignty rapidly developing in the South. From the Northern point of view the Union was (as Edward Everett called it) "a metaphysical and theoretical thing." It was something that defied definition, Daniel Webster said, "a settled conviction, and an habitual feeling, that these twenty-four states are one country."

The issue between these opposing points of view concerning the nature of the Union was most dramatically presented in 1830 during the Senate debate over tariffs. When Senator Robert Hayne of South Carolina advanced and explained the prevailing Southern theory of state sovereignty, he was answered by Massachusetts' Daniel Webster, whose strongly nationalist interpretation represented the consensus of Northern opinion. His "Reply to Hayne," as it became known, soon attained the status of an oratorical classic. It was Webster who first defined the American Union in quasi-religious terms and who first created, with his considerable rhetorical talents, the emotionalist mystique which enveloped it in Northern minds. His motto, "Liberty and Union, now and forever, one and inseparable!" became his generation's slogan in the North.

Webster's presentation was perhaps the most attractive, but the idea of a nationalized union was also given form by many others. Francis Lieber, the Columbia political scientist, helped to provide an intellectual background for Webster's plea by emphasizing the nation as the highest form of political association. William Seward, Charles Sumner, and many others in terms almost as eloquent as Webster's developed and expanded his theme, creating in the North a deification of Union that went far beyond argumentative analysis. Nations, wrote Congressman Owen Lovejoy of Illinois, required "some nucleas thought, some central idea which they could enshrine." For the United States, it was *union,* that "holy instrument around which all American hearts cluster and to which they cling with the tenacity of a semi-religious attainment."

"Union," said a New York editor, was "a divine instrument . . ., the offspring of something more than human wisdom," given to the United States for its progress, or, as Henry Wadsworth Longfellow wrote eloquently in his famous poem, "Building of the Ship" in 1849,

> Then too, sail on O Ship of State!
> Sail on, O UNION, strong and great!
> Humanity with all its fears,
> With all the hopes of future years,
> Is hanging breathless on thy fate!

The New England lawyer and orator Rufus Choate, speaking at a July 4th celebration in Massachusetts in 1858, put this feeling well in the flowery, intense prose of the period. The Union, he said, was "a state of consciousness, as a spring of feeling, as a motive to exertion." The idea

fills your mind and quickens the heart of millions around you. Instantly, under such an influence you ascend above the smoke and stir of this small local strife; you tread upon the high places of earth and history; you think and feel as an American for America; her power, her eminence, her consideration, her honor are yours.

Unionism and *nationalism* were virtually synonymous by Lincoln's time, an identification illustrated most clearly, perhaps, by his attitude toward the issue of war. The concept of a nationalized, unified democracy—represented by the principle of union—was the guiding doctrine of Lincoln's life, one that he erected into an almost mystical principle. "The world's best hope depended on the continued union," he believed, and he hoped that "the chorus of Union," as he said in his First Inaugural, would be swelled by "the mystic chords of memory, stretching from every battlefield, and patriot grave, to every heart and hearthstone, all over this broad land." The war in which he reluctantly engaged was to him a war for the Union, nothing else. Its aim was to preserve the United States as an indivisible unit, a nation and not a federation; his "paramount object," he told Horace Greeley, was "to save the union."

Since the Union furnished the means by which men raised themselves to freedom, the war to Lincoln was "a struggle for maintaining in the world that form and substance of a government whose leading object is to elevate the condition of men." To Lincoln the idea of Union was both political and intensely personal. The covenant which created the Union Lincoln thought of in theological terms as a contract or covenant that since it had divine sanction, was therefore irrevocable. In his First Inaugural he stated this in unequivocal terms, saying, "I hold that, in contemplation of universal law and the Constitution, the Union of these states is perpetual." While there were those in the North, as in the South,

who did not like the idea of a union maintained by the force
of arms, there were a great many more who agreed with
Lincoln that without force there would be no union, and
without union no nation. Why thousands of Northern boys
who had never seen a slave went to war to maintain that
union was expressed directly and simply by a popular song of
the Union Army camps:

> The Union forever, hurrah! boys, hurrah!
> Down with the traitor, up with the star,
> While we rally round the flag, boys, rally once again,
> Shouting the battle cry of Freedom!

The Civil War marked a bloody, anguishing climax to the
American nationalizing process; both victor and vanquished
so recognized, for even the defeated South agreed that whether
or not its cause deserved to lose, it had lost, and the nation
was one. Terrible as the war was, it preserved the Union and
made an end to the constitutional issue of nationalism. As the
Supreme Court put it succinctly in *Texas v. The United
States* (1869), the war decisively proved that the nation was

an indestructible union of indestructible states . . ., [which] began
among the colonies and grew out of a common origin, mutual
sympathies, kindred principles, similar interests, and geographical
relations.

But more important than any legal settlement was the
emotional validity of the victory for the Union, reflected in
the thousands of commemorative orations and celebrations
over the next half-century. The war, Charles Sumner explained
in an oration titled "Are We A Nation?" gave a conclusive
answer, for it had "regenerated and redeemed" the country,
making it "One and Indivisible, with a new consciousness of
national life." James Russell Lowell, writing in 1865 when
national "memories of common danger and common triumph"
were still fresh, concluded that the United States had gained
from the experience a "conscious feeling of nationality, the

ideal abstract of history and tradition" which older countries possessed but which Americans had not, until then, developed in mature form. He went on, with admirable lucidity, to explain what was meant by this new consciousness of nationality:

Loyalty has hitherto been a sentiment rather than a virtue; it has been more often a superstition or a prejudice than a conviction of the conscience or the understanding. Now for the first time it is identical with patriotism, and has its seat in the brain, not the blood. . . . Every man feels himself a part, and not a subject, of the government, and can say in a truer sense than Louis XIV, "I am the state." Every man feels himself a part, sensitive and sympathetic, of this vast organism, a partner in its life or death.

Nobody could have said it better.

American nationalism during the latter half of the nineteenth century was confident and self-assured. The nation had survived the greatest threat in its history to its existence, and it looked ahead with assurance. Albion W. Tourgée, assessing "The Renaissance of Nationalism" in 1887, believed that it no longer displayed the "stridency and urgency" of prewar decades but was now "positive and active, serious and earnest." Francis Walker, writing a few years later, came to much the same conclusion; the United States exhibited, he said, "instincts and feelings of common interests and a common destiny" that together constituted "a positive force" for national progress. As evidence, Walker might have cited, among other things, the large number of flourishing patriotic societies—nearly fifty new ones—founded after 1875, including the Daughters of the American Revolution, the Military Order of the Loyal Legion, and the most powerful veterans' organization of all, the Grand Army of the Republic. Finley Peter Dunne's Irish commentator, "Mr. Dooley," summed up the prevailing temper of his times in a conversation with his friend Hennessy. " 'We're a great people,' said Mr. Hennessy earnestly. 'We are,' said Mr. Dooley. 'We are that. An' th' best iv it is, we know that we are.' "

The emergence of the United States as a world power, somewhat to the surprise of the American people, required a re-evaluation and a re-definition of nationalism within a larger, international frame of reference. Except for the Mexican War, which was only a brief foray into international affairs, the United States for more than a half-century had found it possible to develop its sense of nationality in relative isolation. But beginning about 1870, the nation found itself implicated in a complex and intricate web of worldwide relations; no longer could American nationalism exist in a vacuum, without reference to other nationalisms.

The central principle of American foreign affairs during the latter decades of the nineteenth century rested on an imperialism formed out of a number of factors—the American missionary zeal, the popularity of certain racist doctrines of Anglo-Saxon supremacy, and most of all, an aggressive industrialized capitalism that strongly influenced American foreign policy. New advances in technology brought tremendous increases in industrial productivity, creating a demand for materials and markets not available in the country itself; to find them, American economic interests had to go abroad. The "manifest destiny" of the 1840's was an agrarian imperialism, motivated by the need for new land. The imperialism of the 80's and 90's was business-centered, a search for new sources of markets and investments. Senator Albert Beveridge put it bluntly: "American factories are making more than the American people can use; the American soil is producing more than they can consume. Fate has written our policy for us; the trade of the world must and shall be ours."

The prevailing belief in Social Darwinism was also especially adapted to imperialistic foreign policy, for the idea of natural selection among nations, based on principles of force and competition, contained all the ingredients needed to make it appeal to public approval. The pseudo-Darwinian thesis that certain races and nations were naturally superior to others, and that natural leadership was to be granted to certain peoples, provided a useful vocabulary for imperialism. The Anglo-Saxon peoples were, as Beveridge said, "a conquering race," destined to "occupy new markets and if necessary new lands." The Reverend Josiah Strong's *Our Country* (1885), a book of great popular influence, explained that the United States ought to "exercise a commanding influence in the world's future," since

it is manifest that the Anglo-Saxon holds in its hands the destinies of mankind, and it is evident that the United States is to become the home of this race, the principal seat of his power, the great center of his influence.

Admiral Alfred Thayer Mahan, in his *Influence of Sea Power Upon History* (1892) and later writings, assumed that national self-interest motivated all human activity, and that international relations must be considered always in the light of this fundamental fact. "The principle of independent nationality," he wrote, "has played . . . a great and beneficent part in the history of European civilizations for the past four hundred years." Attempts to reduce its influence as a factor in foreign affairs, he maintained, would simply hamper the United States' ability to deal with the modern world.

Mixed thus with racism, militarism, and imperialism, American nationalism reinforced the outward thrust that characterized American expansion after 1890—the era of "dollar diplomacy," landings by the Marines, and flagwaving speeches about "national destiny." The United States was not alone in this; Britain, France, Germany, Russia, Holland, and Japan were equally at work in the "backward" portions of the world with much the same aims. Nor was there much doubt about America's success at playing the imperialist game. Secretary of State Richard Olney could say with some accuracy and satisfaction in 1896, "Today the United States is practically sovereign on this continent, and its fiat is law upon the subjects to which it confines its interposition."

The great climax of nationalistic imperialism, of course, was the Spanish-American War. This ninety-day military adventure marked a turning point in American history, for it made the United States a major military force, committed it to a colonial empire, and enmeshed it irretrievably in international affairs. As the Philadelphia *Record* wrote accurately and succinctly of the effects of that war, "Willy nilly, we have entered upon our career as a world power." To defeat an ancient European nation (though a sadly decadent one) in an easy and almost bloodless three months, was a tremendous boost to the national morale, but the victory brought with it, as the more thoughtful were well aware, some real questions about the future nature of American nationalism.

Two articles in *The Forum* in 1898, assessed the meaning of the war and put the issue into focus. John R. Proctor stated the dilemma—could the United States return to its historic policy of isolation or must it "take its rightful place among the World Powers and assume the unselfish obligations" demanded by that leadership? Proctor thought the nation ought to follow the second course; the United States, he said, whether it knew it or not, bore responsibility for "a new Imperialism, destined to carry worldwide the principles of Anglo-Saxon justice and peace, liberty and law." William MacDonald took an opposite view. The new American involvement in the world's affairs raised hard-to-answer questions "about our national hopes and desires, about our place and work in the world, about what we want *our* America to become." Entanglement with the rest of the world was "not in harmony with the historic American spirit;" to commit American power abroad would "sacrifice many of the things which thus far have made us great." What was the nature and function of nationalism in an increasingly interlocked and interdependent world? Was simple, though sincere, dedication to one's country's aims—to the exclusion of others'—an adequate instrument for measuring decisions which irrevocably involved other nations in the world?

No prominent person in public life during the period (until the appearance of Woodrow Wilson) was more aware of the problem of nationalism versus internationalism than Theodore Roosevelt; certainly none tried more earnestly than he to work out a set of answers. As President, what Roosevelt said and did was of course national policy, but more than that, Roosevelt's opinions had tremendous impact on the thinking of the times. A reader of Mahan, and more than a little influenced by Anglo-Saxonism, Roosevelt welcomed the Spanish-American war, and made a good deal of his reputation in it. He saw international affairs as a struggle for survival of the fittest, and (in an interesting essay called "Biological Analogies in History") theorized about the biological reasons for the growth and decline of nations. His concept of nationalism was ultimately Darwinian; nations were strong and survived, or they were not strong enough to survive.

On this base he erected a rather sophisticated theory of nationalistic imperialism, in which the mission of the United States was not only to survive, but to do so in order to extend "the ideas of civilization and Christianity" over the world as needed. Nationalism was to him essential for survival, and he hailed (in his essay "True Americanism") that "broadly American and national virtue" as a powerful and desirable attribute of personal life; he could not brook "hyphenated Americans," he said, or that "flaccid habit of mind which its possessors style cosmopolitanism." Patriotic pride seemed to him "the most essential element in the success of a great, free, modern democracy."

Yet Roosevelt was never quite satisfied with this kind of simplistic definition, for he knew that the United States could not maintain its traditional nationalistic isolation in the light of contemporary international facts. "To us is given the privilege," he said in 1901,

of playing a leading part in the century that has just opened. . . . Whether we wish it or not, we cannot avoid hereafter having duties in the face of other nations. All that we can do is to settle whether we shall perform these duties well or ill.

"A great nation must think first of its own internal affairs," he said again in 1911, "and yet it cannot substantiate its claim to be a great nation unless it thinks of its position in the world at large."

Sooner than many of his political contemporaries, and often more clearly than they, Roosevelt located the central dilemma of the turn-of-the-century nationalism—that is, that as the distinction between foreign and domestic affairs broke down, the line separating national interest from international involvement became much more difficult to locate. As Walter Lippmann later remarked, the United States of Theodore Roosevelt's time began to see that very few important problems were wholly domestic, that the current problem was both "to reform and advance our own social order, and at the same time to recognize that we must live in a world beyond our frontiers." Roosevelt was among the first of the influential American political leaders to perceive this fact, and to attempt a sincere (though often ambivalent) synthesis of nationalism and internationalism in response to the challenge it presented.

When Roosevelt was awarded the Nobel Peace Prize, he advocated, in his address of acceptance, the creation of a world organization with strong police powers, in which the United States would play a leading part. But he also bitterly opposed Wilson's League of Nations, for he believed that it forced the nations who joined it to surrender too much of their distinctive and separate nationalities. He envisioned an organization of strongly independent states which cooperated on issues affecting common interests, but which maintained the separate unity and autonomy of each—a league of *nations,* he made clear, not an *international* league. "Let us absolutely refuse to abolish nationalism," he wrote in 1919;

On the contrary, let us base a wise and practical internationalism on a sound and intense nationalism. . . . Let us build a genuine internationalism, that is a genuine and generous regard for the rights of others, as the only healthy basis—a sound and intense development of the broadest spirit of American nationalism.

The United States entered the twentieth century facing the problem much as Roosevelt stated it, and with more or less the same ambiguous answers. The nation had a powerful sense of its identity; "We have come to full maturity with this new century of our national existence," Woodrow Wilson wrote quite truthfully in 1902, "and to full self-consciousness as a nation." Granting this, how could the nation remain national, yet accept its responsibilities for leadership in an increasingly complicated and internationalized world? Over the preceding century the task had been to develop, and then to maintain, a mature and integrated nationalism; now the problem was, how to turn this outward?

From its beginnings, American nationalism had been marked by a strong sense of separation; now the pressures of the world beyond its shores were too great to disregard. Archibald Coolidge, Theodore Roosevelt's friend, stated the problem well in 1908. America, he wrote in *The United States as a World Power*, "may be a world in itself, but it is also part of a larger world. There is no doubt but its power for good and for evil is very great. How that power is to be used is of consequence to all humanity." This became the theme—and the dilemma—of the development of American nationalism in the twentieth century.

The outbreak of World War I in Europe brought Americans to a close and careful re-examination of the problem. When the European nations rushed at each other's throats in the name of nationality, it raised in American minds a good many questions about the morality of nationalism and its function in twentieth-century relationships among states. If a clash of irrational and exaggerated nationalisms caused the war, as many believed it had, what was the lesson to be gained? Some agreed with Edward Krehbiel, who in 1916 after asking "Is Nationalism an Anachronism?" concluded that it was, and a dangerous one, "out of date . . ., no longer in keeping with modern facts, no longer the cohesive unit of society." Historian James Harvey Robinson, that same year in a thoughtful essay called "What Is National Spirit?" doubted if it was "the beneficent thing we have all been taught from the cradle it was," and doubted even more its relevance to the situations of the contemporary world. As Woodrow Wilson put it in his Inaugural of 1917, the facts of modern life made all Americans "citizens of the world," bringing the nation into "cooperation with the wide and universal forces of mankind."

The American entry into World War I, as a member of an allied group joined in a common military effort, of course committed the nation to the closest kind of international cooperations. For the first time since the Revolution the United States engaged in war with European nations as allies; at its close the country woke to the realization that these wartime international obligations were not readily relinquished. The United States was surprised to find, Franklin Giddings wrote in 1919, that it was suddenly an international power; until the war ended, "her own people did not know for what achievements she was ready." America's involvement created, as Giddings observed, a greater public sympathy and perception than ever before of its international power and responsibilities. The United States emerged from the conflict with a better understanding of the interdependence of nations in the twentieth-century world; a revised concept of the implications of foreign affairs as they affected domestic policy and the national interest; and a much clearer realization of the need for the United States to assume a larger role in matters of international security.

But the total effect of the American military experience was far more nationalistic than internationalist. The circumstances of war itself—recruiting, bond drives, new techniques of persuasion and opinion-control, the wartime psychology,— these and other elements of the military effort were powerful nationalizing factors. Poet Amy Lowell sensed this in 1918, when she wrote that

The welding together of the whole country which the war has brought about, the mobilizing of our whole population into a single, strenuous endeavor, has produced a more poignant sense of nationality than has recently been the case. . . . Hyphens are submerged in this solid overprinting of the word "American."

War created national feeling, remarked *The Independent,* which was good—patriotism turned "a mob into a people, a stretch of hills and plains into a country, a place into a home. . . . It must be a religion because it works miracles." Afterwards, the backlash of this warborn nationalism testified to the force of the emotions loosed by the conflict. Military leaders campaigned for preparedness and larger military appropriations; veterans' and other groups supported (often uncritically) numerous attempts to "teach patriotism" and to use the public schools for nationalist ends. The Ku Klux Klan made white supremacy, anti-Semitism, and anti-Catholicism into "one hundred per cent Americanism" and tried to enforce its definition by intimidation and violence. Results such as these were not quite what Miss Lowell and *The Independent* had in mind.

The discussion of the Treaty of Versailles confronted the United States squarely with the issue of isolation versus international participation. Could American nationalism be preserved if the United States involved itself more deeply in international affairs? Would the American sense of identity be endangered or diminished by American participation in what many believed to be the final solution for the historic problems of nationalism? The issue was most dramatically presented in the argument over the League of Nations and discussions of the amount of support that the United States might or might not give the League. The debate was complicated by personalities and party politics, but at the bottom the issue was whether or not the United States was yet ready to surrender something of its traditional nationalistic independence in foreign affairs and launch itself into the world community.

If a major cause of the World War was nationalism run wild, as more than a few thoughtful Americans and Europeans believed, then the maintenance of future peace depended on less nationalism and more internationalism. In Europe a group called The Central Organization for a Durable Peace appeared even before the fighting stopped, while the Fourteenth Point of Woodrow Wilson's famous speech to Congress in 1918 called for "a general association of nations" in the postwar world. As early as 1901 he had spoken of the need for the United States to join "the universal world of commerce and ideas" and of its "peculiar duty . . . to moderate the process" of international cooperation. The American entry into the war was to his mind a commitment to internationalism. Wilson remarked at Versailles that he regarded Allied support of an international organization or league of nations "as the keystone of the whole program which expressed our purposes and ideals in this war."

Yet Wilson's internationalism was of a peculiarly American kind. He no doubt spoke for the majority of Americans when he defined the war as one "to make the world safe for democracy," for the United States saw the ideal postwar world as one safe for *American*-style democracy. If what Wilson proposed was internationalism, it was an internationalism postulated on America extended, assuming that the result would be—someday—a kind of United States of the world. Wilson and his fellow Americans took for granted that people everywhere shared American ideals and goals, that if given freedom to choose ("self-determination of peoples") they would choose to copy the American model. As Daniel Aaron has perceptively remarked, "Wilson's demand that the world be made safe for democracy expressed the nascent American belief that America should become the norm of the world."

Wilsonian internationalism, therefore, was in effect a projection of American nationality into universal terms. Wilson saw American ideals "not as the principles of a province or a single continent," but as "the principles of a liberated mankind," applicable to any society at any time. He believed (as many did) that the nations of the world could establish among themselves a relationship much like that which held together the American states; that each could work out compromises with the others for the good of all under an American-style federalistic system. His ideal was the Americanization of the world. Unfortunately, as it happened, this view did not take into account the revolutionary character of twentieth-century nationalism, the bitter residues of class and racial conflicts left by centuries of war and oppression, or the drive for power and national aggrandizement that less idealistic political leaders might possess. But the vision of Wilson's America had strength and purity of purpose, and more than a few held it with him.

Many, of course, did not. Hostility to Wilson himself, lingering resentment over his narrow and unexpected victory in 1916, massive accumulations of party, personal and even racial animosities persuaded a number of powerful political leaders to oppose any further American involvement in the consequences of the war and to avoid acceptance of any further international responsibilities. The powerful tradition of American national isolation, augmented by wartime emotions, generated strong opposition to the League of Nations. *The North American Review* in 1919 summarized popular suspicion of the League by remarking that if it were a "league of nations, and not of denationalized anomalies," it might favor it—but that unless the United States entered any such organization "as a *nation,* with all the rights and privileges of complete and sovereign nationality unimpaired," it ought not to do so at all. In other words, as Senator Fernald of Maine cried, there would be "no surrender of the national flag."

The champion of isolation who rose in the Senate on February 21, 1919, to challenge Wilson's Versailles speech, was William E. Borah of Idaho, who dedicated much of his long public career to keeping the United States free of international commitments. To Borah, American participation in the League represented "the first distinct effort to sterilize nationalism . . ., yielding our Americanism before the onrushing tide of revolutionary internationalism." No international organization, he believed, could equal the "wisdom and conscience and humanitarianism of the hundred million free and independent liberty-loving souls to whom the living God has intrusted the keeping of the Republic." "I do not want this Republic," he concluded,

its free people and its institutions, to go into partnership with and to give control of the partnership to those, many of whom have no conception of our civilization and no true insight into our destiny. What we want is what Roosevelt taught and urged—a free, untrammeled nation, imbued anew and inspired again with the national spirit.

Though the national election of 1920 was not a mandate by the public for or against the League, since a number of other issues were involved, the results were so interpreted. Warren Harding, the new President, called for a return to "triumphant nationalism," and stated what he conceived to be the national position in his Inaugural: "We do not mean to be entangled. We will accept no responsibility except as our conscience and judgment may determine." This was the mood of the twenties—an isolationist mood, represented quite accurately by Harding and his successors, Coolidge and Hoover. (Coolidge's Secretary of State, Charles Evans Hughes, at first did not even bother to acknowledge communications addressed to him from the League of Nations.) Republican victories at the polls in the elections of 1924, 1926, and 1928 did much to silence the internationalists, although several prominent party leaders—such as Charles Evans Hughes and Henry Stimson—were not ready to accept isolationism as permanent American policy.

One of the most important reasons for the return to nationalism of the twenties was disillusion with the results of the war. The excesses of wartime propaganda backfired badly; the world seemed no more safe for democracy than before. The grand result of the great American sacrifice appeared to be, wrote Herbert Gibbons bitterly, that "three men sat with their tongues in their cheeks . . . and drew a new map of Europe that would suit the foreign policies of Great Britain, France, and Italy." John Maynard Keynes' *Economic Consequences of the Peace* (1919) and other assessments of the Versailles settlement played on the theme that American moral idealism had been betrayed by self-seeking political leaders; as *The Review of Reviews* interpreted recent history in 1926,

The world was moving rapidly in the direction of a better and happier mode of life for the vast majority, when foolish and criminal leaders precipitated the World War. [*These*] governments were chiefly responsible for the war and its incalculable disasters.

It became fashionable to assume, Walter Lippmann wrote, that America entered the war "because of British propaganda, the loans of bankers, and the machinations of President Wilson's advisers." During the two decades following the war they fought together, the distance which separated America from her allies was greater than at any point in the forty years preceding.

To maintain American identity, the twenties and thirties believed, the United States must avoid entanglement with the Old World and re-emphasize its own national purposes. The nation should stay out of the world's troubles; Europe was warlike, not to be trusted, full of intrigue. Beneath the foreign policy of the period ran the traditional American conviction of separateness, superiority, self-reliance—the United States was better than Europe, had little need of it, and risked danger by getting too closely involved with it. Isolation, as the twenties defined it, was a revised version of Washington's Farewell Address. Harding, who had a gift for oversimplification, expressed the prevailing disposition very well. "Call it the selfishness of nationality if you will," he said. "I think it an inspiration to patriotic devotion—a safeguard to America first . . ., to think of America first, to exalt America first." Nicholas Roosevelt was quite correct in concluding an article in *Current History,* in 1929, with the statement that "American nationalism has never been so strong."

The debate over America's position in world affairs extended without diminution into the thirties, brought into sharper focus by the gradual but perfectly perceptible division of Europe into totalitarian and non-totalitarian states. A choice had to be made, but few Americans wanted to be forced into making it. When Ernest Hemingway wrote in his *Notes on the Next War* (1935) that he wanted to stay clear of "the hell broth that is brewing in Europe. . . . We were fools to be sucked in once in a European war, and we should never be sucked in again," plenty of Americans agreed with him. Senator Borah, who headed the Senate Foreign Relations Committee from 1924 to 1933, explained what "American Foreign Policy in a Nationalistic World" ought to be to the Council on Foreign Relations in 1934. The fact was, said Borah, that "hopes that the war was to give us a new world have in no way been realized." Internationalism was wrong and dangerous; it "rests upon a false foundation. And when undertaken, it will fail as in the name of progress and humanity it should." Nationalism, "the strongest and noblest passion, outside of those which spring from man's relation to his God," remains the "great welding, cementing, driving power" of the American people.

American opinion during the thirties was very likely with Borah. Public opinion surveys taken between 1935 and 1939 showed that a heavy majority of those polled believed every effort should be made to preserve American neutrality from Europe's problems. Franklin Roosevelt's "quarantine the aggressors" speech in Chicago in 1937, in which he suggested that the United States ought to commit itself to a positive role in world affairs, drew such violent reactions that Roosevelt felt constrained to explain and modify his position. (Ironically, a public opinion poll taken at almost the same time showed that seventy-one per cent of those asked, answered "Yes" to the question, "Do you think it was a mistake for the United States to enter the World War?") Herbert Hoover in 1939 spoke for a large segment of the public when he warned that "when we take sides in their controversies . . ., we are playing power politics at the European chess table." With the memory of World War I still fresh, the nation wanted neither involvement or commitment. Thus in Congress the opposition to Lend-Lease, "destroyers-for-bases," and other measures to aid the Allies against Germany and Italy met real opposition, based on wide popular support; it should not be forgotten that in 1941 Congress very nearly liquidated the American Army.

As it had in 1914, the outbreak of war in Europe again brought the United States to the edge of decision. A substantial portion of the public believed that the United States should remain neutral, whatever the course of the European war, since the American national interest demanded it. "We have nothing to fear from a Nazi European victory," the

American First Committee said in September, 1941; "When shall we learn that Europe is Europe, America is America, and there are two worlds?" asked the *Saturday Evening Post* that year. "The fight in Europe is not our fight," said Senator Henry Cabot Lodge, Jr., in 1939. "It is theirs. If the British and French empires cannot stand without our help, then they deserve to fall."

Another segment of public opinion, represented by the Committee to Defend America by Aiding the Allies, countered by claiming that the safety of the nation required that it support the Allies, even, as some thought, to the point of intervention. Both were, of course, equally nationalistic in that both set the national interest as the criterion of choice; the debate between them centered on the manner of its protection. Thanks in part to the role played by Wendell Wilkie, the defeated Republican candidate for President in 1940, and to Senator Arthur Vandenberg, a great deal of what might have been bitterly partisan opposition to the nation's international responsibilities failed to develop.

Pearl Harbor, naturally, settled the argument, but the debate over the relationship that the United States should hold to the rest of the postwar world continued throughout the war. The actual entrance of the nation into the conflict came from necessity, not from any assumption by the United States of its international obligations. Yet in the course of the war the nation committed itself more completely to international collaboration than ever before in its history, wartime or peacetime—at Casablanca, Quebec, Moscow, Cairo, Teheran, Bretton Woods, Dumbarton Oaks, Yalta and Potsdam. Would postwar nationalism (as after World War I) bring isolation and separation, or would the United States find the means to align its traditional nationalism with its obvious postwar responsibilities for helping to determine the shape of the postwar world? "The Second World War," wrote Reinhold Niebuhr, "raised the old tension in our national soul—between our senses of virtue, power, and responsibility—to a global dimension."

At the end of the war the United States found itself in a

position of undisputed world power, whether it liked it or not. At the same time, a great number of Americans wished more than anything else to return to the simplicities of prewar isolation. The nation had everything it could desire—wealth, economic and civil liberty, a high living standard, unexploited resources, a stable government—and nothing held more appeal than preservation of the status quo. But it was clear that the disengaged nationalism of the twenties and thirties was unworkable, even dangerous, in the world of the forties. "The contemporary world is *de facto* a community of nations," wrote philosopher Suzanne K. Langer. "The new ideal . . . is a civil world order, [*based on*] transnational thinking, international planning, and supranational administration and law."

All except the most diehard isolationists recognized during World War II that the United States could not reject its internationalist obligations without pushing the world once more to the edge of disaster. Even conservatives such as Raymond Moley of *Newsweek* agreed that "the atoms of the old cosmos have been shattered. Not only must we participate in international affairs, but we must assume a new dominant role." It was irrevocably *One World,* Wendell Wilkie concluded in his book of the same name. The question was, how might American nationalism fit within this single world, without losing American identity, curtailing American freedom of action, or endangering the integrity of American ideals?

There seemed to be general agreement as the war drew toward a conclusion that it must be followed by some kind of a world organization, and that the United States ought to have a major share in it. Herbert Hoover, in his book (with Hugh Gibson), *Problems of Lasting Peace* (1943) argued that misdirected nationalism was one of the major causes of the Second World War. Unless some kind of international machinery were set up after it to divert nationalism into constructive, rather than destructive channels, another war might easily follow. He suggested seven possible plans for some kind of international confederation to preserve the peace, finding in such an organization the only remaining "fleeting chance for the leaders of mankind to bind the wounds, to restore faith, and to bring new hope to the world." Henry Wallace, writing in 1943, saw the situation in much the same way. A narrow and nationalistic isolationism, Wallace believed, was no longer possible: "We of the United States can no more evade shouldering our responsibility than a boy of eighteen can avoid becoming a man by wearing short pants." The postwar world, he continued in his essay, "The Price of World Victory," needed some strong world organization, just as the United States, "before the adoption of the Constitution . . ., realized that the Articles of Confederation had failed and that some stronger union was needed."

Wendell Wilkie, who flew around the world in wartime as President Roosevelt's personal representative, stated the postwar alternatives succinctly in his book:

America must choose one of three courses after this war: narrow nationalism, which inevitably means the ultimate loss of our own liberty; international imperialism, which means the sacrifice of some other nation's liberty; or the creation of a world in which there shall be an equality of opportunity for every race and every nation.

Choosing the last as the only possible alternative, he suggested an international Council of Nations, somewhat on the pattern of the old League. Almost simultaneously the Senate, traditionally the stronghold of isolationist sentiment, pledged the United States to join "an international authority with power to prevent aggression and to preserve the peace of the world." Public opinion polls showed overwhelming agreement; an incredible ninety per cent of those questioned in late 1944 believed that the United States should join some kind of world organization, while more than eighty per cent believed it should contribute actual military assistance to it. (In 1937, for example, only thirty per cent favored such membership.)

One of the more popular of plans for an international organization was that which proposed an Atlantic Community of the United States, Canada, and Western Europe, a group of nations bound together, Walter Lippmann said, "by the ties of indissoluble and irreversible history." A specific proposal to this effect had already been made by Clarence Streit's *Union Now* (1939) which suggested joining fifteen nations in a federalized world government. Streit's book sold ten thousand copies within a few months of publication, and his supporters formed an "Inter-democracy Federal Union" which later became the United Federalists for World Government. The most pressing contemporary problem, wrote Streit, was nationalism; so long as nations dealt with each other as competing sovereignties, no system of alliances or treaties could ever preserve peace and stability. But if different national sovereignties joined in union, each retaining its individuality, they then possessed the machinery needed to realize their common goals.

A poll at the time indicated that eight million people found an organization such as Streit proposed both desirable and feasible. Though the "Union Now" movement did not produce concrete results, the measure of its support indicated that the American public had taken a long step away from the nationalistic isolation of the thirties. The North Atlantic Treaty Organization, though founded as a military alliance in 1949, reflected this point of view, emphasizing the prevailing belief, said Secretary of State Acheson, that the United States was "connected with western Europe by common institutions, and moral and ethical beliefs."

The concept of a league of nations, despite its defeat in 1919, survived the twenties and thirties with sufficient vitality to reappear in the thinking of Franklin Roosevelt. Roosevelt, who never lost faith in the Wilsonian ideal, in 1941 coined the term "United Nations" for the allied powers, seeing in the wartime coalition the genesis of a postwar world alliance. The major aim of the postwar era, Roosevelt wrote in the midst of the war, must be "the establishment of an international order in which the spirit of Christ shall rule the hearts of men and of nations." Sumner Welles drew up plans for such an international organization in late 1941 which Roosevelt took with him to the Teheran Conference in 1943, and which he proposed in his annual message to Congress in 1944.

The United Nations concept, as Thomas Greer has pointed out, was always a central part of Roosevelt's thinking about the postwar world. The creation of the United Nations in 1945 on American soil, American participation in it, and American leadership of it, marked a turning point in American nationalism. For the first time since the appearance of the issue in the late nineteenth century, the United States gave a decisive answer to the question of how it might adjust its powerful nationalism to its global commitments. It was doubly significant that the Senate—the rock on which Wilson's League foundered—ratified the United Nations Charter with but two dissenting votes.

The American entrance into the Korean conflict under United Nations sponsorship in 1950 was a final decision from which the nation has never retreated. In 1953, in the aftermath of the not-wholly-successful Korean military experience, *The Public Opinion Quarterly* reported that more than half of those questioned approved American participation in such UN actions, and the percentage of approval has not decreased since. American political leaders since Roosevelt have similarly expressed confidence in international cooperation, without exception. President Truman named the American decision to enter the United Nations one of the two or three most important acts of modern history. President Eisenhower's victories in 1952 and 1956 vindicated the internationalist wing of his party, which had long been under nationalist-isolationist domination. Eisenhower had strong convictions about American responsibilities in world affairs, and was able to impose them upon the more influential of his party leaders. President Kennedy was equally clear about his convictions; the United Nations, he said, was "our last best hope."

Yet it is true that beneath the surface of the contemporary dialogue there remain some deep disagreements over the nature of American nationalism in the mid-twentieth century, and over the extent to which it should control America's stance in international affairs. If the isolationism of the twenties is a thing of the past, a new variety of neo-isolationism has emerged in the fifties and sixties to take its place. This abjures Europe for "Asia First," looks on the United Nations as a nest of dangerous bedfellows, opposes the principle of foreign aid, and refuses to accept the One World concept on which much of present-day internationalist thinking is based. Some, indeed, such as Colonel Edward Rickenbacker, see internationalism as "the very heart and core of the Communist plan to enslave the human race," an attempt "to dissolve the nationalism of the republic into the United Nations, and then into one-world government," engineered by "a Communist-inspired liberal establishment that has been gunning to destroy the nationalism of this once great republic." This hard-core, heavily-emotionalized nationalism, centered in organizations such as the John Birch Society, the Christian Crusade, and in the ultra-conservative wings of the major parties, may well become an increasingly important factor if encouraged by a few victories at the polls.

However, it seems reasonable to assume, in the light of present opinion, that the majority of Americans are convinced that over the long term free institutions can survive only in the context of a free community of nations; that American policy for its own survival must be involved in world policy; that the United States must, in the words of historian William Langer, "exert its influence and power in behalf of a world order congenial to American ideals, interests, and security," which it can do most effectively through an international organization. American internationalism, then, still may have a legitimately nationalist purpose. Harland Cleveland, Assistant Secretary of State for International Organization Affairs, put the matter quite concisely in 1962:

The power, resources, and influence of the United States place her in the middle of whatever matters come before the United Nations. However desirable it might theoretically seem to let other people stew in their own problems, we find that as a practical matter, we cannot escape the implications of our own power. So—if you are an American, there is a United Nations in your future, for better or for worse. That is both the prize and the price of our own power.

The United States has also found international organization an effective apparatus for dealing with the emergence of non-Western nationalism, one of the great facts of life since World War II. Lenin proposed to build a great alliance between communism and those non-Western nations which stood on the doorstep of the modern world. Through the forties and most of the fifties, as the intensity of Arabian, African, Asian, and Latin-American nationalisms increased, the United States assumed that their choice lay between Russia and the United States, and that if these new nations were right-thinking and right-aspiring, they would choose the United States. The American view of this new world of raw and aggressive nationalism was that it was merely an updated version of the eighteenth-century's age of revolution, and that the result would be the worldwide appearance of a congress of middle-class democracies. The function of the United States was to help this to happen.

That this picture of the modern world might not be accurate, or that all revolutions were not like 1776, seemed inconceivable. When it became clear to some (not to all yet, by any means) American leaders that the new nations refused to restrict their choice, and that they claimed the right to be neither Russian nor American-orientated, the United States needed to find ways and means of dealing with them on other terms. The United Nations provided such means, furnishing mechanisms by which the energy and fervor of the new nations could be channeled into some kind of disciplined direction within an international pattern. The American counter to Russia's proposal to unite communism and nationalism, therefore, has been internationalism, with the United Nations providing the machinery for maintaining a balance among these new, competing nationalisms.

The old-fashioned brand of nationalism is no longer fitted to the needs of the twentieth century. The day of self-sufficiency, when countries could live behind walls in isolated security, has disappeared. American nationalism operates today in another kind of world and under another set of surrounding necessities. Hans Morgenthau has accurately summarized the prevailing view of nationalism as an instrument of foreign policy:

Nationalism was the political principle appropriate to the post feudal and pre-atomic age. For the technology of the steam engine, it was indeed in good measure a force for progress. In this atomic age, it must make way for a political principle of larger dimensions, in tune with the worldwide configurations of interest and power of the age.

So too President Lyndon Johnson, speaking at the fifteenth anniversary of NATO, explained that today

Nations are more and more convinced that their fates are closely bound together; their salvation and their welfare can no longer be based upon an egotistical and aggressive nationalism, but must rest upon the progressive application of human solidarity.

Means have been found, or are being evolved, to harmonize the drive of American nationalism with the requirements of twentieth-century conditions in a fashion compatible both with American needs and with the realities of present-day world alignments. The American public, since Theodore Roosevelt's time, has come to understand the realities of a rapidly-changing world, and has accepted the obligations which rest with the United States as a world power. Nationalism, in its nineteenth-century form, has had its day. While "passionate nationalism" still exists, as Adlai Stevenson remarked, "the rationale of separate, desperate sovereignty has all but vanished" from the contemporary scene. "If we revert to crude nationalism and separatism," continued Stevenson, speaking at Charter Day at the University of California in 1964,

if we turn in upon ourselves . . ., we shall be back in the jungle of rampant nationalisms, baleful ambitions, and irreconcilable conflicts which have already twice in this century sent millions to their deaths. . . . The only sane policy for America lies in patient search for the interests which unite the nations.

BIBLIOGRAPHICAL ACKNOWLEDGEMENTS

Hans Kohn's *American Nationalism* (New York, 1957) is the most complete treatment of the subject, and one on which this chapter has drawn heavily. Charles Beard's "Nationalism in American History," in Waldo G. Leland, ed., *Nationalism* (Bloomington, 1934), and Henry Steele Commager's "Responsibilities of American Nationalism," *Foreign Policy Bulletin* XXVII (January 1, 1958) are both germinal essays. An interesting recent treatment is Yehoshua Arieli, *Individualism and Nationalism in American Ideology* (Cambridge, Mass., 1964). Merle Curti's pioneering study of American patriotism, *The Roots of American Loyalty* (New York, 1946) has also contributed much to this treatment, as has Benjamin Spencer's study of cultural nationalism, *The Quest for Nationality* (Syracuse, 1957). Cushing Strout, *America's Image of the Old World* (New York, 1963) and Edward H. Reisner, *Nationalism and Education since 1789* (New York, 1922) are sources of specialized information. The most useful general study of nationalism is Carleton J. H. Hayes, *The Historical Evolution of Modern Nationalism* (New York, 1949). Nationalist feeling in the colonies is treated well in Max Savelle, *Seeds of Liberty* (New York, 1948), and in William L. Sachse, *The Colonial American in Britain* (Madison, 1956). Savelle's article, "Nationalism and other Loyalties in the American Revolution," *American Historical Review* LXVII (July, 1962) 901-23, is the best of its kind. Albert J. Harkness, "Americanism and Jenkins' Ear," *Mississippi Valley Historical Review* XXVII (June, 1950) 61-90, is useful for early attitudes, and Paul A. Varg, "The Advent of Nationalism 1758-1776," *American Quarterly* XVI (Summer, 1964) 169-81, is an excellent summary. Richard S. Merritt has made an interesting study of colonial newspapers in "The Colonists Discover America," *William and Mary Quarterly* XXI (April, 1964) 270-87.

Merle Curti, "Francis Leiber and Nationalism," *Huntington Library Quarterly* IV (1941) 68-78, is a useful study of early nineteenth-century ideas. For the argument over the nature of unionism, see David M. Potter and T. G. Manning, *Nationalism and Sectionalism in America 1777-1877* (New York, 1956) and Paul C. Nagel, *One Nation Indivisible: The Union in American Thought* (New York, 1964). General studies of nineteenth-century imperialism are Harold Faulkner, *Politics, Reform, and Expansion 1890-1910* (New York, 1959) and Ralph H. Gabriel, *The Growth of American Democratic Thought* (New York, 1940), chapters 26 and 27. Theodore Roosevelt's essays on the subject are collected in *American Ideals* (New York, 1897) and later editions of his writings. Contemporary discussions of later nineteenth-century nationalism include Albion W. Tourgée, "The Renaissance of Nationalism," *North American Review* CXLIV (Jan., 1887) 1-11; Francis A. Walker, "The Growth of American Nationality," *Forum* XIX (June, 1895) 385-400; Bishop William Doane, "Patriotism," *North American Review* CLXVI (March, 1898) 310-23; E. C. Chapman, "The Menace of Pseudo-Patriotism," *North American Review* CLXIV (June, 1892) 250-53; Grover Cleveland, "Patriotism and Holiday Observances," *North American Review* CXXCIV (April, 1907) 683-93; and William Burnham, "Everyday Patriotism," *Outlook* XC (November 7, 1908) 534-40. Representative contemporary discussions of imperialism are John R. Proctor, "Isolation or Imperialism?" *Forum* XXVI (October, 1898) 177-87; and L. S. Rowe, "The Danger of National Isolation," *North American Review* CLXXXV (June, 1907) 420-25.

In addition to the relevant chapters of the general studies of nationalism cited above, the argument over nationalism in the period of World War I may be followed in such articles as Edward Krehbiel, "Is Nationalism an Anachronism?" *Survey* XXXV (June 3, 1916); James Harvey Robinson, "What is National Spirit?" *Century* LXXXXIII (November, 1916) 57-64; Franklin Giddings, "The United States Among the Nations," *Independent*, June 14, 1919; "National Character," *ibid.*, November 16, 1918; B. M. Fernald, "Will Nationality Survive?" *Forum* LXII (October, 1919) 459-63; "Can Internationalists Support National Causes?" *The Nation*, March 8, 1922. The problem of isolation in the thirties is illustrated by such articles as Nicholas Roosevelt, "Nationalism," *Current History* XXX (May, 1929) 181-88; Jane Addams, "The Social Deterrent of National Self-Righteousness," *Survey Graphic* XXII (February, 1933) 98-101, and "Exaggerated Nationalism and International Comity," *ibid.*, XXXIII (April, 1934) 168-71; William E. Borah, "American Foreign Policy in a Nationalistic World," *Foreign Affairs* XII (January, 1934) suppl. 1-5; James W. Gerard, "America Self-Contained," *Scientific American* CLI (October, 1934) 194-5; Christian Gauss, "The End of Nationalism," *Scribner's* LXXXIII (May, 1933) 266-71. An especially revealing study is Selig Adler, "The War Guilt Question and American Disillusionment," *Journal of Modern History* XXIII (1951) 1-28; see also the early chapters of Daniel Boorstin, *America and the Image of Europe* (New York, 1960). The isolationist debates of the pre-World War II period are treated exhaustively in William Langer and S. E. Gleason, *The Challenge to Isolation 1937-40* (New York, 1952) and Walter Johnson, *The Battle Against Isolation* (New York, 1944). Clarence Streit's *Union Now* (1939) is still available; the history of the unionist movement is traced in George Catlin, "A Book and an Idea," *Saturday Review of Literature* XXXI (February 10, 1940)

12-15; and Streit's discussion with Quincy Howe, "Shall We Have Union Now?" *Forum* CII (July, 1939) provides a capsule of the arguments. The internationalist discussions of the forties are represented by Henry Luce, "The American Century," *Life* X (February 17, 1941) 61-5; Russell Davenport, "This Would Be Victory," *Fortune* X (August, 1941) 45-48 ff.; and Suzanne K. Langer, "Make Your Own World," *Fortune* XXXI (March, 1945) 156 ff. See also Raymond Moley, "How To Behave Like a World Power," *Newsweek* XXVI (August 20-October 25, 1945) various pp.; Hadley Cantril, "How Real is America's Internationalism?" *New York Times Magazine,* April 29, 1945, and the essays by Herbert Hoover, Hugh Gibson, Henry Wallace, and Sumner Welles in Henry Seidel Canby, ed., *Prefaces to Peace* (New York, 1943). Three representative recent considerations of nationalism in an internationalized world are William Langer, "The United States' Role in the World," in *Goals for Americans* (New York, 1960); Hans Morgenthau, "Paradoxes of Nationalism," *Yale Review* XLVI (June, 1957) 480-96; and Reinhold Niebuhr, "America the Smug," *Saturday Evening Post,* November 16, 1963.

III

The American Tradition
of Free Enterprise

Our national commitment is to a free economy—to
the belief that an economic system based on freedom
of choice, freedom of opportunity, and freedom of
decision is more productive and creative than any
system devised by man.

—ADLAI STEVENSON

WHETHER THE PHRASE commonly used to describe the
American economic system is "private," "individual,"
or "free" enterprise—or in the language of the classical economist, *laissez-faire*—the concept is a deeply-held, traditional
component of the American credo. The term is also a highly
treacherous one, dependent for its meaning on the situations
in which it is used and the uses to which it is put. It describes,
of course, a capitalistic system, one in which private ownership operates in a market environment for the purpose of
profit-making, in contrast to socialism, communism, or any
other system. But it also describes a whole complex of related
ideas about political, social, and economic organization, with
wide connotations of popular belief.

The terms *"laissez-faire,"* "free enterprise" and their variants
have always carried with them symbolic values for the American people far more important than the kinds of economic

practice they indicate—values identified in the public mind with the Constitution, the Founding Fathers, the flag, natural law, freedom, and the "American Way." These terms, like the American political creed, have deep roots in Calvinism, the frontier experience, and evangelical Christianity.

Americans have traditionally believed that the United States is possessed of a unique economic system built upon a wealth of natural resources, a particular kind of population, a particular kind of historical setting, and a particular set of national motivations. Two factors, however, are considered to have been of especial importance in creating it—representative government and individual liberty, which are irrevocably joined. The pivot on which this system rests is an accepted belief in the essentially competitive nature of man. As economist Donald Richberg once explained, "The only time when the competitive spirit of a human being is stilled is when the human heart ceases to beat."

This principle of competition, or "enterprise," lies at the heart of America's concept of its distinctive economic style. It is assumed that there always exists a free market in which the buyer may choose, and in which a number of private producers may compete to meet his choices, making a profit in the process. The mainspring of this activity lies in the competitive situation, in the relationship of consumers who are free to choose and producers who are free to compete for their choices, the two combining to complete the total enterprise.

From this model there are derived several other suppositions which combine to form the larger pattern of "free enterprise." Because sellers are always competing for the buyer's trade, it is assumed that this relationship inevitably provides the greatest good for the greatest number. Progress is therefore built into the system, because it furnishes a channel for and encourages the release of economic energy and productivity. It is also assumed that the system is self-adjusting because it is rooted in the laws of nature and human nature; it will automatically produce the right products, the right distribution of income and employment, and the fullest employment of resources.

The state, therefore, must keep its hands off economic life and allow it to operate freely, so that economic activity may flourish and society advance. While it is agreed that the state must provide a satisfactory legal and monetary framework within which this economy can operate, the free enterprise system is assumed to be more or less self-contained, self-adapting, capable of functioning in perfect equilibrium if left alone.

While the American free enterprise system has always lacked a definitive, clearly articulated ideology, it is generally accepted that what Americans conceive of as their philosophy of economic life includes at least six related elements.

First, the American philosophy of free enterprise is set deeply within the broad context of political and social freedom. No fact is more fundamental, the president of the National Association of Manufacturers told that organization on its fiftieth anniversary, than the recognition that "competitive enterprise, civil and religious freedom, and political freedom are inseparably bound up together." In almost identical language, the president of the United States Chamber of Commerce defined the free enterprise system in 1961 as "the economic expression of the fundamental principle of human liberty," co-existent with "freedom of speech, freedom of the press, freedom of assembly, and freedom of religion." In its belief that *economic* freedom is one of the major elements of the general framework of American freedom, the American business creed is soundly at one with the American tradition.

Second, the American philosophy of free enterprise emphasizes the importance of the individual. The businessman believes that in economic affairs, as elsewhere, a man's success —or lack of it—is very likely a reflection of his individual ability to make economic decisions. The American emphasis on self-reliance, and the corresponding fear of collective dependence on the state, is clearly reflected in *laissez-faire* economics. Harvey Firestone, Jr., was distinctly within the American tradition when in a Fourth of July speech in 1948 he grouped as vital American liberties "the right to work, to worship, to speak, and to live as we choose." The philosophy of American free enterprise, emphasizing as it does initiative, self-reliance, and resistance to collective pressures, simply accents those broader values of individualism long accepted by American society.

Third, the cornerstone of the free enterprise ideology is competition, which the National Association of Manufacturers points out, is "truly the life of trade and the breeding ground of progress." Competition functions

as a regulator and reducer of prices, as an incentive to improved production efficiency, as a guarantee that we shall get what we want, and as a protector of the freedom of opportunity.

The competitive principle, of course, has long served as an important emotional symbol in the American cultural heritage. In a number of contexts—athletic, social, political, educational, occupational—the American tradition involves a strong commitment to the concept of "may the better man win." The business creed is thus in agreement with the American tradition in making competition an integral part of its ideology, for no principle in American life attracts wider public approval.

The emphasis on the competitive principle as a key symbol of economic life lends a tone of fundamentalist toughness to the American free enterprise philosophy. The businessman feels that he deals in the actualities of life; he knows the "hard facts" of social and economic life. A businessman's life, writes Edgar Queeny in his *Spirit of Enterprise* (1943),

is competition. There must be a winner and a loser in every race. He recognizes this and risks being the loser for the chance of winning; and as the stakes are high, the playing is hard.

The world owes no one a living; you can't get something for nothing; laziness and incompetence never succeed; everybody gets what he deserves these and similar phrases stud the prose of countless chamber of commerce pamphlets and the rhetoric of hundreds of service-club "inspirational" talks.

Weakness has no place in the economic and individualist's creed. There are certain basic truths about the competitive life which may seem unromantic, but to refuse to face them is fatal. As the editors of *Business Week* write, "the realistic businessman" knows "the kind of world that—like it or not— he has to live in and work in," and he "adjusts to it without sentimentalizing it." A salient virtue of the American free enterprise creed, in the eyes of its believers, is that it predicates its view of economic activity on fact and not wishes.

Fourth, as the American business creed stresses realism, so too it emphasizes practicality, another quality highly regarded by American society at large. The private enterprise ideology distrusts abstraction and theory, and trusts experience and "common sense." The principles which govern economic life, the president of Sun Oil once remarked, are "nothing less than the workaday laws we are forced to observe" by experience. American businessmen have great suspicion of "armchair" thinkers and theoreticians; the National Association of Manufacturers prefers to appeal directly, its spokesmen say, to "common sense usage, as against professional refinements." This stress on practicality can and sometimes does turn into an aggressive anti-intellectualism, holding in great contempt, as Edgar Queeny does, "those underpaid and underworked professors of law, economics, and sociology" who "deal in the abstractions and unrealities of the academic world."

Fifth, realistic and practical as it may be, the American business philosophy is highly sanguine and optimistic, in tune with the general tone of American life. Since the days of its earliest formulation, the American business creed has constantly emphasized that the American system has produced the "highest standard of living that the world has ever known," (to use the usual phrase) and confidently affirms its ability to continue to raise it. America is "the richest and most self-contained society in the world," a commentator on The Ford Hour remarked in 1941, "but an unfinished picture, a picture in process, for the glory of America is not finality but fertility." Progress, it is assumed, is built into the American system as an automatic result of allowing it to function un-interruptedly—or, as an advertisement for Burlington Mills said briefly, "Freedom of Enterprise inevitably provides the greatest good for the greatest number." The belief that the American way of economic life will always provide an ever better future is one of the most persistent themes in business ideology.

Free, individualistic, competitive, practical, and optimistic, the American philosophy of free enterprise is, finally, heavily moralistic. The aim of economic activity, as American business sees it, is neither simply material gain nor the satisfaction of selfishness, but the advancement of the general welfare. To be successful, wrote Walter S. Gifford of American Telephone and Telegraph, the national economy must produce "a demo-cratic and widespread prosperity," not "prosperity for the few at the expense of the many." "With all its faults," echoed Congressman Samuel Pettengill of Indiana,

the American economic system has produced and distributed more of the goods and comforts of living to more people over a greater territory and for a longer period of time than any other system in any other country since Adam walked out of the Garden of Eden.

The great moral value of the American way, the Advertising Council once sweepingly summarized it, is that the American system has "done more good for more people than anything that ever happened on earth." Its goal is not only to produce, explained President Clarence Randall of Inland Steel, but to produce for the benefit of all; free enterprise is "a tool to be used by society for its own advancement," for "the achieve-ment of those ends for which Providence has placed us on this earth." Cotton Mather, one supposes, would have thoroughly approved of Randall's view and of the basic moralism of the American business philosophy.

The origins of this ideology of free enterprise strike deep in early American history. They lie originally, perhaps, in the Puritan ethic brought to the colonies by those Calvinist settlers who believed that men were at heart self-interested.

The Puritan, who recognized the inherent defectiveness of human nature, never hesitated to accept a picture of an economic society constructed out of a balanced conflict of self-interests. They believed also, of course, in the doctrine of one's "calling," and that each man had the responsibility so to use his talents as to make himself a successful and good life in this existence as well as in the next, placing great emphasis on the virtues of hard work and application to one's worldly tasks. Their belief in the primacy of self-interest was reinforced, of course, by the view of human nature held by those eighteenth-century philosophers who conceived of an economic society in which the members served each other to be served in turn, thereby translating individual self-interest into a common good. Hobbes, Locke, and the Calvinist heritage prepared the American mind for Adam Smith and the idea of economic *laissez-faire* long before either arrived.

The eighteenth century believed that there were natural laws of society which mirrored the laws of the universe, equally immutable, equally harmonious. One discovered these, the philosophers of the era assumed, and one discovered both how society worked and how to improve it. The Enlightenment saw the world as a galaxy of self-correcting and self-governing units running on a pattern of laws which, when revealed, served as the perfect design for social systems. The law of self-interest seemed to be one of these fundamental laws, the controlling law of economic society. It must, then, be allowed to operate freely, and all economic activity should be organized about its unhampered operation.

The American colonies were also heir to a strong native tradition of economic individualism, deriving from the conditions of frontier life and the colonial experience. As Lord Bryce later remarked in his perceptive analysis of America, in the United States

the circumstances of colonial life, the process of settling the western wilderness, the feelings evoked by the struggle against England, all went to intensify individualism in personal enterprise and pride in individual self-sufficiency.

Most certainly the pursuit of individual self-interest, in one manner or another, was a major cause of emigration to America; the majority of the colonies were themselves founded as private enterprises for profit. At the same time, colonial Americans and Englishmen both, since Tudor days, distrusted centralized governmental authority, a distrust accentuated by the growing acerbity of the colonial's argument with mother country over economic controls. The idea of economic freedom was quite compatible with the American's colonial desires and with his ingrained doubts about Britain's external economic authority over him. American land policy from the beginning meant the creation of a constant frontier, populated with ambitious men who possessed more opportunities for material and social advancement than any society in the world had previously known. The whole atmosphere of settlement, a process which occupied the American for two centuries, was one of open, individual enterprise. Frontier society was committed by its situation to economic individualism.

The Enlightenment stressed the individual's responsibility and ability to take care of himself. If the majority of men were allowed to make decisions freely in those affairs that most directly concerned them, the era believed that life would move in relatively harmonious channels, reflecting the order of the universe around them. Franklin's "Poor Richard"—the industrious, shrewd, independent businessman—was an authentic American creation, developed directly out of the American Enlightenment. Franklin himself, in fact, seems to have been the first in his *Principles of Trade* (1774), to use the term *laissez-faire* in English.

The idea of free enterprise also evolved in opposition to British mercantilism, which by the eighteenth century no longer fitted colonial needs or interests. Under mercantilism, the aim of economic life was to build British power by means of strict regulation of trade, industry, and production. Mercantilist polices were intended to benefit the nation at large; the national interest was held to be paramount over individual interests, the well-being of the mercantile class paramount over that of others within the state. Mercantilism not only seemed best for imperial interests, but reflected the prevailing economic philosophy by which the western world lived. Neither John Smith nor William Bradford brought the idea of free enterprise with them, for both came from a governmentally-controlled, mercantilist society.

By the middle of the eighteenth century, however, the American colonies no longer fitted easily into the mercantilist framework. Land was plentiful in America, labor scarce, regulations difficult to enforce, the colonists themselves restive, adventurous, individualistic. The American land provided tremendous resources, so much that there seemed no conceivable need to control its exploitation. Utilization of the continent's natural resources, in fact, was the chief economic end of American life; all the colonist ever asked of England was the privilege of being let alone to make the best of the opportunities the land offered in such profusion.

The American position *vis-a-vis* English economic policy received reinforcement in the later eighteenth century from a group of French economists who found their own native brand of mercantilism as unsatisfactory as Americans found the British. Known as "physiocrats," such men as Quesnay, Mirabeau, Turgot, and du Pont de Nemours (who eventually emigrated to the United States) argued that individuals, if left to themselves to pursue their interests within the natural order, would merge them into a common social good. The state, they believed, should provide only the simplest legal framework for economic life; its motto should be *"laissez-faire, laissez-passer"*—whatever laws passed to influence economic life should do no more than reinforce the laws of nature, and erect no barriers to individual activity.

What the eighteenth-century American demanded of Crown and Parliament, then, was a system which gave him an open opportunity to compete for economic advantage, in contrast to the closed and restricted systems of a less well-endowed Europe. The mercantilist concept of trade met increasingly heavy colonial opposition as the century progressed; violations of the laws governing colonial economic life became so common under the British policy of "salutary neglect" that obedience was almost the exception rather than the rule. When Parliament decided to enforce the laws, it was too late. Colonial merchants and shippers and producers were already conditioned to the pleasures of a relatively free economy, demanded to be let alone to pursue it, and were willing to support a revolution to prevent interference with it.

By the time of the American Revolution, the American colonies presented the picture of a country unique in the world—rich in resources, all of them available by contemporary techniques of exploitation, lacking in economic restrictions or controls, without a privileged class, already possessed of a strong tradition of economic freedom. It was extraordinarily underpopulated but growing fast. It had little industry and a rapidly-expanding market, it was predisposed to political and economic individualism, and its governmental institutions were relatively weak. Under the Articles of Confederation economic authority was widely dispersed; even under the Constitution, power over economic life was granted to the national government carefully and selectively.

Adam Smith's great book, *The Wealth of Nations,* appeared in 1776, providentially suited to the American situation. Smith's belief, that "all governments which thwart the natural course are unnatural," agreed with the image of the world that Americans accepted. His model of the ideal economic society expressed clearly and vividly the dimly-understood but powerfully-felt concepts of economic life already inherent in the American situation. Adam Smith, like the physiocrats, advocated "a system of natural liberty" under which "every man, so long as he does not violate the laws of justice, is left perfectly free to pursue his interest his own way." He opposed most government interference in the economic life of the nation, but not all. What he repudiated was that which was discriminatory, which benefitted the few and not the nation at large. If the actions of "a few individuals," he wrote, "might endanger the security of the whole society," then they "ought to be restrained by the laws of all governments."

If government action in economic life proved to be for the good of society at large, Smith favored it; what he opposed was government action which served special economic privilege. Government intervention in the economic process was therefore, in Smith's view, not of itself bad, if it served useful social and national ends. His version of *laissez-faire* was thus a recoil from the misuses of mercantilism, which created monopolistic advantages for the few and restricted the natural economic freedom of the individual. As colonists and as revolutionaries, the Americans found Smith's views particularly attractive; what he had to say fitted in exactly with their hopes for a much freer kind of economic life, in a society of tremendous untapped resources.

The incentive to wealth-producing labor, Smith contended, lay in the basic human drive to self-interest. If one removed obstacles to this most powerful of human forces and kept the government from interfering with its free play, all elements of harmonious economic life fell into place. If let alone, he argued, the general interests of society and the particular interests of individuals merged. Prices and competition, if let alone, would determine the allocation of society's resources in the most efficient way, as by the direction of "an invisible hand." Smith's program was clear: eliminate the restrictions of mercantilism on free enterprise; develop the kind of competition which protected the consumer from monopolistic exploitation; then, with the state serving as an umpire, release the inherent power of the free economic system to assure individual liberty and economic well-being for the nation.

Smith's book was a detailed application to economic life of the Enlightenment's concept of a unified natural order of natural law, which, if left alone, produced results generally beneficial to mankind. All of his concepts suited the prevailing contexts of American thought. *The Wealth of Nations,* in fact, might almost have been written to supply the American need for an economic theory. Smith's view of economic life was based on the same ideas of natural right and individual liberty which in one form or another appeared in every aspect of American eighteenth-century thought; his book rejected all those governmental and monarchical activities which the colonies had long protested—bounties, duties, restraints on foreign trade, legal monopolies, laws of primogeniture and entail. The image of economic man that emerged from Smith's book—the independent, energetic entrepreneur, making his own way to the benefit of himself and society—reflected the ideal of the Puritan, of the Poor Richard tradition, and of the Enlightenment.

It is little wonder that Adam Smith became by adoption an American Founding Father. Few men have had a more powerful influence on American life. As the editor of *The Boston Monthly Magazine* wrote in 1826, fifty years after the appearance of *The Wealth of Nations,*

The novelty and boldness of his general tenets, the easy, natural, and expressive style of his composition, the many important truths he disclosed, the lucid explanations he gave of many points previously deemed obscure and difficult, the general ignorance of the people concerning the subjects considered by him, all these circumstances conspired to give his work a speedy and extensive celebrity.

The economist C. F. Dunbar, writing fifty years later still, found no reason to change this view. The foundations of American economic thought, he wrote, were

laid deep and solid by Adam Smith; the great men who have since carried forth the work have declared themselves his followers, and in developing and extending the science have kept to the lines of discussion which he laid down with such vigor and insight a century ago.

Smith's theories, to which the French label of *laissez-faire* became attached early in the nineteenth century, soon became the standard explanation to Americans of the facts of their economic life. *The Wealth of Nations* went through three American editions before 1820, but the core of its ideas was more widely disseminated by the translations of the French economist Jean Baptiste Say's *Treatise on Political Economy* which appeared in 1817, 1821, and 1827. Say (who also translated Franklin's "Poor Richard" maxims into French) was a devoted admirer of Smith; in Jefferson's opinion, he presented Smith's ideas in "a shorter and more lucid manner." His became the standard textbook in American economic theory after 1820, hailed by an American editor as "unquestionably the most methodical, comprehensive, and best-digested treatise on the elements of political economy that has yet been presented to the world." Simultaneously, the *laissez-faire* economics of Smith and Say was reinforced by the British economist David Ricardo, whose *Principles of Political Economy* appeared in 1817. Such was the impact of Say and Ricardo on American thought that by the middle of the nineteenth century every leading economic theorist in the country merely played variations on their themes.

The economic situation of the new nation, after the adoption of the Constitution stabilized its political life, encouraged a revival of the old free enterprise-mercantilist controversy in a new context. The *laissez-faire* economics of the physiocrats and Adam Smith was in part a reaction against eighteenth-century mercantilist policy; however, some of the doctrines of mercantilism—especially its policy of favoring the merchant and trading elements of society—continued to appeal to those who were most likely to be advantaged by it. The American businessman wanted no more of the minute and never-ending supervision of economic life that European mercantile practice entailed. At the same time he observed the benefits of a strong, active government that could grant favors to him, exert controls when he wanted them, and keep trade and fiscal policies stable and profitable. Despite his enthusiastic reception of Adam Smith, he did not wish either to reject mercantile economics entirely, or to accept absolute *laissez-faire*. What the new American merchant class needed was a way to balance the thrust of individual *laissez-faire* energy with the control and the direction of the national interest. These men conceived of the nation in commercial and industrial terms; they believed that, given the problems of an untried, fledgling economy, it would be necessary for the government to play a positive role in solving them.

The spokesman for this neo-mercantilist group was Alexander Hamilton. Hamilton did not believe in too much *laissez-faire,* for he recognized, he said, that the individual possessed "a certain activity of speculation and enterprise" which "if left entirely to itself, may be attended with pernicious effects." The point was, therefore, to make this energy "subservient to useful purposes" by properly controlling and redirecting it. The state, in Hamiltonian terms, was to exert a powerful positive influence on the course of economic events, favoring "those economic groups which could contribute most toward building a rich and powerful nation." He did not approve of the all-powerful authority of British Crown and Parliament over economic life; neither did he want the anarchy of an uncontrolled economy. There ought to be a balance, for, as he wrote,

In matters of industry human enterprise ought, doubtless, to be left free in the main; not fettered by too much regulation; but practical politicians know that it may be beneficially stimulated by prudent aids and encouragements on the part of the government.

Hamilton's *Report on Manufactures* (1791) and his subsequent reports and policies as Secretary of the Treasury illustrated how this was to be accomplished by striking the proper combination of individual enterprise with governmental supervision and assistance.

The Federalist version of mercantilism developed by the Hamiltonians did not appeal to the farmers, artisans, small businessmen, and planters who made up the bulk of the national population and whose entrepreneurial ambitions had been largely frustrated by British mercantilism. Suspicion of centralized government was strong among a people who had just completed a war to escape one, and who could see little to gain from Federalist economics. As an admirer of the French physiocrats, Thomas Jefferson found the free enterprise ideology admirably suited to his democratic political interests and his innate Virginia agrarianism. While he did not oppose Federalist versions of the new mercantilism with the zeal of such men as John Taylor of Caroline, he too was hostile to the urban and industrial expansion that the Hamiltonians encouraged, and in his belief that that government governed best which governed least, he was kin in spirit to the *laissez-faire* of Adam Smith.

Neither Jefferson nor his political followers could conceive of a way to grant authority to the state that would not endanger, as British mercantilism had, the interests of agriculture and small business. He visualized government as playing little more than a negative economic role, believing that its authority ought to be kept at a minimum and distributed among the states where it was amenable to popular control. His First Inaugural described a government

which shall restrain men from injuring one another, which shall leave them otherwise free to regulate their own pursuits of industry and improvement, and shall not take from labor the bread it has earned,

granting it no more power than that required to accomplish these limited ends. "Agriculture, manufactures, commerce, and navigation," he said, "the four pillars of our prosperity, are the most thriving when left most free to individual enterprise."

At the same time, the Jeffersonians conceded that complete *laissez-faire* was neither wholly possible nor desirable. The infant nation needed things which only the state could provide, for the private sector of the economy was not yet able to furnish either the capital or the leadership to develop a mature economy. A rapidly expanding nation, forced to compete in world markets with the powerful nations of Europe, one that had suddenly acquired the tremendous spaces of Louisiana and that was shortly to begin a second war against England, obviously needed something more than a government which governed as little as possible. The scarcity of capital demanded active government aid to supply certain necessities of economic life—such as transportation—for only the government possessed the resources needed to underwrite such ventures. The businessmen of the new nation had simply not had sufficient time by the opening of the nineteenth century to build up accumulations of private capital large enough to do those things which capital was needed to do. Albert Gallatin, Jefferson's Secretary of the Treasury, pointed out in his *Report on Roads and Canals* in 1808 that if these were to be built as the nation needed them, the governments would have to provide the wherewithal to do it; he advocated both a system of land grants and a sixteen million dollar federal program of internal improvements to finance them. Whatever his belief in Adam Smith, the Jeffersonian was willing to suspend the rules of *laissez-faire* if it were necessary to do so to build the infra-structure of a strong economy in which *laissez-faire* could operate successfully.

The Jacksonian years were boom years for business. Alexis de Tocqueville, that sharp-eyed observer of American life as it was lived in the 1830's, saw bustle and wealth everywhere. "Nothing is greater or more brilliant than commerce," he wrote of the United States. "It attracts the attention of the public, and fills the imagination of the multitude; all energetic passions are directed toward it." The times produced a great many rich men who were willing and eager to risk their money to make more, for the rewards of success in the new republic were very great. As private capital accumulated in sufficient quantity to supply some of the nation's needs, the relationship between the private and public sectors of the economy gradually shifted. The government no longer needed to furnish quite so much capital as before; the entrepreneur, in return, wanted less competition from government and a clearer field for his investments. Meanwhile, as private corporations gained strength and assurance, they demanded greater autonomy. The Astors, Vanderbilts, Morrises, Biddles, and others like them who were making money wanted no interference from either state or national governments—except on their own terms.

At the same time, it was evident that there were certain capital needs which even the great private financial accumulations still could not satisfy, particularly in internal improvements. Financing the Erie Canal, for example, was far beyond the capacity of any private fortune or combination of fortunes. It was clear that in certain other areas, such as tariffs and currency, business still required and desired direct government action. Neither business nor government, during the Jacksonian years, could quite find a satisfactory balance of interests. Business and industry needed government's help in some areas and not in others; government for its part was not content to intervene in the *laissez-faire* process only when asked.

As a result Jacksonian economic theory was uncertain and confused. A believer in strong government and decisive executive power, Jackson used the authority of his office to intervene in economic life when he believed the situation warranted. Although he declared that the government "ought to leave individuals and states as much as possible to themselves," he was quite willing to engage in direct battle with either or both if needs be. His destruction of the Second Bank of the United States was an almost symbolic reflection of the reversal of Hamiltonian and Jeffersonian roles of government—with Jackson using the powers of his office to smash what he believed a monopoly, and Biddle, for his part, claiming the right of private interests to operate without government interference.

Under Andrew Jackson the businessman was no longer certain that government was always his ally, as the Hamiltonians had assumed; perhaps it might be his enemy, as the Jeffersonians suggested. The Jacksonians, unlike the Jeffersonians, seemed to be interfering with the *laissez-faire* pattern. Businessmen, unlike the Hamiltonians, seemed to be demanding protection from government power. Business often turned to the state for assistance, and the state in turn regulated private activity in certain sectors, both by mutual consent. There often seemed to be no clear line of demarcation between private and public enterprise.

The confusion of economic theory that characterized the early decades of the nineteenth century arose from the fact that the nation under Jackson was neither ready to declare in favor of governmental control of economic life, nor ready to demand complete *laissez-faire* freedom from government's assistance or interference. On the one hand, the national government during Jackson's time appropriated more funds for roads and canals than any previous administration; while the state governments, many of them controlled by Jackson's party, were even more enthusiastic in their support of internal improvements. The federal government not only built roads, canals, and railroads, but subsidized manufacturing and shipping, gave bounties to fisheries, and even gave land for schools. It regulated the conditions of trade and labor in a number of enterprises, and in the case of so-called monopolistic concentrations, (as the Bank crisis illustrated) did not hesitate to use its authority to regulate credit, currency, and business conditions. The government used its licensing and chartering powers to restrict certain enterprises, and at the same time, by the use of loans, subsidies, tax exemptions, and land grants, it encouraged others. Recent studies have shown that federal and state governments during the pre-Civil War era, in one fashion or another, eventually paid perhaps as much as two-thirds of the cost of building the national railway system, and that they paid perhaps the same percentage of the cost of road, canal, and port facilities.

Yet on the other hand, the Jacksonians were strong proponents of *laissez-faire* non-interference. Jackson himself, who vetoed a bill for the extension of the National Road into Kentucky, declared that the function of government was to guarantee an open field for competitive enterprise and to grant special advantages to no one. Like Jefferson, he opposed governmental limitations on economic opportunity, nor did he want government interference with open entry into *laissez-faire* competition. If the government, he said, would stay out of economic affairs and "confine itself to equal protection, and, as heaven does its rains, shower its favors alike on the high and low . . ., it would be an unqualified blessing."

A great deal of the governmental activity in the business sector at this time was on an *ad hoc,* unplanned basis, deriving not from any comprehensive theory of the function of the state, but from the practical needs of the moment. During the panic of 1837, when a number of business leaders appealed to the Federal government for aid, President Van Buren explained that it was not the government's function to intervene in the natural economic process, and that governmental powers were limited and ought to remain so. "All communities," he said in his message to Congress in 1837,

are apt to look to Government far too much. The Federal Government will find its agency most conducive to the security and happiness of the people, when limited to the exercise of its conceded powers. In never assuming, even for a well-meant object, such powers as were not designed to be conferred upon it, we shall in reality do most for the general welfare.

He refused, therefore, to ask for measures "relieving mercantile embarrassment" because it was not within the province of government to do so, and because the economy ought to be allowed to operate itself out of its own difficulties.

One of the great objectives of Jacksonian economics was to liberate business from those governmental restrictions and favoritisms that remained from the mercantilistic era, and to open the field for the great upsurge of the new industrialism. In this it was signally successful. Yet, far from being merely a "let-alone" state, the Jacksonian economy was an intricate, flexible, and at times confused interplay of private and public activity. One problem was that there existed no single unified theory to explain American economic practice.

While the majority of American economic thinkers busily repeated or paraphrased *The Wealth of Nations,* a few tried to evolve a revised theory of *laissez-faire* to describe what was going on and clarify its development. Daniel Raymond, whose *Thoughts on Political Economy* appeared in 1820, proposed that government should take a middle position in economic affairs, neither assisting nor neglecting the economy too much. It "should be like a good shepherd," he explained, "who supports and nourishes the weak and feeble ones in his flock, until they gain sufficient strength to take their chance with the strong." Governments should not do those things which "have a tendency to cramp and paralyze the energies of man," and must do those things which are "calculated to develop the faculties of man, and to stimulate his native energies."

Raymond's adaptation of *laissez-faire* coincided with the neo-mercantilism of Henry Clay's "American System," which he strongly supported. Clay, who consistently advocated the employment of governmental powers to stimulate the economy, planned to use the tariff, subsidies, and internal improvements to develop a balanced, self-sufficing national economic structure. Throughout his career he served as spokesman for those who, like Raymond, believed that government should be an active partner in economic life, especially as its resources were needed to provide those improvements "before there is, in the hands of individuals, the necessary accumulation of capital to effect them." A thorough believer in private enterprise, Clay at the same time believed equally in the responsibility of government to furnish the conditions, and even at times the direct aid, necessary for its successful operation.

The most original attempt to develop a body of economic theory to fit the times was that of Henry C. Carey of Philadelphia, whose *Principles of Political Economy* (1837-40) was the first major American publication in the field. Carey tried to redefine and re-balance Hamiltonian and Jeffersonian economics, working out an adaptation that would serve to align contemporary economic theory with what were obviously new and different practices. Unrestricted *laissez-faire,* in Carey's opinion, led toward "declining civilization and approaching anarchy." A mature economic society needed some "coordinating and regulating power," a center of authority "so coordinating the movements of the individual members of a society, as to enable all to become more productive." Too much control stultified individual energy and restricted economic growth; too little simply meant that "markets . . . became fields of battle, strewed with the corpses of slaves and paupers."

In the present situation, Carey believed, the American economy required neither excessive restraints nor excessive freedom from restraints. It did, however, need tariffs to protect America's infant industries against foreign competition until they had developed to the point at which they could compete equally with the more mature industrial establishments of England and Europe. Carey's *Principles* tried to clarify, more accurately than any other book of its period, the most troublesome areas of prevailing economic thought, but unfortunately he became more involved with economic specifics than with theory. As he turned his attention to tariffs, banking laws, rents and wages, and other contemporary political and economic issues, he became less interested in general economic problems and less the Hamiltonian revisionist.

Despite the assaults against it, the dominant force in American economic theory until the 1870's was still Adam Smith. Smith's teachings, in their various mutations, permeated economic instruction in the colleges of the country, popular writing in the journals, and all branches of economic speculation and research. The "dynamics of American political economy," a reviewer quite accurately wrote in *The North American Review* in 1856, "are all comprehended in the maxim, *Laissez-faire*"—as interpreted, he might have added, by the Frenchman Frédéric Bastiat and the Englishman John Stuart Mill.

Bastiat's *Harmonies of Political Economy* (1848-50), which explained more easily than Smith the concept of a harmonious economic world, was extremely popular. A great admirer of Smith and Say, Bastiat taught that government must allow for the economic process "free play of those laws of harmony which God has provided for the development and progress of the human race." The Frenchman's clarity and simplicity lent themselves admirably to academic explication, and his *Harmonies* not only exerted a powerful influence on American textbooks but was itself, in translation, standard equipment for the customary college course in political economy.

More influential in shaping American economic thinking, however, was John Stuart Mill's *Principles of Political Economy* (1848) which dominated the scene for the next half-century. Mill's book both reaffirmed Smith's basic belief in the primacy of self-interest in economic life and renewed his attack on economic restrictions. At mid-century, certainly, the majority of American economic thinkers accepted without question Mill's theory that national prosperity was based on three principles—free competition, representative government, and international amity. Free competition, in Mill's view, furnished individual motivation for work and savings, opportunity for fair profit, and a reasonable assurance that the rewards for economic activity would be equitably distributed. Mill's economic philosophy seemed to describe accurately the kind of nation and world both business and government hoped to attain; his economic theory not only explained what economic life was, but what it hoped to be.

Francis Bowen, the American economist, spoke for his profession and the public at large when in 1852 he called the Englishman "unquestionably the ablest living writer upon Political Economy." Every American book on political economy during the latter portion of the nineteenth century showed the influence of Mill (or of his disciple, J. E. Cairnes) and Bastiat. Arthur Latham Perry, at Williams College, wrote in his *Elements of Political Economy* (1866) that the study of economic activity demonstrated "The harmonious mechanism of society, by which, through the agency of liberty and property, God has designed the progressive amelioration of mankind." Professor Amasa Walker, of Amherst, in his *Science of Wealth* (1860) was convinced that "all limitations of the rights and powers of capital or labor, not required by the public morality and safety, are useless and mischievous."

The American concept of *laissez-faire* was most clearly exemplified, perhaps, by Francis Bowen's *American Political Economy*, first published in 1856 and periodically revised. Like Smith and Mill, Bowen based his economic theory on the belief that men are "weak and imperfect creatures," whereas society is "a complex and delicate machine, the real Author and Governor of which is divine." God, wrote Bowen,

turneth their selfishness to good; and ends which could not be accomplished by the greatest sagacity, the most enlightened and disinterested public spirit, and the most strenuous exertion of human legislators and governors, are effected directly and incessantly, even through the ignorance, the willfulness, and the avarice of man.

Man cannot interfere with this work, Bowen continued, without marring it; "the attempts of legislators to turn the industry of Society in one direction or another . . . are invariably productive of harm." *Laissez-faire*—"these things regulate themselves"—means

of course, that God regulates them by his general laws, which always, in the long run, work to good. . . . Let the course of trade and the condition of society alone, is the best advice that can be given to the legislator, the projector, and the reformer. . . . Do not meddle with the general laws of the universe.

As for government, Bowen believed it had but one general function, to "remove all casual and unnatural impediments from that path which society instinctively chooses for itself . . ., to remove all stumbling blocks . . ., and to prevent interference with the natural order of things."

Bowen's description of *laissez-faire* constituted the received definition of the American economic system as it was perfected by the 1860's. Drawn from English and French sources, modified by the American past and the emergencies of the American experience, the American concept of economic life stressed sacredness of individual effort, maximum of individual choice, openness of individual competition, and a minimum of interference by the state. And the system seemed to be a success. In not much more than a half-century the nation had grown from three million to a booming, dynamic society of twenty million, with no limit in sight. Looking at itself, the United States believed it had the right to assume that *laissez-faire* worked as Smith and Mill said it would.

At the close of the Civil War, Smith and Mill and their explicators seemed to have explained everything, and what they explained seemed to be exemplified in the kind of life the American saw as he looked around him. *Publisher's Weekly*, at the hundredth anniversary of *The Wealth of Nations* in 1876, compiled a list of the ten "most saleable works on political economy" which showed Mill's *Principles* first, Adam Smith's book second, and Arthur Latham Perry's popularization of Smith and Mill third. There was little need of developing economic theory any further; C. F. Dunbar, surveying "Economic Science in America 1776-1876" in that year, could see no point in going beyond Smith, Ricardo, and Mill, and concluded that American economic theory was really little more than "the sagacious application of rules of thumb," derived from these three great sources. Yet at the same time that *laissez-faire* was receiving its clearest exposition by Bowen, Walker, and the rest, a number of changes in American society had already taken place (with others in process) that were soon to necessitate a complete re-examination of it.

During the first half of the nineteenth century the United States was predominantly a rural, agrarian society. Prior to 1860 little more than sixteen per cent of the population lived in towns of more than eight thousand, and the sources of national wealth were primarily agricultural. The typical American businessman was a banker, a merchant, or a shipper, and the American enterprise found its outlets in trade, mining, transportation, or speculation. Industrial production by 1840 was still relatively small, with the factory system formed in only a few industries such as iron, textiles, machinery, or leather products.

After 1850 the growth of the factory system was spectacular. In the next thirty years industrial investment increased four hundred per cent, in some areas of manufacturing from six hundred to nine hundred per cent. By 1880 the United States was an industrialized nation, with a tremendous network of railroads, a growing labor supply, a widened domestic market, and a burgeoning mass-production system. David Wells' *Recent Economic Advances,* published in 1889, listed more than a hundred important "inventions, discoveries, and applications" over the preceding half-century that had virtually revolutionized American industrial production. After 1850 American economic life was in a continuous process of transformation from a rural-agrarian to an urban-industrial society.

These changes meant, of course, a complete reshaping of American economic life. The individualistic, competitive *laissez-faire* concepts of Smith and Mill no longer satisfactorily explained the increasingly concentrated nature of business. Such giants as Carnegie's empire in steel, and Rockefeller's in oil, which narrowed down the area of competition available to smaller units, seemed destined to be the dominant form of economic life. The wheels of "free enterprise" and "open competition" turned very slowly in a number of segments of the economy in the 1870's and 1880's; and *laissez-faire* was ill equipped either to explain or to justify the monopoly, the pool, the trust, and the combination. There was competition, of course, among these business behemoths, but there was little place in it for the individual. "Free" enterprise was lost in corporate enterprise, and Smith's "invisible hand" seemed to be at the end of the long arm of the trust.

In 1885, therefore, the facts of American economic life were far different than in 1855. The profound changes wrought in the nation brought with them a whole new set of economic problems. After 1860 Americans were forced to re-think, with some care, the implications of *laissez-faire* and to re-study the relations between governmental authority and economic activity. The basic issue remained much the same as in Hamilton's day or Jackson's—what was the role of government in the national economic life?—but the framework of discussion was quite different. What had been implicitly accepted as a law of God and nature now had to be examined, articulated, and designed. Both *laissez-faire* and government intervention had deep roots in American practice, but the existence of a number of powerful, large-scale business enterprises which exerted massive influence on large segments of the American economy placed the problem within a new context. What most needed re-examination was the central doctrine of competition itself, regarded as the balance wheel of the *laissez-faire* system and the manner of its operation in the new industrial society.

The businessman of the seventies and eighties had no intention of giving up his freedom of enterprise, or of reversing the trend of economic affairs. The last thing he wanted was government intervention (especially through taxation and regulation) except on his own terms—as in government assistance to railroads, or easy access to land and natural resources, or legislation preventing labor organization. The enactment of anti-trust measures in some states, and the successful passage in Congress of the Interstate Commerce Act of 1887 and the Sherman Act of 1890, showed how desperately the businessman needed to erect defenses against further governmental restraints. He needed a philosophy of private enterprise, one which updated Adam Smith and John Stuart Mill, and one which justified the trends of economic life. He needed, in fact, a new philosophy of *laissez-faire* which would allow him to continue to do what he had been doing so successfully.

Business found exactly what it needed in contemporary science, where the evolutionary hypothesis provided a new manner of looking at the old economic ideas. The "survival of the fittest" principle, suggested by Darwin, became the keystone of the re-formed business philosophy; businessmen used it to describe a new kind of *laissez-faire* which did not replace Smith or Mill, but which extended their ideas into a modern "scientific" setting. The Darwinian explanation of life as struggle seemed to show that the advocates of *laissez-faire* had been right all along—that *competition,* economic and otherwise, was a law of nature, that a free and open struggle for survival was a necessary condition of social progress.

The most influential figure in the formation of the new *laissez-faire* philosophy, developed by the later nineteenth century, was Herbert Spencer, the Englishman whose *Social Statics* (1851), *Synthetic Philosophy* (1862-96), *Man Versus the State* (1884) and other books and essays supplied the arguments that business needed to make its case. What Spencer did was to formulate a version of Darwinism applicable to social and economic life in such a manner as to appeal to the American individualistic tradition on the one hand, and to the profit-motive on the other. What he suggested about the facts of life was particularly relevant to the American experience; as Henry Ward Beecher told Spencer in 1866, "The peculiar condition of American society had made your writings far more fruitful and quickening than in Europe."

As a result, Spencer's impact on American thought was greater, probably, than that of any philosopher since Locke. No authority was cited more frequently by economic writers between 1880 and 1900. As Andrew Carnegie said, when he first read Spencer, "Light came as a flood and all was clear;" when Spencer visited the United States in 1882, he was welcomed as a conquering hero. Edward L. Youmans, editor of *Popular Science Monthly,* and Harvard professor John Fiske became his tireless expositors to the public, so that his name and ideas were by 1890 virtually household words—Appleton's edition of Spencer's works, over a fifty year span, sold more than 300,000 copies.

Herbert Spencer's appeal to economic philosophers lay chiefly in the fact that his model of economic life, since it derived from the new Darwinian biology, was therefore authoritatively "scientific." In its essentials, Spencer's ideas were also surprisingly easy to summarize and explain; dozens of commentators presented his philosophy to the public and numerous magazines extracted or paraphrased his essays. He provided, Spencer said, "a basis for a right rule of life, individual and social," which rested on two laws, the "law of equal freedom" and the law of "survival of the fittest." The first gave an individual the right to do as he wished, if his actions did not interfere with the right of others to do so. The second gave each individual the freedom to attempt to survive, so that those best adapted would succeed, those least adapted fail. These two laws, said Spencer, together form "an ultimate ethical principle."

Like Adam Smith, Spencer drew his philosophy on the pattern of nature, but it was Darwin's, not that of Newton's eighteenth-century world. Like Smith, Spencer used nature as a design for economic society but with a new explanation of how nature worked. Smith's generation and that of the early nineteenth century saw the universe as an orderly collection of laws which, if let alone, operated in smooth and beneficent harmony. Economic life, it was assumed, worked the same way. Spencer's view of the world, adapted from Darwin, showed nature to be the scene of a bitter and implacable struggle in which species either adapted to a changing environment or failed to survive. Allowing nature to take its course—the "let-alone principle"—meant something quite different than Adam Smith's original dictum, if one saw nature in Darwinian terms. Spencer freely transposed Darwin's conjectures about the survival of biological organisms into social terms; just as in the struggle for existence the best-adapted (or "fittest") plants and animals survived, so to Spencer those competitors in society who best adjusted to conditions lived while the others died.

Spencer was not an economist, but what he wrote was quickly translated into economic terms. The results of economic activity, if one allowed Spencerian nature to take its course, were quite different from the consequences which the classical *laissez-faire* economists had assumed. But the language of Spencer, as well as his ideas, were swiftly inserted into the vocabulary of *laissez-faire*. What Spencer implied was —keep the state's hands off, allow the natural laws of economics to operate, let the struggle for survival proceed in business as it did elsewhere. William Graham Sumner, the great Yale sociologist, wrote:

Society needs first of all to be free from these meddlers—that is, to be let alone. Here we are, then, back at the old doctrine—laissez-faire. Let us translate it into blunt English, and it will read Mind your own business. It is nothing but the doctrine of liberty.

John D. Rockefeller, Jr., speaking to a Sunday school class, put the Spencerian *laissez-faire* doctrine even better in an inspired image:

The growth of a large business is merely a survival of the fittest. . . . The American Beauty rose can be produced in the splendor and fragrance which bring cheer to its beholder only by sacrificing the early buds which grow up around it. This is not an evil tendency in business. It is merely the working-out of a law of nature and a law of God.

Working from the evidence supplied by Spencer, the business community of the eighteen-eighties and nineties constructed a solid, tight structure of *laissez-faire* theory on this new base. It was understood that the activities of the state in the field of business should be severely limited; that the law of supply and demand should be allowed to operate without hindrance; that wages should reflect the productivity of the worker; that competition in the marketplace was to operate under only the most minimal restrictions; that the primary responsibility for the workings of the economic system rested on "natural law." Economist David A. Wells, writing in *Practical Economics* (1885) put the case for *laissez-faire* individualism very well:

In point of natural resources, Providence has given us all that we desire. And that these resources may be made productive of abundance, great and overflowing, to all sorts and conditions of men, there must be, *first*, industry and economy on the part of the individual; and *second*, on the part of society, a guaranty that every man shall have the opportunity to exert his industry, and exchange its products, with the utmost freedom and the greatest intelligence.

These were primary economic truths. "Oh these grand immutable all-wise laws of natural forces," exclaimed Andrew Carnegie, "how perfectly they would work if human legislators would only let them alone!" James Bryce, the English political analyst whose study of *The American Commonwealth* appeared in 1888, found "laissez-aller to be the orthodox and accepted doctrine" of United States business to a degree unknown in England or Europe. The high point of the Spencerian "let-alone" philosophy probably came with President Cleveland's 1887 veto of a bill to appropriate ten thousand dollars of federal funds to buy seeds for drought-stricken Texas farmers. In the best Spencerian terms, Cleveland killed the bill because it violated the "limited mission" of the government's "power and duty" to extend "relief of individual suffering" from state funds.

In the main, both business and the public accepted the new

laissez-faire as a viable, workable, and superior economic system, the one best suited to American needs and productive of the best results. The approved version had powerful support from all segments of society. It had the sanction of the leading American economists; it was taught in all classrooms and permeated all the popular text-books; it was officially accepted by business groups as the only sound doctrine. Among intellectuals, William Graham Sumner was undoubtedly the most commanding and influential of the Spencerians; the only law of business, he told a student at Yale, was "root, hog or die," the only sound economic system "was the contract-competition system, all others are fallacies."

Spencerian doctrines were written into legal interpretations by the leading jurists on both state and federal courts. Meetings of the American Bar Association, as Edward S. Corwin has written, were a "sort of juristic sewing-circle for mutual education in the gospel of laissez-faire." The cases argued before state and federal courts during the eighties and nineties were so filled with explanations and justifications of *laissez-faire* that the opinions of judges such as Field, Brewer, Peckham, and Sutherland, to name a few, still remain the best exposition of the *laissez-faire* economic philosophy as it flowered in these decades.

Ministers were as enthusiastic as lawyers in their support of the conventional business doctrine. The Reverend Julian Sturtevant, who among other duties taught economics at Illinois College, thought that "the foundation of our free society was that great law of human nature, the law of competition." Henry Ward Beecher, one of the two or three most influential of American divines, wrote that "God has intended the great to be great, and the little to be little." "The American doctrine," he continued, "is that it is the duty of the Government merely to protect the people while they are taking care of themselves—nothing more than that. 'Hands off,' we say to the Government."

The greatest defense of the new *laissez-faire* came naturally from the ranks of business, articulated in hundreds of speeches, editorials, essays, and business journals. Andrew Carnegie, who was unusually verbal for a tycoon, established in his writings, especially in *The Empire of Business* (1902) and *The Gospel of Wealth* (1900) —the most careful elaboration of the businessman's point of view, but many others explained *laissez-faire* in day-to-day, popular terms. How correct the system was, they affirmed first of all, had its proof in how it worked. There was a visible advance in living standards after 1870, whatever else the era's problems; *laissez-faire* delivered the goods on at least some of its promises, and business leaders never failed to point it out. Nor did they fail to point out how *laissez-faire* fitted with the deeply-ingrained tradition of self-reliance, with the Poor Richard, Honest Abe, log-cabin-to-White House, Horatio Alger myth of individual initiative and responsibility. John D. Rockefeller's rise from clerk to multimillionaire, or Andrew Carnegie's from bobbin-boy to Steel King, were proof of the values of competitive *laissez-faire* as well as of the values of the American way of life.

Laissez-faire, the spokesmen of business explained, coincided with the natural law as Spencer and Darwin demonstrated it. "Competition in economics," R. R. Bowker said in 1886, "is the same as the law of the 'survival of the fittest' or 'natural selection' in nature." Andrew Carnegie, drawing on his knowledge of Spencer, decided that concentration of power in a small number of business firms was a clear example of "evolution from the heterogeneous to the homogeneous, and is clearly another step in the upward path of development." Competition, he wrote in his essay on *Wealth* in 1889,

insures the survival of the fittest in every department. We accept and welcome, therefore, as conditions to which we must accommodate ourselves, great inequality of environment, and concentration of business, industrial and commercial, into the hands of a few. . . .

The state, therefore, must keep out of the economic process. Its sole duty, according to President C. W. Eliot of Harvard, was simply that of "enforcing the sanctity of contracts and preventing cheating," or as Judge Gary of United States Steel wrote, the public must say to government, "Keep your hands off, let men work; protect, encourage, but do not interfere." It was an accepted fact, Jay Gould said, that no matter what kind of business was involved, "individual enterprise can do things more economically and efficiently than the government can." If only for no other reason, wrote Abram Hewitt, the New York ironmaster, "the invasion of government into the domain of industry must be met with uncompromising opposition."

This was the accepted doctrine of the dominant economic group in American society before 1910. Charles A. Dana probably spoke for most of the men in his class when he called criticisms of the prevailing *laissez-faire* philosophy "absurd, unpatriotic, and dangerous;" so too did Grover Cleveland, who thought such critiques "the bane of republican institutions and the constant peril of government by the people." Attacks on the official doctrine were likely to generate a good deal of heat and a spirited defense, not only from business leaders but from a sympathetic public who accepted, more or less intact, the revised Spencerian version of *laissez-faire* that Carnegie and his fellows cultivated. As President Nicholas Murray Butler of Columbia explained, *laissez-faire* meant progress, intervention by the state confusion and retrogression:

Nature's cure for most social and political diseases is better than man's, and without the strongest reasons the government should withhold its hand from everything that is not, by substantially common consent, a matter of governmental concern and governmental action.

But not everyone agreed. Opposition to the received version of *laissez-faire* after 1870, though it represented a minority position, was nevertheless spirited. The Social Gospel movement within the Protestant churches attacked the basic morality of the survival of the fittest doctrine. "The let-alone theory of society," said the Reverend Graham Taylor of Chicago, "bears the mark of Cain." The Reverend C. W. Clark felt that "Christianity means cooperation and the uplifting of the lowliest; business means competition and the survival of the strongest." Josiah Strong, one of the ablest of the Social Gospel theologians, accused the business system of being "thoroughly selfish, and therefore thoroughly unchristian," while the crusading Reverend George D. Herron of Iowa called it "economic waste . . ., destruction of life . . ., the deformity, brutality, and atheism of civilization."

Others believed that the state should intervene to establish the conditions of Christian life in economic affairs by regulating such things as wages, hours, working conditions, perhaps even profits, so that business had an ethical basis—for, as the Reverend Washington Gladden of Ohio wrote, "Economics without ethics is a mutilated science." The Reverend Lyman Abbott, one of the most respected and popular contemporary ministers, felt that *laissez-faire* was outmoded, that what was needed was a "new conception of the function of government and consequent enlargement of its powers, and the sphere of its operations." The state, said the Reverend Heber Newton, ought to pass any and all laws needed to make her citizens "healthful, vigorous, wealth-producing factors." Some of the Social Gospellers, among them Gladden and Herron, came perilously close to socialism.

Attacks on the *laissez-faire* system also came from some economists themselves. A group of younger men, many trained in Germany, believed as Richard T. Ely of Wisconsin did that economics was "a distinctly ethical science." Ely, Edwin Bemis, Henry C. Adams, Simon Patten, John Bates Clark, and others criticized the principles of the *laissez-faire* school as "unsafe in politics and unsound in morals," (in Ely's words) or as "a tool in the hands of the greedy and avaricious." They questioned the assumption of accepted economic theory in respect to competition and the role of the state, and refused to accept the Spencerian version of natural law as applied to economic life. "In our worship of the survival of the fit under free and natural selection," wrote John Bates Clark,

we are sometimes in danger of forgetting that the conditions of the struggle fix the kind of fitness that shall come out of it . . ., that survival in predatory competition is likely to mean something else from fitness for good and efficient production, and that only from a strife with the right kind of rules can the right kind of fitness emerge. Competition is a game played under the rules fixed by the state to the end that, so far as possible, the prize of victory shall be earned, not by trickery or mere self-seeking adroitness, but by value rendered. It is not the mere play of unrestrained self-interest; it is a method of harnessing the wild beast of self-interest to serve the common good—a thing of ideals and not of sordidness. It is not a natural state, but like any other form of liberty, it is a social achievement, and eternal vigilance is the price of it.

In 1885 this group of recalcitrants founded the American Economic Association, whose platform declared that "We regard the State as an agency whose positive assistance is one of the indispensable conditions of human progress." "The very object of our association," Simon Patten said, "should be to deny the right of individuals to do as they please."

American sociologists, representing a relatively new discipline among the social sciences, joined with the economists in their critique of *laissez-faire* as a social principle. Was "let-alone" such a primary law of life that it was to be copied in society as a reflection of nature? Sociologists such as Lester Ward of Brown, Albion Small of Chicago, and Edward A. Ross of Wisconsin said No—men had always progressed by interfering with natural processes. The so-called "law" of competition, in their opinion, was not only one that *could* be interfered with, but *ought* to be. They recommended what Ward called "positive social action as against the negativism of the dominant *laissez-faire* school of politico-economic doctrinaires," so that society might curb what Ross called "the lawlessness, the insolence, and the rapacity of overgrown private interests" that unregulated competition had produced in American economic life.

The dissident economists and sociologists were seconded by a number of reformers who wrote and lectured tirelessly against the ills they believed a *laissez-faire* philosophy fastened on society. Henry Demarest Lloyd, whose *Wealth Against Commonwealth* (1894) was a stinging indictment of prevailing business practices, pointed out that "the golden rule of business . . ., the weakest must go first" was a rule of action allowed "in no other field of human associations." The Spencerian ethic, said Lloyd, was "a race to the bad, and the winners are worst . . .; a system in which the prizes go to meanness." True *laissez-faire,* in contrast, was to "let the individual do what the individual can do best, and let the community do what the community can do best," a sentiment echoed by other critics. Henry George's *Progress and Poverty* (1879), which sold two million copies by 1905, suggested using the power of the state, in the form of a single tax on rents, to solve many of the social problems created by inequitable distribution of profits. Edward Bellamy's *Looking Backward* (1888), a tract in the form of a utopian novel, attacked the excessive individualism of *laissez-faire* and the "immoral, wasteful, brutal scramble for existence" that passed for competition in business.

The most powerful protest against the prevailing concept of *laissez-faire,* however, came in politics. As an older, simpler, rural society changed into a complex, urbanized and industrialized one, economic problems emerged which the *laissez-faire* theory of progressive prosperity simply did not explain. The system, whatever the optimistic claims of the business community, did not seem to be working for the farmer, who found his path to wealth apparently blocked by concentrations of mercantile and financial power which controlled his markets; nor for the immigrant factory worker, lost in a huge and invulnerable industrial enterprise; nor for the small business entrepreneur who found it impossible to compete with the corporate behemoths who surrounded him.

They found an outlet for their grievances in political activity, chiefly in third party movements, since the major parties were solidly controlled by supporters of the status quo. The Grangers, Anti-Monopolists, Greenbackers, and Populists of the period had one thing in common—the conviction that government must assume a larger share of responsibility for the general economic welfare, that it should use its authority to regulate the economic process, and that it should take action to insure a better distribution of income, guaranteeing a fair share to all of the benefits of an expanding economy. No economic system, in the opinion of the Populists, ought to produce so many "tramps and millionaires." The Greenbacker platform of 1876, for example, declared it to be "the paramount duty of the government, in all its legislation, to keep in view the full development of all legitimate business. . . ."

Whether it be problems of currency, credit, political representation, a fair market price, or corruption in politics, the discontented elements of the third parties which dotted the national and state elections in the closing decades of the nineteenth century asked for positive action by the state, and an end to unrestricted *laissez-faire*. None of these parties was more than temporarily successful, but the combined total of their critical attacks on the status quo was impressive and effective. It was quite clear by the turn of the century that the accepted doctrine of economic *laissez-faire,* almost at the moment of its most successful and widely-accepted articulation, was under severe attack from several directions.

Despite the solid front presented by the advocates of Spencerian economics, the doctrine of *laissez-faire* seemed increasingly unable to put up satisfactory defenses against its critics. Public faith in the classical economic view rapidly declined; by 1914 the traditional philosophy of business had changed so drastically that it barely resembled the doctrine once so confidently espoused by Carnegie and Sumner. When the American Economic Association, the American Sociological Association and the American Political Science Association met in Philadelphia for their annual conventions in 1918, their common theme was, according to *Survey Magazine,* "Laissez-faire is dead! Long live social control!" and at the meeting Professor John R. Commons, the magazine reported, "gave its funeral sermon" in his presidential address.

There was more than a little truth to the report, though *laissez-faire's* epitaph was not yet final by any means. But two things were true: first, that the concept of the relationship of the state to economic life, the key principle of the traditional *laissez-faire* position, was changing; and second, that there was a wide gap between the theory of *laissez-faire* as most Americans accepted it and its actual application to American economic life. During the early years of the twentieth century the American people began what soon became the common practice of praising "free enterprise" as a treasured patriotic belief while paying it less than lip service in practice.

The *laissez-faire* system owed its decline after 1900 to a number of factors, internal and external. For one thing, its critics found a responsive public. As people became more aware of the social and political problems that came in the wake of the nineties, they tended to listen to the reformers who claimed that the state needed to do more than simply to guarantee an open field of competition. Far from keeping its hands off society, wrote the economist Edwin James, "Government should interfere in all instances where its interference will tell for better health, better education, better morals, and greater comfort for the community." There were many, and not all of them economists, who agreed with this point of view, particularly after they surveyed the wreckage of the depressions of 1892 and the panic of 1907.

In addition, the logical outcome of the "survival of the fittest" principle seemed to show that apparently the biggest was fittest, since it survived. Not everyone believed this. Smith and Mill had assumed that self-interested capitalists, competing with one another, would create fair wages, prices, interest, and profits. What happened instead appeared to be that as smaller businesses failed, competition was in the end reduced to the few or eventually lost entirely as only one survived. Though some economists claimed that no monopoly was ever really safe from competitive attack, the creation within less than a half-century of fifty of the largest corporations the world had ever known pointed another direction. When any combination of economic forces became so powerful that it eliminated all its competitors, or when competing combinations agreed to cooperate rather than compete, the only agency with sufficient authority to restore competition was the state. By the eighteen-eighties both industrial and financial monopolies had developed to the point that the public was willing to ask for state intervention to retard them. The Sherman Act of 1890 rejected *laissez-faire* in order to maintain competition, an irony that has yet to be resolved.

For that matter, in reality, ever since the wartime controls of the Civil War, both federal and state governments had been deeply involved in economic regulation. Unhindered, pure *laissez-faire*—whatever the illusion—did not exist in actual practice. Lord Bryce, analyzing the American scene in 1888, shrewdly noted that the strongest proponents of *laissez-faire* did not hesitate to demand government intervention when it suited their purposes. "Though the Americans conceive themselves to be dedicated to *laissez-faire* in theory, and to be in practice the most self-reliant of peoples," he wrote, "they have grown no less accustomed than the English to carry the action of the state into ever-widening fields."

The fact was that over the years that the business creed of Spencerian "let alone" was finding its fullest expression, the state and federal governments were gradually assuming a variety of economic duties and powers. The states by degrees took over regulation of banking, railroads, insurance, public utilities, laboring conditions, access to natural resources, and communications—sometimes after bloody battles with the *laissez-faire* entrepreneurs, but eventually with the sanction of public opinion. Farm leaders during the period wanted and got cheap government credit, low-priced public lands, favorable tariffs, subsidies for agricultural research and education, and federal support of farm organizations. Mercantile interests asked for and received commercial treaties and discriminatory shipping and inspection laws to give them advantages over foreign competitors. Manufacturers wanted protective federal tariffs, subsidies, and patent protection; railroads and shippers asked for construction aids and outright grants. Ironically, it appeared that each group which defended *laissez-faire* economics at the barricades at the same time requested some kind of governmental aid, intervention, or protection.

While the influence of state and federal authority was gradually being extended in economic life, the popularly-accepted version of *laissez-faire* was being replaced by a different idea of the function of the state, much as the critics of the status quo were suggesting. A good many of these suggestions were about to be translated into legislation after 1900. The nation was in a critical and self-examining mood, "looking itself over," Woodrow Wilson said, "from top to bottom . . ., questioning its oldest practices as freely as its newest." *Laissez-faire* economics was one of these practices.

The so-called "progressive era" of American politics, dominated by Theodore Roosevelt and Woodrow Wilson, brought a major change in the concept of the proper relationship of state to individual in social and economic affairs. The key issue in the discussion was competition, still the basic element of *laissez-faire* economics. The eminent sociologist Charles Horton Cooley had already devoted a brilliant book, *Personal Competition* (1894) to the study of the destructive effects of the Spencerian struggle on society and the individual, and economic and political theorists more and more looked on the competitive principle with skepticism. The American Academy of Political and Social Science, for example, devoted its entire session of 1912 to the issue. "The age of unregulated competition has passed," one speaker concluded, and the time has arrived when it "might wisely be supplemented by some man-made law to protect and maintain competitive spirit against monopolistic power." "Unregulated competition," said another, "induced and forced immoral business methods;" the times demanded "correction of competition by governmental regulation."

This new belief in the need for closer coordination between governmental authority and business practice was most clearly reflected in the attitudes of Roosevelt and Wilson, who, though neither was willing to give up the idea of *laissez-faire,* agreed that unbridled competition in the Spencerian sense was no longer possible or desirable. The national economy, in Roosevelt's opinion, should be made "to administer to the needs of the many rather than be exploited for the profits of the few."

In his *Autobiography* Roosevelt explained how it might be possible to handle the problem of economic concentration. It

could not be done simply by "busting the trust," since one
could not "remedy by more individualism the concentration
that was the inevitable result of the already existing individualism." Instead, Roosevelt continued, one must recognize
that "corporations and combinations had become indispensable in the business world, that it was folly to try to prohibit
them, but that it was also folly to leave them without
thoroughgoing control." His plan therefore was, he wrote, to
use the power of the government "to protect labor, to subordinate the big corporation to the public welfare, and to
shackle cunning and fraud exactly as centuries before it had
interfered to shackle the physical force which does wrong by
violence." "Whenever it is possible," he once said, "we propose
to preserve competition, but where under modern conditions
competition . . . cannot be successfully restored, then the
government must step in."

Woodrow Wilson was equally critical of unregulated competitive economics. "Our thought has been," he said in his
first inaugural,

"let every man look out for himself, let every generation look out
for itself," while we reared giant machinery which made it impossible that any but those who stood at the levers of control
should have a chance to look out for themselves. . . . We have not
. . . studied and perfected the means by which government may be
put at the service of humanity.

"Freedom today," he said in a 1912 campaign speech, "is
something more than being let alone. The program of a
government of freedom must in these days be positive, not
negative merely." Government must "set the stage . . . for
the doing of justice to men in every relationship of life" by
guaranteeing to every individual "a fair chance to live and to
serve himself, to see that injustice and wrong are not wrought
upon any." Wilson, like Roosevelt, believed in the competitive
principle, but he wanted it free and open—"All the fair competition you choose, but no unfair competition of any kind."
His solution, like Roosevelt's, was control of the economic

process by the state to the extent that competition was neither erased nor unregulated.

Laissez-faire, in the Progressive view, could be carried to self-defeating ends. As Justice Brandeis, Wilson's friend and adviser phrased it, "Regulation is essential to the preservation and development of competition. . . . The right to competition must be regulated in order to preserve it." Neither Roosevelt nor Wilson, nor any of their political generation, had any intention of destroying the *laissez-faire* system. Both, within the boundaries of their respective party traditions, accepted *laissez-faire* under proper control; both hoped to preserve individualism, competition, and open entry into a competitive market against the pressures of corporate concentrations. Their aim, as William Diamond described it, was "to restore the American economy to a Golden Age of competitive capitalism: an age in which . . . the small business class had been free from the pressures of monopoly." In books such as Charles Van Hise's *Concentration and Control* (1912) and Herbert Croly's *Promise of American Life* (1909) progressive theorists provided political leaders with blueprints for economic legislation. During Wilson's terms these bore fruit in such things as the Underwood Tariff, which attempted to equalize rates heretofore rigged for the advantage of protected industries; the Clayton Act, which prescribed certain limits for competition; and the Federal Trade Commission, which controlled methods of competition in interstate commerce.

The most effective criticisms of unlimited *laissez-faire* during the 1920's came from within the ranks of the professional economists. Economists such as John M. Clark and Frederic Benjamin Garver explained that economic individualism could not maintain the same form in the twentieth century as it had in the nineteenth, since the conditions under which uncontrolled *laissez-faire* might satisfactorily work were long since gone. Clark pointed out in *Social Control of Business* (1926) that *laissez-faire* as the nineteenth century had known it was finished—"It is not a question whether our great-great-grandfathers were right or wrong; the thing they defended no longer exists." The point was, said Garver, underlining the Wilsonian view, that the intervention of the state in economic affairs was not intended to abridge the individual's liberty, but rather to assist him in dealing with new economic questions. Government had "certain advantages arising from its greater power and wider scope of action" which allowed it to handle larger economic problems in ways which individual enterprise could not.

The rise of "institutionalist" economics marked another step away from *laissez-faire* theory. The Institutionalists attacked *laissez-faire* from a different angle, criticizing it because it was chiefly a theory, and at that a theory which did not take actual economic life into account. As the label attached to the school implied, these economists recommended abandoning theory in favor of studying actual economic behavior. The economist must see economic life as events rooted in reality; economics, they said, is how men act, not an explanation of events by reference to a theoretical model which might be called *laissez-faire*. Institutionalists such as Wesley C. Mitchell, Thorstein Veblen, and John R. Commons (who was perhaps more the sociologist) opened the way for a critique of traditional *laissez-faire* theory from a new academic direction.

In addition, the course of twentieth-century economic theory was irrevocably influenced by the work of two Englishmen, first by Alfred Marshall, later by his pupil John Maynard Keynes. Marshall, whose work spanned the period from 1890, when his *Principles of Economics* appeared, to 1919, was a brilliant synthesizer and an original thinker. He agreed with the classical *laissez-faire* school that competition was the mainspring of trade and the best guarantor of economic growth; he also believed that unregulated competition could never exist in a real economic situation, no matter how well it fitted into pure theory. He could not accept pure *laissez-faire*, nor could he approve complete state control; *laissez-faire* needed constant regulation, governmental authority should never be absolute. Economic life, in Marshall's view, existed in balance between freedom and restraint, between competitive freedom and the state's interference with it.

Marshall's view, rather accurately called "neo-classical" by economists, harmonized with the atmosphere of the post-World War I years wherein both large-scale business and government controls were accepted facts of economic life. His ideas spread rapidly throughout Britain and the United States, until by the 1930's Marshallian economics was standard fare, in one form or another, in almost every college or university. It satisfied the theorists who needed a device by which to explain American economic life, and it satisfied the businessman and politician who lived it. But the fact was that Marshall's concept of the economic process was by no means the traditional concept of *laissez-faire,* and that his acceptance marked the beginning of *laissez-faire's* final phase. John Maynard Keynes' two articles in *The New Republic* in 1926, titled "The End of Laissez-faire," were prophetic.

Keynes supplied the *coup de grâce,* assisted by The Great Depression. His economic speculations, begun in the twenties, culminated in his *General Theory of Employment, Interest and Money,* published in 1936. Classical economic theory, deriving from Adam Smith and the nineteenth century, held that the normal state of economic life was full employment and prosperity; hard times were abnormal deviations which would be rectified if only the natural laws of economics were allowed to operate—or at least if given a little governmental help. Keynes argued that twentieth-century civilization was so sophisticated and complex that in it economic stagnation was perhaps more normal than prosperity. To maintain a state of economic well-being demanded more than merely minimal government assistance. What Keynes suggested, in effect, was that private investment alone was insufficient to keep the national economy running at full power, and that as a matter of public policy the government should follow a constant spending policy to fill out the private sector of the economy.

Keynesian economics meant, some of his interpreters believed, that the government should become permanently involved in the economic process as part of its public responsibility. This was the intervention with a vengeance. Yet it was apparent, once Keynesian economics was stripped to its essentials, that it fitted into a long American tradition of using fiscal policy to regulate the economy, familiar since the days of tariff battles, "internal improvements," Greenbackers, Silverites, and the rest. Keynes' arguments for deficit spending, for that matter, justified many of the anti-depression measures already introduced by the first Roosevelt administration. Though Franklin Roosevelt apparently did not know Keynes' work sufficiently to be influenced by it, the idea that in time of crisis the government should intervene with its full financial power was one of long standing, certainly dating back to the depression nineties. Keynes' ideas served to explain what the New Deal policy-makers were already doing, and to give academic respectability to rule-of-thumb attempts to defeat the depression.

The greatest blow to the old *laissez-faire* tradition, of course, came not from any economic theories but from the brutal reality of the depression that struck in 1930. During the depression, the argument over whether or not the government should keep hands off seemed quite unreal, as day by day the federal government tried to restore some order to economic society. Whatever one believed about individual enterprise and government intervention, it was clear that *laissez-faire* was not enough to combat depression. The federal government was the only agency which had the power to act effectively (even that seemed occasionally in doubt) and whatever one believed of Smith or Spencer or Sumner, action by the state seemed the only way out of the emergency. Though A. C. Miller of the Federal Reserve Board said in 1932 that if the economy were sick, government should "keep hands off and stay out of the sick room" the nation could not afford to risk his advice.

Franklin Roosevelt later explained that the federal government intervened during the depression because it had to. His aim, he said, was to have the government "use affirmative action to bring about its avowed objectives rather than stand by and hope that general economic laws alone would attain them." Roosevelt was merely repeating what a good many

businessmen had already admitted—that *laissez-faire* was unequal to the crisis. *Business Week,* in a strikingly candid editorial titled "Do You Still Believe in Lazy Fairies?" put the
matter bluntly in 1931:

This deflation has let the wind out of a good many grand old ideas.
The grandest is the philosophy of letting George do it, summed up
in that fine French phrase, laissez-faire. . . . The one thing clear
to men of candor everywhere, and at last to us in our maturity, is
that it no longer works. . . . The legend of an "automatic equilibrium" upon which we can rely to correct chaos lingers only in the
myth and magic of those financial air-castles where the enchanted
princesses of political economy lie.

One of the most important results of the depression, therefore, was the acknowledgement by the American public (including much of the business community as well) of the
necessary influence of government on economic affairs. The
mobilization efforts of World War I and the tentative policies
of Theodore Roosevelt and Wilson had already accustomed
the nation to accept the national government as a factor in
the economic process; the depression experience confirmed it.
There was general agreement that the federal government
held the primary responsibility for stabilizing the economy
and restoring prosperity, and as the depression continued, the
government expanded its activity into sectors of the economy
heretofore regarded as exclusively private.

When in the later thirties the depression began to abate,
the question of whether or not the government should with-
draw touched off sharp controversy. Should the nation go back
to its pre-depression philosophy of modified *laissez-faire,* or
for that matter, could it do so? How much governmental control could the nation afford in normal times? The heated debates of the New Deal thirties and after involved two issues:
first, the efficacy of government planning; and second, the re-
examination of the theory of competition, the chief ingredient
of a system which, some felt, had failed.

No matter what economic theories one held, it was agreed
that the depression should not happen again. An effective

weapon against a recurrence, in the opinion of some economists, was a broad program of national economic planning,
for the debacle of the thirties showed that the firemen very
nearly arrived too late. Only by anticipating and controlling
economic trends in pragmatic, rational fashion, they believed,
could the nation's economic future be made secure. John M.
Clark, for example, proposed a national planning board which
would bring together "all the elements whose movements
must be fitted into each other if the whole national economic
machine is to work smoothly."

There were economists who agreed, and those who disagreed
violently. The case for planning was stated most clearly, perhaps, by Rexford Guy Tugwell in his address to the American
Economic Association in 1932, titled "The Principle of Planning and the Institution of Laissez-faire." Economic planning,
Tugwell said, was no more than a normal extension of recent
developments in business organization, accelerated by the prevailing crisis. For *laissez-faire*'s "lack of purpose," the nation
"must substitute plans born of intellectual effort" and imposed by governmental authority. The "chaos and chance" of
the classical economists, with its "explosive possibilities" of
boom-and-bust, must disappear before the rational organization of economic society. Tugwell himself in 1932 became an
adviser to the Roosevelt administration, along with others of
the same views. There were bitter attacks on these "New Deal
planners," and cries of "socialism," but the fact remained that
the full participation of government in the economic order, on
a planned, continuing basis, was there to stay.

The depression experience also brought about a good deal
of revised thinking about the principle of competition. The
pre-depression concentration of industrial power in big corporations, some believed, might have had something to do with
the causes of the depression; economists therefore felt that the
whole matter of competition and monopoly might well be restudied. The two most influential studies appeared simultaneously, Edward Chamberlin's *Theory of Monopolistic
Competition* in the United States in 1933, Joan Robinson's
Theory of Imperfect Competition in England the same year.

The chief characteristic of modern economic life, they agreed, was the existence of a small number of giant firms ("oligopolies") which controlled a large share of the industrial production. A few firms, for example, might produce similar products with separate identities (such as automobiles) in a market which was neither purely competitive nor purely monopolistic but a combination of the two. The prices set in such situations were, in Chamberlin's language, "administered prices," set not by competition but by the industry itself with self-defined limits. Such prices, it was suggested, provided justification for governmental interference in the price-setting process for the protection of the consumer, where "imperfect competition" provided little or none. While not all economists, by any means, accepted fully the implications of the Chamberlin-Robinson thesis, the concept of imperfect competition had noticeable effects on anti-trust theory and legislation.

Though he was neither an economist nor a social theorist, Franklin D. Roosevelt had greater influence than any other man on the direction of thought and practice in these fields during the thirties and forties. Roosevelt himself embodied a pragmatic kind of approach to economic issues that belonged in the old Progressive tradition, and in his attitude toward *laissez-faire,* he often looked much like Theodore Roosevelt and Woodrow Wilson. Like them, he recognized the existence of monopolistic concentration of power as well as its dangers and responsibilities. It was the duty of the state, he wrote, to "bring private autocratic powers into their proper subordination to the people's government," and to "preserve the American ideal of economic as well as political democracy against the abuse of concentration of economic power that has been insidiously growing up among us in the past few years."

Roosevelt's aim, in essence, was to work out a scheme of business regulation that prevented over-concentrations of capital and their misuse, but one still consistent both with the aims of political and economic democracy. It was the same policy, actually, that Theodore Roosevelt and Wilson searched for in their day. The answer, Frankin Roosevelt wrote in 1934, was "a coherent body of law protective of the large consuming interests and yet broad enough to afford the necessary play for industry to act as a unit, free from the pressure of unrestrained and wasteful competition." "We seek," he said another time, "to guarantee the survival of private enterprise by guaranteeing the conditions under which it can work."

To Franklin Roosevelt, then, the struggle against concentrated industrial power was "a struggle for, not against American business . . ., to preserve individual enterprise and economic freedom" from the restraints of "private monopolies and financial oligarchies." He wanted to free industry from itself, to eliminate the curbs placed on business activity by monopolistic concentrations much as his predecessor T. R. had. "Once it is realized that business monopoly in America paralyzes the system of free enterprise on which it is grafted," he wrote in 1938, "action by the Government to eliminate these artificial restraints will be welcomed by industry throughout the nation." The point was to have a balance of competition and combination in American industrial life, not too much of either, just enough of both.

There were two strands, actually, in the New Deal's attitude toward business. One, represented by the National Recovery Administration, was the result of Roosevelt's drive to end the depression by giving business all the freedom from restraint it could use. Under the NRA the New Deal was willing to accept price-fixing by industry, exemptions from the Sherman Act, industrial self-regulation, and almost any device in a somewhat fumbling attempt to raise prices and combat depression. The other was represented by the Temporary National Economic Committee, which under the chairmanship of Senator O'Mahoney held three years of inquiry on the possible effects of monopoly on business operations. The TNEC investigations, Roosevelt said, were part of "a program to preserve private enterprise for profit by keeping it free . . ., to stop the progress of collectivism and turn business back to the democratic competitive order." But beyond producing thirty-one volumes of testimony, the TNEC proved disappointing as a trust-busting agency and provided no effective recommendations for legislation.

Roosevelt, it is clear, quite truthfully wanted a controlled, *laissez-faire* economic system, not "individualism run wild" (as he called it in 1936) but *laissez-faire* individualism under regulation. "I believe in individualism," he once said, "up to the point where the individualist starts to operate at the expense of society." In his speech to the Commonwealth Club of Chicago in 1932 he explored quite carefully the relations of governmental authority to economic individualism, concluding that under twentieth-century conditions, government must exert some controls and restrictions on economic life, "not to hamper individualism but to protect it," to maintain the conditions under which free enterprise might operate. The aim of the national economy, he said again in Detroit in 1932, "should not be the survival of the fittest," but rather "the fitting of as many human beings as possible into the scheme of surviving."

Franklin Roosevelt believed in private enterprise, but he believed also that its field of operation should not be narrowed by undue concentrations of economic power. He sought, therefore, a modified *laissez-faire* under which private, individual enterprise might be kept alive by the sort of regulation that limited its potential capacity to stifle itself. The whole economic system was to him a problem in balance—"balance between agriculture and industry, and balance between the wage earner, employer, and consumer." But since it was born and developed within the context of economic emergency, Roosevelt's New Deal was much more prone than Theodore Roosevelt's Square Deal, or Wilson's New Freedom, to augment individual enterprise with government assistance when regulation alone seemed insufficient.

Had Roosevelt been able to develop his somewhat vague and unformed economic ideas during prosperity rather than depression, they might have turned out otherwise, and his attitudes toward *laissez-faire* might have been quite different. But working in *ad hoc* fashion in a race against crisis, he felt the urgent need to rescue the economy rather than adapt it. All "our concepts . . ., created for the old civilization," he said in 1935, "are being modified to save our economic structure from confusion, destruction, and paralysis." New Deal economic policy was always made in haste.

Nevertheless, the New Deal brought about certain major changes in American economic life. One was the swift extension of the planning function of the federal government. "No one could study the history of our industrial advance," said Roosevelt, "without being struck by its haphazardness." To him the nation's paramount problem was "the problem of controlling by planning the creation and distribution of those products which our vast economic machine is capable of yielding." The early New Dealers planned with great energy. By 1934 there were roughly fifty bureaus or commissions responsible directly to the President. These in turn involved dozens of sub-bureaus, boards, and committees—forty-five in the Agricultural Adjustment Administration alone, for example, thirty-five in the National Recovery Administration. The list of "brain trusters," as the newspapers aptly named the New Deal's army of official and unofficial planners, reached into the hundreds.

A second result was the extension of the federal authority into new areas of economic activity and its consolidation in those areas already penetrated. Obviously, because one of the New Deal's major problems was to bring the nation out of the doldrums, Roosevelt believed that government should play an active, positive part in improving economic life. The federal government first assumed the task of levelling out the peaks and valleys of the historic economic cycle. It next expanded its regulatory functions, reinforcing or extending its control over railroads and banks, securities issues and exchanges, industrial and agricultural production, agricultural prices, and broad areas of transportation and communication. Government under Roosevelt also extended its service functions into such areas as unemployment relief, housing, credit and loans, and conservation of natural resources. In the Social Security Act of 1935, the government also assumed a new kind of responsibility for personal economic security that marked a turning point in American social history.

Whether the New Deal was an economic "revolution," as some claimed, or whether it represented a normal movement of the American economy into its next phase, is beside the point. The fact is that the New Deal moved rather swiftly away from the *laissez-faire* tradition of the earlier century, far beyond the modified economic individualism of the Progressives, even beyond the neo-classical economics of the Marshallians. Jim Reed, at the Democratic convention of 1932, appalled at Roosevelt's views on government-in-business, trumpeted the last call of the old guard: "There has been no improvement in the philosophy—the economic philosophy—of John Stuart Mill, and *there never will be an improvement!*" But the course of twentieth-century events had left Mill, as it had Spencer and Carnegie, long gone by. William Orton, writing in *Harper's* in 1935, assessed the results of three years of Rooseveltian economics quite accurately:

To whatever strange ports we are wafted on the warm breezes of the New Deal, we shall not see the lotus land of laissez-faire again. That is probably the major historical fact of our generation.

The impact of the second World War on the *laissez-faire* tradition reinforced what the depression had already accomplished. The trend toward nationalization of the economy was accelerated by the necessities of wartime spending, controls, and postwar readjustments. What began in the turmoil of World War I, intensified by the depression, came to completion in World War II. As Elliott Bell wrote in 1941, a few days before Pearl Harbor, "The economy of the United States is undergoing a revolution under the impact of the rearmament program. We are passing in swift steps away from our traditional system of free individual enterprise and deeper into a system of government planning."

The signs of change in the forties were unmistakable. Business leaders themselves agreed that the postwar economic world would never be the same. (The term *laissez-faire,* in fact, began to pass out of fashion. *Reader's Guide* in 1941 replaced it as an indexing category with "free enterprise.") That the forties would be a "dangerous decade" for the free enterprise system, C. E. Wilson of General Electric wrote in 1941, was generally accepted. The earliest indication of the changing attitudes of business toward traditional *laissez-faire* came with the formation in 1942 by some 200 businessmen and economists of the Committee for Economic Development, which marked the most important shift in business thinking since the early decades of the century.

The CED began by accepting the fact that the intrusion of governmental authority into economic life was permanent, and even likely to enlarge. In accepting the fact that in modern America business shared responsibility with government for the national welfare, the CED stressed (as Carnegie's generation had) the role of the businessman as a trustee of private and public interests. The CED emphasized, therefore, the role of business as benefactor, rather than survivor—as Robert Gaylord of the National Association of Manufacturers remarked, free enterprise did not mean "the law of the jungle," but "business carried on in competitive fashion, facing the tests of the marketplace . . ., yet subject to the impartial restraints necessary to respect the rights of others." *Fortune* magazine, which became the spokesman for the Committee, explained in 1944 that "free enterprise is not, never has been, and never should be a system of complete *laissez-faire* . . ., the freedom to profit by any and all means." What it should mean is

maximum dependence upon competition and the free play of prices to determine who shall produce what; maximum dependence on profit as an incentive rather than on compulsion or prestige; and maximum emphasis on free personal choice among the economic opportunities—be they goods or jobs—that are available to men.

Business itself, CED pronouncements made clear, had crossed the great divide. Nineteenth-century *laissez-faire* was gone, Spencer dead beyond recall. At the bottom of the CED philosophy lay what economist John Kenneth Galbraith called "the rejection of automaticity," of the idea that the economy worked automatically and should be left alone except in dire emergencies. The relationship of government to business should be, *Fortune* said, to "police it without obstructing it, encourage it without pampering it, and help provide it with a balance wheel in times of business boom or depression."

Another important sign of the passing of *laissez-faire* came with the approval by Congress of the Employment Act of 1946, which literally ended the concept of a self-regulating, individually-operated, *laissez-faire* economic system. It was apparent that through such things as federal spending, veteran's benefits, and control of fiscal and credit policies, the federal government had already assumed partial control of the economic cycle. But with the Employment Act the national government undertook explicit responsibility for full employment, production, purchasing power, control of the business cycle, and the preservation of economic stability.

The Act also established a Council of Economic Advisers who were to make continuing studies of the economy in order to report to the President and to recommend legislation. As President Truman remarked in signing the bill, the Employment Act repudiated the traditional *laissez-faire* idea that the economy is governed by "unchangeable economic laws, that we are powerless to do more than forecast what will happen to us." Instead, he continued, it assumes that "our economy is within reasonable limits what we make it," and that the nation can maintain "a full, bountiful, and growing economy" as a matter of course. In 1946 the American people took a decisive step away from *laissez-faire*.

The United States at mid-century operates under neither free enterprise nor a planned economy, but rather under a mixture of both. It is what economist Alvin Hansen has called a "dual economy," in which government and private enterprise share the responsibility for its operation and in which both make vital decisions. A. A. Berle calculated in 1962, in fact, that perhaps no more than one-quarter to one-third of the volume of American industry is still administered in the classic *laissez-faire* manner, and this in the least important sectors of the economy. "No longer does *laissez-faire* constitute the ideal relationship between government and the economy," writes Robert Heilbroner. "Slowly there has arisen the conception of active public intervention to insure the orderly operation of the system."

It seems quite clear in the sixties that the state has assumed ever-greater responsibilities. Much more than simply a driver at the wheel, the national and state government furnishes a large share of the power that drives the economy forward. At the same time the competition provided by Soviet Russia has encouraged—and in some cases forced—governmental action in a number of fields heretofore regarded as sacrosanct for private development. Noticeably, in creating a communications satellite system, the United States turned not toward the traditional free-enterprise, open-competition methods of *laissez-faire,* but to an arrangement involving one near-monopolistic firm (American Telephone and Telegraph), and two government agencies (the National Space Administration and the Federal Communications Commission). In the light of such developments, one must agree with Professor Arthur Larson that "the old days of *laissez-faire* are gone:"

A new age or system is in the making . . ., in which control and planning are largely in the hands of government and only routine management to any great extent remains to private business. This growing union of business and government is probably no temporary development—the changes represent not only current difficulties but a new situation.

What most Americans call their "free enterprise" economy, on examination, turns out to be quite different from the classic model of *laissez-faire* constructed in the nineteenth century. Senator Robert Taft, writing in 1949, expressed as succinctly and authoritatively as any the essentials of what "free enterprise" means today. It does not mean to businessmen "complete freedom to do anything they please in business," nor does it mean "a system of special privilege for business." It means, in Taft's terms, that a citizen has "the right to engage in any occupation or business he wants to engage in and run it as he sees fit so long as he doesn't interfere with the right of others to do the same." Yet at the same time Senator Taft recognized several important restrictions on this economic individualism—government should intervene to "protect any one business from suppressing the liberty of others;" to "maintain equality of opportunity" for all businesses; to "reduce hardship and poverty . . ., putting a floor under the necessities of life;" and to "prevent or alleviate depressions."

The search by business leaders for a satisfactory definition of "free enterprise" that realistically describes contemporary economic facts, and at the same time agrees with the hallowed American *laissez-faire* tradition, remains a difficult one. The problem, writes Theodore Houser, chairman of Sears Roebuck and of the Committee for Economic Development, is to find "the vital balance" between government and private business, a balance maintained when government works "in and through the market, as buyer and seller," not as "suppressor and controller." Thus the apparent desire of the American people to send an expedition to the moon, expressed through government rather than through the private sector of the economy, does not impair the function of private business nor disturb the efficiency of the market. But government actions that keep business from producing what people want, or that keep it from producing at the lowest cost, Houser explains, damage business functions and suppress free enterprise.

Gabriel Hauge, president of Manufacturers Hanover Trust, in 1964 approached a definition of this "vital balance" by setting the limits beyond which governmental participation in the economy should not go; the power of the government may be used, he wrote,

to strengthen the operation of free markets, to promote vigorous and steady economic growth . . ., to supplement the market system . . ., to provide a floor under living levels . . ., to give protection from abuses of private economic power from whatever sector, to bring opportunity within the reach of all through education, to open the door to all careers, to guard freedom, to dispense justice . . .,

but always it must stop short of infringing on "the freedom of the individual" or his "opportunity and responsibility."

Peter Drucker has found that the term "free enterprise" in contemporary usage carries with it six generally accepted principles: first, that "it sees the function of government in setting the limits within which business is to be conducted rather than in running business enterprises," with certain exceptions; second, it means that "business is to be in the hands of men who are neither appointed by the political authorities nor responsible to any political agency other than courts of law;" third, it assumes that "the productive resources of the country are to be privately owned;" fourth, it accepts "profit as motivating and controlling business actions;" fifth, it means that "prices are to be based on supply and demand, with a free consumer choice;" and sixth, it is founded on "the concept of the privately owned, independently managed corporation producing for profit goods to be sold on a competitive market." To this definition, however, some economic conservatives would strongly object. The "Chicago school" of economists, represented by Professors Milton Friedman and George Stigler and supported by the politically conservative wing of the Republican party, interprets "free enterprise" much more vigorously; their model of the proper economy is built on ideally perfect competition, whose preservation is almost the sole aim of government.

The modern concept of "free enterprise," then, has moved far from Carnegie and Sumner. Business and public alike now consider normal kinds and amounts of governmental assistance, regulation, and intervention that fifty years ago would have been termed dangerous, or even subversive. They have approved a federally-subsidized highway system (as they did turnpikes, canals, and railroads) as well as aid to farmers, veterans, small business, schools, students, hospitals, airlines, newspapers, and utilities, among others. They have adopted wage and working minimums, collective bargaining under government supervision, price floors, and fair trade regulations. They have accepted a host of regulatory boards which control great segments of American life, including such powerful agencies as the Federal Trade Commission, the Federal Communications Commission, the Civil Aeronautics Board, the Federal Power Commission, the Interstate Commerce Commission, the National Labor Relations Board, and the Securities Exchange Commission, to name a few. And they have also accepted the direct entrance of government into business, with the Tennessee Valley Authority and its descendants, any of which would have been unthinkable not many decades ago.

There are a number of reasons for the gradual transformation of the traditional nineteenth-century concept of *laissez-faire* into what the mid-twentieth century accepts as "free enterprise." The older doctrine could not prevail in the face of twentieth-century facts. Depression, cyclical unemployment, the pressures of population, social and technological change, the rising expectations of mass society and its demands for more of the "good life"—these and other manifestations of modern living left the simplistic *laissez-faire* ideology of the 1880's and 1890's outmoded and inapplicable. Nor in the light of twentieth-century life did the state seem to be quite the same enemy to private business as before; the experience of two world wars and a cold one within two generations has helped to convince the public to the fact that business and government can successfully cooperate.

It would be safe to say that Americans no longer necessarily believe that that government governs best which governs least, and that *laissez-faire* economics survives more as tradition than actuality. Government today plays two different kinds of roles, at different levels, in economic affairs. Within the overall economic framework it makes general decisions—on such things as credit, currency, budget, spending, and so on—which have much to do with prosperity, stability, full employment, and the economic climate. At the same time, through legislation and regulation, government makes specific judgments which affect individual and corporate decisions practically and directly. All but the most unreconstructed of *laissez-faire* individualists recognize that government has, in the larger economic context, a vital part to play in the maintenance of prosperity. It is in the narrower context, that of specific decision in particular instances, that the issue of government-and-business almost always arises in contemporary disputes.

The American still believes, certainly, in the values of individual enterprise, assumes that it is part of the basic law of the United States brought into being by the Founding

Fathers, and is determined to maintain it wherever it can be applied—though he recognizes also that the areas of twentieth-century economic life in which it can operate as before may be rapidly shrinking. The American also believes that the state should promote the general welfare by supplying such services as the private sector of the economy does not provide, by guaranteeing economic and social security to the general citizenry, and by assuming an overall responsibility for the stability of national economic life. How he proposes to align these two sets of beliefs, both of them strong and pervasive in the American mind, fails to concern him greatly.

BIBLIOGRAPHICAL ACKNOWLEDGEMENTS

Good general historical treatments of American business include Thomas C. Cochran and William Miller, *The Age of Enterprise* (New York, 1956) and Sidney Fine's study of nineteenth-century economic thought, *Laissez-faire and the General Welfare State* (Ann Arbor, Michigan, 1956). Stuart Bruchey's *Roots of American Economic Growth: 1607-1861* (New York, 1965) is by far the best summary of scholarship regarding economic growth in the nation prior to the Civil War, with brilliant insights of its own. Joseph Dorfman's *The Economic Mind in American Civilization* (Five volumes, New York, 1946-1961) is encyclopaedic in its information of American economic theory; valuable background material is to be found in Richard Hofstadter's *Social Darwinism* (Philadelphia, 1944) and Clinton Rossiter's *Conservatism in America* (New York, 1955). Contemporary discussions of the issue are numerous. Among those which have proved useful are Edgar Queeny, *The Spirit of Enterprise* (New York, 1943); *The American Individual Enterprise System,* published by the Economic Principles Commission of the National Manufacturers' Association (New York, 1946); Peter Drucker, *Big Business* (New York, 1947), and *The Concept of the Corporation* (New York, 1964); Russel W. Davenport, *USA: The Permanent Revolution* (New York, 1951); Clarence B. Randall, *A Creed for Free Enterprise* (Boston, 1953); Walter Adams and Horace Gray, *Monopoly in America* (New York, 1955); F. X. Sutton, S. E. Harris, Carl Kaysen, and James Tobin, *The American Business Creed* (Cambridge, Mass., 1956), John K. Galbraith, *American Capitalism* (Boston, 1956); Louis Kelso and Mortimer Adler, *The Capitalist Manifesto* (New York, 1958); Roger Blough, *Free Man and the Corporation* (New York, 1959); Robert L. Heilbroner, *The Making of Economic Society* (New York, 1962); R. Joseph Monsen, *Modern American Capitalism* (Boston, 1963); and Michael Reagen, *The Managed Economy* (New York, 1963).

Three useful brief treatments of the American *laissez-faire* ethic are Arthur Schlesinger's "Ideas and the Economic Process," in Seymour Harris, ed., *American Economic History* (New York, 1961); Max Lerner's "Triumph of Laissez-faire," in Schlesinger and Morton White, eds., *Paths of American Thought* (Boston, 1963); and Overton Taylor, "The Free Enterprise Ideology and American Ideals and Institutions," *Daedalus* CX (Summer, 1963) 415-32. Articles pro and con, and analyses and discussions of *laissez-faire, free enterprise*, and government authority occur in profusion, as reference to any volume of *Reader's Guide* or *Vital Speeches* will illustrate. Some which are both typical and helpful, however, are C. F. Dunbar, "Economic Science in America 1776-1876," *North American Review* CCL (January, 1876) 124-54; Richard T. Ely, "Political Economy in America," *ibid.*, CXLIV (Feb., 1887) 114-18; John Maynard Keynes, "The End of Laissez-faire," *New Republic* XLVIII (August 21, September 1, 1926) 13-51, 37-41; Samuel Pettengill, "The Future of Free Enterprise," *Vital Speeches* III (Feb., 15, 1937) 275-81; Rexford G. Tugwell, "The Principle of Planning and the Institution of Laissez-faire," *American Economic Review* XXII (March, 1932) suppl. 75-92; Charles A. Beard, "The Idea of Let Us Alone," *Virginia Quarterly Review* XV (October, 1939) 500-14; E. G. Nourse, "Free Enterprise," *Vital Speeches* VIII (Dec. 5, 1941) 153-60; Charles E. Wilson, "Can We Save Free Enterprise?" *American Magazine* CXXXII (November, 1941) 37-64; Elliott V. Bell, "Planned Economy and/or Democracy," *New York Times*, Nov. 23, 1941; Thomas Nixon Carver, "Government's Place in Business," *Nation's Business* XXXI (February, 1943) 45, 75-6; The Committee for Economic Development, "The Economics of a Free Society," *Fortune* XXX (October, 1944) 163 ff.; Symposium, "Free Enterprise," *American Economic Review* XXXIV (March, 1944) 288-304; Wendell Berge, "Free Enterprise Lost?" *Forum* CVI (October, 1946) 322-5; Robert A. Taft, "How Much Government can Free Enterprise Stand?" *Colliers* CXXXII (October 22, 1949) 16, 74-6; Clarence B. Randall, "Free Enterprise is not a Hunting License" *Harper's* CLXXXIX (March, 1952) 38-41; Courtney C. Brown, "Toward a New Business Philosophy," *Saturday Review of Literature* XXXVI (January, 1953) 11-12, 38 ff.; "The New Competition," *Readings in Economics from Fortune* (New York, 1957) 99-104; Kenneth Boulding, "The Jungle of Hugeness," *Saturday Review* XLI (March 1, 1958) 11-14; David Bazelon, "Facts and Fictions of United States Capitalism," *Reporter*, Sept. 17, 1959;

C. F. Darlington, "Not the Goal, Only the Means," *New York Times*, July 3, 1960; Kenneth Watson, "The Myth of the American Way," *Christian Century* LXXX (March 13, 1963) 328-31; Theodore V. Houser, "Government and Business: The Vital Balance," *Saturday Review* (Jan. 11, 1964), and Gabriel Hauge, "Accent on the Individual," *ibid.*, 41.

IV

The American
Sense of Mission

And we Americans are peculiar, chosen people, the
Israel of our times; we bear the ark of the liberties
of the world.

—HERMAN MELVILLE

THE SEARCH by Americans for a precise definition of their
national purpose, and their absolute conviction that they
have such a purpose, provide one of the most powerful threads
in the development of an American ideology. All nations, of
course, have long agreed that they are chosen peoples; the idea
of special destiny is as old as nationalism itself. However, no
nation in modern history has been quite so consistently
dominated as the United States by the belief that it has a
particular mission in the world, and a unique contribution to
make to it. This American sense of direction has been consistently strong and surprisingly uniform from the outset of
American history; from the beginning of settlement they have
expended a great deal of thought and effort on the task of
formulating and confirming it. It is an idea deeply embedded
in the grain of American thought, from scholar to layman,
from the most articulate orator to the most mute, inglorious
Milton. Deep within the American mythology lies the con-

viction that a new free form of government was introduced into this continent by people chosen of God, in order to found a society in which the individual would possess all that liberty to which God thought him entitled, far from the interferences of Europe, free from the burden of the prejudiced past, to serve as an inspiration and a model to the world.

Since its beginnings, this conviction of mission and of special providence has provided the core of America's definition of itself. Edward Johnson, who came to Massachusetts in 1630, saw the new country as "the place where the Lord will create a new Heaven, and a new Earth, new Churches, and a new Common-wealth together." Johnson and his fellow settlers were convinced that God had brought them to New England for providential purposes as He had once directed Moses and the children of Israel. From the Puritans, awareness of the parallels between their transatlantic adventure and the Book of Exodus, to John Adams' belief that the American Revolution was an essential piece of "a grand scheme and design of Providence," to Woodrow Wilson's commitment of the United States to the "universal dominion of right," and beyond him to the present day this deep belief in the national destiny has been perfectly clear. Throughout their past, Americans have tended to think and behave in certain ways because they have always believed that they were, as a people, divinely designated for certain great achievements.

The development of a conviction of national purpose was, for Americans, a historical necessity. First, it was necessary in a new land, which possessed no cohesion, to develop some such sense of continuity. American colonists had to ask questions about themselves and their society to which their transplanted traditions provided no answers. British and Europeans lived with a ready-made ancestral heritage which yielded guides and controls for society. This was not true of America, for nobody (or few) had ever been there before, and the implications of living in a new land were profuse and puzzling. The American, therefore, felt the need to establish (even as a *British* colonist) some concept of the meaning of his life and his institutions, to ask something of his purpose and destination.

He needed to have a set of long-range principles with which to handle immediate problems and issues arising out of the utter novelty of his peculiarly American situation.

Second, the diversity of the American population demanded some sort of definition of this new society. As an ethnocentric expression of national pride, the identification of a national purpose was one way of transforming a bundle of colonies into a unit, providing for them some sense of coherence. It gave something for each American to aspire to, and national culture a meaning and point. Every American was literally an immigrant, a fact which continued to influence the psychology even of those who might be several generations removed from their British and European origins. American society was a mixture of attitudes, traditions, and ideas, all imported and at different times; it became imperative for Americans who had no single identifiable tradition to attempt to evolve one out of what was borrowed, old, and new. To establish a sense of national purpose was one method of providing American society with the unity and security it needed, a way of giving it status among other nations.

Lastly, the development of an American sense of mission and purpose helped to compensate for the American lack of a past. Among the cultures of the world, even in comparison to the more recent countries of Europe, America was embarrassingly new. The American colonists were extremely conscious of this and properly respectful of their cultural elders; as members of a new country (after 1776) they were equally aware of their infancy, and often aggressively sensitive about it. But if the nation had been chosen to do something no other nation could do, it obviously possessed a distinction granted to no other. Jedidiah Morse, the scientist and historian, explained this in the preface to his *American Geography* in 1789:

Here the sciences and the arts of civilized life are to receive their highest improvement. Here civil and religious liberty are to flourish, unchecked by the cruel hand of civil or ecclesiastical tyranny. Here Genius, aided by all the improvements of former ages, is to be exerted in humanizing mankind—in expanding and enriching their minds with religious and philosophical knowledge, and in planning and executing a form of government, which shall involve all the excellencies of former governments, with as few of their defects as is consistent with the imperfection of human affairs, and which shall be calculated to protect and unite, in a manner consistent with the natural rights of mankind, the largest empire that ever existed.

The American could say with Morse, in effect, we are new and young and fresh, but we have a unique and special destiny; we have a brief and perhaps negligible past, but we have a long and significant future ahead.

For the most part, the shaping of the national purpose was evolved out of the American people at large, through various channels and groups, within the context of a relatively loose and permissive society. Unlike Europe, America never had an established set of leaders to articulate or judge the national aims, or to control the methods of attaining them. It possessed no spokesmen—in the British and European sense—to whom society might turn for statements of the national purpose, or who might provide (as a nobility or an established church might) some kind of authority in setting national goals. As a result, early expressions of the national aims were not always accurately formulated, nor clearly defined, however earnestly held.

Yet America, over the span of its existence, always possessed consistency of national purpose and awareness of its importance. The United States has possessed, for almost two hundred years, a concise statement of its aims, specifically enumerated in writing, periodically re-affirmed, and carefully re-examined. This of course exists in the preamble of the Declaration of Independence, which Archibald MacLeish has called "the most precisely articulated statement of national purpose in recorded history." It is probable that only in the United States would a national body, appointed by the head of the state, embark on a study of the national purpose, as President Eisenhower's Commission on National Goals did in 1959. It is also significant that the Commission's report, published in 1960 as *Goals for Americans,* opened with a reaffirmation of those aims first stated in the preamble of the Declaration. "The paramount goal of the United States," the report begins, "was set long ago."

It is to guard the rights of the individual, to ensure his development, and to enlarge his opportunity. It is set forth in the Declaration of Independence, drafted by Thomas Jefferson and adopted by the Continental Congress on July 4, 1776.

The American national purpose, as defined over three hundred and fifty years, has remained remarkably constant. It is divided into three parts:
   —that the United States lead others toward a future world-state of freedom and liberty as yet unknown, and that it serve as surrogate or agent for the rest of mankind in achieving it.
   —that the United States serve as an example to the rest of the world of God's plan for mankind, and as proof that man can govern himself in peace and justice.
   —that the United States serve as a haven for the oppressed of the world, and as a place of opportunity for the deserving, ambitious, and godly.
Each aim, it is noticeable, is related to the other, the three comprising a whole. Each presupposed a specific function: the first exemplary, the second evangelical, the third exoteric.

In the first instance, the goal of the United States is to furnish to the world a model of democracy, and to convince others of its worth and workability by the force of the American example. The mission of America, Albert Gallatin told his fellow-citizens, was

to be a model for all other governments and for all other less-favored nations, to adhere to the most elevated principles of political morality . . ., and by your example to exert a moral influence most beneficial to mankind.

Combined with this is a missionary spirit which leads Americans to believe that if the American system of government is the best for mankind, it therefore ought to be extended to others. Thus when Tom Paine remarked that "My country is the world; my countrymen are all mankind," he succinctly expressed how American revolutionaries meant to extend their principles to universal application. So too Jefferson, in his belief that his generation "acted not for ourselves alone, but for the whole human race," implied that those ideals which motivated their revolution were ultimately exportable.

Americans have always conceived of their civilization as exemplary, or, as George Bancroft gracefully expressed it, they believe that the United States will eventually "allure the world to freedom by the beauty of its illustration." Puritan John Winthrop expressed the hope that this new society would be so constructed that "men shall say of succeeding planta- tions: the Lord makes it like that of New England. For we must consider that we shall be as a city on a hill, the eyes of all people upon us." The Revolutionary generation, too, was acutely conscious of the responsibility which rested upon the new nation to provide a model for the world. The Declaration of Independence carried with it the feeling that its framers had an overpowering sense of the importance of the document, that they believed that they were doing something of great significance to the future of mankind—certainly it must have been issues of far greater importance than taxes or parlia- mentary authority which led them to ask the judgment of "The Supreme Judge of the World" and "the protection of Divine Providence." The Reverend Timothy Dwight believed the United States to be "by Heaven designed, th' example bright, to renovate mankind." Philip Freneau had a vision of America as "a new Jerusalem sent down from Heaven" to serve "a pattern for the world beside," while his fellow-poet Joel Barlow hailed the founding of the Republic as "the mild morning, where the dawn begins, the full fruition of the hopes of man." Continental Congress expressed the idea con- cisely and accurately in 1789:

If justice, good faith, honor, gratitude, and all the other qualities which ennoble a nation and fulfill the ends of government, shall be the fruits of our establishment, then the cause of liberty will acquire a dignity and lustre it has never yet enjoyed, and an example will be set which cannot but have the most favorable influence on mankind.

But, Congress also warned, if this "last and fairest experiment of human nature fail," the cause of liberty were lost, silenced forever "by the votaries of tyranny and oppression."

Subsequent expressions of this idea remained much the same. Washington, in his First Inaugural Address, pointed out that "the preservation of the sacred fire of liberty and the destiny of the republican model of government" rested on the success of the American example. Alexander Hamilton believed that the American Revolution set a precedent that would force Europe to "inquiries which may shake it to its deepest foundations." Jefferson called the American experiment "the last best hope of mankind," and "a barrier against the returns of ignorance and barbarism."

The idea has never since lacked for Presidential expositors. Lincoln believed the Declaration of Independence gave "hope for the world for all future time," and of course his Gettysburg Address gave classic expression to the idea that America was charged with the responsibility for showing mankind whether a nation conceived in liberty, and dedicated to the proposition that all men are created equal, could long endure. Theodore Roosevelt, in language reminiscent of Washington, believed it to be an American duty "to show that under a free government a mighty people can thrive best." "Upon the success of our experiment," he continued, "much depends, not only as regards our own welfare, but as regards the welfare of mankind." Woodrow Wilson echoed Lincoln; the American mission, he wrote, "was to show men the path of liberty and mutual serviceability . . ., to set responsible example to all the world of what free government is and can do. . . ." Harry Truman, in 1950, wrote in the same vein that the United States stood always in "a conspicuous place" before the judgments of history. "The world is watching us," he said, "because all the world knows that the fate of civilization depends, to a very large extent, on what we do."

Not only Presidents, of course, have expressed this aim with eloquence and understanding. In the opinion of John L. Sullivan, the Jacksonian editor, the United States was

destined to manifest to mankind the excellence of divine principles; to establish on earth the noblest temple ever dedicated to the worship of the Most High—the Sacred, and the True . . ., governed by God's natural and moral law of equality, the law of brotherhood.

Southerner Hugh S. Legaré, speaking to a Fourth of July celebration in Charleston in 1823, defined America as an example to the world of "an imperial republic . . ., founded in the maxims of common sense, employing within itself no arms but those of reason, blending in one divine harmony various habits and conflicting opinions." William H. Seward, in an 1853 oration devoted entirely to "The Destiny of America," believed that it was among other things "to advance most effectively the common cause of human nature among men" by "establishing and maintaining the principles on which the recovery and preservation of their inherent natural rights depend." Carl Schurz felt that "the great mission of true Americanism" was to answer by the national example the question, "Has man the faculty to be free and to govern himself?"

The later nineteenth-century centennial celebrations called forth innumerable definitions of national purpose. Charles Sumner, in preparation for the Centennial of 1876, prepared in 1874 a volume called *Prophetic Voices Concerning America* consisting of hundreds of statements about America's destiny, mission, and function in the congress of nations, ranging from pre-Columbian prophecies to his own time. He closed the volume with his own explanation of the American mission, which was by "the national example" to "exert an irresistible attraction" on the rest of the world "to seek new life" through the recognition of "the basic principles of human brotherhood." "It is my first conviction," U. S. Grant said at his second inauguration as President, "that the civilized world is tending toward republicanism . . ., that our great Republic is destined to be the guiding star for all others."

Only minor differences in style separate Sumner's and Winthrop's statements from Herbert Hoover's Constitution Day address of 1935, which fixed the national purpose as the responsibility to illustrate "the highest conception of the Christian faith—the conception of individual freedom with brotherhood," or from Walter Lippmann's definition of the American mission in 1944 as the obligation "to make the New World a place where the ancient faith can flourish anew, and its eternal promise at last be redeemed." Nor should it be forgotten, for that matter, that Bartholdi's bronze Statue of Liberty, placed on Bedloe's Island in 1886 and visited by thousands of Americans each year, is actually titled "Liberty Enlightening the World."

The second portion of the American destiny, to lead the world actively toward the millennium of liberty, has been equally clearly articulated since the beginnings of settlement. It was conceived from the beginning that America would be not only the model, but the laboratory wherein men everywhere learned how to govern themselves. Edward Johnson, in his *Wonderworking Providence* (1654), characterized the settlers as "forerunners of Christ's army" who would soon "proclaim the near approach of the most wonderful works that ever the sons of man saw." Jonathan Edwards, a century later, agreed that God has chosen America to be his minister to some as "glorious renovator of the world," just as he had chosen certain human ministers to renovate souls. Thomas Paine, a professional agitator against Kingship, remarked that his home was "where liberty was not," and he spent much of his life in an attempt to transfer the American revolution elsewhere.

Simply to serve as an example of the ability of men to govern themselves, admirable as that might be, was however not enough. The mission of the United States, Paine said, was "to excite emulation throughout the kingdoms of the earth, and meliorate the conditions of the human race"—by serving as the model for other revolutions, if needs be. "America's purpose," echoed David Ramsey in 1794, "is to prove the virtues of republicanism, to assert the Rights of

Man, and to make society better." The responsibility of the nation was to extend the concepts of liberty, equality, and justice over all the earth; this, said James Wilson at the Constitutional Convention, was "the great design of Providence in regard to this globe."

This evangelical spirit, the belief that the fundamentals of the American way ought to be extended and exported, remained through the nineteenth century as conformable as Johnson's early vision of it. William H. McGuffey's *Eclectic Reader,* the most widely used textbook of its time, taught American students that the United States "holds out an example . . . to those nine-tenths of the human race who are born without hereditary rank or fortune," showing the world "that it is practicable to elevate the mass of mankind . . ., to raise them to self-respect." "In our endeavor to maintain our existing forms of government," said Daniel Webster, a tireless exponent of the idea, in an address at Worcester in 1832, "we are acting not for ourselves alone, but for the whole globe. We are trustees holding a sacred treasure, in which all lovers of freedom have a stake. . . . The gaze of the sons of liberty, everywhere, is upon us, anxiously, intently, upon us." Orestes Brownson, obviously steeped in Hegel, worked the concept out carefully in an essay called *The American Republic:*

Each people had a mission selected by God, he wrote, some great, some small. Of those entrusted with great duties, the Jews' was to establish worship of a single God, and belief in the Messiah. The Greeks were chosen to develop beauty in art and truth in philosophy. The Romans to develop law, order, political systems. The US has divine orders to continue these, and to contribute its own, that is, "its mission is to bring out in life the dialectic union of authority and liberty, of the natural rights of man and society.

Ralph Waldo Emerson, in quite un-Brahminlike language, wrote that "the office of America is to liberate, to abolish kingcraft, priestcraft, caste, monopoly, to pull down the gallows, to burn up the bloody statute book . . .," wherever these may be. His contemporary Marcius Wilson, writing a spreadeagle patriotic American history in 1847, was equally certain that the American example was "destined yet to regenerate the world upon the principles of universal intelligence, and eventually to overthrow the time-worn system of tyrannical usurpation of the few over the many." William H. Seward conceived of America's duty as facilitating the spread abroad of Christian principles of government, making "a new and further development of the Christian system of the introduction of the golden rule of benevolence in the science of human government." An editorial in the *United States Magazine and Democratic Review* in 1840 summarized the matter perfectly:

To us much has been given, and much will be required of us. We have been placed in the forefront of the battle, in the cause of Man against the powers of evil which have so long crushed him to the dust. The problem of capacity for self-government is to be solved here. Our mission is to elevate him to a sense of his native dignity, and to prove that . . . he should be left to the individual action of his own will and conscience.

For this reason, nineteenth-century Americans were quick to welcome revolutions elsewhere which seemed to reflect the example of their own. The American experience of 1776, said John Quincy Adams in 1821, stood as a model for all others, as "a beacon . . . on the summit of the mountains, to which all the inhabitants of the earth may turn their eyes." It would be but a short time, a Massachusetts orator told his Fourth of July audience in 1827, until "the spark kindled in America, shall spread and spread, until all the earth shall be illuminated with its light." The reaction in the United States to the upheavals in Europe early in the nineteenth century was therefore one of expectant approval; it was commonly hoped, historian George Bancroft wrote, that within twenty years not a crowned head would be left in Europe. The Greek uprising against Turkey enlisted the passionate support of hundreds of prominent Americans; mass meetings were held in major cities to raise funds for arms, and men of the stature of Webster, Clay, Monroe, and Calhoun spoke out for Greek independence.

The overthrow of Louis Philippe's government in France in

1848 produced a sensation throughout the United States, eliciting dozens of speeches, celebrations, and orations in Congress. This second French Revolution, they stressed, was lit from the sparks of 1776; the American Revolution was the "leaven to the millions of the world," according to the New York *Sun,* "a light and a fire, illumining their souls and warming their hearts until they have dared to shout in the ears of tyrants, 'we too are men—we will be free!' " More revolutions could be expected, and in happy anticipation Senator William Allen introduced a resolution into Congress congratulating the French on their "efforts to consolidate liberty by imbodying its principles in a republican form of government."

The Hungarian revolutionist leader Louis Kossuth, called by the American press "the General Washington of Hungary," came to the United States in 1851 on a ship officially furnished by the American government, and his subsequent tour was a wild success which provided him with a hundred thousand dollars in contributions and left streets and statues in his honor all over the nation. Italy, Germany, Switzerland, Prussia, and Belgium were soon to follow in America's path, the New York *Sun* predicted; England's monarchy might be the last to go, but go it must. The mission of the United States at this point in history, the *Sun* continued, was "by our sympathy and counsel, to nerve and help guide the sinews of the liberty-seeking masses," to serve as "the watchword, the polestar of their struggle"—even, perhaps, "if freedom were in *danger . . .,* to fly to her rescue."

This millennial strain has remained strong in American thought. Walt Whitman, in his poem, "Thou Mother With Thy Equal Brood" (1872), saw emerging a

> Beautiful world of new superior birth that rises in
> my eyes,
> Like a limitless golden cloud filling the western
> sky . . .,
> By history's cycles forwarded, by every nation, lan-
> guage, hither sent,
> Ready, collected here, a freer, vast, electric world
> to be constructed here.

That America would lead the way to it, there was no doubt. "We have no choice," wrote Theodore Roosevelt in 1901, "we people of the United States, as to whether or not we shall play a great part in the world. That has been determined for us by fate, by the march of events."

The outbreak of war in Europe in 1914 caused many Americans to re-examine the American role in the world as it was related to the European conflict. Commentator Wallace Rice, writing in *The Forum* in 1914 about the American duty to serve as "the conscience of the world," felt that it must work toward "that shining goal" of world peace to "create a United States of Europe" at the war's end. In this same spirit Woodrow Wilson, taking America into World War I with heavy heart and an idealistic moral intensity, told Congress in his war message that he did so with full recognition of the nation's mission to enter the contest as a war

for democracy, for the right of those who submit to authority to have a voice in their own governments, for the rights and liberties of small nations, for a universal dominion of right by such a concert of free peoples as shall bring peace and safety to all nations and make the world itself at last free.

American participation in the war, he told his audience at a Fourth of July celebration held at Mount Vernon in 1918, was actually an extension of "the spirit of '76" to "the great stage of the world itself." No one of his time gave the American concept of national mission a greater personal dedication than Wilson.

In the same vein Franklin Roosevelt, both in his Third Inaugural of 1941 and his famous wartime "Four Freedoms" speech, spoke of those "fundamental freedoms and liberties" which the American nation was obligated to protect and diffuse throughout the world. Adlai Stevenson, speaking in 1952 during the frustrations of the Korean conflict, phrased the same thought in language of which Wilson and Roosevelt would have approved:

God has set for us an awesome mission: nothing less than the leadership of the free world. Because He asks nothing of His servants beyond their strength, He has given to us vast power and vast opportunity. And like that servant of Biblical times who received the talents, we shall be held to strict account for what we do with them.

So too the President's Commission of 1960 reiterated that it was still the historic function of the United States

At all times, to exert its influence and power in behalf of a world order congenial to American ideals, interests, and security, a world in which the peoples of all nations can find the opportunity for freedom and well being.

John F. Kennedy, in 1963, put it more directly:

The iron of the new world being forged today is now ready to be molded. Our job is to shape it, so far as we can, into a world we want for ourselves and our children and for all men.

The concept of America as missionary, and the concept of America as model, however, have historically met in distinct contradiction. If the United States is to fulfill its destiny, it bears the responsibility of promoting the cause of liberty everywhere. It then must certainly assist the victims of oppression wherever they may be, perhaps even intervening in behalf of justice and liberty wherever it is endangered. Yet at the same time Americans consider themselves a chosen people, separated geographically by a wise Providence from the rest of the world, placed in a bountiful land where they are self-sustaining and self-sufficient, and where they may pursue without interference the destiny intended for them. These two beliefs here long presented the United States with a dilemma in its foreign policies. If the United States is to serve as an example to the rest of the world, it must think of itself in relation to others and must become involved with them. Certainly what the United States does at home should have consequences abroad. Yet neither should it become so involved with others that it loses its purity of purpose or its ability to work out its own salvation independently.

The concept of mission and the concept of example, therefore, have always pulled both ways. Thus Joel Barlow in 1792 could exhort the people of the Piedmont to revolt against their tyrannical governors as the Americans did, while Washington in his Farewell Address of 1796 explained that the best way to keep the American mission inviolate was to avoid entanglement in Europe's affairs. Americans have always felt that they have a special mandate to develop and maintain democratic values and institutions at home; they also feel that they have a particular function in extending the benefits of the American system abroad. If Americans are to be committed, as Theodore Roosevelt thought, "to promote justice, freedom and the rights of man" everywhere, how can they keep free of the world to keep themselves, as Robert La Follette said, from "becoming a party to every political scheme that may be hatched in the capitals of Europe," thereby "losing our right to control our destiny as a nation?"

Throughout the nineteen-thirties, these two historic traditions—the one isolationist, and the other internationalist—clashed repeatedly over America's concern with European affairs and their effect on American policy. The America First Committee, with a few exceptions, clung to the respected tradition of avoiding foreign entanglements, believing that the nation should pursue its separate course of internal development. The Committee to Defend America by Aiding the Allies pursued an equally historic policy by explaining that since the United States had a clear responsibility to encourage freedom and self-determination everywhere, it must assist others to resist anti-democratic governments. Both traditions had ample precedent, and both belonged directly to the mainstream of America's missionary past. Only by sudden involvement in the war itself, as in 1917, was the conflict between them resolved.

Americans have never found these positions absolutely irreconcilable. The President's Commission on National Goals, for example, in 1960 solved the issue by adopting both views—

the American aim, its report states, is not only "to preserve and enlarge our own liberties," but equally "to extend the area of freedom throughout the world." "Our enduring aim," the report continued,

is to build a nation and help build a world in which every human being shall be free to develop his capacities to the fullest. We must rededicate ourselves to this principle and thereby strengthen its appeal to a world in political, social, economic and technological revolution. . . . Our goals abroad are inseparable from our goals at home.

The one road leads toward deeper and deeper implication in the affairs of the world, the other points toward isolation.

The third portion of the American concept of mission, that the country should serve the world as a refuge for the oppressed, appeared with the first settlers. The Puritans saw the New World as a haven: they welcomed the opportunity to worship in it without interference and to govern themselves with as little hindrance as possible. Quaker William Penn, for his part, helped to make his colony a retreat from all those "anxious and troublesome solicitations, hurries, and perplexities of woeful Europe." Growing out of the "Come to America" theme of the promotional literature of early settlement, the belief took shape quite early that the American scene offered men an equal chance for a fair share and a fresh start. Franklin's "Poor Richard" praised the colonies as a place

> Where the sick Stranger joys to find a Home,
> Where casual Ill, maim'd Labor, freely come,
> Those worn with Age, Infirmity, and Care,
> Find Rest, Relief, and Health's returning fair.

Thomas Paine in *Common Sense* pictured America as "an asylum for the persecuted lovers of civil and religious liberty from every part of Europe," while Schubart, in Germany, likened the new States to "thirteen golden doors . . ., open to the victims of intolerance and despotism."

The "asylum" theme was commonplace in the public literature of the later eighteenth century. Lafayette, speaking after the Revolution, hoped that "this great temple which we have just erected to liberty will always be an instruction to oppressors, an example to the oppressed, and a refuge for the rights of the human race." Philip Freneau agreed that America was a place where,

> From Europe's proud, despotic shores,
> Hither the stranger takes his way,
> And, in our new-found world, explores
> A happier soil, a milder sway.

Congress told the Irish that "the fertile regions of America would afford you a safe asylum from poverty, and, IN TIME, from oppression also." Washington believed the new nation to be "a capacious asylum for the poor and persecuted of the earth," while Jefferson too, in his First Message to Congress, considered it "an asylum for oppressed humanity" and a refuge for "unhappy fugitives from distress." Nor was it only the poor who received attention, but the prosperous as well. Tench Coxe in 1787 assured the British and Europeans that there was a place in the new society for the entrepreneur, and Jefferson believed that the United States would "draw the wealth and wealthy men of other nations into our bosom, by giving security to property and liberty to its holders."

Hundreds of Fourth of July orations delivered through the nineteenth century, as Merle Curti's study of them has shown, emphasized the idea that America had been and still was a harbor from oppression. Wendell Phillips' invitation to the world of 1852 was typical—"Let every oppressed man come; let every poor man come; let every man who wishes to change his residence come—we welcome all!" The Senate periodically renewed its invitation to Irish revolutionaries to immigrate to "the hospitable shores of the United States," and to others such as Kossuth's defeated Hungarian patriots. This concept of America as asylum, expressed over and over throughout the century, left powerful marks on the European imagination. Carl Schurz, one of the most famous of the century's emigrants, told in his memoirs how this vision of the United States impressed him as a youth in Germany. The country, he wrote, seemed to his mind's eye

a land covered partly with majestic trees, with flowery prairies, immeasurable to the eye, and intersected with rivers and broad lakes—a land where everybody could do what he thought best, and where nobody need be poor, because everybody was free.

Ironically, however, nineteenth-century America did not particularly want to be a haven for certain religious groups, nor for Chinese, Japanese, and Africans, although both major political parties for sixty years included strong statements in their platforms of the principle of free entry. Nor did the twentieth century seem more receptive. Woodrow Wilson, at the same time that Congress was preparing to restrict immigration quotas, welcomed to America "the strong men and the forward-looking women of all nations." Although in ensuing years the welcome was not so generous as Wilson's invitation presumed, most Americans nevertheless felt the essential rightness of Emma Lazarus' poem, inscribed on the Statue of Liberty as expressive of the belief that the country offered to the Old World the "golden door" of opportunity:

> Give me your tired, your poor,
> Your huddled masses yearning to be free,
> The wretched refuse of your teeming shore.
> Send these, the homeless, tempest-tost, to me.

Although his philosophy differed widely from Jefferson's, it is notable that Henry Ford, in the midst of the Nazi terror of 1938, believed that the United States must "maintain its traditional role as a haven for the oppressed." During these years, and afterwards in the chaos of post-World War II in Europe, American organizations such as the American Friends Service Committee, the National Refuge Service, the American Committee for Christian Refugees, and many other organizations carried on the deep, historic American tradition of offering asylum and refuge to the homeless of the world.

If Americans really were a chosen people—the Israelites of

the New World—the richness and variety of the land itself gave ample evidence to support the analogy. The land seemed so fair and bountiful that its settlers could not help but draw the likeness to Canaan. Thomas Morton of Merrymount, when he "seriously considered the bewty of the place, with all her faire indowments," did not think "that in all the knowne world it could be paralleled." God had meant great things for such a land. "Rome and Paris," he wrote in 1722, "had not such considerable beginnings, were not built under such happy auspices, and their founders met not with those advantages . . . which we have found on the Mississippi." Divine generosity in providing more than enough land, in contrast to crowded Europe, Jefferson took as proof of God's special providence to Americans; theirs was a "*chosen* country, with room enough for their descendents to the hundredth and thousandth generation."

Americans decided quite early that their country had been blessed with all the attributes needed to make it the final scene in the unfolding drama of a free mankind. The fertility and variety of the country, its beauty and salubrity, its vast reaches and unlimited resources, all seemed to show its fitness for great events. Benjamin Smith Barton, the naturalist, thought that every American should "glow with emotions of a virtuous pride, when he reflects on the blessings his country enjoys." Certainly the land itself, viewed in its unspoiled majesty, seemed to make the United States a mighty stage for new developments in human history. Washington, in his Circular Letter of 1783, remarked that because of its qualities of soil, climate, and resources, the new nation was undoubtedly blessed with a "fairer opportunity for political happiness" than "any other Nation had ever been favored" by the Deity. Joel Barlow agreed, in his epic poem "The Columbiad" (1809), that American nature itself was the final proof of God's favor:

> For here great nature with a bolder hand,
> Roll'd the broad stream and heaved the lifted land;
> And here, from finish't earth, triumphant trod,
> The last ascending steps of her creating God.

Succeeding generations of Americans echoed the same conviction. The country's "mighty rivers, vast sea-like lakes, and noble and boundless prairies" presented a tremendous challenge to the imagination, the Albany *Argus* pointed out to those settling the new territories:

To live in such a splendid country . . . expands a man's views of everything in this world. Here everything is to be done—schools to be established, governments instituted. These things fill their lives with great enterprises, perilous risks, and dazzling rewards.

The editor of a volume of engravings, titled *Scenery of the United States* (1855) believed that "nowhere else on the globe is Nature lovelier, grander, less austere, and more varied and picturesque, than upon this continent."

Not only was the land beautiful, it was imperially large; as W. H. Seward wrote, the United States occupied "a compact and indivisible domain, peculiarly adapted to internal commerce, seventeen times greater than France, and a hundred times more extended than that of Britain." The Reverend John Johnson believed in 1794 that the American soil had been "marked by the special hand of Nature;" so too was Thomas Starr King, two generations later, convinced that God had designed the country "to be the home of no mean people and the theater of no paltry destiny." Senator Albert Beveridge saw God in 1900 as a "Master Strategist" who "enthroned the United States between the two great oceans of the world" in order to furnish its people with the perfect environment for their government.

Another evidence of God's special partiality for Americans was the relative isolation of their continent from Europe. It was almost, Americans felt, as if God meant to remove their land from the contaminations of less favored societies, so that in the New World men could make a fresh beginning. "Nature having separated us, by an immense ocean," wrote George Mason in 1783, "from the European nations, the less we have to do with their quarrels and politics, the better." The idea received its most eloquent statement, perhaps, in Washington's

Farewell Address, in which the retiring President spoke of "our detached and distant situation" which "invites and enables us to pursue a different course" from Europe's "ambition, rivalship, interest, humor, or caprice."

The thought was repeated endlessly by subsequent generations. Gouverneur Morris, cosmopolitan sophisticate though he was, believed that the "great gulph which rolls its waves between Europe and America" formed a valuable barrier against the Old World's troubles. The Reverend Andrew Lee of Connecticut thanked God in 1795 for the Atlantic Ocean, which might "forever guard us against the violence, and separate us from the vices, follies, and politics of Europe." To Hugh S. Legaré, fifty years later, it seemed that "a whole continent has been set apart, as if it were holy ground, for the cultivation of pure truth—for the pursuit of happiness upon rational principles—for the development of all the sensibilities, and capacities, and powers of the human mind." Jefferson rejoiced that "America has a hemisphere to itself," a conviction which President Monroe and his Secretary of State J. Q. Adams turned into a basic element of American foreign policy. The Monroe Doctrine merely formalized a principle already traditional in American thinking—that Europe was politically and morally different from America, and that the physical fact of separation established an irrevocable distinction between the Old and the New Worlds. John L. O'Sullivan, the Democratic editor, in remarking that the United States occupied "a disconnected position as regards any other nation," was grateful that this meant it had "little connection with antiquity, its glories or its crimes." James Russell Lowell's couplet in his *Fable for Critics* put it pungently:

> O my friends, thank your God, if you have one,
> that he
> Twixt the old World and you sets a gulf of a sea.

This implicit antagonism toward Europe, and the belief that by design of an approving God their land had been separated from it, was given especially cogent expression by Boston's William Ellery Channing. "We cannot admit the thought," he wrote in 1830,

that this country is to be only a repetition of the old world. We delight to believe that God, in the fullness of time, has brought a new continent to light, in order that the human mind should move here with a new freedom, should frame new social institutions, should explore new paths and reap new harvests.

"All the past we leave behind," said Walt Whitman a generation later. "We debouch upon a new and mightier world. . . . I hold it to be the glory and pride of America not to be like other lands, but different, after its own different spirit."

The American sense of difference, ingrained in the consciousness of the settler from the beginning and constantly re-emphasized by the colonial experience, reached its culmination after the Revolution. The American came to realize that to be different from Britain and Europe was not necessarily a disadvantage, that in fact those differences might well be important qualifications for America's missionary destiny. It was possible that the United States, because it *was* new and different, was really superior to Europe, and that God had willed it so for a purpose. There was convincing proof of this in world history, Americans believed, for it seemed to show a divinely-arranged sequence of events, marching toward one goal—the separation and creation of the United States. Dr. Richard Price, Franklin's friend, went so far as to suggest that the American Revolution ranked in historical importance second only to "the introduction of Christianity among mankind." American writers were quite familiar with the contemporary cyclical theory of history which taught that nations rose and fell in sequence by dependence on universal natural and moral law. They were convinced that the United States was on the rising curve of this cycle, and that the whole sweep of the past was but a prelude for the God-ordained emergence of the United States.

It seemed plain, therefore, that in being created distinctively by divine design, Americans possessed certain advantages not given to other men. There was evidence to show, a contributor to a Connecticut magazine wrote in 1786, that God had "reserved this country to be the last and greatest theater in the improvement of mankind." Nowhere else had a kindly deity given man the chance to put into practice those principles of government and society He favored, nor had He ever granted another nation such opportunities to work out its ideals. The United States was special—in the sense that it had been chosen to build a society on values fundamental to all men but never before given this chance to operate. What happened to America was for this reason of utmost significance; the results of the American experiment were of great consequence to the whole human race. The United States was superior to England and Europe because it was not like them, because it had been chosen to be the model for the new kind of New World. Nothing good or new could be built on Europe's "moldering pillars of antiquity," wrote Noah Webster. The future lay with America.

This concept of the American as separate and exceptional carried with it certain advantages and disadvantages. It led, perhaps too often, to the belief that as a special case the United States was immune from those forces which shaped the courses of other nations. The conviction of speciality caused a certain reluctance to integrate the American destiny with that of the rest of the world, or to accept the challenges of change from without. The American, the French traveller Marie Dugard once observed seems always to have the feeling of "collaborating with God in a grand humanitarian work." What others do, or have done, is sometimes assumed to provide no lessons of experience for America; *sui generis,* it can claim exemption from history.

But this same feeling of separation has also led to the belief that because the United States is not bound to the past, it *can* do things differently. Americans, perhaps more than other peoples, tend to break out of the pattern, to experiment; they feel that the laws of probability need not always hold. The same spirit of risk which led a handful of men at the head of a weak confederation of thirteen colonies to challenge history successfully is still part and parcel of the American way of life. The American ideology of risk, the "let's-try-it-and-see-if-it-works" pragmaticism that has so often characterized American procedures, stems from this same sense of difference.

The Puritan settlers were convinced that they were a people chosen of God, a conviction which generations of Americans since have never quite lost. As William Stoughton wrote succinctly in 1668, "God sifted a whole nation that he might send choice grain over into this wilderness." This belief in divine selection, which was by no means restricted to the Puritans, pervaded the minds and attitudes of those who followed them. Revolutionary ministers were especially fond of comparing Americans to the ancient Jews, with the implications, as one explained, that both "had an indefeasible title to peculiar divine favor." During the war, scriptural texts for sermons found the parallel very useful—"Happy art thou O Israel: who is like unto thee, O People Saved by the Lord." . . . "Hitherto the Lord had helped us . . . He hath not dealt so with any nation." Americans had been commanded "by the behest of God almighty," wrote John Quincy Adams, "to make the wilderness blossom as the rose, to establish laws, to increase, multiply, and subdue the earth."

The comparison remained popular long after the Revolution. The Reverend Joseph Twichell, Mark Twain's friend, phrased it concisely by saying in a sermon, "We believe our nation is a creation of God, that He ordained it for an object . . ., demonstrating that men are equal as God's children." The historian George Bancroft, who was fascinated by the idea of divine guidance in human affairs, could never quite refrain from commenting on one of his favorite analogies—that the colonial settlers, "Like the Jews, fled to a wilderness; like the Jews, they looked to heaven for a light to lead them on; like the Jews, they had heathen for their foe"—and returned to it often.

Less elaborately but with equal force, Emerson once wrote in his *Journals* that "the Divine Providence has a sneaking fondness" for Americans, an attitude often noted with irritation by foreign travellers. "Our whole history," he once wrote, "appears like a last effort of the Divine Providence in behalf of the human race." The English historian E. A. Freeman, visiting the United States in the 1880's, spoke impatiently of those natives who

seem really to think that the United States, their constitution, and all that belongs to them, did not come into being by the ordinary working of human causes, but sprang to life by some special creation or revelation. They think themselves wronged if it is implied that they are not absolute *autocthones* but that they are the kinsfolk of certain other nations.

The most definitive compilation of evidence, however, was that of Robert Ellis Thompson, of Philadelphia, who after making a careful study of *The Hand of God in American History* in 1902 found undeniable proof "that God's hand has shaped the course of our national history for his own ends." First, Thompson pointed out, God endowed the American continent with resources sufficient to make it "the most valuable division of the earth's surface possessed by any people." Second, He "kept the whole continent from discovery until Europe had reached the point of social development at which its people were competent to become successful emigrants." Third, He entrusted settlement to "a picked and gifted element," and fourth, He gave American leadership, in time of crisis to a group of "the modern world's great men," the Founding Fathers. Having thus launched the nation, God has ever since continued, Thompson showed, to intervene in its affairs and to guide its destiny as a kind of special project.

The concept of Americans as a divinely-chosen, unique people was a strong force in developing their sense of national mission. If God had chosen them, it must be for an undoubtedly exalted purpose. It was necessary for the early colonists to believe in their special selection if they were to survive the rigors of settlement and to evolve the feeling of cohesion needed for the development of a colonial personality. The more they were unlike other peoples, the more they were free to realize their own integrity. During the eighteenth century, as tensions increased within the empire, this conviction of divine and separate choice helped substantially to reinforce the colonists' belief that because they were special people with a particular mission, they deserved a special place within the imperial framework, and quite possibly special treatment.

The idea of the colonist as a distinctive kind of Anglo-American breed is easily discerned in American thinking by the mid-eighteenth century. After the Revolution and the launching of the new nation, preservation of this conviction of God-elected uniqueness was part of the country's apparatus of survival. The kind of government these Americans established was markedly different from any that had ever preceded it—it violated, as a matter of fact, almost all traditional accepted rules for successful governments—and if it *were* to succeed its founders realized that they had to preserve their conviction of God's guidance. Quite accurately, they considered their society irreconcilably different from Europe's; they knew that to survive they must continue to emphasize the differences. Crèvecoeur put it perfectly: "The American is a new man, and acts upon new principles; he must therefore entertain new ideas and form new opinions." There was no other way for Americans to think and act, if they were to accomplish their mission.

It always seemed logical to assume, therefore, that Americans were governed by God's providences, in order that the purposes for which He had chosen them were to be realized. The titles of Edward Johnson's *Wonderworking Providence of Sion's Saviour in New England* (1654) or Increase Mather's *Remarkable Providences* (1684) illustrate the antiquity of this belief. Mather remarked on God's diligence in punishing those enemies of the Puritans "who have sought the hurt of the people of God in New England," and Governor Winthrop in his journals also noted instances of how the Lord "preserved and prospered his people here beyond any ordinary ways of providence."

The eighteenth-century American was equally convinced

that he enjoyed God's preferment in his national affairs. The Reverend Samuel McClintock, meditating in 1784 on the incredible victory of thirteen weak colonies over the world's greatest military power, could only ascribe it to "the government of Providence." The Reverend Isaac Keith of Charleston, in 1789, felt the same way about the Constitution, concluding that its ratification proved that "citizens of the United States are the object of divine providential care." Toward the close of the Civil War, another minister, the Reverend A. D. Mayo of Boston, expressed a common Federal conviction in telling his congregation that "there has indeed been a Divine Intelligence guiding the destiny of our republic . . ., God Almighty is shaping a free and exalted civilized nation out of it." So too the Reverend William Aikman of Detroit, preaching his Centennial Sermon in 1876, concluded, "We may safely say that no nation but one [*Israel*] has had a history so marked by the superintending Providence of God."

Even those misfortunes which befell the nation, such as the Civil War were often viewed as divine interventions intended to discipline and educate God's chosen people. Lincoln saw the Civil War as "a punishment inflicted upon us for our presumptuous sins." "The war itself was an act of God," he wrote, "No mortal could have brought it to pass or stayed its occurrence." In the same frame of reference, President Truman in 1951 believed that although the Korean War seemed to bear only superficial relation to the American destiny, yet the United States' decision to support the United Nations meant that the nation had "finally assumed the leadership which Almighty God intended us to assume. . . ."

The most thorough exploration of the concept of the American mission as part of the responsibilities of divine guidance was made by George Bancroft, who began writing his *History of the United States* in 1834 on the assumption, he said, that "a favoring Providence, calling our institutions into being, has conducted the country to its present happiness and glory."

Behind and beneath the surface of American history, he wrote in volume III, one could clearly discover the hand of

God at work in the colonies' growth from feeble wilderness settlements to powerful nation,

the mysterious influence of that power which enchains the destinies of states, overruling the decisions of sovereigns and the forethought of statesmen, and which often deduces the greatest events from the least commending causes.

Nor could Bancroft resist detecting the hand of God elsewhere in the colonists' affairs—in the fortunate alliance of English and Iroquois rather than Iroquois and French; in the Treaty of Utrecht, which would have changed the course of American events had it not occurred when it did; in the marvellous voyage of the Mayflower, which was surely steered by Providence to port; in the miracle of the Pilgrims' survival against starvation and sickness. He discerned "the footsteps of Providential Intelligence everywhere," he wrote, in the history of early America. There was some truth to the critic's jest that Bancroft "wrote the History of the United States as if it were the Kingdom of God," because Bancroft himself believed the two were, in a sense, congruent.

The Puritan and Enlightenment idea that the American people were divinely chosen for a special purpose received powerful reinforcement in the nineteenth century from the development of new theories of nationalism in Europe. The seventeenth-century Calvinist believed God simply chose certain peoples to do His work. The eighteenth century, following Montesquieu, Burke, and others, suggested that the choice was more likely to be a secular one, that nations developed particular characteristics out of natural conditions; each state, therefore, existed for certain purposes by reason of natural law. However, some of the late eighteenth-century philosophers, notably Hegel and Fichte, postulated that a nation was an organic expression of an inward "national spirit," a *Zeitgeist* or soul in which its seeds of creation lay.

Comte, and later Spencer, supported this concept of nationalism by suggesting that nations, like organisms, developed by natural evolutionary growth out of their own special circumstances. Each nation, therefore, was an individual entity, unique, peculiar, endowed with its own distinctive, special qualities and possessing a life of its own. Extending the analogy, scholars assumed that like organisms, nations had qualities in common but others which differentiated them, that each had "its own distinctive Force or Idea." This squared perfectly with the American seventeenth-century theological sense of mission, as well as with the eighteenth-century American ideal of secular purpose, and buttressed them both.

American thinkers swiftly seized German nationalistic philosophy and appropriated it to their use. George Bancroft, who heard Hegel lecture in Germany, based much of his nationalistic historical theory on German models, while William T. Harris, the St. Louis Hegelian, worked out a theory wherein the purpose of Greek civilization was to provide mankind with beauty and order, Anglo-Saxon to provide it with self-government, and American to bring the world self-reliance. Dozens of others elaborated the Hegelian synthesis and used it both to establish the existence of a national American purpose and to define it. Thus the traditional American belief that the United States had a special position in history, and a particular contribution to make to world civilization, absorbed Hegelian nationalism and coincided with current theories of national mission.

The seventeenth-century Puritan's vision of the place of America in the divine providential design was clear and unequivocal, for the Puritan was, of all things, confident of his purposes. Thus on shipboard, in 1630, John Winthrop could write firmly, "The work we have in hand, it is by mutual consent through a special overruling Providence . . . to seek out a place of cohabitation and consorting under a due form of government both civil and ecclesiastical." John Smith, for his part, also knew what drew men to Virginia, "for I am not so simple to think," he wrote, "that ever any other motive than wealth, will ever erect there a Commonwealth." And although the reasons why men came to America were obviously more diverse and complex than either Winthrop or Smith revealed, the rationale of removal in each case was plainly

put. The New England settlers, in particular, were a sophisticated and purposeful group, well able to articulate their aims;
accustomed to living by rules, they disciplined themselves to
advance in an orderly way toward their goals, convinced that
what they were doing in America was of very great importance
to the world. As one of them said, "The very finger of the
Lord" pointed their way out to them. Yet the New England
Puritans, despite their importance, were a minority. The majority of the other early Americans, like Smith, came with a
variety of purposes in mind, often less well-formed and
intelligible, usually much less exalted. To own land, to make
money, to colonize for King and country, to lead a better life,
to escape responsibility, debt, or boredom, or simply to see
what the new country was like—the grounds of personal decision for migration must have been endless.

Whoever came to America had to have a reason for coming;
at one time or another, he had to declare the intention (at
whatever level of consciousness) of exchanging one set of
conditions for others in another land. The American, then,
was purposeful from the outset; each of the first generation,
as he decided to emigrate, did so with a sense of resolution.
Even the transported pickpocket or the indentured servant
must have speculated on how he happened to be where he was,
and must have sought, perhaps idly, some kind of answer.
Everyone who made up the first waves of migration felt that
his presence in America had some purpose in it. They all
arrived with an expectation whether dimly or precisely formed.

During the later seventeenth and the eighteenth century the
quality of this sense of purposefulness changed. The original
Puritan belief that Americans were a chosen people, charged
with constructing a Biblical state, no doubt still remained,
but the ideals of the second and third generations were much
more secular than religious. By 1700 the majority of colonists
were American-born; they no longer needed to explain their
comings or stayings, as their fathers had. The native-born
American asked a different question about his Americanism—
What is our purpose *now*? We know what the first generation
had in mind to accomplish, but what do we? It became neces-

sary, then, for these generations to identify the American purpose all over again—not to reject, but to transform it.

The second and third generations of colonists were at home with all those things which their fathers and grandfathers found new, strange, and even dangerous—the savages, the forest and sea, distance, climate, remoteness from Europe and the sources of the old civilization. They possessed much greater control over their environment, and what had once seemed chance and hazard appeared to them as opportunity—space, land, the forest, waterways, the frontier. The eighteenth century's feeling of command over the country evidenced itself in a number of ways—in an American sense of direction, pride, self-confidence, and most of all in the colonial's perception of *differentness*. The Americans of that era did not look back to Europe, for they did not come from there; to them the Old World was simply a place one left. As their fathers' mission was to construct a commonwealth of virtue, so theirs was to build one of power. If the first settlers had been designated by God to construct a civilization by reason of their superior morality, these colonists believed they had been selected to continue the work because they possessed superior strength and purpose. Theirs was the confidence of power and control, born of a secular rather than religious drive. The sense of national mission was the same and equally strong—to build a new society this side of the Atlantic—but they intended to accomplish it by different means.

What had happened over the first century and a half of American existence was that the secular aim of establishing an ideal free society had displaced the original purpose of building a New Jerusalem. The goal of founding the perfect society still remained, but the model of God's commonwealth gave way to the Enlightenment's. The design was Newton's nature, not Scripture's. But the challenge was equally great, and the stakes of success equally high. The eighteenth century was an exciting era, filled with new formulations of purpose—national and individual—of building a new nation, framing new ways of governing, rejecting one empire and beginning another.

The shift of ideals continued through the confused decades of unrest and revolution, the years of experimentation and peril, to the successful conclusion of the War of 1812, when the nation seemed at last secure. The celebrations of 1826, marking the fiftieth year of national survival, struck a loud and consistent note of satisfaction. As an Ohio orator that year summarized the national mood in fashionable contemporary rhetoric,

We have, by the grace of God and the miracle of Providence, survived the buffetings of fate, the ill-chance of misfortune, the hatred and infections of Europe, the malevolence of kings and tyrants, in a half-century of unparalleled progress. We have, as a nation, fulfilled the initial promise of our destination, pledged by those brave and noble men who first set foot on the soil of Massachusetts and Virginia; and we have made the New World bloom in freedom, justice, and the sweetness of right. It is now to the future we look, to the next half-century's fulfillment, for our glorious destiny, ordained by God and Nature since the beginnings of time.

The mission of the eighteenth century had been accomplished. During the Era of Good Feeling and the Jacksonian years the United States was certain of its purpose and confident of success in attaining it. As it turned out, the nation was, in fact, willing to fight a long and bitter war to preserve its chances of doing so. To Lincoln, the Civil War was a crisis in the course of the national mission, a battle for the kind of future Americans "felt in the blood and felt along the heart." To him the concept of the nation for which the war was fought gave "hope to all the world, for all future time," and he articulated in his Gettysburg Address the final symbol of that mission in the hope that what the nation represented "shall not perish from the earth." The Civil War marked a final agreement among Americans that their society must exemplify the justice of democracy as a political system, affirm the creative powers of individual liberty, and fix in that society the democratic virtues. What, then, came next?

The nineteenth century had two answers to the question, involving two related concepts of the national purpose. First, it was conceived that the aim of the United States was to achieve the moral regeneration of the world by the force of its example; second, that its ultimate destiny was to expand its authority over the western hemisphere, and perhaps beyond. The first objective derived from the conviction that the United States, by reason of its faith in the integrity of the individual, was meant to provide the pattern for other governments to heed and do likewise. American democracy, it was believed, would make its proselytes by the success of its example. Robert Breckenridge, speaking in Kentucky in 1837, felt that the American mission was

to elevate and improve the individual, to establish in the highest degree on the scale of human progress the standard of national greatness—to teach man to govern himself, to love his fellow, to love his God, to teach the nations that all are equal . . ., to reverence human rights and bestow human privileges, to raise up the downtrodden, [and] to sheathe the sword. . . .

The United States, therefore, was to serve as proof to the world of what happened when the potential power of the individual was released by reform. The great reforms of the day—disparate in kind as they were, temperance, women's rights, evangelical religion, communitarian living, a ten-hour day, healthful clothing, abolition of slavery, world peace, and a nutritional diet—were all intended to set free the power of the person. In practice, all the reforms of the earlier nineteenth century merged into one single national mission, to make American society perfect by re-forming the individual.

With the ideals of the founders seemingly secured by the Jacksonian political state, and the dangers from aristocratical Europe apparently past, the nation turned its attention to the removal of all possible obstacles in the path of national purpose. The democratic and the humanitarian reform movements melted together, pooling methods, efforts, and objectives. Emerson summed up the movement best, perhaps, with the remark that the cause of it all lay in the belief that "there is an infinite worthiness in man, which will appear at the call of worth, and that all particular reforms are the

removing of impediments." The reformers were simply interested in removing impediments. They trusted the individual
and believed in his ability to better himself; seeing to it that
he was able to do so became the national purpose. The
American future, in Walt Whitman's expansive view, should
be built upon "the fused and fervent identity of the individual, whoever she or he may be, and whatever the place."

The second concept of national purpose which emerged in
the nineteenth century was that concerned with America's
"manifest destiny"—that is, with the necessity of extending
the physical and political authority of the United States over
the continent, so that it might in turn exert control over the
entire hemisphere. Taking its name from Editor John
O'Sullivan's statement in 1845 that it was but "the fulfillment
of our manifest destiny to overspread the continent allotted
by Providence for the free development" of the United States,
this centripetal flow of energy led the American for the first
time to define his national mission in external terms.

The Reverend Theodore Parker, Emerson's friend, thought
that Americans were "involuntary instruments of God" in a
divine plan to absorb not only Canada but Central and South
America, "uniting the waters of the Mississippi and the
Amazon." (Another friend of Emerson's, however, Henry
Thoreau, had little patience with this talk of "manifest destiny." "The whole enterprise of this nation," he wrote with
annoyance, "is not an *upward,* but a westward one.") Editor
Parke Godwin believed that the conquest of Mexico and the
South American continent was part "of that high destiny
which Providence has plainly reserved for our race." Manifest
destiny meant playing the role of Rome in the modern world,
as Thomas Hart Benton once said, as "the reviver and re-
generator" of other peoples and civilizations. It meant extending American domination not only over Texas and
Oregon, but over the Caribbean, Mexico, South America, the
Pacific, and perhaps beyond. The United States, composed
"of forty to fifty great states, among them Canada and Cuba,"
must serve, Walt Whitman wrote exuberantly, as "the cus-
todian of the future of humanity."

Defining the national objectives in such imperialistic terms influenced American foreign relations, swiftly and directly, and provided a new base for American foreign policy. Since fate had "placed a continent before us to spread our free principles, our language, our literature, and power," said Congressman Edward Baker of Illinois in 1846, obviously "we had a present right to provide for this future progress" anywhere in the Americas. For this reason Senator H. V. Johnson interpreted the Mexican War as a conflict ordained by "the All-wise Dispenser of events, [as] the instrumentality of accomplishing the great end of human elevation and human happiness." (The dying Calhoun could not agree, pointing out that the United States would "do more to extend liberty by our example over this continent, and the world generally, than would be done by a thousand victories.") Before the close of the century, this belief in the nation's manifest destiny to expand its sphere of influence coincided with the concept of Anglo-Saxon superiority to produce the racist-tinged imperialisms of such men as Josiah Strong, Albert Beveridge, John W. Burgess, Theodore Roosevelt, Admiral Mahan, and others. As Strong put it in his book, *Our Country* (1885), "It is manifest that the Anglo-Saxon holds in his hands the destinies of mankind, and it is evident that the United States is to become the home of this race, the principal seat of his power." For this reason, he wrote, the United States must accept the responsibility for "guiding the world . . . as a trust for civilization."

Throughout the latter years of the century the nation continued to probe the idea of "manifest destiny" in relation to its purpose. John Fiske, the popular Harvard historian and lecturer, found the concept a challenging one, for to him it proved that the United States had been charged by Providence to federate the world. Writing in *Harper's* in the same year Strong's *Our Country* appeared, Fiske gave an entirely different meaning to the term. He believed that in the federalistic system the United States had discovered the single vital principle by which disputes among clashing national interests might be amicably resolved for all time. The constitutional

pattern of state-to-state relationships within the federal framework, he explained, might well furnish the model for a permanent world organization. If under the American system
disputes among states were settled by compromises and alignments of interests, why could not the same system settle disputes among nations? "This we have seen to be the real
purport of American federalism," he wrote. "To have established such a system over one great continent is to have made
a very good beginning toward establishing it over the world."
It would be difficult, Fiske conceded, to impose the American
example on "the immense complication of prejudices" that
constituted Europe, but he felt confident that "the pacific
purpose" of the American system would, in time, force
Europe toward some kind of federalized global organization
which would render war outmoded. There seemed no reason
to doubt, Fiske concluded, that eventually "the whole of mankind should not constitute politically one huge federation"
of the American design, in which all conflicts would be decided not by military might but "by the decision of one central
tribunal, supported by the public opinion of the entire human
race." Toward this goal, "America has set the example and
indicated the method."

Others, however, used the doctrine of "manifest destiny" as
justification for other kinds of leadership. By 1900, after the
"splendid little war" with Spain, Josiah Strong summarized
its meaning in his book, *Expansion*, by saying "It is time to
dismiss 'the craven fear of being great,' to recognize the place
in the world which God has given us and to accept the responsibilities which it devolves upon us in behalf of Christian
civilization." Speaking that same year, Senator Albert Beveridge was even more explicit about what those responsibilities
were. "American law, American order, American civilization,
and the American flag," he believed, were "agencies of God"
intended by Him to make "shores hitherto bloody and
benighted . . . henceforth beautiful and bright."

God has made us the master organizers of the world to establish
system where chaos reigns . . . He has marked the American people

as his chosen nation to finally lead in this regeneration of the world. This is the divine mission of America and it holds for us all the profit, all the glory, all the happiness possible to man.

Just as John Quincy Adams was convinced that the North American continent was "destined by Divine Providence to be peopled by *one* nation," so exactly a century later in 1911 Speaker of the House Champ Clark believed that the American flag ought to "float over every square foot of the British-American possessions clear to the North Pole."

It was not the "manifest destiny" of imperialism that took the United States into World War I, however. The nation entered the war, certainly, not to extend its dominion in the Strong-Clark-Beveridge sense, but with a strong realization of its responsibilities in making the world safe for its kind of democracy. Like Fiske, Wilson saw in the peace to follow an opportunity for establishing a better-organized world, one based (hopefully) on such American principles as self-determination, equality of rights, protection of minorities, and adjudication of opposing interests. It is clear from Wilson's speeches and letters that he believed that the United States entered the World War not simply to preserve itself, but to lead the postwar world toward democracy as part of the obligation inherent in the American mission. "America is the only nation which can sympathetically lead the world in organizing peace;" he wrote early in the war. "It is surely the manifest destiny of the United States to lead in the attempt to make this spirit prevail." Since the United States was "of necessity the sample democracy of the world," it seemed to him uniquely fitted to guide the world toward that permanent peace that only the principles of democracy might bring. The United States, Wilson believed, had been chosen by history to assert ". . . the rights of peoples and the rights of free nations . . ., to set a responsible example of what free government is and can do for the maintenance of right standards, both national and international." If the World War was justified to make the world safe for democracy, it was the duty of the United States to show the world that this democracy was worth saving. To Wilson, the League of Nations was to be the instrument by which the United States might fulfill this mission, the tool with which American democracy might "prove its purity and its spiritual power to prevail." What Fiske had seen in 1885, as Freneau and Barlow had seen the vision before him—a United States of the World —Wilson hoped might find fruition through the League.

The disillusion that followed World War I cracked the American's faith in the terms and dimensions of his national mission for the first time in history. Things did not work out the way they should have; victory did not mean what it was supposed to; the sacrifice of thousands of lives, so it seemed, advanced the world not one whit nor the American cause one iota. "The war has destroyed not only men, money and goods," wrote one of the young veterans of 1917, "—it is no great problem to restock the world with these—but faith, a faith that our fathers held as firmly as they held that two and two are four." The hard facts of the postwar world belied all the sense of mission and obligation that had gone into the conflict, and Wilson, the very symbol of American idealism, died a failure in his own terms. The onset of history's most brutal economic depression, of another world war, and the swift revival of once-rejected modes of force, deceit, and cynicism, shook faith in the American mission and in its chances of success even more. The United States existed in an "attitude of recoil," Walter Lippmann wrote in the thirties. "The American people suffer," he continued,

from accumulated disappointments. They believed with Wilson that they could help to make a world that was safe for men living in peace under just laws. They believed with Coolidge and Hoover that they had arrived at a New Era of certain and advancing prosperity. They believed with Roosevelt that they were organizing securely an abundant life for all the people but none of it seemed to have come true.

"We feel that we've lost our way in the woods," poet Archibald MacLeish said later, "that we don't know where we are going, if anywhere."

But the American sense of national destiny, shaken by the tempest of the twentieth-century events, has not lost its roots in the sixties. It has been changed, naturally, by the impact of two world wars, an undeclared one, and a continuing cold one. For one thing, the United States has come to recognize that it cannot successfully export its brand of democracy to a world that does not fully understand it and apparently does not want it. The nation has "abandoned the fond belief," wrote William K. Langer in 1960, "that it could by its own influences and efforts, make the world safe for democracy." No one has expressed this view more cogently than President John Kennedy, who told the nation in 1963 that "in a world of contradiction and confusion we must acknowledge the realities of the world," which are that

the United States is neither omnipotent nor omniscient, that we cannot always impose our will on the other ninety-four percent of mankind, that we cannot right every wrong or reverse every adversity, and that there therefore cannot be an American solution to every world problem.

The American way of life, in other words, is no longer considered to be convertible currency; Americans have begun to conceive of their destiny in private terms. The black-and-white clarity of purpose which once led Woodrow Wilson to propose solving certain problems of foreign relations by "teaching the Mexicans to elect good men" has nearly disappeared.

On the other hand, if the national purpose has lost much of its earlier missionary—or imperialistic—coloration, it has gained conviction and force since World War II as an energizing principle within the nation itself. The shock of war and fascism, each wholly concerned with cancelling out the individual's importance to himself and his society, led to a renewed recognition of the individual and his value as the chief aim of government. "After World War II," wrote one survivor of it, "it would seem difficult for anyone ever to believe that the individual would be important again, yet on reconsideration I can see that was what it was all about." The national mission, therefore, has shifted direction back toward the nineteenth century's interest in releasing the individual potential. Its emphasis has again turned inward.

If present-day America has a settled and agreed purpose, it surely lies in the encouragement and development of the individual's inner self. The focus of the national effort, wrote Charles Lindbergh in 1954, "lies in each individual, and through the standards he holds. . . . Our parties, movements, codes, and laws are important, but they are only outward manifestations of our inward values." The President's Commission on National Goals, reporting in 1960, was clear enough about it. The nation's primary concern, it stated, must be "to further enhance the dignity of the citizen, the maximum development of his capabilities, stimulate their responsible exercise, and widen the range and effectiveness of opportunities for individual choice."

In this vein John F. Kennedy defined the American national purpose for the sixties in specific, individual and domestic terms. Any complete statement of the American mission, he wrote, must include

The fulfillment of every individual's dignity and potential

The perfection of the democratic process

The education of every individual to his capacity

The elimination of ignorance, prejudice, hate, and the squalor in which crime is bred

The elimination of slums, poverty, and hunger

Protection against the economic catastrophes of illness, disability, and unemployment

The achievement of a constantly expanding economy, without inflation or dislocation, either in the factory or on the farm

The conquest of dread diseases

The enrichment of American culture

The attainment of world peace and disarmament, based on world law and order, on the mutual respect of free peoples and on a world economy in which there are no "have-nots" or "Underdeveloped" nations.

President Lyndon Johnson summarized it by saying that "America was created to help strike away the chains of ignorance, misery, and tyranny," in every society.

The American sense of mission is still embodied in its vision of an ideal state, constructed on those terms defined so glowingly by the Declaration. But well aware (as Jefferson himself was) of the impossibility of attaining perfection, the American knows that unfortunately he must always be satisfied with something a little less. This has lent American life a quality of stress, deriving from the perpetual tension between the ideal and the practical. The American lives with a constant compromise of his dream, caught between what ought to be, in terms of his ultimate goals, and what it is possible to obtain at any given place in his national history. Despite his sincere dedication to his mission, the American must continually reconcile himself to imperfection, and concede to the actual, no matter how exalted his purpose. Since his national ideal has always been expressed in *moral* terms (whether it be those of the Puritan Commonwealth, or of the harmonious Newtonian state, or of the progressive organic society of Spencer) the American's commitment always outruns his attainment.

Americans therefore must continue to attempt to meet their own high standards, and suffer when they do not; they are no doubt the only people in the world who blame themselves for not having finally created the perfect society, and who submit themselves to persistent self-examination to determine why they have not. Because they have set themselves such an elevated task, they are less willing than others to accept anything less than its accomplishment. The nation spent nearly a century, for example, rationalizing its acceptance of slavery, fought a bloody war to eliminate it, and has since subjected itself to an agonizing self-appraisal because it has not completely rid itself of the consequences of having once tolerated the system. No other nation has quite the same feelings of guilt over its failures.

This constant tension between the ideal and actual in American life has led the United States to view its mission essentially in dramatic terms. The Puritans saw their unfolding history as the manifestation of a mighty conflict between God and Satan, quite literally carried out in an American

theater. Eighteenth-century America saw itself as chief protagonist in a giant struggle between liberty and tyranny; the
nineteenth century engaged in an equally mighty crusade
against injustice and want, treason and secession, the infec-
tious evil of Europe, and the dead hand of the past. Americans
have pitted themselves from their beginnings in a struggle
against space, nature, and the elements—against the problems
of spanning a continent, bending it to control, using it. The
fact is that Americans have always tended to see their past,
present, and future as a moral drama, with the nation as
protagonist, beset by many enemies but driving onward.
American life has a peculiarly histrionic quality, for Americans see their mission as a contest, and themselves as a people
besieged by mighty forces, triumphing over obstacles and
enemies. The United States has a mission to accomplish; there
are those who would divert or impede its progress toward
completion; the nation must, like Christian, overcome.

This dramatic element has lent American life a quality of
expectancy—the belief that, in President Kennedy's phrase,
the United States is "unfailingly confident of winning through
all obstacles to realize our dream." Americans anticipate,
whatever the impediments may be, a better future. Every
American expects things to be better in his time as well as in
his grandchildren's; this he takes as a matter of course. This
tradition of expectancy had its origins in the hopes of the
seventeenth-century settler, grew in strength during the confident eighteenth century, and perhaps reached its climax in
the exuberant decades following the Civil War.

The seventeenth century succeeded in surviving in a new
and hostile land; the eighteenth century created a new state
against all the forewarnings of experience; the nineteenth
won a continent and conquered its imperial distances; the
twentieth survived too, expanded, enriched itself beyond all
visions. Well might Walt Whitman both summarize and pre-
dict, in 1874,

> The promise of thousands of years, til now deferr'd,
> Promis'd to be fulfilled, our common kind, the race.

The new society at last, proportionate to Nature . . .,
Fresh come, to a new world indeed, yet long prepared,
I see the genius of the modern, child of the real and
  ideal,
Clearing the ground for broad humanity, the true
  America, heir of a past so grand,
To build a grander future.

It is difficult to reduce this sense of certainty to precise and accurate terms, but it has been a strong strain in American life imparting to it a special quality of assurance. There is little recognition in the American view of things of the alternatives of failure; the American assumes success, here and now, and often enough finds his assumptions rewarded.

The central American myth has always been this myth of anticipation, of the search for opportunities, the quest for El Dorado, the unenclosed land of the frontier, the gold of California, the success story of Alger, the prospect of the open future. Expectancy is the mark of the American temper, which has found its classic expression in the quest, the mission, the journey toward destiny—whether it be the journey of Elizabethan adventurer, Puritan settler, pioneer woodsman, Kansas emigrant, or space traveller. It has been sometimes clothed with certain ambiguities and reservations (as in Cotton Mather, Melville, Hawthorne, Dreiser, or Faulkner) but the American mood is optative, the national purpose founded in confidence.

BIBLIOGRAPHICAL ACKNOWLEDGEMENTS

The best and most inclusive treatment of the American sense of purpose is that of Edward McNall Burns, *The American Idea of Mission* (New Brunswick, N.J., 1957) from which this chapter derived a number of quotations and ideas. Oscar Handlin, *The Americans* (New York, 1963); Merle Curti, *The Growth of American Thought* (New York, 1943); Curti's *Roots of American Loyalty* (New York, 1946); and Frederick Merk, *Manifest Destiny and Mission in American History* (New York, 1963) and Albert K. Weinberg, *Manifest Destiny* (Baltimore, 1935), contain general discussions of interest which contain additional information. Henry Luce, *The American Century* (New York, 1941), and Walter Lippmann's "American Destiny," *Life* V (June 5, 1939) 47, 72-3, are representative modern discussions. Robert Ernst's article, "Asylum for the Oppressed," *South Atlantic Quarterly* XL (January, 1941) is an excellent brief treatment of one aspect of the American mission. The series of essays edited by Oscar Handlin, *American Principles and Issues: The National Purpose* (New York, 1961), and the report of the President's Commission on National Goals, *Goals for Americans* (New York, 1960), are careful and extended treatments of the problem of purpose in the contemporary world. John K. Jessup, *et al., The National Purpose* (New York, 1960) is a useful collection of essays written especially for *Life* magazine, to "close the gap," Walter Lippmann's contribution states, "between the new realities and the old formulations of national purpose." Walter Reuther's "A Sense of National Purpose," *Business Topics* XII (Spring, 1964) 15-21, is an interesting treatment by a prominent labor leader, while Clinton Rossiter, "The American Mission," *American Scholar* XIX (Winter, 1951) 19-28, is a useful summary of historical trends. Frederic Saunders, ed., *Centenary Addresses* (New York, 1882) and Charles Sumner, ed., *Prophetic Voices Concerning America* (New York, 1874) reprint dozens of speeches, sermons, and commemorative addresses from the beginning to the mid-nineteenth century, which deal with the national purpose.

V

America and the Individual

In all my lectures, I have taught one doctrine,
namely, the infinitude of the private man.
—RALPH WALDO EMERSON

PERHAPS no ideal is more characteristic of American culture
than the emphasis the American places on the importance
of the individual and his ability to identify and solve his
problems. In Walt Whitman's phrase, individualism is "the
compensating balance-wheel of the successful working machinery of aggregate America." The American believes that
the pursuit of happiness is an individual quest; that in the
United States each individual is free to carry out his own purposes as nowhere else; and that no boundary should be set by
any authority to the individual's self-expansion, save by his
own inadequacies. However, as Ralph Barton Perry has explained, this individualism is not a cult of solitude, for American individuality is the opposite of singularity. It is a collective
individualism—not isolation or withdrawal, but participatory
and cooperative, conceiving the individual not as separate, but
as one of many.

The chief end of American society, in the American view,
is to provide unlimited opportunity for self-development. The
"paramount goal" of the United States, the President's Commission on National Goals reported in 1960, is to "guard the
rights of the individual, to ensure his development, and to

enlarge his opportunity." Nowhere is this stated with greater clarity than in the Declaration of Independence, with its affirmation of the unalienable rights of all men. The individualistic strain in American thought, however, antedates the Declaration by more than a century; Jefferson's preamble is only a re-phrasing of what Americans believed long prior to the Revolution but never before expressed with such remarkable appropriateness.

Calvinism, of course, was one of the three great historical sources of American individualism. The Calvinist idea that the salvation of man's soul was a matter concerning himself and God played a large part in establishing the American concept of individual worth. The unique individual soul, in the Puritan view, was the subject and object of salvation, the most important single fact of human existence. How the individual was saved—or was not—rested solely on the degree of his self-fulfillment. In the process of searching for grace, the Calvinist emphasized the importance of private judgment; the individual stood or fell in this quest on his own attributes and by his own decisions. Church, state, and society might assist and advise, but their intervention was kept at a minimum.

Each man, the Puritan believed, held the key to his destiny in his own hands, for the ultimate moral unit was the individual soul. The fact that salvation was never sure nor complete lent an activist quality to Puritan individualism. One achieved a state of grace not by passive receptivity, (though this were possible at God's will) but by working at it. The search for salvation was dynamic as well as personal. The arrival of Quaker and pietist sects in America simply reinforced this trend, since they were perhaps even more rigorously individualistic than the Calvinists.

Calvinism gave the individual judgment and conscience the same position in which traditional modes of thought placed the authority of the King and the state. For this reason it was revolutionary, carrying within it the seeds of explosive change. However, despite its powerful emphasis on personal responsibility, Calvinist individualism was not anarchistic. Theirs was a tight-knit commonwealth. Each Puritan was strongly aware of the associative element in society, quite conscious of the fact that he was one of a chosen people, working under a social agreement for God's glory. The terms of his agreement with society were as important to him as those of his covenant with God.

The American Puritans possessed a strong corporate sense—amounting almost to a kind of theological nationalism—which tended to counterbalance their equally strong feeling for individuality. If the Puritan's religion stressed the validity of the person, his social theory emphasized the importance of the individual as part of a covenanted group. His legacy to the American stream of thought was therefore two-fold: on the one hand, he left to posterity an activist philosophy of individualism, based on his idea of one's personal responsibility for his fate; and on the other, an awareness of social involvement and collective destiny. He saw society as an aggregate of free-standing individuals, joined in a compact for God's purposes.

A second major source of American individualism was the continued renewal of the frontier, particularly over the first four generations. As Frederick Jackson Turner pointed out in his famous essay in 1893, the frontier instilled an "intense individuation" in the national character, implanting in Americans "traits that made for aggressiveness, individuality, and an impatient habit of self-assertion." The frontier held out tremendous promise to the individual, whether he be settler, trapper, farmer, miner, cattleman, trader, or entrepreneur. The frontiersman depended on himself, not society, for his survival and advancement. Both the relative weakness of institutions on the frontier, and the simplicity of its society, encouraged individualism and self-reliance. Just as Puritanism stressed the sufficiency of the individual, so too did frontier thinking carry within it a rooted dislike of administrative supervision and control. The British imperial policy of "salutary neglect," followed over almost the entire first century of its administration, reinforced the impact of frontier permissiveness and further encouraged individualism in American colonial life.

One may agree with the thesis that the frontier situation imparted to American life all those qualities of initiative, optimism, and equality of which Turner wrote, but the individualism it engendered had broader implications than simple self-reliance, when placed in the perspective the frontier American had of his world. The decision to follow the frontier, to exchange a settled way of life for an uncertain one, presented the person who made it with the prospect of formidable obstacles as well as of great rewards. The challenge of empty land, limitless in expanse and incredibly rich in resources, involved the risk of failure as well as the opportunity for success. What was lost in culture, security, and order by removal to the frontier was often more than made up by the different meaning it gave to the life of each man who chose to do it.

The act of decision to move to the frontier was itself a powerful assertion of individualism. The determination to go west—whether it be Bradford's New England, Smith's Virginia, Boone's Kentucky, or Bridger's Rockies—was a personal one; frontier settlement from Plymouth on was a collective migration which arose out of initial individualism. Individualism was not simply one of the values which men found on the frontier; it was one of the motives that sent them there. The promise of a new and open society inspired self-confidence in those who decided to go, and expressed itself in the rewards of their individual efforts once they arrived.

The individualistic heritage of Calvinism and the frontier was transmitted to the eighteenth century with undiminished force. The third major source of American individualism, the Enlightenment, like the Renaissance, emphasized the liberation of the individual from the restraints of tradition, authority, and dogma. The man of the Enlightenment had confidence in his ability to reason out solutions to his problems, to gain knowledge and control over himself and his universe. He threw off the shackles of the paternal state and the straitjacket of mercantilist economy as well as the curbs of ecclesiastical authority. In England, the political tradition of Locke and Hobbes stressed individualism (though they reached opposite conclusions) while the English revolutionaries of 1642 and 1688 both assumed man to be politically self-sufficient under the laws of nature.

Men entered into social contracts, the eighteenth century believed, from their own free will, a fact which increased the importance of the individual in the contract and decreased that of the state. The new economics of Adam Smith and the physiocrats pointed in the same direction. Social philosophers agreed on the economic necessity of allowing the individual to pursue his self-interest. "Free enterprise" meant individuals free to follow enlightened self-interests.

By the middle years of the eighteenth century, therefore, the American colonist possessed a strong, highly-developed tradition of individualism, drawn from a variety of indigenous and imported sources. His concept of individualism rested also on a powerful belief in the intrinsic goodness of human nature. Despite their Calvinistic heritage, Americans were never at ease with the doctrine of the total depravity of man, and no matter how much they tried to convince themselves, not even the Puritans could wholly acquiesce to it. The facts of American history, of American geography, experience, temperament, all pointed toward faith in individual man—or at least *American* man, whose accomplishments one could proudly and plainly assess.

Paine, Barlow, Jefferson, Rush, and Franklin (in his more sanguine moments) conceived their fellowmen to be essentially trustworthy. Americans of their generation, in fact, tended to hold far fewer reservations about the reliability of ordinary man than did the Europeans or British. This was the result, perhaps, of a long frontier heritage, a successful revolution, and a new, incomplete, open society of opportunity. Whatever the reason, American thinkers of the later eighteenth century were much more confident of man's virtue and rationality than the majority of contemporary British philosophers—much closer, in their faith, to the French. What the British Romantics considered a *qualified* trust in the individual, the Americans (and the French *philosophes*) took as absolute conviction.

There was no reason, many Americans believed, why the heavenly city of the eighteenth-century philosophers could not be built by good men on this earth, on this side of the Atlantic, here and now. Dr. Benjamin Rush, throwing caution aside, was "fully persuaded that it is possible to produce such change in the moral character of man, as shall raise him to a resemblance of angels—nay more to the likeness of God himself." When Joel Barlow asked rhetorically in *The Columbiad* (1809), "Where shall we limit the progress of human wisdom, and the force of its institutions?" he implied his own answer.

Out of this confidence in individual humanity, the political theorists of the new republic contrived a government built about the individual's "natural" rights, his inherent wisdom, and his ability to rule himself. There were those, of course, such as Timothy Dwight of New England, or John Adams, or Alexander Hamilton, or Fisher Ames, who did not fully share the easy confidence of the times; even the usually optimistic Franklin, now and then, had uneasy glimpses of men as "a set of Beings badly constructed." Nevertheless, there were more believers than doubters in the young United States.

The change which took place in American thought after 1750 in its attitude toward the individual was the result, among other things, of certain new decisions reached by philosophers and theologians about the availability of truth. The eighteenth century was convinced that man, by exercise of his reason, could locate truth and act upon it. As individuals seized upon fragments of truth, society put them together in order to provide patterns and standards for life and belief. The early eighteenth century, quite certain of this, placed its reliance on Reason as the prime quality of mind by which the truth was found. Later eighteenth-century thinkers, though still confident of man's rationality, began to have doubts.

At the same time, the generation of Americans who were busy justifying a revolution and building a government on "self-evident" principles, found some difficulty in substantiating those so-called "self-evident truths." How could one "prove" the individual's right to the pursuit of happiness, when there was still legal question in some quarters about his right to liberty? Since they were forced by necessity to accept and act upon *unproveable* truths—self-evident truths—American thinkers revised their opinions of how one located truth, and the qualifications for its discovery. If a truth were self-evident, how could it be verified? Could it be also self-originated, perhaps not a product of the reason or subject to it? Joel Barlow, the American poet-soldier-diplomat-philosopher who had a facility for phrasing contemporary intellectual issues, wrestled with the problem. He finally concluded that there were three kinds of truth—*rational* truth (capable of proof by logic within the mind), *scientific* (capable of empirical demonstration), and *self-evident,* which Barlow defined as those truths "as perceptible when first presented to the mind as our age or world of experience could make them."

James Wilson, the brilliant Pennsylvania jurist, concluded like Barlow that there were three kinds of verifiable truth. First, Wilson accepted those "truths given in evidence by the external senses" which provided knowledge of the physical world. Second, he said, were truths "given in evidence by our moral faculty," which supplied men with moral and ethical knowledge. And third, he recognized a puzzling kind of truth "which we are *required* and determined by the constitution of our nature and faculties to believe." But neither Barlow, Wilson, nor others who struggled with the problem could quite define this unproveable truth; they simply knew such truths existed, and the individual man somehow possessed the power to find them.

By degrees, then "self-evident truth" turned into a kind of knowledge which no one needed to justify. The intuitive and unprovable, in the opening years of the eighteenth century, became as valid to the philosopher as the rational. And as American thinkers revised their ideas of what truth was and how men might find it, so they concluded that individual man himself was the *source* of truth. From where else, they asked, might "self-evident" truth come? The standards of society, the codes of tradition, the rules of universal reason, all these might serve as the bar to which ordinary logic could be brought, but to judge the validity of the self-evident truth, only a man's inner sense could suffice.

For example, James Marsh of the University of Vermont thought in 1829 that one might discover truth "by those laws of the understanding which belong in common to all men" (a good, orthodox, eighteenth-century dictum), but he also suggested that one must always "try the conclusions by one's own consciousness as a final test." "It is by *self*-inspection," he continued, "that we can *alone* arrive at any rational knowledge. . . ." Emerson wrote, "I have taught one doctrine, namely, the infinitude of the private man." Out of secluded, intimate moments of perception, he believed, came that sudden conviction of enlightenment which men knew was true. What a man must do to find the truth, Emerson wrote in *The American Scholar,* was "to learn to detect and watch that gleam of light which flashes across his mind from within."

This was the popular, pervasive point of view of Emerson's time; others repeated the theme with variations. Philosopher Caleb Sprague Henry explained that "the instantaneous but real fact of spontaneous apperception of truth" took place in "the intimacy of individual consciousness." Theodore Parker believed that truth could be perceived best in those "great primal Institutions of Human Nature, which depend on no logical process of demonstration, but are rather facts of consciousness given by the instinctive action of human nature itself." Orestes Brownson recognized in man "the capacity of knowing truth intuitively, or of attaining to a scientific knowledge of an order of existence transcending the reach of the senses, and of which we can have no sensible experience." George Bancroft, the historian, explained that each man possessed "an internal sense . . . not that faculty which deduces inferences from the experience of the senses, but that higher faculty which from the infinite treasures of its own consciousness, *originates* truth and assents to it by the force of intuitive evidence." Henry David Thoreau, of course, lived out at Walden Pond the practical experiment which tested the entire concept of early nineteenth-century individualism.

By the eighteen-thirties, then, the existence of self-evident truth—meaning that truth evident only to the individual self-consciousness—was an accepted and accomplished fact in American thought. In such fashion Coleridge, Kant, Carlyle, and Cousin displaced the great Mr. Locke and the eighteenth-century world of Reason; in this manner the world of Jefferson, Paine, and Rush gave way to the world of Emerson, whose belief, and that of his age, in the integrity and worth of individual man formed the foundation of the American political, intellectual, and social structure. "Every spirit builds its own house," wrote Emerson, speaking to his era, "and beyond its house a world, and beyond its world a heaven. Know then that the world exists for you."

Of course, there were those who saw neither life nor man with the unclouded vision of an Emerson or the confidence of a Jackson. Even some of the faithful, now and then, expressed doubts about what Emily Dickinson aptly called "freckled human nature." Alcott argued for years with Emerson and Channing over what he called their "excessive individuality." Orestes Brownson, rebel though he was, decided that an individual must be subject to some sort of authority, joined the Catholic Church, and concluded that individual freedom was to be obtained only within the realm of the imaginative.

The age also had its men who saw shadows in the universe, and knew the power of blackness. Where Emerson could say that "God himself culminates in the present moment" and concern himself solely with the personal intuitive instant, Hawthorne instead spoke of "that visionary and impalpable *now,* which if you look at it closely, is nothing." Melville's Pierre followed Longfellow's confident advice to "Act, act in the living present!" and met sheer disaster. In the same way, as Thoreau found certainty and sufficiency in the Individual Self, so Melville's theme is the insufficiency and alienation of Self. Neither Hawthorne nor Melville could accept the Emersonian dictum, "Know thyself," for what they found, when they searched within, was the desperate self-destruction of Ahab and Ethan Brand. *Pierre, Moby Dick, Young Good-*

man Brown, and *The Marble Faun* were dark books that did not belong with the optimism and hopefulness of Emerson's *The American Scholar* or *Self-Reliance*. These were the underside of the intellectual pattern of the age.

The earlier nineteenth century sought to maintain the validity of the individual against those forces of society and history which, it seemed, tended to deny or suppress his freedom of action. Bronson Alcott summed it up by writing in a rebellious mood, "Individuals are sacred. The world, the state, the church, the school, all are felons whensoever they violate the sanctity of the private heart." The spokesmen of the period—Emerson, Jackson, Thoreau, Theodore Parker, and others—succeeded for the most part in what they set out to do, or at least as much as any group of theorists had a right to expect. But no sooner did it seem that they had succeeded than a new set of conditions, both historical and intellectual, placed the problem of individualism in a different context. The evidence seemed to show that the Age of Emerson and Jackson was either wrong in its estimate of the individual, or that its conclusions were inadequate to satisfy the new circumstances. The whole question of individual and society had to be reviewed after 1870; the question of the relations of the individual to nature had to be re-examined; the question of the relation of the individual to his deity had to be reassessed.

The period of revision lay between 1870 and 1914, from the close of the Civil War to the beginning of World War I, which serve as convenient bench-marks in measuring the dimensions of the problems that era faced. Over this span of years, there were several important changes in the concept of the individual—first, because of the plain fact of war. Of the generation of Americans who served as leaders of American thought and society from 1870 to the turn of the century, almost every one was affected by the war, as a veteran of a mass action in which the individual counted for very little, if at all. What chance did the tradition of Emersonian self-reliance have in this great amorphous struggle that lasted four long years?

Second, because of changing concepts in science. There was a marked shift, after 1870, in the attitude of both scientist and public toward what science was and did. To the eighteenth and to an earlier nineteenth century, science had close ties with philosophy, ethics, and theology. The growing divorcement of science and society became apparent in the late eighteenth century, and by the time of Thoreau—to cite a spectacular example—protests about the dehumanizing and de-socializing effect of science on the individual were common. The impact of the "machine age"—the popular terminology used to identify it—was one which, in the eyes of its critics, tended more and more to impersonalize society and nullify the individual. The business of science, the scientists themselves suggested, was to formulate laws and to apply them to the production of uniform results; they were concerned not with individual instances but rather with numbers of instances. The drift of scientific speculation, as it appeared in the later nineteenth century, moved inevitably away from the individual toward the statistical.

Third, because new approaches to the materials of certain specific sciences shattered the traditional image of the individual. Psychology, a comparatively new science which emerged after the Civil War, had a tremendous impact on those concepts of individual human nature held by philosophers, theologians and the general public. Even before Freud, speculations about the biological and physiological bases of human nature and such things as *will, perception, emotion,* and *conscience,* seemed to be changing the entire picture of what an individual was and what he might be capable of.

William James' *Principles of Psychology* (1890), the most widely-used text of its time, suggested that the individual mind was perhaps not, as men had assumed, a wholly free agent, but rather a "function of the physical organism in time and place." A little later, John B. Watson suggested that an individual action was very likely the result of predetermined patterns and not of thought at all. There was doubt, according to the behaviorists, that man really was a "thinking" being in the older sense of the word; perhaps he was, in

Watsonian terms, simply "a reaction mass." At the turn of the century, Sigmund Freud's ideas began to filter into the public consciousness (Freud lectured in the United States in 1909 and his work appeared in an American edition in 1911) with an explosive effect on the traditional idea of individuality. Freud postulated many things about the human personality, but one thing he seemed most clearly to show was that the individual was not in command of himself. There were too many dark and subterranean forces at work within a man, Freud suggested, to make self-reliance—in the Emersonian and Jacksonian sense—reliable.

The sum of these new points of view on the psychology of the individual added up to an emphatic loss of belief in the efficacy of the individual will. The popular contention that "I am the master of my fate . . ., the captain of my soul," faded away under Freudian analysis. A Watsonian behaviorist had different and startling ways of explaining Emerson's ringing dictum, "Trust thyself. Every heart vibrates to that iron string." William James put the answer concisely by saying, "The concept of will has passed into partial eclipse. In psychology it has lost its position as a primary mental function, and has become an epiphenomenon. We have gained determinism and have lost determination." The German biologist Ernst Haeckel, who was immensely popular among American intellectuals, was more decisive: "Consciousness, thought, and speculation are functions of the ganglionic cells of the cortex of the brain. The human will has no more freedom than that of the higher animals, from which it differs only in degree, not in kind."

More than psychology, new developments in the biological sciences served to revise previous estimates of the individual's nature, motivations, reliability, and freedom of action. Certainly the date of Darwin's *Origin of Species,* 1859, marked a drastic change in the direction of human thought about itself. The combined work of Darwin and his explicator, Herbert Spencer, seemed to indicate that nothing was changeless except change; that the aim of all activity was simply survival and the continuation of the species; that the species was more important in nature's view than any individual within it. It was not that the drift of Darwinian-Spencerian thought was away from individualism. Rather it redefined the word in terms of a wholly different concept of the individual, his function, and his aims. The individual existed to compete and survive; he had but one inherent natural right, "only the right of the fittest to survive," to use a popular paraphrase of Spencer. The idea of individualism in America, after Darwin, existed within the context of the animal world, where biological science seemed to place mankind. Jack London, the popular novelist, wrote, "Civilization had spread a very thin veneer over the surface of the soft-shelled animal known as man. It is a very thin veneer. Let him miss six meals, and see the animal beneath."

In addition to the disclosures about man made by biology, there were also important changes in those ideas about the individual that derived from the physical sciences. Developments in astronomy and physics, especially, seemed to change the individual's relation to nature and to lose him in an illimitable universe. As one commentator put it, a man was possibly less important in the universe than a speck of dust on the skin of an apple floating in a void that was five thousand eight hundred and fifty-nine plus seventeen zeros of light years wide. In the face of such implications drawn from science, it became difficult to believe that what happened to an individual was of any great consequence, or that he possessed any intrinsic importance in the scheme of things.

As a result of these changing views of science toward the individual, there was in the later nineteenth century a shift of responsibility for individual action from the individual to his environment, or his inward composition, or the forces of chance and accident. There was a comparable shift in the position of the individual *vis-a-vis* the universe and society, and a consequent loss of certainty concerning the individual's capacities and capabilities. Was man so capable of receiving truth as he once thought? Was he capable of acting upon it, if he could perceive it, accurately? A great part of American intellectual energy in the later nineteenth century and the early twentieth was directed toward answering such questions.

The society of the United States, in common with that of the western world, experienced during the closing decades of the nineteenth century a relatively sudden and powerful concentration of power in certain segments of society. The position of the individual in relation to government—that is, to the economic, political, and social aspects of the state—was by 1910 quite different than it had been in 1810, or even in 1870. Marks of this change lay everywhere on the surface of American society through the post-Civil War years.

For one thing, between 1850 and 1900, the United States increased tremendously in population, with effects not really understood for another half century. In fifty years the population of the nation more than tripled; in Theodore Roosevelt's time there were three Americans to every one in Jackson's, a rate of increase which dipped from 1900-1950 but has since continued to rise. This fact had far-reaching implications for the period. The spectacular growth of American society brought a new set of mass problems stemming from the sudden appearance of a mass society—problems of housing, education, health, economy, politics, of all the machinery of living. A mass society makes demands which can be adequately met only by standardization, not individuation; nor can such a society afford to give priority, in the same way or as before, to individual needs. The late nineteenth century found that where there are more people, each one counts for less.

At the same time, the United States, like other nations in the final phases of the Industrial Revolution, experienced a swift massing of economic power. In 1783 there were only seven commercial corporations in the new nation. In 1883 the primacy of corporate economic power was an accomplished fact, and its control, function, and aim the greatest single problem facing American society. One major result was to translate a great deal of American thinking about individualism into economic terms, since the American of the late nineteenth century confronted a concentration of economic power never before known to history.

As part of the same social and economic pattern of events, the United States after 1870 experienced a similar concentration of political power and control. The extension of governmental authority into hitherto untouched areas, and the gradual transformation of the United States into an urban society tended to change the relation of the individual to the state. It seemed difficult, after 1870, if not wholly impossible, to think about the state at all in terms of the Jeffersonian or the Jacksonian individual.

As a result the traditionally individualistic American, of the nineteenth century, confronted a society expanding in size, increasing in complexity, and displaying greater and greater concentrations of power. The problem became, as the era perceived it, to find ways of controlling and managing that society so that the individual who lived within it might still retain some measure of autonomy, identity, and authority. The change, as compared to the central issue which concerned the earlier nineteenth century, was quite significant. The problem facing the American of Jackson's time was to establish the individual's ability to perceive truth and to act upon it—which created tangential problems of will, ethics, and knowledge. The problem of the age of Carnegie and Theodore Roosevelt was to preserve the individual's identity and to maintain him as a unit. To put it differently, the earlier nineteenth century was concerned with confirming the validity of individualism. The later nineteenth century was concerned with preserving a sense of individuality in a new context of complexity and concentration. Ironically enough, it seemed to many who considered the problem that if individuality in America were to survive, it might have to be done by banding together in an increasingly interdependent society.

The tremendous burst of energy that blew American society outward in the three decades following the Civil War—with a swiftness unmatched in any other nation's history—is difficult to comprehend in ordinary terms. In the ten years between 1870 and 1880, for example, the amount of farm land under cultivation in the United States increased by the size of an area equal to France; during the next twenty years the total area of farm land increased to an extent equal to France, England, and Germany combined. Villages became cities; states doubled and tripled population; industrial production increased twenty, fifty, and then a hundred-fold. The exploding population and the growing complexity of society meant that the state, the nation, and even local units of government had to assume a multitude of responsibilities for the welfare of the individual which had not existed prior to the Civil War, and all within the space of a generation. The place of the individual within this new social complex was yet to be fully determined; a number of factors helped to determine it, but the passage of the Fourteenth and Fifteenth Amendments to the Constitution (1868, 1870) was a most important one.

Primarily, both amendments were intended to translate into law the results of the Civil War by providing a place within the political structure for the freed Negro. They were in effect a re-affirmation of the traditional belief in individual liberty, of the belief that individual freedom was the most effective and desirable element in the social process, that in it lay the keys to the future of American society. These two amendments were, in more than a casual sense, what a great deal of the war had been about. The first section of the Fourteenth Amendment provided that no state shall deprive a person of life, liberty, or property without due process of law, or deny to any person the equal protection of the law. Neither amendment specifically referred to Negroes or freedmen as such; they placed these rights under *national* jurisdiction (thereby settling another issue of the late war) and made the national government their protector.

The Fourteenth Amendment raised a series of difficult questions of interpretation concerning the individual's protection. Having guaranteed the individual political and economic freedom by these constitutional devices, how much social control was compatible with these guarantees? In a growing, complicated society, how far ought the amendment to be used as a guarantee for every man to do as he chose until checked by national authority or brought under due process of law? The thrust of nineteenth-century industrial and social problems demanded—or seemed to—some kinds of controls in an era of rapid change and rapid development. The disputes which arose under the first section of the Fourteenth Amendment revealed the nature of the problems of individualism raised by the emergencies of the times. How far could legislatures go, under guise of the police power, in controlling the individual's use of property or of political power? What rights did the states have, for example, in regulating rates and charges which directly affected the individual's profits and therefore his property rights? To preserve the historic theory of individual rights, reaffirmed by the Fourteenth Amendment, and at the same time to preserve the right to limit individualism for desirable social ends, was not an easy task. By hundreds of minor decisions, and a few major ones, the courts worked out adjustments. If there were to be restraints on the free exercise of individual power, they eventually agreed, there must be some reasonable relationship between that restraint and the larger welfare of society; individual action (especially corporate action interpreted as such) should be controlled for social advantage. The Fourteenth Amendment's affirmation of individualism, validated by the Civil War, could yet be adjusted to the new social, economic, and political situations that the eighties and nineties encountered. The adjustment opened up a wide domain of legislation and administration hitherto unknown to earlier generations. Jefferson's ideal—to "complete the circle of our happiness" by instituting "a wide and frugal government" which would leave the individual alone to pursue his own affairs—no longer held the same force. The *public* welfare, as occasionally distinct from private and individual, could now become a prior objective of legislation.

In educational circles, the problems of adjusting individual needs to the requirements of a new industrialized mass society took on increased priority. There was in American educational thinking a strong tradition of treating education as an individual as well as a social need, dating back as far as Horace Mann, who in the pre-Civil War decades believed in treating each child as a separate educational problem. Although Mann drew much of his psychology from the pseudo-science of phrenology, his criticisms of current educational practices— which, he said, consisted "in telling, not training . . ., in hearing, not doing"—he learned from phrenology the importance of individual differences and the necessity of preserving them. This individualistic strain continued in educational philosophy through the century, backed by the psychology of such men as William James and G. Stanley Hall, whose findings seemed to confirm the belief that the aim of education was to develop the individual's capacities as well as to adjust him to society.

The integrity of the individual, in James's view, was a primary requisite for the advancement of society. The mutations of social change, James wrote, originated in "the accumulated differences of individuals, of their examples, their initiatives, and their decisions." It has been estimated that nine-tenths of all teachers in the United States who studied any psychology at all between 1890 and 1910 read William James, learning from him, no doubt, what he called "the well-known democratic respect for the sacredness of individuality," translated into educational terms.

This emphasis on individualism in education was restudied and reaffirmed in the early years of the twentieth century. Psychologist Edward Lee Thorndike's theory of individual differences helped to substantiate James, and pointed directly toward what became known as "progressive" educational theory. Since it was widely held that the pressures of modern life threatened to submerge the individual in mass conformity, educators stressed the fact that a most effective way of preserving individuality was to emphasize the importance of personality throughout the educational process.

In 1916, in *Democracy in Education,* John Dewey laid down some of the principles of this philosophy of educational individualism. Society, he wrote in echo of James, "counts individual variations as precious, since it finds in them the means of its own growth." Hence in its educational philosophy, society must "allow for intellectual freedom and the play of diverse gifts and interests." Individual capacities and abilities are to be developed individually, each child to be treated as one and educated as such. Thus the trends of mass society may be counteracted, the paramount individual preserved. Although the nature of "progressive" education has long since changed, it is still the primary aim of the American educational system, to use the words of the National Educational Association, "to educate the child as an individual, to the limits of his abilities to learn." Modern American education is an organic expression of this American individualism, and remains one of the chief instruments by which it is maintained.

One of the most striking reflections of the change in the issues raised by individualism in the late nineteenth and early twentieth century was the shift in those values assigned to the word *individualism*. What it meant in the prose of Emerson and Dewey, or Jackson and Woodrow Wilson, is quite different. After 1870 the term *individualism* normally carried either strong economic or political connotations, sometimes both. It was generally agreed after 1870 that the chief aim of individual activity was to improve the economic or political condition of each person; there was much less interest in individualism as individuality, as self development, as personal distinction.

A number of men during the later nineteenth and early twentieth century recognized and measured this new issue. Frederick Jackson Turner, the historian, stated it in perhaps the clearest terms, in his famous essay of 1893 on "The Significance of the Frontier in American History," which brilliantly synthesized the individualistic tradition and the frontier experience. Continuing his exploration of the frontier, Turner came to the conclusion that "the most significant product" of the frontier within the American democratic tradition was "the unchecked development of the individual." American democracy, he wrote in 1903, was "fundamentally the outcome of the experience of the American people in dealing with the West," producing a society "of which the most distinctive fact was the freedom of the individual to rise under conditions of social mobility, and whose ambition was the liberty and well-being of the masses."

It was the transfer of this frontier spirit to American business that had much to do with the changed quality of post-Civil War economic life. American businessmen did not

imitate the pioneer, but they developed their style of operation during the latter decades of the nineteenth century out of
conditions strikingly similar to his. The land offered the
frontiersman a vast, sparsely populated expanse with few if
any curbs on its exploitation; the world of business offered
the Horatio Alger hero (a kind of *laissez-faire* pioneer) both
colossal opportunities and colossal rewards relatively unhampered by regulations. The American businessmen shared
with the settler and the woodsman, therefore, many of the
same characteristics identified by Turner with the frontier—
optimism, expansiveness, acquisitiveness, mobility, a willing-
ness to risk, and most of all, a massive individualism.

The emphasis on individuality in the business world made
the American entrepreneur a gambler of imperial proportions.
The old business adages simply did not work. The facts of
economic life showed that a rolling stone *could* gather moss,
that a penny saved might lose a dollar, that waste did not
necessarily mean want. "Nothing venture, nothing lose" had
little relevance to a society when men stood to gain mag-
nificently by venturing boldly. The individual won or lost on
the basis of his own skill, luck, or what have you, and that was
the way it was. Walter Weyl called American business of the
period "one huge gambling joint, where money, success, and
prestige were the counters, and the players were devoutly
reading conventionalized biographies of famous men." And
it was true that a man might spend a fortune on advertising
his product and lose it all; another might coin a brand name
and win millions. The farmer's land might cover oil or coal
unbeknownst; the worthless mine might suddenly cash in.
The individual took the chance and the consequences—this
was the core of American business psychology.

This individualism was the product of frontier conditions—
in *all* sectors of American society—of open land, open society,
free opportunity, social volatility, minimum regulations. But,
as Turner pointed out, many of these conditions no longer
existed in 1900, either in economic or in political life.
America was no longer primarily a frontier society. The question became, therefore, could the ideals of the old individual-

ism survive under new conditions? Could the individualistic spirit of the frontier be preserved as the frontier itself disappeared? Americans tended, he noted, to turn away from individualism toward organization to meet the problems of a changed society. "More and more," wrote Turner, "have found it necessary to combine under the leadership of the strongest."

The new conditions also brought new leaders. Instead of George Rogers Clark, William Henry Harrison, or Andrew Jackson, Turner's America found its leadership in James J. Hill, John D. Rockefeller, and Andrew Carnegie. Whether this was bad, or wrong, Turner did not imply; but he did believe that it meant that any consideration of the role of the individual in American society must take realistic account of these new conditions if individualism of any kind were to survive.

The American of the turn-of-the-century years, therefore, in his attempt to maintain his individualistic ideal, was forced to deal with certain basic issues of economic, social, and political life in terms of new problems of business and political organization, and of new issues of social responsibility. Everyone recognized this; the issue appeared in the cartoons, editorials, debates, campaigns, and discussions as part of the continuing dialogue of daily life. How could America redefine and relocate the individual in this new, vaguely-discerned, difficult, and complicated kind of world? Four Americans who grappled with this problem indicated the possible alternatives of its solution—a businessman, Andrew Carnegie; a political leader, Theodore Roosevelt; a philosopher, William James; and a social-political analyst, Herbert Croly. They represented separate reactions to the three major issues confronting late nineteenth- and early twentieth-century individualism: the assimilation of recently-changed concepts of science and society; the acceptance of new forces in an attempt to preserve the old ideals; the adoption of new means of retaining older values by evolving a new way of meeting changed conditions.

Andrew Carnegie believed in old fashioned individualism.

He believed in the virtues of bigness and power; he believed deeply in democracy. A devout Presbyterian who recognized the conflicts between traditional Christianity and the Darwinian-Spencerian ethic, he made a delicate and surprisingly sophisticated adjustment between these contradictory forces and made it clearly. First of all, he affirmed the validity of the individual, while he at the same time fixed the individual's relation to society. "A man's first duty," he wrote in *The Empire of Business* (1902), "is to make a competence and be independent. But his whole duty does not end here. It is his duty to contribute to the general good of the community in which he lives." Thus Carnegie recognized the necessity of considering man as a unit, and as part of a group—as an individual and as a social creature.

Carnegie emphasized, as well, individualism as the key to progress. Diversity, he explained, not uniformity, is the law of life: the "exceptional" individual is a social necessity, for it is he who directs his fellows upward. "The race is not led by the multitude," he explained, "but by the few *exceptional* natures," and he accepted the Darwinian-Spencerian explanation of how those exceptions were chosen—by survival of the fittest. Each individual, Carnegie wrote, must be permitted to develop

his unusual powers, tastes, and ambitions in accordance with the laws which prevail in everything that lives or grows. The "survival of the fittest" means that the exceptional plants, animals, or men which have the needed "variations" from the common standard are the fructifying forces which leaven the whole.

However, since Carnegie was a devoutly religious man, he gave the Darwinian struggle a Christian and progressive cast. The basic law of life, he went on to say, was "progress, [*which*] from the lower to the higher has prevailed from the time this earth cooled and life began to appear." The survivor of the struggle, the "exceptional" man on whom progress depended, must recognize the responsibilities of leadership; it is central to "our God-like mission, that every individual in his day and generation push on this march upward, so that each generation may be better than the last."

Andrew Carnegie, then, placed the issue of individualism in Christian perspective. It is a law of life, he believed, that individualism (or, using economic terms, competition) be recognized as primary so that exceptional leaders may emerge (the survivors of the struggle for the fittest) who will lead society onward and upward (Christian duty and progress). He succeeded in assimilating the older concepts of individualism into the new nineteenth-century economic and scientific environment, and made a reasonable explanation of how it was done. Carnegie was not alone in so doing, of course. He simply achieved his synthesis more adroitly than most and lent credulity to his explanation by the force of his own personal example.

Carnegie's age tended to agree with him. Echoes of the Carnegie philosophy of Christian individualism were everywhere. Abbott Lawrence Lowell, in his *Essays on Government* (1889), explained that three "principles of utility" lay beneath the American system: first, the belief that "individual enterprise is the mainspring of all human progress;" second, that the individual must "enjoy unmolested the fruits of his labor;" and third, that the individual must be protected in his right to plan and calculate "the results of a course of conduct." These three principles added up to a total of individually-chosen destiny, and the survival of the individually best-adapted. Economist Thomas Nixon Carver put the matter bluntly, saying, "The laws of natural selection are merely God's regular methods of expressing his choice and approval. The naturally-selected are the chosen of God"—a sweeping assimilation of Darwinism, Calvinism, and individualism that even Carnegie did not attempt. Russell Conwell, whose lecture "Acres of Diamonds" became the most popular lyceum and Chautauqua presentation of the era, expressed the same idea in striking terms. "The idea is," said Conwell, "that in this country of ours every man has the opportunity to make more of himself than he does, in his own environment, with his own skill, with his own energy, and with his own friends."

This was the theme of Elbert Hubbard's famous essay "The Message to Garcia," which he published in *The Philistine* in 1899 (and sold forty million copies) to attack what he called the "current incapacity for independent action," closing with the stirring words, "The world cries out for a man to carry a message to Garcia!" It was also the theme of William Mathews' best-selling book, *Getting On in the World: Or Hints on Success in Life* (1893) which told young men that self-reliant individualism was "a vital element of success—a determination to be one's own helper. . . . It is the secret of all individual growth and vigor, the master-key that unlocks all difficulties in every profession or calling." Horatio Alger struck the same theme. This adjustment of the old individualistic values to the new social and economic situation satisfied some of the needs, certainly, of later nineteenth-century America. As historian Ralph Gabriel has summarized it, the individualism of the Carnegie School was "an effort to implement the old democratic doctrine of the free individual to make it useful to a developing industrial capitalism. The new version of the philosophy of individualism, supported by Protestant theology or by Darwinian naturalism, became the rising intellectual pattern of the period."

What Carnegie and the others educed, however, was a conception of individualism whose primary function was to explain contemporary economic life. The same pattern of adaptation and assimilation did not work half so well—and some felt not at all—in making sense of contemporary political life. Carnegie's theory of the leadership of the "exceptional" individual, if applied to politics, seemed to produce (or at least to justify) the political boss, the machine, the purveyor of political privilege. One could accept, perhaps, the business leadership of Carnegie, of Rockefeller, or even (with some strain) of Jim Fisk, but it was impossible to regard Boss Tweed or Hinky-Dink McKenna as the finest flowers of a competitive society or the "exceptional" survivors of a noble struggle for eminence. Politically, the formulae of individualism accepted by the economic thinkers would not work. What would?

The person who came closest, perhaps, to working out a political rationale for the new individualism was Theodore Roosevelt. He, more than any other single figure at the turn of the century, represented the image of the politician. With his colorful, emphatic personality and his gift for phrase, he served his age as Andrew Jackson served an earlier one. Roosevelt was neither a deep nor consistent political thinker, but he captured the public imagination and symbolized the political spirit of the times. What he had to say the public accepted as important.

We must recognize, Roosevelt explained, the existence of those forces in the contemporary world which threaten the individual's sense of identity and authority both in economic and political life—the trust, the machine, the "big business" man, the political manipulator. We must accept bigness as a fact of life, and concentration of power as characteristic of modern society. Having thus placed our feet on the rock of reality, he continued, we must then find ways of controlling those forces so that they do not destroy or corrupt the individual, and so that they serve social ends. Roosevelt, like Carnegie, hoped to retain all the old values and principles by adjusting—and no more—to a new set of circumstances and by introducing limits and controls. He reduced the crucial problem of his era, that of the relation of the individual to the state, to three major issues.

First, Roosevelt re-affirmed self-reliance as the primary principle of American individuality. Each man, he said, "has his own qualities which must determine in the last resort that man's success or failure. . . . In the last resort, nothing can supply the place of a man's own individual qualities." He repeated this idea many times, until it became a recognizable theme in his public statements of political policy. Speaking at Provincetown in 1907 (significantly enough at the commemorative ceremonies at Plymouth Rock) he concluded that the "all-important factor for each of us must be his own character," and again at Memphis the same year, "The vital factor in each man's effort to achieve success in life must be his own character, his own courage and uprightness and intelligence."

Second, Roosevelt believed it to be the aim of government to preserve open opportunity for self-reliant action. Government must clear the field for the proof and testing of individuals; the aim of government, he said succinctly, is "to secure for each man a fair chance." In his famous "New Nationalism" speech of 1910, he explained his point carefully, saying,

Proper government means that every man will have a fair chance to make of himself all that within him lies, to reach the highest point to which his capacities, unassisted by special privileges of his own and unhampered by the special privileges of others, can carry him.

Government is therefore a device to guarantee the individual an opportunity for his self-realization; whatever might close off that opportunity is to be eliminated. This helps to explain what seemed to be an inconsistency in Roosevelt's attitude toward wealth and big business. Neither the act of getting rich, nor the bigness of business in themselves were, in his view, wrong; it was not rich men but "malefactors of great wealth," not the trust but the bad trust, that he opposed. The men who gained great wealth or who built giant corporations were "making of themselves all that in them lay." It was unbridled, uncontrolled individualism, the kind of competition that nullified a "fair chance," that he objected to. For this reason Roosevelt could never satisfy Robert La Follette, who thought that trusts ought to be "busted," or Jim Hill, who thought they ought to be left alone.

Third, Roosevelt believed in keeping the state at arm's length from the individual. Its machinery should be employed for police or educational purposes, its activity exerted always in partnership with individual effort. "Much can be done by *association*," Roosevelt once remarked, "but each man should work for others by working for himself, by developing his own capacity." Speaking at Logansport, Indiana, in 1902, he expanded his comment:

Work in combination may help and the State can do a great deal in its own sphere, but in the long run each man must rise or fall on his own merits; each must owe his success in life to whatever of hardihood, of resolution, of commonsense, and of capacity for lofty endeavor he has within his own soul.

The key principle of Roosevelt's belief in the individual was, in his words, to realize "the ideal of social progress in individualistic terms;" his problem was to find out how to counteract all those forces which seemed to threaten traditional American individualism without surrendering the quality itself. He meant to do this by affirming the worth of the individual, and by employing the forces of government to keep his opportunities for action forever open.

What Roosevelt perceived politically, William James perceived philosophically, for philosophers too were equally concerned with discovering and mapping out the contours of the individual. James' father, William Senior, had already pointed out in his 1861 oration on "The Social Significance of Our Institutions" that "the undeniable spiritual difference" between Europe and America was the American regard for the individual, "this exquisite honor which is due to man alone" in the United States. James carried this speculation further. He searched for answers to two questions, he wrote in *The Energies of Men* (1906): "First, that of the possible extent of our powers; and, second, that of the various avenues of approach to them, the various ways of unlocking them in diverse individuals." (Ironically, Emerson had asked the same questions more than a half century before, and he and his generation were certain they had found solutions.) James found in pragmatism a satisfactory answer for some of his questions' implications. Pragmatism, in granting the individual a choice, was fundamentally an individualistic way of approaching truth and an affirmation of individual worth.

As James explained the pragmatic philosophy, each individual made decisions with the will to believe that he could make them; an important element of choice is the conviction that one *has* a choice. It is the individual who made James' pragmatic proofs of truth, he who tests hypotheses and judges results. John Dewey, who carried pragmatism into its next phase, called James' philosophy

a faith in individuality, in uniquely distinctive qualities in each normal human being; faith in corresponding unique modes of activity that create new ends; with willing acceptance of the modifications of the established order entailed by the release of individualized capacities.

Thus there is something of the Emersonian individualism in pragmatism—what the transcendentalist granted man the chance to find within, James and Dewey granted him the opportunity to discover by use, experience, and instrumentality. The mode and means were different, the end the same.

A fourth reaction to the problem of individualism in the period was that of a group of political and social thinkers, encompassing university professors, journalists, political analysts, and ministers, who hoped to retain the enduring values of the American individualistic tradition under the new conditions of life at the turn of the century. The chief social problem that the period presented was simply this—granting the individual complete responsibility for his own success or failure meant that the state should not interfere with the competitive process, whatever its undesirable results. The state therefore did not interfere with child and female labor, with strike-breaking violence, with unemployment or industrial speed-ups, with stock-market riggings and mass depression, with tenements and poverty. Walter Weyl pointed out in 1912 that the same tradition of individualism which produced the millionaire, through "the serenely stupid indifference of the state" also produced the slum, "the apotheosis of the individual." What Weyl and others like him suggested, paradoxically enough, was that the individual surrender something of his own autonomy to save it. There ought to be a greater balance between the individual's responsibility for himself, and the state's for his welfare—more emphasis, wrote Weyl, on the *common* action and the *common* lot, so that the individual's interest might be protected and advanced.

These "reformers," a word loaded with pejorative connotations after 1900, reasoned that since bigness and complexity in contemporary society were apparently combined to crush individuality, therefore individuals must combine through the state to exert a countervailing force. One must use collective means to secure individual ends, they decided—or, in other words, men must use concentrated power to obtain individual good. By combining in group action, the individual yielded some of his individuality to the group for the purpose of retaining the most of it. It seemed better to give up a bit of one's freedom of action voluntarily, they suggested, than to lose it all to opponents more powerful than the individual alone. This seemed, after all, an intelligent recognition of a new set of circumstances which could not be met by absorption (Carnegie) or by control (Roosevelt).

The most convincing exposition of this position was made by Herbert Croly, a brilliant journalist and commentator whose two books, *The Promise of American Life* (1909) and *Progressive Democracy* (1914) remain strangely neglected classics of political thought. A tough-minded man who wrote knotty and compressed prose, Croly represented a point of view which took on increasing importance.

The Promise of American Life began with a statement fixing the position of the individual in contemporary society. First of all, the individual who lived in the early twentieth century, wrote Croly, faced the menace of specialized, organized politics—epitomized in the boss, whose expertise and political skill he could not cope with. Second, the individual faced organized, specialized economic power, personified by the "plutocrat" (if you did not trust him) or the "captain of industry" (if you did), again with experience, skill, and resources that the individual could not match. Yet the focus of American life was still rested on the individual, based on the fond belief that "a democracy is composed of individuals, and must be organized for the benefit of its constituent members." Granted the contemporary situation, what must the nation do, Croly asked, "to maintain and improve conditions for individual fulfillment?"

It cannot, he explained, continue to operate politically within the Jeffersonian-Jacksonian tradition of individualism, a concept which, admirable as it might be, was no longer relevant to the twentieth century. Attempts to adapt this older tradition to contemporary needs, Croly explained, simply played into the hands of the social Darwinists, who used it to justify unlimited economic competition and produce the "destructive individualism" of Carnegie. The "devil-take-the-hindmost" school of thought that traced its origins to Jacksonian-Jeffersonian liberalism, according to Croly, simply provided its enemies with the tools to destroy it. We must, he believed, remove the whole issue of individualism from its eighteenth- and early nineteenth-century context and think about it in twentieth-century terms. He proposed, then, a new kind of "constructive individualism" which involved two important modifications of the older nineteenth-century tradition.

First, Croly advocated the use of the state as a collective means of advancing individual progress, not merely by controlling the forces of concentration as Roosevelt suggested, but by planning for individual needs and using the power of the state to satisfy them. Second, Croly explained that society had its own needs, as important as those of the individual. Society had a right to exist for itself; there existed "a social ideal which differs from," he wrote in *Progressive Democracy*, "and is independent of any collection of individual ideals." The older tradition of Jeffersonian and Jacksonian individualism, as well as the newer adaptations of Carnegie and Roosevelt, both postulated a separation—almost an antagonism—between the individual and society. Croly suggested that this separation was false, even destructive, and that by the proper balance of individual and group needs, both profited.

What Croly called "constructive individualism" in politics, others in economics, social thought, and religion called by different names, but what they believed was much the same. Richard T. Ely, the Wilsonian economist, believed that it was the goal of economic studies "to direct the economic, social growth of mankind [*to*] the most perfect development of all human faculties in each individual which can be attained in harmony with the ethical idea of Christianity." Its aim was, he said, to re-direct the goals of economic society toward individual well-being and progress, away from the threat of bigness and concentration. If to attain this meant using the collective agencies of society and the state, as Croly indicated it might, so be it. The American Economic Association, founded in 1885, wrote in its declaration of principles, "We regard the state as an agency whose positive aid is one of the indispensable conditions of human progress."

Charles W. Eliot's Barbour-Page Lectures, given at the University of Virginia in 1909, provided a striking example of the acceptance by some of the old guard of the new attitudes toward social collectivism. Published the following year as a book, *The Conflict Between Individualism and Collectivism in a Democracy,* Eliot's talks showed a keen understanding of contemporary society by a man who, though a life-long believer in the old fashioned individualistic virtues, was yet able to comprehend the meaning of recent change and even to welcome it. Eliot, recently retired as president of Harvard, was seventy-five years old when he accepted the invitation to lecture, choosing for his topic what seemed to him the most significant alteration in American society that had occurred during his lifetime. The development of the factory system, new relationships between capital and labor, the creation of corporations, the consolidation of education and the professions, the emergence of "unprecedented inequalities of comfort and wealth"—these were some of the reasons, in Eliot's opinion, for the trend toward collective social and political action over the past half-century. As he shrewdly noted, there were simply more Americans than ever before, and in an expanding population there was less chance for individuality; the growth and concentration of population, he pointed out, "has forced government to assume many new functions, to increase public expenditures, and therefore taxes, and to interfere frequently with individual rights formerly considered very precious."

Eliot was acutely aware of the velocity and breadth of those shifts that had taken place in the America of his youth. "All business is now done," he remarked, "in ways which men in active life before 1850 had no conception," a fact which made corresponding changes in society inevitable. Government now "touches many of the most fundamental interests of the individual citizen, affecting favorably or unfavorably his property, his earning capacity, his mode of life, and his family concerns." Like Ely, Eliot refused to be disturbed. American society, far from losing, had gained in the exchange of social for individual action; the increased activity of government and the assumption by society of ever greater responsibilities for the individual led him to "a strong expectation of improvement and progress, and a welcome for new ideas and new hopes." The trend away from the individualism of a simpler, earlier age toward the collectivism of an intricate and complex modern society, he concluded,

has been constructive, not destructive, inevitable in consequence of other profound social and industrial changes, beneficial in the present, and hopeful for the future. It tends neither to anarchy nor to despotism. . . . Its object is that stated in the preamble of the Federal Constitution—"to promote the general welfare, and secure the blessings of liberty to ourselves and our posterity."

Religious thinkers of the Social Gospel school absorbed all this into their theology. The late nineteenth-century movement among the Protestant sects, called informally "the Social Gospel movement," tried to remove the emphasis from competition among individuals as a law of life and to place it instead on cooperation, stressing the group aspects of society. Theodore Munger, writing in *Freedom of the Faith* (1883), explained the Social Gospel point of view on individualism with great clarity and conviction. Christianity, he wrote, contained two principles: the traditional individualistic belief that "every man must live a life of his own, build himself up to a full personality, and give an account of himself to his God;" and second, "the blurred truth that man's life lies in his relations, that it is a derived and shared life . . ., that in origin and character and destiny he cannot be regarded as standing in sharp and utter individuality." Contemporary religion, too much under the spell of *laissez-faire* economics and Spencerian ethics, in Munger's opinion, overemphasized the first and neglected the second. "We must have more Golden Rule Christianity," said President John Bascom of Wisconsin; or as the Reverend Washington Gladden of Columbus, wrote, we should emphasize "the other-regarding motive" so that "cooperation, not competition, must be the basis of social action." The Federal Council of Churches, a product of the Social Gospel social ethic, was founded in 1908 to accomplish exactly this end.

There were, in summary, certain perceptible trends in the way Americans thought about individualism during the period between 1870 and 1914. The most marked of these trends was toward what the political philosophers called "social politics," what Lester Ward termed "sociocracy." There was a growing awareness of the function of the state as a social and economic agency, and of the necessity of evolving a new definition of individualism, as well as a new set of relationships among individual and social and economic values and needs, all within a changing set of social and economic conditions. Summing it up, Herbert Croly wrote in *The Promise of American Life* that the principle of twentieth-century individualism hereafter must be "Live and help live," not "Live and let live."

The underlying assumption of live-and-let-live is an ultimate individualism, which limits the power of one human being to help another, and which binds different human beings together by allegiance to an external authority. The underlying assumption of live-and-*help*-live is an ultimate collectivism, which conceives different human beings as part of the same striving conscious material, and which makes individual fulfillment depend upon the fulfillment of other lives and upon that society as a whole.

The prevailing pattern of thought about the relationship between the individual and society which characterized the period 1870-1914 can be summarized as follows:

Society is made up of individuals whose welfare and fulfillment is of greater importance in the long run, than society's. Among these individuals the strongest, the best adapted, and those with the most desirable human and social qualities, emerge as leaders by a kind of natural process of selection. The best modes of action are those which, within reasonable limits, allow this process of competitive elimination to operate.

This concept, during the later years of this period, came under heavy criticism. Its critics refused to recognize the implicit analogy of human and animal worlds, and doubted that the Darwinian-Spencerian ethic was applicable to human activity. They countered by saying in effect:

Society is not an aggregate of separate individuals, but a unit, with its own kind of organic existence. While it is true that men are individuals, the relatedness of men, one to another, is equally a fact. One must recognize the powers of cooperation for the production of both social and individual good, and the usefulness of collective action—especially in economic and political life—in attaining socially desirable ends which are also congruent with desirable individual goals.

The argument between these two schools of thought, suspended by World War I, continued afterwards with greater vigor and urgency. After the war, most of the major factors which had influenced American thinking about individualism in Roosevelt's and Carnegie's time were still in operation. The tradition of Darwinian-Spencerian ethics was so deeply ingrained in the American mind that the phrase "survival of the fittest" was still almost universally used to describe and justify the course of American economic and political life.

At least two new elements, however, were inserted into the argument over individualism during the first thirty years of the new century—World War I, and the great depression of the nineteen thirties. Whatever conclusions Americans had begun to evolve about the issues of individualism and the forces which seemed to threaten it, after 1917 they were forced to reassess and redefine. The war itself was a tremendous group effort, the most complex and mighty mass exertion in which the nation had ever engaged. The individual, as many noted, was simply lost in the magnitude of it. Fabian Franklin, writing in 1917, concluded that the American entry into the conflict marked "the definite passing of that individualism which has hitherto been an essential part of our national life." Reinhold Niebuhr saw the war as "a tragic climax" to the individualistic tradition—first because it "convinced us that the forces of history have not favored individual life as much as we thought," and second because it fostered an aggressive nationalism from which the individual identity might never survive. The position of the individual in postwar American society, critics concluded, would not be the same again.

The impact of the depression, intensified by the euphoria of prosperity that preceded it, was almost equally shattering. To quote a popular song of the period, on "the day the merry-go-round broke down" the individual suddenly realized that there was apparently little he could do to repair it and for that matter not much he could do by himself to survive the damage. For more than four years, no matter what anyone wrote or said, the historic tradition of individualism failed to provide satisfactory answers to one of the great crises of American history.

More than war and depression shook the average American's faith in his individual capacity to direct and control his destiny. At about the time of the First World War there also began a re-evaluation (which is still in process) by Protestant theologians of the capabilities of human nature. The first few decades of the twentieth century found the Social Gospellers emphasizing the social responsibilities of the church in making possible the development of personal individualities in an age of concentrated power. These men believed deeply in the perfectibility of man, in progress as a law of history, in man's ability to create a kind of Kingdom of God on earth here and now. This has remained a strong element in American religious thought, but it was soon sharply challenged.

After World War I there began to emerge a contrasting,

critical realism in religion which found certain Protestant thinkers stressing, instead of man's individual worth, his fallibility, his propensity to sin, the ambiguous character of "progress" (which might be only another word for purposeless change), and the finitude of the individual. They emphasized that the will had limits, that much of human action was irrational, that human nature was fallible and unpredictable—all leading to the conclusion that individualism, as a way of life, was of uncertain value. The contemporary technological culture, in this view, submerges the individual with the machinery of life. Reinhold Niebuhr wrote in *Reflections on the End of an Era* (1936):

The individual draws the sustenance of his self-conscious individuality from his organic relation to his social group, his family, his craft, and his community. . . . A mechanical civilization weakens these organic relationships and thereby destroys robust individuality. The completely modern man has no social relations sufficiently organic to give his life real significance.

Thus the question is not merely how to preserve individualism in the twentieth century, but more likely the question of whether it can survive at all, and if so, whether it deserves to.

War, depression, and changing concepts of individual worth have added new elements to the continuing dialogue concerning the place of the individual within the context of twentieth-century life. There has also been added to the mixture a confusion and perplexity never present in the same manner before. However they differed, Carnegie, Roosevelt, and Croly were certain that answers to the problems of the individual were available; by the thirties, no one was quite so sure. If there was one thing certain about the twentieth-century world, said John Dewey, it was "the reality of uncertainty." Where was a place for the individual in what poet Louis MacNeice called "an incorrigibly *plural* world?" Walter Lippmann put it in prose: "We are unsettled to the very roots of our being. There are no precedents to guide us, no wisdom that wasn't made for a simpler age." Archibald

MacLeish, in a poem ironically titled "The Land of the Free," believed that

> We don't know
> We're not sure
> We cut our way in the bark of a big tree
> "We hold these truths to be self-evident . . ."
> Now we don't know
> We're wondering.

It was no accident that John Donne's quotation that "No man is an island," popularized by Ernest Hemingway, became almost as familiar to Americans of the forties as the aphorisms of Poor Richard.

Within this framework of discourse, the debate over individualism continues into our time. There are two main streams of this debate, each as strong and each as divided as they were a half-century ago. Within the first are those who have reaffirmed, in much the same fashion and language, the individualism of Carnegie and Roosevelt. The best statement of this point of view occurs in the writings of Herbert Hoover, particularly his *American Individualism* (1922) and *The Challenge to Liberty* (1934). The greatest source of power and success in the American way of life, he wrote in the earlier book, is the freedom of the individual. American progress depends on "an abiding faith in the intelligence, the initiative, the character, the courage, and the divine touch in the individual," words which might have come directly from Ralph Waldo Emerson.

Twentieth-century American Individualism, wrote Hoover, must be based first on an open acceptance of the competitive basis of existence, of self-interest as the mainspring of human activity, and of the law of survival as a rule of life. We cannot ignore, he wrote in *The Challenge to Liberty,* "the biological foundations of human action. No economic equality can survive the workings of biological inequality. This is a hard, commonplace truth." The only guarantee that can honestly be offered to the individual by the state is the right of open competition—"all that we can assure to the individual is liberty, justice, and equality of opportunity." The business of the state is "to safeguard to every individual an equality of opportunity to take that position in the community to which his intelligence, character, ability and ambition entitle him."

But economic individualism is not the whole of life, Hoover believed. Although the individual must "stand up to the emery wheel of competition" to survive, for his fullest development he must also express *himself*. The innate "yearning for individual self-expression, the desire for the creation of something," wrote Hoover, exists in every man and is as much a part of life as the competitive principle. Hoover emphasized the individual's social responsibility, his obligations to his fellow man, his responsibility to add a bit to the advancement of the race; "the progress of the nation, is the sum of the progress in its individuals." While life is competition, it is neither savage nor brutish; though the aim of a successful society is to "stimulate effort of each individual to achievement," it must also contribute to "an enlarging sense of responsibility and understanding."

Herbert Hoover was the last President to enunciate so clearly the fading philosophy of nineteenth-century individualism, but as he did so the world which produced it, and shaped him, suddenly collapsed. There was nothing wrong or cheap or insincere about the individualistic creed which he represented and which he explained so well; it was only that what had been a noble faith, under other conditions, overnight became inapplicable and unintelligible. Yet the point of view Hoover explored in his writings and speeches is still perhaps the most pervasive view of individualism held in contemporary America.

Competitiveness has long been a key principle in the American credo, implanted there by the facts of history. The battle of settler with frontier began it; the desire for betterment that brought forty million immigrants into the country over a century and a half encouraged it; an open, fluid society which consistently offered rewards to those who competed for them, placed a premium on it. Almost any copy of *Vital*

Speeches echoes it today as Chief Justice Maxey of the Pennsylvania Supreme Court did in 1944:

The Creator made life a competitive game and wherever there is competition there will be those who succeed and those who fail. . . . Without the law of gravitation we would have celestial chaos; without the law of struggle we would have weakness and decadence.

In the classic individualistic tradition, sociologist Horace Kallen explains, the American still believes that "the individual comes first, the establishments of society second; that freedom and fellowship of individuals is the goal, the institutions of government, religion, and affairs are but instruments to attain this goal, valid not by what they are, but by what they do." Leo Durocher, one-time manager of the Brooklyn baseball team, put it into the American argot (and certainly the majority of the public approved) by saying, "Nice guys finish last."

The opposite stream of modern individualistic thought, a continuation of the tradition of Ward, Croly, and the Social Gospellers, strives to balance social against individual requirements and places greater emphasis on the role of society in meeting individual needs. It has been strongly influenced by the development of social psychology over the past quarter century; one reason, perhaps, that the nineteenth century stressed the importance of the individual over society was that so much more was known about the individual, who it was therefore assumed must be more important. Herbert Croly's chapter on the need for an adequate, modern social psychology in his *Progressive Democracy* stated the situation clearly. We can never advance our society, he wrote in 1914, until we recognize that the factor of association always adds a broader dimension to our problems; men live in groups, whose fulfillment is as important as that of the individuals who comprise them.

As Croly wrote, a set of much more usable concepts of social psychology were already in the making through the work of such men as Charles H. Cooley, James Mark Baldwin, and others. The individual and society, they explained, exist not in separation but in interdependence; the individual cannot be withdrawn from the group, nor can he be fully understood except in terms of his participation in it. As Baldwin phrased it, "The individual is a product of his social life, and society is an organization of such individuals." Cooley, in agreeing, put it differently by saying, "We cannot divide man's psychical outfit into the social and the non-social."

Those who belonged to this second strain of thinking found hope for the individual in social planning, in an increased use of collective action for individual ends. The old myth of "rugged individualism," represented by Hoover and his predecessors, came under heavy fire. Charles A. Beard, in an essay in 1931 called "The Myth of Rugged Individualism," argued that it was simply "not applicable in an age of technology," and that attempts to apply it to modern problems were in fact "principally responsible for the distress in which Western civilization finds itself." James Truslow Adams, writing three years later, felt that the "myth of rugged individualism," born in "a past of farm and frontier," would never work in an era of "flibbers and factories." In the simple agricultural society, said Adams, repeating Croly's critique,

for which Jefferson alone predicated his system, what he called "restraining men from injuring one another" required the merest minimum of governmental interference at any point. In the America of today and the future the demands must of necessity be wholly different.

Other critics agreed that "the rugged variety of individualism will no longer work as a principle of conduct for citizens in a democratic state." But if old fashioned individualism was no longer relevant to twentieth-century problems, what should take its place? Social planning—the intelligent, controlled use of all of society's agencies, set forth in orderly phases of development leading to a greater and more successful level of individual development. The thirties were alive with plans, ranging from Technocracy to the New Deal, which in its early phases was itself a tremendous *ad hoc* planning agency. One of the first acts of the first administration of Franklin Roosevelt was the creation of the National Planning Board, whose aim was to devise ways for the best use of national resources.

Of the numerous critiques of the "rugged" individualistic school of thought, perhaps the most cogent was that of John Dewey, whose series of essays published in *The New Republic* in 1930 were later collected as a small book called *Individualism: Old and New*. The old individualism will not fulfill twentieth-century requirements, wrote Dewey, for modern life in its bigness and complexity has created "a mental and moral corporateness . . ., without formal or legal status," which has caused a marked "decline of the individualistic philosophy of life." Individual persons can no longer "find support and contentment in the fact that they are sustained and sustaining members of society." "The lost individual," said Dewey, "lacks secure objects of allegiance," while his society is "organized and orderly" as never before because of improved technology and new methods of social organization. We have, then, the paradox of an age in which life has never been more secure or better organized, in which the individual exists without inward organization or coherence.

It is also obvious, Dewey explained, that the twentieth-century individual exists in a world much more interdependent than ever before. Industrialization, by greatly increasing the collective productive effort, has created new problems which can be solved only in collective terms, not those of the frontier's "rugged individualism." Therefore modern society, as Dewey saw it, was "split between the idea of an individual inherited from the past, and the realities of a situation that is becoming increasingly corporate." His solution lay in using collective planning to solve the problems created by the collective tendencies of modern times.

The dialogue has continued in much the same pattern over the past thirty years, tending to focus on two prevailing problems. The first of these is the problem of the individual versus the social majority, of individual values and directions versus a mass and mechanized culture. Contemporary thinkers hope to find ways to develop the greatest possible variety among people—to encourage independence of thought, superiority of the talented, freedom for the individual intellect—while at the same time recognizing the existence of mass culture. The second problem is that which involves the individual and the state, raised by the necessity of balancing political equality and independence of action against the need for planning and regulation for the common good.

The problem of the existence of the individual in a mass culture is not solely an American problem, but one belonging to the entire twentieth century. Charlie Chaplin's classic cinematic statement of it, *Modern Times* (1936), struck a responsive note from audiences all over the world, and still does. William Whyte's book, *The Organization Man* (1956) has recently stated the problem so well that it added a phrase to the American vocabulary. Whyte's study, which found that individuals try to find stability and values in a sense of clan and status, is paralleled by the work of the social psychologist Erich Fromm, who in *Man For Himself* (1947) and *The Sane Society* (1955) introduced the thesis that many of the individual's problems today arise from the strain of living in a frighteningly complex society that submerges him. The individual fears freedom, Fromm wrote earlier in *Escape from Freedom* (1941), for it forces him to take responsibility for his choices, and he attempts to shift that responsibility to other agencies of society. He "escapes" toward an authoritarianism which precludes choice, or toward conformity, which allows him to "adopt a self which is not his" by agreeing with "distant and anonymous authorities."

Social philosopher Henry Murray, however, has taken issue, as have others, with the theory that mass conformity has smothered individualism. There is more individuality today, he suggests, than we realize; it has simply taken different forms. We tend to put more imagination, creativity, and individuality into our *work* than into *self* (as the nineteenth century interpreted individualism) thus creating a new kind of individuality. We have also found how to be individually expressive through a group; scientists, for example, have found ways to think fruitfully in groups, and we may be evolving, in a mass culture, such devices as the "team" to express individuality. Russell Davenport, in *The U.S.A.: The Permanent Revolution* (1951) agrees that the "team" concept has become a new kind of outlet for individual creativity, for it "challenges the individual to seek his self-expression, not along purely egoistic channels, but in dynamic relationship to others. . . ."

Discussions of the second contemporary problem, political individualism—the position of the individual *vis-a-vis* the state —still create the highest temperatures of all. So it has always been, whether it was Hamilton versus Jefferson, Jackson versus Calhoun, Bryan versus McKinley, or Taft versus Franklin Roosevelt. Beginning in the 1870's, American politics found the older nineteenth-century individualism politically unworkable in a swiftly growing, interdependent mass society. Maintaining a balance between governmental interference with individual independence, especially in the economic sphere, became an increasingly moot political issue, debated by Antimonopolists and Greenbackers, Bellamyites and Georgists, by Populists, Progressives, Socialists, and New Dealers, down to the "anti-collectivist" Conservatives of the sixties.

Eric Johnson, president of the United States Chamber of Commerce in the 1940's, felt that the most decisive fact of twentieth-century political life was "the duel between individualism and statism," the issue "at the core of the political and economic turmoil of the two decades between the world wars, intensified under the pressures of postwar problems." We "must candidly accept" he believed, the possibility that under certain circumstances central planning and control might in fact bring increased efficiency," but we must also resist every day, in every way, the "direct operations of the government on the individual" as "peculiarly abhorrent and dangerous to the American system."

From the opposite point of view, Franklin Roosevelt's famous speech of 1932 to the Commonwealth Club of San Francisco stated another concept of the correct relationship of government to the individual. The task of government, he explained, was to maintain individual opportunity and equality against those forces which, in the development of an industrial and concentrated society, tend to destroy them. We must create between the individual and his government

a form of organization which will bring the scheme of things into balance, even though it may in some measure qualify the freedom of action of individual units within the society. . . . We know that liberty to do anything which deprives others of those elemental rights is outside the protection of any compact; and that the Government in this regard is the maintenance of a balance, in which every individual may find safety if he wishes it; in which every individual may attain such power as his ability permits, consistent with his assuming the accompanying responsibility.

According to the *Oxford English Dictionary*, the word *individualism* came into the vocabulary in 1840 when Henry Reeve translated part II of Alexis de Tocqueville's *Democracy in America* and transferred the word *individualisme* into English unchanged—since, Reeve said, it had no English equivalent. Tocqueville was describing a uniquely American concept, the idea of organizing society around the individual person, which he believed a risky and radical departure from European and British practice, admirable though its intent might be. Tocqueville respected the American experiment, and hoped it might succeed, but he could not help but view the American belief in *individualisme* with some apprehension, for, as he pointed out, it severed the vital relation between man and society. There must be, he thought, an ideal combination of social harmony with individual liberty, providing the means by which individuals and society might exist separately, yet in mutual balance.

Americans have never found, perhaps, the perfect balance that Tocqueville hoped for, but they have approached it closely enough to exist as a society, and their form of it has survived systems based on different terms. They first developed an individualistic ethic which reached its climax in the age of Emerson and Jackson, one which deified the individual at society's expense. The later nineteenth century, and the twentieth, found that so to separate the individual from society left him vulnerable to the power and impersonality of modern industrial life. The unaffiliated person in the twentieth century is the most defenseless of men.

The present need of Americans is to find a workable definition of individualism to fit contemporary conditions, a continuously successful way to integrate the individual with the community so that both gain. As Adlai Stevenson phrased it in 1952, the questions facing Americans are "how far government must impair some individual freedom to preserve more," and "how far is government to go to attain the economic and social atmosphere in which the utmost individual can thrive?" The mission of individualism through the first half of American history was to liberate the individual from controls, to release and direct his powers. The question to be solved by the later nineteenth and the twentieth centuries has been what controls needed to be restored, and how.

"Getting along with bigness," writes Senator Joseph Clark of Pennsylvania, is the great task of the individual in today's world. The development of big corporations, associations, unions, government, and even the emergence of Megalopolis have created issues which differ in degree (though not in quality) from those presented by the same factors in earlier twentieth-century life. Bigness is a modern fact; so too is the need for the individual to learn to live with it so it need not be a curse. What the contemporary individualist must solve, therefore, is the problem stated accurately by James P. Dixon, writing in the Report of the President's Commission on *National Goals for Americans* in 1960. The individual, wrote Dixon, is still and will continue to be the focus of the American effort, for "we believe that the individual is central to our society, that the principal asset of human society is human life itself, and that society must therefore help to protect the lives and interests of every individual." The "deep conviction that the individual and his productivity are basic to our free society make us reluctant to meet human needs in a fashion which might reduce individual initiative and self-reliance."

Yet these human necessities must be met within the context of modern mass society. Americans, some social psychologists have suggested, are learning to express their individuality by learning to work through organizations—corporations, government agencies, cooperatives, societies, presssure and protective groups, and so on—which represent multiplications of individual energies. This is of course nothing new, but rather the "principle of association," evolved in Emerson's and Channing's nineteenth century and adapted to modern uses. Some, as Channing did, fear the disappearance of the individual in the group; others believe that the individual may, through participation in the group, find full and rich personal development. But the dilemma still remains—of equalizing individual and group needs, in balancing individual freedom and self-reliance against the need of society at large.

The search for what Allen Wheelis, writing in *The Quest for Identity* (1958) has called "a coherent sense of life" related to "the supporting framework of life," has presented twentieth-century American society with its most pressing problem. The dilemma has been most acutely perceived and sensitively explored, perhaps, by the modern novel; it forms the theme, for example, of Ralph Ellison's *Invisible Man,* William Styron's *Set This House on Fire,* Saul Bellow's *Augie March* and *Henderson The Rain King,* John Updike's *Rabbit, Run,* among others. In novel after novel the question recurs, "Who am I, and where do I belong, and what are my relationships to others and the world?" Nor are the novelists alone in attempting to locate the individual somewhere within the structure of contemporary life—as witnessed by the popularity of such books as Vance Packard's *Status Seekers,* David Riesman's *Lonely Crowd,* Peter Viereck's *Unadjusted Man,* or Paul Goodman's *Growing Up Absurd.* The novelist Herbert Gold leaves it with an unanswered question: "When am I free and when am I merely isolated? When am I alone and independent? When am I responsible? When am I groupy, togethered into socialized isolation? When am I selfished into insignificance?"

BIBLIOGRAPHICAL ACKNOWLEDGEMENTS

For the attitude of the Puritan toward the individual, see Ralph Barton Perry, *Puritanism and Democracy* (New York, 1944), and Stow Persons, *American Minds* (New York, 1958), Part I. The discussion of eighteenth- and early nineteenth-century individualism is adapted from R. B. Nye, "The Search for the Individual, 1750-1850," *Centennial Review* V (Winter, 1961) 1-20. The American concept of individualism is also a continuing thread in Ralph H. Gabriel, *The Course of American Democratic Thought* (New York, 1940). For comments on the idea in the later nineteenth and early twentieth centuries, see Andrew Carnegie's "Variety vs. Uniformity," in B. J. Hendrick, ed., *Problems of Today* (New York, 1933); William Jennings Bryan, "Individualism vs. Socialism," *Century* LXXI (April, 1906) 856-9; Samuel Orth, "What of the Individual?" *North American Review* CLIV (October, 1911) 517-28; F. J. Turner, "Contributions of the West to American Democracy," *Atlantic Monthly* (January, 1903) 83-96; Ralph Barton Perry, "William James and American Individualism" *Characteristically American* (New York, 1949) 70-93; Charles W. Eliot, *The Conflict Between Individualism and Collectivism in a Democracy* (New York, 1910); Walter Weyl, *The New Democracy* (New York, 1912); Herbert Croly, "The Individual and Society," *Progressive Democracy* (New York, 1914); Fabian Franklin, "Individualism After the War," *Atlantic Monthly*, CXX (August, 1917) 270-76; and Reinhold Niebuhr, "The Nation's Crime Against the Individual," *Atlantic Monthly*, CVIII (November, 1916) 609-14. For the controversies of the thirties, see Charles A. Beard, "The Myth of Rugged Individualism," *Harper's* CLXVIV (December, 1931) 13-22; J. T. Adams, "Rugged Individualism Analyzed," *New York Times*, March 8, 1934; J. A. Nolte, "The People vs. Individualism," *North American Review* CCXXXVII (June, 1934) 545-53; Everett Dean Martin, *The Conflict of the Individual and Mass in the Modern World* (New York, 1932); John Dewey's *Individualism Old and New* (New York, 1931) and his *Quest for Certainty* (New York, 1929), and Horace M. Kallen, *Individualism: An American Way of Life* (New York, 1933). Merle Curti, *The Social Ideas of American Educators* (New York, 1935) contains material on individualism in American education. Excellent modern treatments of the problem are Gordon Mills, ed., *Individualism in Twentieth Century America* (Austin,

Texas, 1963), and John W. Ward, "Individualism Today," *Yale Review* XLIX (March, 1960) 380-92, both of which contributed substantially to the latter portions of this chapter. A recent study, Yehoshua Arieli, *Individualism and Nationalism in American Ideology* (Cambridge, Mass., 1964) contains a number of interesting interpretations.

VI

The American View
of Nature

The land was ours before we were the land's . . . .
—ROBERT FROST

THE DISCOVERY of America created quite literally a *new* world. In contrast to a Europe that had long been thoroughly catalogued, the American continent presented nature still in pristine bloom, fresh and unspoiled, filled with strange and wonderful things. Columbus wrote enthusiastically of the "fields very green and full of an infinity of fruits as red as scarlet, and everywhere there was the perfume of flowers, and the singing of birds very sweet." Though Columbus, and later others, found the new land did not always live up to that first intoxicating promise, the impact of American nature on the new arrival remained much the same. It seemed to another observer in New England a century later as "beautiful a land as ever the sun shined upon," as comely as "that pleasant land described by Moses." Few who came failed to be struck by the land's immensity, its fertility, its incredible variety and richness. "This is as God made it, when he created the worlde," exclaimed John Smith of Virginia, and his fellow Jamestown colonists, seeing "faire meadows and goodly tall Trees . . ., the ground all flowing over with faire flowers," were "almost ravished at the first sight thereof."

The explorer's second response to American nature was usually of a much more practical kind. Columbus, after his first reaction to the Caribbean paradise he described, was more interested in reports of "gold found among the roots of trees, along the banks, and among the rocks and stones left by torrents," and so were most of those who followed him. Sixteenth- and seventeenth-century explorers and settlers, stirred as they were by American nature, also knew quite well what it was good for. The Virginia colonists, according to Challon's *Voyage* (1606), intended "both to seek to convert the savages, as also to seek out what benefits or commodities might be had in those parts." Christopher Smith, returning to London from the Jamestown settlement, wasted little time describing its beauty but brought instead a sample of what purported to be gold dust and an "expectaunce and assurance of great wealth."

America was beautiful, but more important, it was profitable. It could be appreciated and enjoyed, but it was to be conquered, controlled, and used. Thomas Morton, on his arrival in New England in 1622, saw it both ways. A sensitive and observant man, Morton was immediately taken by the fair prospect before him. "I had more seriously considered the beauty of the place," he wrote, "with all her fair endowments, I did not think that in all the known world it could be paralleled." But at once his mind turned to how it might be used—"If this land be not rich, then is the whole world poor." While certainly not unaware of the charms of American nature, Morton and others like him were much more interested in its merchantable products. Thomas Heriot's report to Raleigh, preserved in Hakluyt's *Voyages,* was a practical account of what Virginia could profitably offer the settler. John Smith's *Description of New England* (1616) , William Wood's *New England's Prospect* (1634), Morton's *New English Canaan* (1637), and John Josselyn's *New England's Rarities* (1672) emphasized the utility of the country, the presence of arable land, pure water, available timber, abundant game, and little else.

Besides their normal human desire for wealth, the settlers

brought with them the European attitude toward the wilderness. To them uncontrolled nature was an ever-present threat. Over the centuries Europe and Asia had worked out a kind of symbiotic relationship between man and nature, but those who first settled on the edge of this huge, unknown expanse possessed no knowledge of wildness nor an understanding of how to live with it. American nature was new, strange, and hostile, not at all so responsive and predictable as the Old World had become over generations of mutual acquaintance with man. Nature had to be subjugated, if the Colonists' goals —ranging from the Puritan's desire for God's commonwealth to the adventurer's search for jewels in Virginia's sands—were to be realized.

The contrast between the American forest and the tailored, subdued landscape of Europe was frightening. Father Hennepin, viewing Niagara Falls in 1679, had nothing in his experience to prepare him for it; he could therefore find no beauty there, but only "a horrible Precipice" whose waters "foam and boyl after the most hideous manner imaginable." Accustomed as the early settlers were to a settled and peaceful land, the untamed, uncouth American wilderness alarmed them. Nathaniel Morton of Plymouth Colony recorded that the *Mayflower* travellers, arriving in a cold and gloomy November, found before them only "a hideous and desolate wilderness, full of wilde beasts and wilde men." Michael Wigglesworth, a generation later, saw it the same way as

> A waste and howling wilderness,
> Where none inhabited
> But hellish fiends and brutish men
> That Devils worshipped . . . .

Beyond the strip of settled shoreline there were savages and animals, starvation, cold, violent death. "Only here and there," wrote John Smith of the land's awesome immensity, "we touched or have seen a little of the edges of those large dominions which do stretch themselves into the Main (land) God doth know how many miles." Smith, who loved the new country as well as any and better than most, knew very well "the furie of savages, famine, and all manner of mischiefs and inconveniences" it held. The settler, to make the land trustworthy and livable, had to subdue this wilderness as soon as possible. The man with a living to make and a family to protect had very little chance to reflect on the meaning or the beauty of the natural scene before him. His concern with nature was strictly utilitarian; he needed to know it only insofar as he could subjugate it.

The Puritan colonist, however, unlike the majority of others, brought with him certain theological equipment which, while it did not substantially alter his attitude toward the physical facts of American nature, did provide him with a different way of understanding it. He saw nature, of course, as a resource for man's use (and especially for *his* use) placed at hand by a helpful God to insure success for His holy experiment in Calvinist society. But beyond practicality, the Puritan also saw nature as a great and ordered hierarchy, intricately related in one vast whole, itself a testimonial of God's perfection. To the Calvinist colonist, nature revealed divine law. "When a man looks on the great volume of the world," commented the Reverend John Preston, "those things that will have known, are written in capitall letters." In nature one found infinite evidences of God's designs. "When God wrought the works of Creation," said Samuel Willard, "he had a Design in every Creature;" through an understanding of nature one comprehended something of God's providence and power. Compared to that of the Bible, of course, such natural revelation was incomplete, but it was neither to be slighted nor ignored.

To the Puritan, then, the natural world had a symbolic function. Every natural fact was an emblem of the divine law which governed spirit as well as thing; every object, creature, and event in nature held a moral purpose over and above its scientific or temporal meaning. The world contained, wrote one New England divine, "numberless Lessons of Morality, which by the Help of the Analogy between the Natural and Spiritual World . . ., we may learn from them." So Cotton

Mather, bumping his head on a low doorway, might mutter to himself, "Be not too proud," or Samuel Sewall meditate on a spilled glass of wine as a reminder of life's transitory pleasures. The Puritan observed and interpreted nature so that from it he might receive spiritual and moral guidance.

Before the first generation of American colonists had gone to their graves, they had already established two major attitudes toward nature. First, they regarded nature as a commodity, a source of food, fiber, wealth, power and physical and social well-being, to be utilized for man's comfort and profit. Second, they considered nature to be a source of knowledge, a visible lesson designed by a wise and beneficent Creator for man's instruction. Nature had both use and meaning. It was to be both *exploited* and *contemplated*; it was tool and symbol. These two attitudes have controlled the pattern of Americans' reactions to nature ever since.

By the closing decades of the seventeenth century the colonists were much more accustomed to the American land and in much less fear of it. The wilderness was still an antagonist to be respected, but the sense of struggle between man and land was less urgent, the conflict not so sharply defined. There was less direct danger (though by no means none) from the Indian; improved use of the soil and rapid clearing of new land had removed much of the threat of starvation. The development of a brisk trade with England and Europe provided economic securities lacking in the early years of settlement, but the colonists faced a constant shortage of capital. They rarely possessed enough capital to support a full-scale productive economy, and in order to accumulate it they turned to their natural resources. Nature was the chief source of wealth, the most easily used, the most abundant. The psychology of exploitation imported by the explorers fitted perfectly the needs of a burgeoning society.

By the eighteenth century, too, Boston, Philadelphia, Baltimore, and other cities had established an English-European pattern of urban life. A substantial percentage of city-dwellers after the turn of the century had little more contact with the land or the forest than the average Londoner. Franklin, a cosmopolitan at home in American, British, or French society, was no more a "man of nature" than his Parisian counterpart, no matter if he did elect to play the role. Furthermore, the majority of these colonists were native-born. Since American nature had always been a part of their lives, nothing seemed strange or unfamiliar about it. Never having seen the neat hedge-rows and tamed brooks of the English countryside, to them the great dark forests and wild cataracts of America were neither unnatural nor frightening. They knew the European model of nature only from books, hearsay, and parental memories. Wildness was part of their heritage.

The eighteenth-century American had a much different, and a much closer kind of relationship with the natural world about him than his grandfather's. A century of acquaintance with the American scene gave the farmer, the explorer, the traveller, the entrepreneur, and most of all, the scientist, a kind of familiarity with it that the previous generation had never possessed. The era's great technological and scientific advances meant that eighteenth-century man knew more about nature than ever before; Newton and his successors took much of the mystery and terror out of it. As the scientist penetrated farther into the recesses of nature's laws, as the farmer brought more of the land under control, and as the merchant dipped more deeply into nature's bounties, Americans found less reason to fear or fight their natural environment. For that matter, their subjugation of nature seemed to be nearly complete; swamps were drained, forests cut down, roads conquered isolation, wilderness produced wealth. The colonists learned with each passing decade how to exploit the land more efficiently, and their success in so doing was to them a source of considerable pride.

For these reasons the eighteenth-century American could consider the land as something other than an adversary. Having once been mastered, nature now became interesting in a number of different ways. During the early years of settlement, the American's reactions to nature were conditioned by either the settlers' conflict with it or the theologian's emblematic use of it. Now, a century later, it became possible to respond to nature intellectually and emotionally. One could find in nature qualities surpassing physical or theological utility; one could discover profits and pleasures beyond mere service—the kinds of pleasures that Colonel William Byrd of Westover drew from "a Garden, a Grove, and a Purling Stream."

Lord Shaftesbury, the English philosopher, taught the age that "wilderness pleases," that "things of a natural kind" elicited complex and interesting inner responses. Where Wigglesworth saw a howling wilderness, William Penn saw a great garden—nor was it accidental that he chose to call his colony "Penn-sylvania," with all the connotations of natural peace and beauty that the Latin word brought from the pastoral tradition. It was Penn, also, who sensed the reality of the relationship between man and nature in this new world that exceeded simple utility; one of his first orders to his settlers was that one acre of trees must be left for every five acres cleared.

Since he no longer needed to look at nature as merely an obstacle to be overcome, the American of Franklin's generation began to evolve a new set of attitudes toward his environment. First, he reacted to it intellectually; nature, he believed, was *knowledge*. The Age of Reason described the world as an eminently rational place. The word *nature* meant the whole orderly system in which everything existed, that perfect, harmonious machine which reflected the supreme rationality and skill of the Great Engineer who created it. "If we form in our imagination an idea of the harmony of the universe," wrote Ethan Allen in *Reason The Only Oracle of God* (1784), "it is the same as if we called God by the name of harmony." Nature, wrote one of Newton's disciples, leads man

to the knowledge of the Author and Governor of the universe. . . . To study nature is to study into His workmanship; every view of discovery opens up to us a new part of His scheme.

This natural machine exhibited certain qualities which were assumed to be qualities of the Divine Mind itself: order, for nature was a vast collection of compatible laws; beneficence, for all natural processes were progressive and benevolent; knowledge, up to certain finite limits, for nature was accessible to the reason. Like the Puritans, the deists saw evidences of God in nature (though their picture of nature led them to see a different God) since, as Allen wrote, "As far as we understand nature, we are become acquainted with the character of God, for the knowledge of nature is the revelation of God." Nature was no longer subordinate to the Bible as the channel of revelation—as Thomas Paine wrote succinctly in his *Age of Reason* (1794) "The Word of God is the Creation we behold."

The scientist looked into nature for patterns, laws, predictabilities. In order to understand it, he observed, identified, and classified it; nature neither frightened nor puzzled him. Nature was a storehouse of phenomena and matter, wrote Charles Wilson Peale, "a great school, an institute of laws eternal." Professional scientists such as Franklin, Benjamin Rush, Cadwallader Colden, and David Rittenhouse (or gifted amateurs like Jefferson and Crèvecoeur) probed the natural world to find ways of controlling and using it, and of harmonizing it with society. They opened the way for the next generation of scientists who penetrated it more deeply— chemists such as Samuel Mitchell, botanists such as Benjamin Smith Barton, Thomas Nuttall, Asa Gray, ornithologists such as Alexander Wilson and John James Audubon. Scientists though these men were they also saw nature as a fountainhead of knowledge about man and God. Their combination of intellectual and spiritual interest in the natural world was soon to become a part of the great effloration of art and philosophy and poetry that was American Romanticism.

William Bartram, the Pennsylvania naturalist, exemplified this eighteenth-century approach to nature. Born in 1739, the son of a famous Quaker naturalist, Bartram read Burke and the philosophers of taste while he trained himself rigorously as a scientific observer. He saw natural facts and events as evidences of God's order and benevolence, and equally as objective realities to be scientifically classified and analyzed. He observed nature, and he was at the same time personally involved with it, which helped to make his *Travels* (1794) a highly popular book with philosophers and scientists alike. Moralist, scientist, and part-poet, Bartram found the natural world to be "the glorious apartment of the boundless palace of the sovereign Creator," an "inexpressibly beautiful and pleasing world of gay, vociferous, and tuneful birds," as well as a scientifically exact world of order, composed of "a variety of qualities . . ., designed for different purposes and ends."

The Enlightenment, far from being a sterile and cold age, responded both emotionally and intellectually to the natural world. The Age of Reason reasoned with nature, but it was also deeply stirred by it. Jefferson, who as a scientist described Virginia in clear, profuse detail in his *Notes on Virginia,* carefully measuring miles and calculating rainfall, also reacted quite unscientifically to Virginia's Natural Bridge, relating in purely subjective terms his "really indescribable rapture" at the view of "so beautiful an arch, so elevated, so light, and springing up as it were to heaven!" Alexander Wilson's great multi-volumed *American Ornithology* (1809-1813) had two aims, Wilson said—the one scientific, to observe, describe, and classify American birds; the other

to draw the attention of my fellow-citizens . . . to a contemplation of the grandeur, the harmony, and the wonderful variety of nature, exhibited in this beautiful portion of the animal creation.

As the application of reason to nature produced a new scientific picture of the universe, so the application to it of emotion produced a new sense of its meaning. If the intellect furnished new ways of comprehending the natural world, so did the fancy.

The man who did most to show the eighteenth-century American how to look at nature was the English philosopher Edmund Burke, whose *Inquiry of the Origin of our Ideas of the Sublime and Beautiful* (1750) provided him with ways to organize his feelings and with means of expressing them. Burke's book appeared in a new American edition every ten years over the next century. For additional assistance, the educated American turned to William Gilpin, whose *Upon Prints* (1778) and other essays outlined more precise methods of observing nature, establishing relationships with it, and extracting from it aesthetic and emotional values. From Burke, Gilpin, and other contemporary aestheticians (among them Kames, Blair, Shaftesbury and the English school) the American learned reliable methods of gaining information from the natural world, and of transmuting it into materials useful to the poet, the painter, the philosopher, and the theologian. He knew that what he saw in nature had measurable connections with what he felt; he knew also how it should make him feel.

When the eighteenth-century American traveller saw Niagara Falls (or the falls of the Cohoes, Trenton, Passaic, or Potomac), Natural Bridge in Virginia, Franconia Notch, Lake George, the White Mountains, or the Catskills, he knew what to look for and how to express it. Travel accounts of the period are filled with explanations, dutifully recorded in great detail, of exactly how one responded to particular scenes; Abraham Lincoln, for example, once prepared a lyceum lecture on Niagara Falls' "power to excite reflection and emotion." Magazines published scores of articles on America's natural wonders, filled with words such as "sublime," "picturesque," "awful" (meaning awe-inspiring), "wild," and "magnificent," each of which carried a precise meaning. Occasionally some traveller tried to penetrate a little more deeply than usual into the process by which natural objects impressed the viewer, or exactly how the emotion grew out of the sensory impression. One such account was that of Dr. Archibald Alexander, president of Hampton-Sydney College, who wrote an unusually perceptive essay in 1797 on his visit to Natural Bridge in Virginia, in which he hoped to demonstrate, he said, how "natural scenery exerted considerable effect on the character of the mind."

First, Alexander suggested, nature impressed the mind by "the novelty of some object, not before seen." The element of surprise, he believed, was quite important in initiating a reaction. Those who lived near Natural Bridge, for example, "might be pleased with the object, but would experience, after a while, nothing of the vivid emotion" attached to its original view. Second, the natural object or scene must have "some fancied resemblance to something familiar" to serve as a point of reference to some concrete memory lodged in the viewer's previous experience. That the rock formation resembled a bridge, Alexander felt, was the primary reason that it elicited a *meaningful* response in those who saw it. This association of novelty and familiarity in a single scene produced a double reaction in the viewer—a sensory, almost visceral response, followed by and combined with an emotional one. Alexander analyzed the impact of this first visit to the Bridge thus:

Having stood at the top, and looked down into the deep chasm above and below the bridge, without any new or strong emotions, as the scene bore a strong resemblance to many which are common to that country, I descended by the usual circuitous path to the bottom, and came upon the stream or brook some distance below the bridge. The first view which I obtained of the beautiful and elevated blue limestone arch, springing up into the clouds, produced an emotion entirely new; the feeling was as though something within sprung up to a great height by a kind of sudden impulse. That was the animal sensation . . ., accompanied by the genuine emotion of the sublime,

which, he pointed out, was of a higher order than that "mere wonder or admiration" (not to be confused with "grandeur") evoked in the viewer by lesser scenes.

The accounts of travellers to Niagara Falls, the most popular of all American scenic attractions, form a case history in changing perspectives on nature. The majority of the early accounts were descriptive, concerned primarily with information about the formation and function of this natural phenomenon. Beginning about 1750, the accounts take on a more subjective cast, until by the end of the century the reflections of the viewer became much more important than the sight itself. The proper emotions evoked by the Falls were almost always "sublimity" and "grandeur;" the sight almost always spoke to the viewer of "God's power." (However, a New York lawyer in 1806 remarked "Is *that* all?" and rode on.) Ann Powell, who visited the Falls in 1789, experienced "strange emotions of wonder and solemnity."

To Isaac Weld, in 1796, "Your mind is forcibly impressed with an awful idea of that mighty Being who commanded the waters to flow." A visitor in 1801 saw the Falls as "grand, awful, sublime;" another "wept with a strange mixture of pleasure and pain;" still another felt "wonder, delight, and awe." Margaret Fuller's response involved "lofty emotions" of "grandeur, mutability, awe and divinity." John Brainerd, a very obscure poet, after his visit dashed off, in fifteen minutes, one of the most popular poems of the period concluding that

> It would seem
> As if God poured thee from His hollow hand
> And hung his bow upon thine awful front
> And spoke in that loud voice . . . .

Mrs. Lydia Sigourney, another highly regarded poet, thought that the Falls "point always to God;" James Graham called it "a primeval altar;" Thomas Grimfield was reminded of "the thunder of God's omnipotence," and so on. Until the latter decades of the nineteenth century, there was a predictable pattern that ran through what was, in effect, a literature of Niagara Falls.

The philosopher Archibald Alison and the poet William Wordsworth furnished the nineteenth-century American with the rest of the equipment he needed to assess it fully and organize his attitudes toward it. Alison's book, *Essays on the Nature and Principles of Taste,* published in 1790 (with its first American edition in 1812) immediately became a popular college text. He built on the philosophical tradition of Burke, and much of what he said was implicit in Wordsworth, but in his logical Scottish way Alison arranged the somewhat diffuse Romantic concepts of nature in an understandable whole. Nature, he said, calls up certain associations in the mind, because natural facts symbolize abstract qualities—*innocence, sublimity, peace, beauty* and so on. Nature, therefore, has an important function in evoking ideas and emotions in the beholder. Nature also contains a moral discipline; it elicits "moral sensibilities." The ultimate effect of nature on the observer, he continues, is to arouse in him a consciousness of God; nature is "a temple of worship" which contains "the throne of the deity."

Alison's contribution, then, was to give men such as William Cullen Bryant, Thomas Cole, and Ralph Waldo Emerson (all of whom knew his book well) a useful and coherent theory of nature from which to proceed to poetry or painting or philosophy. Nature educated men, and healed their emotional and spiritual hurts. Nature was a religious and moral force, for the perception of beautiful objects and combinations in nature inevitably set in motion a chain of associations which suggested the power and love of God. Nature was a symbolic storehouse of inspiration and association, its doors open to all who wished to enter.

Wordsworth's impact on American thought came later. Not until the eighteen-twenties did Americans discover that Wordsworth gave the natural world moral as well as emotional meaning (as Alison had already suggested) and upon discovering this, American poets and essayists eagerly embraced him. R. H. Dana, in a famous essay for *The North American Review* in 1819, marked a turning point in American critical theory by dethroning Pope and crowning Wordsworth the new king; in Wordsworth, wrote Dana, there is "a moral sense to all things, and the materials of the earth become teachers of our minds and ministers of good to our hearts." In Wordsworth, wrote a commentator in *The Atlantic Magazine* in 1821, "all natural forms are symbolical of the high and holy truths which the Universal Mother is perpetually unfolding." The great majority of critics and poets agreed. For them Wordsworth reaffirmed in Romantic terms the traditionally American, Puritan-rooted conviction that the natural fact had moral meaning.

By the first quarter of the nineteenth century, Americans

had developed a cohesive theory of nature, built on older precedents of science and rationalism, absorbing within it the newer intuitive, emotional approaches of Romanticism. Four major principles supported this theory. It rested first on the assumption made famous by Wordsworth's statement that "the meanest flower that blows can give/Thoughts that lie too deep for tears"—that is, that nature aroused in man certain subjective convictions which in themselves constituted truth. Because man held "an intimate connexion and grand alliance with nature," wrote Benjamin Welles in *The Boston Monthly Anthology* for 1806, contact with it under proper conditions produced "a passion of the soul . . ., a sublime energy, without the violence of animal impulse." William H. Furness, speaking to the American Institute of Instruction in 1835, carefully described how natural scenery evoked these emotional truths and how they were verified within the mind. A "sublime and beautiful" scene, he explained, produced in the viewer a primary reaction of satisfaction, followed by a secondary and higher response deriving from "the felt presence of a power, a mind, a spirit, cherishing beauty and sublimity," which touched the emotions and released through them "an intense, uncalculating, unbounded love of truth, beauty, and good." These were the truths that lay too deep for tears.

Second, it was assumed that nature exerted a beneficent and useful force on the course of human affairs. "Kind mother" Nature, wrote R. A. Wellington in 1809, watched over her children, "helped them in their endeavors, and taught them useful lessons." The world's "great sublimity" remarked Furness, "has been prepared solely for us." Nature exists, wrote a contributor to *The Southern Review* in 1828, for "the immediate benefit and improvement of our own species." Not only do human wealth and power "depend on the skilful appropriations of the productions of nature," but nature furnished man with invaluable moral guides:

In the study of nature we tread in the footsteps of wisdom, listen to a voice which is the same yesterday, today, and forever. And while the erring opinions of man . . . pass away and are forgotten, the empire of nature is accurate, forever true . . ., forever useful.

Wordsworth's line, that "nature never did betray the heart that loved her," of course said it best, but Americans endlessly rephrased and repeated the idea. The Reverend Timothy Flint's *Lectures on Natural History* (1833) made the point that God through His creation tells man, "I have given you the faculties to perceive, and reason to reflect—the book of nature is before you . . ., replete with moral and religious lessons." Dr. William Channing (not William Ellery Channing of Boston), speaking on *The Moral Uses of Natural History* in 1835, explained that both "the smallest hand specimen of a mineral species, and the congregation of Alps . . . are related to the moral, designed to act upon it, and for the highest ends."

"The outward universe is a splendid system of signs," wrote the Reverend William Hague in 1855, by means of which one sees "the moral qualities which are beaming forth from all surrounding objects." Elihu Holland, in his *Reviews and Essays* (1849) explained how this worked. A view of the Susquehannah River, for example, furnished an analogy to life. It presented "the image of unity, a representative of human tendencies, wherein many separate strivings unite in the main current of happiness and success." The image of the river, therefore, taught the observer to "concentrate himself like a river in plans and purposes, and seek his unity in some chief end as the river seeks it in the sea."

Third, nature supplied man with proofs of God's existence, purposes, and power, and served as a primary source of His revelation. Unlike the Enlightenment, which sought this revelation through the measured teachings of the Reason, the Romantics of the nineteenth century found it in flashes of intuitive insight which rose out of the "feelings" or "sensibilities." As the Newtonians saw "evidences of Divinity" in nature, so did the Romantics; the means of perception were different. What man learned from nature came not as rational knowledge, but through what William Ellery Channing called "the sympathy that exists between the mind and the outward universe." The *Southern Review* writer of 1828, for example, found visible marks on the natural world of "the omnipotent and omniscient Creator" who had impressed his "design on the animate and inanimate portions of the material world" for the perceptive observer to find. Essayist Henry Wood found Nature "a continued Deific manifestation . . .," in which all natural forms were "visible draperies which in graceful folds thinly veil the invisible One." The minor (but popular) poet Alfred B. Street in "A Forest Nook" (a poem duplicated in any of a hundred similar collections) explained that Nature

> Tells the beauty and the harmony
> Of even the lowliest things that God hath made . . .,
> That God hath formed
> All, from the cloud-wreath'd mountain, to the grain
> Of silver sand the bubbling spring casts up,
> With deepest forethought and severest care;
> And thus these noteless, lonely things are types
> Of His perfection and divinity.

Poet David Humphreys saw "the footsteps of a present God" marked on the "vast wilds where human foot ne'er trod."

Fourth, nature satisfied man's innate aesthetic sense of beauty; it provided standards of taste and materials for the creation of beauty. "The productions of nature," wrote a critic in 1828, "are in themselves so beautiful, so diversified, so innumerable, their arrangements are so harmonious, their combinations so wonderful," that the mind eternally finds "pleasure and beauty in the contemplation and understanding of them." "Nature's volume, read aright," wrote poet George Morris,

> Attunes the soul to minstrelsy,
> Tinging life's clouds with rosy light,
> And all the world with poetry.

The Reverend William Hague thought that "to study the laws of nature is to develop the taste for beauty;" Samuel Taylor, considering "The Aesthetic Influences of Nature" in *The Christian Review* for 1856, concluded that

Just as the contemplation of the agencies which are employed by nature in producing the transformation of matter developes the reason of man (as in Chemistry, Botany, etc.) so does the contemplation of the beautiful forms which cover the surface of the earth awaken his imagination.

All this, of course, was nature seen through the prisms of the Romantic movement. It was expressed perhaps most concisely by Dr. William Channing in 1835. In answer to the query, "What does nature teach us?" he replied that through "its perfection and vastness," it teaches humility; since "it is never at fault" it teaches truth; its repose and efficiency teach "tranquillity, and harmony." Because it presents "a scene in which everything, by universal law, is active and progressive," it is proof of progress; because it "speaks of the internal Power," it is "the visible representation" of God's reality. Nature gives man rest and refreshment, "solace for the perturbation and discomfort" of life; it gives him guidance, for it "raises and purifies the affections" and teaches him "perception and employment of the beautiful." How could anything provide more, or of greater value, for man?

This view of nature dominated American writing for the next half-century. It was the concept of nature reflected by most of the major literary figures of the era (with the exception of the great nay-sayer Melville, and of Hawthorne, who explored human nature instead) and by the majority of its philosophers. This view of nature, and of its functions and meanings, infused Emerson's philosophy and gave it wholeness. His address on "The Uses of Natural History" (1833) duplicated—in better prose than most of his contemporaries could command—what his age felt about the connections that existed between man and the world. His small book *Nature,* published three years later, carried in it the germs of that religio-philosophical system called "transcendentalism," in which he worked out the full implications of the "occult relation," as he called it, that bound man and nature within the One. "Every natural process," he said, "is a version of a moral sentence. . . . All things with which we deal, preach to us." But Emerson was an ethical philosopher, rather than nature lover alone; he felt nature incomplete without man or God in it. "In the divine order," he wrote, "intellect is primary, nature secondary." And again, "The beauty of nature must always seem unreal and lacking until the landscape has human figures as good as itself."

To Emerson's younger contemporary, Henry Thoreau, nature served as law and guide; he discovered at Walden Pond the natural virtues of self-reliance, "the tonic of wildness, the inexhaustible vigor" that nature transmitted to those who understood the messages of "this vast, savage, howling mother of ours." Cooper's Leatherstocking, and his Indians too, possessed a mystic attunement with "the wonder of the woods" and saw "the hand of God in the wilderness." Natty Bumpo, wrote Cooper, "loved the woods for the impress they everywhere bore of the Divine hand of their Creator." There he communed "without the aid of forms of language, with the Infinite Source." "An open spot in a mountainside," mused Natty in *The Deerslayer,*

where a wide look can be had at the heavens and the 'arth, is a most judicious place for a man to get a just idee of the Manitous.

These ideas, which reverberated through the literature of the first half of the nineteenth century (and beyond, for that matter) were articulated most effectively in terms of the public taste by William Cullen Bryant, the American nature poet *par excellence*. In his field of nature-poetry, nobody approached Bryant in popularity; from him the average man learned how to look at nature and what to see there. Longfellow had a wider audience, but whereas Longfellow was the public poet of ethical and social attitudes, Bryant was nature-poet solely. A man of uncomplicated mind and blessed with a gift for appealing simplification, Bryant gave shape to what still remains, to a great extent, the popular American attitude toward nature. Lines from his verse fell easily from thousands of lips over the next century, and the portrait of the benign, white-bearded author of "To A Waterfowl" has looked down on thousands of schoolrooms.

What Bryant had to say about nature was easily understood. To him nature provided "a various language" (as Emerson likewise explained with greater subtlety) for the expression of human moods and values. Flowers gave Bryant analogies to deal with themes of death and transience; woodlands and trees were symbols of peace and worship; oceans and rivers were emblems of past and future. "The calm society" of nature held a curative power which refreshed and restored those bruised by the world's "guilt and misery;" the shade of the forest, he wrote in *Inscription for the Entrance to a Wood,* brought "a kindred calm" to the observer, healing his "sick heart."

Anticipating what was soon to become a major theme in American literature—the conflict of city and country values in a swiftly-urbanizing society—Bryant also saw nature as a sanctuary where the city's "sons of strife" might find refuge from "the jostling crowd." Nature too was God's "visible smile," a "visible token of the upholding love" which filled the universe, for behind the rich variety of the world of birds, flowers, and forests in which Bryant's imagination moved, he always glimpsed the Creator. "Thou art Love," he addressed God in *A Forest Hymn,* "Thou art in the soft winds/That run along the summit of these trees," speaking through Nature's "mighty voice of many tones." Thus the forest flower became "an emanation of the indwelling Life," a symbol of "the soul of this great universe" that guided man and waterfowl to their heavenly destinations.

What Bryant was to Romantic poetry, Thomas Cole was to American landscape painting. There were a number of painters, of course, of the so-called "Hudson River" school— among them Asher Durand, Thomas Doughty, Henry Inman, and George Inness—who looked at nature in the new Romantic way. Of the group Cole was the one most concerned with formulating a theory of nature and best able to articulate it. Though paintings of the American scene had been popular throughout the eighteenth century, neither painters nor purchasers seemed to be interested in nature for its aesthetic values. Artists painted particular places—farms, country houses, harbors, rivers, cities, mountains—for purposes of identification, so that the viewer might say "That's my house," or "That's Whiteface Mountain," or "This is Cohoes Falls." In the nineteenth century, however, painters began to see scenery as valuable in itself, recognizing (like the poets) that an imaginative understanding of nature produced certain artistic and moral values.

Cole read Burke and Alison, knew Wordsworth and the Lake poets well, and was a close friend of Bryant's. He knew the face of the land intimately from numerous walking tours in New York and New England, even into Pennsylvania and the Ohio backcountry. "The sublimity of untamed wildness and the majesty of eternal mountains," he wrote, furnished "an index to feelings and associations;" experience with the outside world gave the artist a means of identifying his inward topography. When Cole painted nature, it was (as he wrote in his *Essay on American Scenery* in 1836) in the belief that it yielded "an unfailing fountain of intellectual enjoyment . . ., delight and improvement, pleasure and consolation." Like Bryant, he saw in nature proof of "the harmony of creation" and "the pure creations of the Almighty;" the woods were "a fitting place," he said, "to speak of God." Asher Durand, when he put Bryant and Cole together in his famous painting, "Kindred Spirits," showing the two intent upon the view of a mountain glen spread before them, for all practical purposes summarized the concept of nature held by their generation.

While the Romantics might find sermons in stones and books in running brooks, there were other Americans (and probably many more of them) who saw nature somewhat differently, and with less sentiment. Unappropriated nature had always been a challenge to the American; taking the wild out of wilderness was part of the American ideal of progress.

To some nature might symbolize God and bring thoughts too deep for tears, but to others it spelled opportunity. It was certain to Jacksonian America that God had providentially supplied it with a plenitude of natural endowments, and it was equally the American destiny to utilize them to build a great power.

Emerson thought "commodity" the lowest of nature's uses to man; his contemporaries in business, agriculture, and industry ranked it quite possibly as the highest. Thoreau might write that nature was "more beautiful than it is useful, more to be admired than used," but the majority of his generation was busy extracting wealth and power from the land. Andrew Jackson stated the other side of the issue in his Second Inaugural very clearly:

What good man would prefer a country covered with forests and ranged by a few thousand savages to our extensive Republic, studded with cities, towns, and prosperous farms, embellished with all the improvements which art can devise or industry execute, occupied by more than twelve million people, and filled with the blessings of liberty, civilization, and religion?

Walt Whitman, who felt the good and beautiful and true in nature as much as any man, conceded in his "Song of the Redwood Tree" that the fall of the forest giant cleared the ground for progress; the spectacle was sad, perhaps, but needful for "a true America, heir to the past so grand, to build a grander future."

Thomas Ewbank, a New York engineer who made a fortune in metallic tubing and who served as United States Commissioner of Patents from 1849 to 1852, explained the Jacksonian point of view at some length in his book, *The World a Workshop: or the Physical Relation of Man to the Earth* (1855). Nature, wrote Ewbank, is "a complete machine-shop, as made manifest in its construction and factory appurtenances," to which "God its builder" has "called in man to take possession and go to work." God made all natural resources available to man, "their properties specially and wonderfully adapted to the exercise of his faculties;" nature, in other words, was meant to be exploited to the full. Proper employment of earth's "cheap store of inorganic resources" would eventually make human labor unnecessary; God placed in nature all those elements needed "to meet civilization's demands for agricultural and mechanical motors." What Ewbank said, the farmer, lumberman, miner, trapper, and entrepreneur believed—the American continent was meant by God to be used, and fortunately God had chosen them to use it. They did not hesitate to do so.

The assault on American nature that came during the latter half of the nineteenth century originated in what Stewart Udall has called the Myth of Superabundance—that peculiarly American belief that the continent contains so much of everything that anything can be infinitely used. The early settler and colonist always believed that just to the west of civilization there was more; but the eighteenth century did not possess the technology to exploit the land fully, nor the needs of a rapidly-expanding industrial society to demand its full exploitation. Crossing the Appalachian mountain barrier brought the first wave of migration to the edge of the continental heartland, facing a sea of forest and land stretched out ahead in apparently limitless expanse. Since American nature seemed inexhaustible, the pioneers acted as if it were.

The impact of the West, especially, on the American concept of superabundant nature was tremendous. The West introduced a new and distinctively frontier kind of mass attitude toward the land and its resources that continued to influence the westbound American until he reached the Pacific, and after. Francis Parkman observed, during his few months on the Oregon Trail, that the emigrants were almost wholly unaware of the country, except as something through which to pass on the way to getting some of it. Very little time was ever wasted on contemplating nature by the Western settler or politician; the Eastern intellectual's belief that nature had more uses than one simply did not hold beyond Pittsburgh. While Thoreau was at Walden, sturdy Western pioneers were already plundering the land.

The land belonged to no one and never had—neither to Church, Crown, nobility, or community. It was vulnerable; unprotected, and limitless; there were no restrictions on its use and no one responsible for its protection and preservation. Nature, in the form of land, was the West's most available resource. It served as reward for military service, as compensation for damages at law, as support for education, as source of capital to underwrite roads, canals, and railroads. It was like money in the bank, and Americans spent it for all sorts of purposes. With neither rules nor guidelines to follow, the settler had no reason to consider the West as anything more than so much raw material to be exploited here and now. A man's time and effort and profit seemed much more important than the resources at hand, so he used the resources as he pleased. Since wood ash was commercially more valuable than trees, Ohio settlers burned whole sections of forest for the ashes alone. Passenger pigeons, killed by the thousands, became hog food. California loggers, John Muir found, burned out smaller sequoias to get at the big ones, which they blasted into manageable pieces with gunpowder, wasting half the tree. If nature was to be used, the Americans used it with a vengeance, literally ripping the land to pieces, leaving the evidence still visible in the West today.

"Conquering" the West, after all, was the great American destiny. The favorite American heroes—Boone, Crockett, Carson, Buffalo Bill, the Forty-niners—were the men who could subdue it. Since the resources of the land were apparently superabundant, using them in the swiftest and most profitable manner was not considered waste, but efficiency, and much to be admired. As Gifford Pinchot wrote later, the entrepreneurs of the seventies and eighties believed that "the man who could get his hands on the biggest slice of natural resources was the best citizen," so he went West "grasping with both hands, reaping where he had not sown, wasting what he thought would last forever."

At the same time, the needs of nineteenth-century American society demanded an ever-larger utilization of the land's resources, more and more goods, machines, food, and materials.

The Myth of Superabundance came through Cumberland Gap with the first westward wave, travelled across the Mississippi with the wagons to South Pass, and moved on to the Pacific. The plainsman exploited nature as his New England and Southern colonial ancestor never did; he had better tools to do it with, and what seemed to be unlimited space to do it in. The fate of the American forest, which at the beginning of settlement covered half the American continent, showed how it was done. Prime timberland in the nineteenth century sold for five cents an acre; loggers simply burned over twenty-five million acres of forest each year and succeeded in cutting four-fifths of it all in less than a century. (Of what was once two million acres of redwoods, the United States now owns four hundred and fifty.) The buffalo hunters were mercilessly efficient, killing more than one hundred million in less than forty years and virtually extinguishing the species. The claim that "there's always more" ranged from the denuded forests of Maine to the overgrazed prairie grasslands to the redwoods of California.

There was of course bound to be a reaction to this frighteningly swift depletion of nature's resources. The word "conservation" did not appear in American usage until nearly the end of the century, but the Superabundance Myth was under fire long before that. Eroded lands, ravished forests and denuded grasslands yielded mute evidence that nothing in nature was really inexhaustible. The first stirrings came from New England and the Midwest, where lumbermen had already stripped the forests. A few state legislatures, notably in Maine, New York, and Wisconsin, began surveys of forest lands in the late eighteen-sixties; the American Forestry Association, founded in 1875, each year thereafter called attention to the need for forest management. The Federal government established a Division of Forestry in the Department of Agriculture in 1887; in 1891 Congress passed the Forest Reserve Act, under which the President could set aside timberland as national preserve. It was too late to save more than a few trees east of the Mississippi, but the movement helped to save something, at least, from the despoilers in the West.

It was not wholly accidental that Frederick Jackson Turner formed his historical thesis of the frontier at about the same time that the American conservation movement was getting under way. The vanishing wilderness called attention to the need to study and preserve something of it. That nature was useful no one doubted; that it was not inexhaustible many suspected; that it had other than commercial values Bryant and his followers had long maintained. Since the disappearance of the great American forest provided the most visible example of unchecked exploitation in action, it was the first to receive serious public attention, but interest soon shifted to other natural resources as well. In the ensuing argument over these, two schools of thought soon emerged. One believed that nature ought to be used (albeit wisely) but conserved so that it could continue to be used. The other believed that nature ought to be saved from use, preserved in its original state, kept more or less inviolate from change and interference. The differences, of course, were in matters of degree as well as aim, but they were deeply held.

Niagara Falls, the great American natural attraction, furnished a test case. Mills were established near the Falls in the eighteen-fifties, the first power plant in 1853. By the end of the Civil War, the area was so industrialized that the Falls themselves were in danger. Public petitions for their preservation, sent both to Congress and Canadian Parliament, were strongly opposed by resident business interests who hoped eventually to utilize the Falls completely. In 1879 the New York State Legislature commissioned a study of the situation, and finally, in 1885, the Falls area came under the joint protection of New York and Ontario, with the understanding that both its commercial and aesthetic importance would be recognized in future developments. Local industrial interests fought the plan bitterly, but its success marked a precedent in that it found a way to compromise opposing demands for utilization and conservation. In effect, the Niagara agreement marked the first major break in the hitherto solid front maintained by the exploiters of Superabundance.

Niagara, though, was an isolated victory. The era badly

needed new controls over obvious misuses of natural resources. That nature had spiritual and aesthetic values none doubted, for the Romantics had done their work well. Yet the public also believed that nature existed to be used, and seemed to approve unwise and wasteful methods of using it. What Americans needed was a methodology of use which combined the moral and the utilitarian, an application of the Niagara principle on a broader, even national scale. George Perkins Marsh, a New England lawyer turned geographer, believed these two aims should be combined. Man could, he said, "derive not only great instruction from studying the ways of nature, in her obscurest, humblest walks, but great material advantage for stimulating her productive energies."

Marsh's essay, "The Study of Nature," published in 1860, represented a new attitude toward nature. Marsh was willing to accept most of the Romantic apparatus of nature-philosophy, agreeing that it taught man, rejuvenated him, served him as a symbol of divinity, and so on. He also recognized that nature was a force to be mastered and utilized for man's material and social advantage. There seemed to him no reason why these concepts need be mutually exclusive. Nature, he believed, could be *both* commodity and inspiration. It could add to man's "full development and perfect growth, to his physical enjoyments and his higher aspirations" without interfering with his practical use of it. How wisely and thoroughly man employed it, Marsh concluded, was "a measure not only of his civilization, but of his progress in the highest walks of moral and intellectual life."

The results of Marsh's reflections appeared in an epoch-making book, *Man and Nature,* published in 1864 (with a revised version in 1874) in which he introduced the concept of a biotic interdependence between man and nature. Man, it seemed to Marsh, was rapidly destroying that balance; some way had to be found to restore harmony between the way man lived and the land he lived on. He should live with his natural environment as co-worker, not adversary. Marsh's book was an important scientific contribution, but beyond that it prepared the ground for compromise between the users and the savers, between conservationists and exploiters. Nature was God's gift to man, Marsh suggested, but at the same time God meant man to use it well, for "the nobler ends of his creation." Both sides could accept his conclusions, and most of all, *Man and Nature* gave the first convincing answer to the Myth of Superabundance. Nature did not automatically give up her rewards forever; it was meant to be used, but never meant to be used up.

The final stages of the settlement of the West brought the conflict to a boil. The railroad made natural resources and wonders much more available than ever before, and their despoliation that much easier. The Rockies, Yosemite, and Grand Canyon were now accessible to ordinary travellers (even Brahmin Henry Adams went west to see it) and so were the forests, streams, grasslands, minerals, and game. Painters such as George Catlin, Karl Bodmer, and Albert Bierstadt (later Remington and Russell) found new scenes worthy of their brushes in the West, while improved engraving and lithographing techniques put Western prints into thousands of homes. In the hands of such masters as T. H. O'Sullivan, Alexander Hessler, and William H. Jackson (who first took a camera to Yellowstone in 1871) photography made the West familiar to people who would never see it. The Yosemite Valley, in fact, became the first great rival to Niagara Falls as a national attraction. Horace Greeley visited it with appropriate publicity in 1859, and in 1863 Frederick Law Olmsted (who later helped to create New York's Central Park) started a successful campaign to have it made a state park—the first scenic area in the United States to be so designated. Whether this new land was to be exploited or conserved, and how it was to be used, became a major issue in the period, incidentally raising other issues still not yet solved.

The growth of cities in the late eighteenth century, combined with the rapid depletion of land in the older Eastern settlements, served to foster a "back to nature" movement in the early nineteenth as a kind of sentimental protest against an increasingly urban-centered society. The Rousseauistic conception of the "corruptions" of civilization and the virtues of "innocent" country life, augmented by the popular Romantic ideas of nature, helped to produce in Jefferson's generation a conviction that rural life was better than city life, that direct contact with nature instilled virtue, that farmers were more likely to be "good" than city-dwellers. Cities, since they were artifacts, were violations of the natural order—necessary perhaps, but artificial as opposed to "natural" in the literal sense. Jefferson thought that small landholders, not city men, were "the chosen people of God . . ., whose breasts he had made his peculiar deposit for substantial and genuine virtue." James Kirke Paulding was equally certain that since rural dwellers were "more closely connected with those operations of nature, which lead us more directly to a contemplation of the Deity," they constituted "the real wholesome strength and virtue" of the country.

Nearly everybody seemed to agree, even city-dwellers themselves. The most popular poem at the turn of the century was Englishman Robert Bloomfield's "Farmer's Boy," which went through five American editions in three years and inspired hundreds of native imitations. The "nature-heals-and-teaches" theme popularized by Bryant and his followers reinforced this refurbished pastoral tradition; Thoreau put it pithily by writing that "man's improvements simply deform the landscape and make it more and more tame and cheap." Drummed into the public by poem, essay, and oration, it became conventional to assume that country and city were unalterably opposed; natural life in the country was innocent and harmonious; soullessness and vice lived in cities. Daniel Boone, the natural man, could not abide the sound of his neighbor's axe; Cooper's Leatherstocking kept moving west toward wilderness. Like them, Americans believed that they could escape the corrosive influences of civilization by constantly renewed contact with unspoiled, original nature. There must always be a haven, wrote N. P. Willis, one of the more fashionable poets, from "the city's feverish hum" where the "prison'd soul will lift its eye" to "the immortal dream" that nature contains.

The clash of values involved in this conflict between nature and civilization was to be observed most dramatically in Henry

David Thoreau's experiment at Walden and the book which grew out of it. *Walden* established a design in nature-writing, (followed by a number of writers who did not read Thoreau deeply enough) which in turn continued the Bryant tradition and adapted it to later nineteenth-century tastes. To those who read him quickly, Thoreau seemed to stress—as Bryant had—the curative, educational, and moral uses of nature, put into convincing and muscular prose. "The stillness, solitude, and wildness of nature," he wrote in 1857, "is a kind of thoroughwort, a boneset to my intellect." Again, "Our life would stagnate if it were not for the unexplored forests and meadows which surround it. We need the tonic of wildness. We can never have enough of nature." Or, as he saw the wreckage left by loggers in Maine, he wrote in a passage still quoted by conservationists:

The pine is no more lumber than man is, and to be made into boards and houses is no more its true and highest use than the truest use of a man is to be cut down and made into manure. There is a higher law affecting our relation to pines as well as to men. A pine cut down, a dead pine, is no more a pine than a dead human carcass is a man. . . . Every creature is better alive than dead, men and moose and pine trees, and he who understands it aright would rather preserve its life than destroy it.

What Thoreau said seemed especially appropriate to an era beginning to question the Myth of Superabundance and disturbed by the ravages of exploitation. The Concord rebel's example encouraged a whole new school of nature writers who filled the magazines with essays patterned on *Walden*. The nature-essay, in fact, soon became an established literary form; an article in 1902 listed among its practitioners such once-popular, now half-remembered names as Ernest Ingersoll, Mary Austin, E. H. Forbush, William Leon Dawson, F. Schuyler Mathews, Charles G. D. Roberts, James Lane Allen, Ernest Thompson Seton, Frank Chapman, and of course the two best-known of all, John Burroughs and John Muir.

Burroughs, born in 1837, was the first of the later nineteenth-century nature writers to attract a wide audience. A clerk in the Treasury Department, he retired to an upstate New York farm in 1873 to turn out a succession of popular volumes, among them *Birds and Poets* (1877), *Indoor Studies* (1889), and *Ways of Nature* (1905), until his death in 1921. He knew Bryant like a book, and admired Emerson and Thoreau, though he penetrated but little beneath the surface of either. Burroughs was an "appreciator," he said, an observer who had a knack for expressing in misty language what the average man might see in nature in his more reflective and sentimental moments. What he did best was to identify for his readers the significant point about a natural fact or event, much in the manner currently made fashionable in Europe by Fabre and Maeterlinck. Burroughs humanized and personalized nature, once remarking to a friend that the nature-lover could "have but one interest in nature, namely to see himself reflected and interpreted there." Like Bryant, he saw parallels between "life" and "nature," and drew from them "nourishing truths." Though Burroughs did little more than restate most of the themes already common to American nature-writing since the eighteenth century, his popularity did a great deal to preserve them in their traditional form after Bryant and his school fell out of fashion.

A much more influential figure was John Muir, who, while more of a mystic than Burroughs, was less the sentimentalist. Unlike Burroughs, Muir was a naturalist with sound scientific training in botany, zoology, geography, and geology. He did field work in the South, Alaska, South Africa, Switzerland, and Australia, but his heart always belonged to California and the Sierras. Burroughs once said that Muir was "mountain drunk," with "a far-away look in his eyes," and it is true that he was capable of writing oleaginous prose about his beloved mountains, such as his description of the Sierras as a place where

peace will flow into you as sunshine flows into trees. The winds will blow their own freshness into you, and the storms their energy, while cares will drop away like autumn leaves.

Nature, Muir believed, responded to the scientist and to the philosopher (as he used the term) by showing both a world created by a loving deity for man's benefit. "I invite you to join me," he once wrote Ralph Waldo Emerson (who could not come) "in a month's worship with Nature in the high temples of the Sierra Crown beyond our holy Yosemite. It will cost you nothing save the time, and very little of that for you will be mostly in eternity."

Muir's constant theme was man's meanness in contrast to Nature's perfection; the ideal harmony and balance of the natural world should be the pattern for man's. Commercialism, vanity, insensitivity, fear, meanness of soul—these keep man from knowing nature and from utilizing her resources of vitality and virtue. An organizer and publicist of no small gifts, Muir threw himself into the battle for conservation and became one of the movement's most powerful leaders. As it turned out, he had an important role in the establishment of eight national parks, Sequoia, Yosemite, Mount Rainier, Crater Lake, Glacier, Mesa Verde, Olympic, and Grand Canyon.

The vogue of the Burroughs-Muir school of nature-writing encouraged the parallel development of a nature-study program in the schools. If an acquaintance with nature had educative and sanitative effects, as the naturists claimed, it seemed imperative that instruction in how to know nature be included in the educational curriculum. The first courses in "nature study" were introduced during the eighties into schools in New York and Illinois by H. H. Straight and Wilbur Jackman; Jackman also published a set of study aids for nature classes in 1890 and the first textbook in the field, *Nature Study for the Common Schools,* in 1894. Another popular text, William Lange's *Handbook of Nature Study,* appeared in 1898, aimed at teaching the child "the relations of plant and animal life to the welfare and happiness of man;" a thorough understanding of nature, said another text, lay at "the foundations of an education," since it helped the child "to orient himself in his environment, discover its relationship to him, and his relationship to it." David Starr Jordan, president of Stanford University and a noted scientist, made "Nature Study and Moral Culture" the subject of his address to the National Educational Association in 1896, a thoughtful and penetrating analysis of the place of nature-study in the curriculum. The movement grew so swiftly in the schools that Columbia Teachers College in 1905 founded a journal, *The Nature Study Review,* to serve the teachers who formed a professional association, The American Nature Study Society, in 1908. John Burroughs gave the movement his approval, emphasizing the need to train children in "that sympathetic and emotional intercourse with nature which soothes and enriches the soul." The value of nature-study in the schools, *The Outlook* explained in 1901, was

> to give to the child an idea of the great world in which he lives, to help him to understand and appreciate its beauty and wonder, and by a contemplation of the relations of living things to each other, to enable him to get a broader conception of his own life . . ., the laws of right living, and of good government.

The most influential figure in the nature-study movement was Liberty Hyde Bailey, a brilliant agronomist who had a wide following as a nature-writer. His approach to nature, like Burroughs', was essentially didactic and emotional, tinged with pantheistic overtones reminiscent of early nineteenth-century Romanticism. "Earth is good, it is kindly, it is holy," he wrote in *The Holy Earth* (1915), replete with "objects of moral significance" which give man "spiritual refreshment" and "moral strength." Returning to nature "cured the ills of civilization," he wrote in his *Outlook to Nature* (1905), as "one of the means of restoring balance and proportion to our lives." Bailey had nothing new to say about nature, but his book, *The Nature-Study Idea* (1905) made a strong argument for teaching the Burroughs-Muir-Bryant concept in the schools, not as science, he wrote, but as "nature-sympathy, whose very essence is spirit. All the senses should be so trained that all our world becomes alive to us."

"It is due every child," Bailey wrote in his book, which became a kind of Bible to nature-study teachers, "That his mind be opened to the voices of nature . . ., to put the pupil in a sympathetic attitude toward nature for the purpose of increasing his joy of living." Since Bailey taught at Cornell, whose School of Agriculture published and distributed hundreds of thousands of copies of nature-study pamphlets to schools, his influence on the teaching of such courses was very large. However, by the time of the World War their popularity had begun to wane in favor of general science courses, whose aim was less to arouse sympathy with nature than to stress the functional understanding of some of the principles and generalizations of the natural sciences. During the nineteen-twenties "nature study" became largely absorbed into science, geography, or biology courses. In 1963, a curriculum survey could find fewer than twenty courses resembling "nature study" taught in the entire country.

The same public interest that provided an audience for Burroughs, Muir, and other popularizers (such as Ernest Thompson Seton, whose *Wild Animals I Have Known* was a wild best-seller) furnished the impetus for the growth of public parks, where the populace might find relief from the presumed pressures and vices of city life. The belief that natural virtues were lost in urban surroundings—deeply rooted in the city-country conflict of the eighteenth century—encouraged nature lovers to agitate for the creation of places where, as Frederick Law Olmsted said, "tired workers" could retire to observe "specimens of God's handiwork." Many Eastern cities possessed a commons, preserved from the seventeenth and eighteenth centuries, which by accident (after sheep and cattle no longer grazed in cities) turned into parks. Vacant lots and undeveloped sections on the city's fringes served the same purpose, but by the eighteen-forties such open spaces were fast disappearing, and what remained was usually too valuable to be turned over to public use.

In New York, Boston, and Philadelphia it was necessary to travel far out of the city to find an expanse of greensward for strolling. Weekend visitors thronged the cemeteries—the only open spaces easily available within the cities—so much so that Boston's Mount Auburn cemetery, for example, drew nearly 60,000 visitors in 1849. If the natural attractions of cemeteries brought thousands each week, it seemed obvious that parks for live people should attract more. "Plant spacious parks in your cities," wrote the famous landscape architect Andrew Jackson Downing, "and unclose the gates of morning to the whole people." If city dwellers could have direct experience with nature, Downing believed, it would "civilize and refine the national character," throughout the land.

Through the efforts of Bryant, Downing, Washington Irving, and like-minded New Yorkers, the city in 1851 began to purchase the land which two years later became Central Park, usually considered the first large public area specifically designed as a city park. The Report of the Park Commission in 1857 clearly stated what the commissioners believed to be the advantages of providing such urban contacts with nature—to make "necessary sanitary provision for the inhabitants of all such large towns, and the extension of natural enjoyment—regarded as a great preventive of vice and crime." Philadelphia's Fairmount Park opened in 1867, Boston's Franklin Park in 1883, and other cities established parks thereafter. Olmsted's landscape firm of Olmsted and Vaux in 1882, for example, handled park projects in fifteen cities; Olmsted himself did the National Capitol grounds, the Chicago World's Fair, and major park systems in Boston, Pittsburgh, and Baltimore. It was generally agreed that such parks, as Frank Waugh wrote in 1912, were "great curative agencies" for urban social ills, with "almost unthinkable sanitative powers of regeneration . . ., when a man's brains and nerves have become so clogged and worn by city excitements that they can no longer perform their functions."

The concept of nationally-owned parks, dedicated to the preservation of natural surroundings and striking natural scenes, was of course implicit in American nature-writing from Audubon on. Congress in 1832 made Hot Springs, Arkansas, a "national reservation," the first official congressional act conserving a natural resource, but no one considered it as the beginning of a national policy. Thoreau and Marsh both made recommendations for some kind of federally-controlled system of natural reservations, but the germ of the national park system really lay in a report made by the ubiquitous Frederick

Law Olmsted, *The Yosemite Valley and the Mariposa Big Trees,* in 1865. Olmsted visited Yosemite, the first of the Western natural wonders to attract wide attention, in 1863, and, anxious to preserve it for the future, initiated efforts to have it made public property. His report, based directly on contemporary attitudes toward nature, formulated a philosophy for a national park system still generally accepted as valid. Constant reference to nature, wrote Olmsted, is necessary to man's well-being:

The occasional contemplation of natural scenes of an impressive character . . . is favorable to the health and vigor of men, and especially to the health and vigor of their intellect beyond any other conditions which can affect them. . . . If we analyze the operation of scenes of beauty upon the mind and consider the ultimate reaction of the mind upon the nervous system and the whole physical economy, the reinvigoration which results from such scenes is readily comprehended.

Olmsted was not alone in his admiration for Yosemite, for Congress ceded the Yosemite Valley to California, which retained it as a state park until the Federal Government took it back as a national preserve in 1890. Meanwhile, agitation over the fate of Yellowstone led Congress to create Yellowstone Park in 1872; Mackinac Island was so designated in 1875, Sequoia and General Grant Parks in 1890, and a succession of others followed, totaling thirty-seven by 1916. That year, in creating the National Park Service, Congress finally tied the entire system of separate parks together and made it possible to evolve a unified park policy, whose dominant purpose, as the Service still defines it, is to provide for the public that "refreshment of mind and spirit" of which Olmsted wrote in 1865.

It is clear from the historical record that beginning about 1870 there was a growing public consciousness of the rate at which the nation's natural resources were being consumed. Efforts to protect and preserve the country's natural endowments came from many sources, public and private, though with far more determination from the latter. The forces of exploitation, represented by lumbering, mining, cattle, and industrial interests, were well-organized, well-financed, and solidly entrenched in the state legislatures and in Congress. The opposition was scattered and without effective political influence.

Still, there were signs of encouragement. Men such as Burroughs and Muir, and the school of nature writers that grew up around them in the eighties and nineties, carried weight with the public. A few influential men in political life were aware of the problem and tried, without much success, to do something about an answer. Congress in 1872 passed a Mineral Lands Act and in 1878 a Timber and Stone Act, both vaguely worded and easily eluded, but their passage showed that Congress had some glimmerings of understanding concerning the issue. Carl Schurz, who served briefly as Secretary of the Interior under Hays, in his report of 1877 pointed his finger directly at the lumber industry's gargantuan theft of the American forests, and though Congress squelched him, still for the first time a governmental agency had named names and placed responsibility for the nation's natural resources where it belonged.

For thirty years after the close of the Civil War, however, the naturalists and conservationists accomplished little except to begin the task of organization. The American Association for the Advancement of Science memorialized Congress in 1873 and 1875 on forest preservation, and the American Forestry Association, organized in 1875, began active work as a pressure group. The Appalachian Mountain Club, founded in 1876, was the earliest of a number of private groups dedicated to saving the national domain, among them Muir's Sierra Club (1892), the American Scenic and Historic Preservation Society (1895), and the American Park and Outdoor Society (1897). Meanwhile, Secretary John Noble of the Interior Department, by attaching a last-minute rider to a public lands bill in the Congressional session of 1891, obtained one of the most important pieces of conservation legislation ever passed—the Forest Reserve Act by which the President could set aside timberlands as national preserves. (At the time, ironically, the entire Federal Government employed exactly one professionally-trained forest specialist.) But for the most part, there were few victories for conservationists before 1900.

It was also clear after 1890 that there were two different—though not necessarily opposed—attitudes toward American nature, both deriving from respectable historical precedents. On the one hand were those who thought that nature should be considered as a sanctuary, a place where men might find the curative, educative, and moralistic values of nature, and through it perhaps make contact with deity. Unspoiled natural surroundings, Alfred Baker said at the National Conservation Congress of 1910, was "a moral tonic for a failing America." This group, of which Muir was the acknowledged leader, comprised the lineal descendants of Bryant, Emerson, Thoreau, and the nineteenth-century Romantics.

The other school of thought derived from Marsh and the utilizers. To them nature was perhaps a temple, but more importantly it was a workshop, as Ewbank had considered it long before. Nature was something to be controlled, managed, and used in a fashion consistent with the highest and broadest public interest. Though by no means unmindful of the moralistic and aesthetic qualities of the natural world, they were also well aware of its utility. Make nature serve man, said Marsh—but use it intelligently and efficiently. Use, not abuse—contemplate it if you will, but preserve and protect it so that it may continue to have a useful function.

Leadership in this group came chiefly from professional and scientific men from engineering, economics, forestry, geology, anthropology, and so on. To them the issue of conservation was an economic and social, not a sentimental or aesthetic one. Richard T. Ely, the crusading Wisconsin economist who had a hand in almost every reform of the period, defined conservation as "the preservation in unimpaired efficiency of the resources of the earth." Natural resources, said the National Conservation Association in 1908, should be "developed for the promotion of the public welfare, without waste, destruction, or needless impairment." Their aim, wrote another conservation leader, was "to insure society at least as great a future benefit from the exploitation of natural resources as is now enjoyed." None of this was language that John Muir and his fellow nature-writers could understand or approve.

The outstanding example of this "scientific" attitude toward conservation was Gifford Pinchot, a young Yale graduate who was appointed Chief Forester in the Department of Agriculture in 1898. An intense, scholarly, aggressive man, Pinchot had studied forest management in Europe, where there were few national parks and no tradition of preserving areas in their natural state. Though no man had a greater feeling for nature than he, Pinchot believed that conservation meant *use*. The word stood, he wrote, "for the same kind of practical common sense management of this country by the people that every business man stands for in the handling of his own business." As Chief of the Forest Service from 1898 to 1910, and especially by reason of his close association with Theodore Roosevelt, Pinchot was by any measure the second most powerful figure in the successful conservation movement of those years and after.

First, of course, was Roosevelt. Before he entered the Presidency he had been traveller, sportsman, avid nature-lover, and better-than-average amateur scientist. (His first publication, in fact, was a Long Island bird-list, done as a boy.) He had camped and hunted through the East and West, raised cattle in North Dakota, and visited almost all the natural wonders of the United States. He knew Burroughs, Seton, Muir, and others of the naturist school of writers well; his own attitudes toward nature, until the late nineties, tended to reflect theirs. As President, however, and perhaps under the influence of Pinchot, he began to see the conservation issue in other terms. The California redwoods, he said in 1903, ought to be preserved for their aesthetic and spiritual values, certainly, but also because it was the *practical* thing to do—"There is nothing more practical," he wrote, "in the end than the preservation of beauty." Later he paid less attention to the contemplative and more to the utilitarian aspects of nature. Conservation, he said in 1908, involved "the problem of national efficiency, the patriotic duty of insuring the safety and continuance of the nation." A year later he wrote that the Federal Government should, in handling its natural resources, "proceed as a private businessman would. . . . He will regularly take account of stock so that he may know just where he stands."

The inevitable clash between these two different attitudes toward American nature came quite early in Roosevelt's second administration. San Francisco (and as it turned out, a number of private companies too) wanted to flood a portion of the Yosemite Valley called Hetch Hetchy for purposes of the city water supply. Proponents of the plan (who later included Senator George Norris, the father of TVA) were not by any means all of them greedy capitalists. The Hetch Hetchy valley, they agreed, was virtually inaccessible to recreational use, extremely hot in summer, snowbound in winter, and not necessary to the beauty of Yosemite itself.

Precisely because it *was* primitive and wild, the opponents of the plan protested. John Muir, Frederick Law Olmsted, Junior, most of the conservation organizations, and several influential journals opposed the idea bitterly, until by 1906 the Hetch Hetchy issue had attained national prominence. Muir, in the forefront of the battle, inveighed against "the temple destroyers, devotees of a raging commercialism," who had "a perfect contempt for nature, and instead of lifting their eyes to the God of the mountains, lift them to the Almighty dollar." Speaking for the other side, Representative Martin Dies of Texas claimed that since "God Almighty has located the resources of this country in such a form that his children will not use them in disproportion," they ought to use them. Amid cries of "nature lover" and "desecrator" the dispute dragged on, with Pinchot and Roosevelt, the two most powerful national figures in the conservation movement, pointedly remaining out of it. Finally in 1913 the Hetch Hetchy Bill passed Congress, a year before Muir died.

Most of the principles which have governed the conservation of natural resources during the twentieth century were laid down during the period of Roosevelt's administrations, and reflect the point of view held by Roosevelt, Pinchot, and the scientific conservationists. There is still strong opposition to them from the descendants of Muir, who have won more than a few victories. Clubs and societies sprang up in profusion after 1900, dedicated to one or the other point of view—the American Civic Association, the National Association of Audubon Societies, the American Game Association, the Save the Redwoods League, the American Shore and Beach Association, and the Izaak Walton League, to name a few which still exert tremendous influence on legislation. Roosevelt effectively channeled the stream of public opinion toward conservation and helped to make the nation nature-conscious. His most dramatic act, no doubt, was the White House Conference of 1908, at which state governors, representatives of various associations, government officials, and scientists gathered to discuss conservation policies. (John Muir was not invited.) This conference, planned and executed by Pinchot, published three volumes of reports and laid the groundwork for legislation for years to come. From it came the National Conservation Commission and later the National Conservation Association.

What Roosevelt did, in effect, was to merge the American feeling for nature with his crusade for popular democracy; he made conservation a part of progressivism, and put it into party platforms as an actual political plank. For too long, he told the voter, big-money raiders had stolen the public's natural birthright; the despoiler must not be allowed "to injure the future of the Republic for his own present profit." Roosevelt gave conservation a kind of moral commitment and put the exploiters on the defensive. He never said, nor did he believe, that the land should not be used; the issue simply was, who should gain most from its use, public or private interests?

The attitude toward nature represented by the conservationists of Roosevelt's and Pinchot's time has continued to dominate the policies of both Federal and state governments. The term *conservation,* and what it implies about nature's use and function, retains today much the same meaning that Pinchot gave it—that is, the managed utilization of nature and the maintenance of its productivity in the public interest. Conservation is "the wise use of nature," writes one authority, "for the proper purpose at the proper time;" it means "maximum benefit from the use of natural resources," writes another. R. C. Lynch, speaking to the Sierra Club of Wisconsin in 1964, summarized it by saying:

Natural resources, it must be emphasized, have no value, either economic or esthetic, except as they are useful to people. Conservation cannot have any real meaning other than wise use. But this should not mean use merely for monetary profit. The use may vary from the mere viewing of natural beauty to the excavation of ore, the damming of a river, or the harvesting of timber to satisfy human needs.

The most comprehensive illustration of this point of view is the Tennessee Valley Authority. Though TVA's chief function may have been the production of power, it became almost equally one of conservation, involving the restoration of depleted resources and the more efficient use of them for public benefit. In 1964 the proponents of Rampart Dam in Alaska advanced the same arguments as those justifying Hetch Hetchy in 1910 and TVA in 1933. A dam "in this isolated wilderness," wrote Senator Ernest Gruening, "would provide Alaska with a prosperous economy, enhancing the natural resources of the Yukon Flats, adding recreational values . . . and new opportunities for water sports." "As a conservationist," the Senator continued, "I believe it is folly to allow waters of the Yukon to flow wastefully to the sea. . . . Alaskans, strong believers in conservation, know Rampart Dam will further this cause while greatly benefiting the species known as *homo sapiens.*"

In effect, the contemporary concept of conservation, and the attitude toward nature that it implies, is an extension of the ancient and honorable American tradition of exploitation —conceived with breadth and sophistication certainly, but still rooted in the belief that nature is a commodity that exists to be used. It is the question of how, and how much, and for whom it is to be used, of course, that separates the modern conservationist from the Jamestown settler, but those are differences of degree rather than of intent.

The contemporary view holds that the overriding interest

in the exploitation of nature is public rather than private; it holds too, that the Myth of Superabundance is only a myth, and a dangerous one at that. The American of today, much as he hopes to profit from the utilization of nature's goods, knows that the supply is not inexhaustible and that certain kinds of natural damage are irreparable. As it did not do until Theodore Roosevelt's time, both Federal and state governments have assumed direct and powerful roles in creating and executing conservationist policy. It is the responsibility of government, wrote President Kennedy in 1962, to guarantee to the people "the wise use of our natural environment [by] the prevention of waste and despoilment while preserving, improving, and renewing the quality and usefulness of our resources." Kennedy not only appointed Stewart Udall of Arizona, a leader in the conservationist movement, to the Secretaryship of the Interior, but called the first White House Conference on Conservation held since Roosevelt's in 1908. President Lyndon Johnson not only gave over a Presidential message to the cause of conservation, but called a "national beauty" Conference for 1965.

Contemporary attitudes toward nature and its use, however, have been complicated by economic, social, and technological factors at work since Pinchot's time which have powerfully influenced the American's use of this natural environment. An expanding population and higher living standards have increased modern society's demands on nature to the point that—even with protection—its resources are being used faster than they can be renewed. Studies such as Fairfield Osborn's *Our Plundered Planet* (1948) and William Vogt's *Road to Survival* (1948), have pointed out the rapid depletion of natural resources, while Rachel Carson's *Silent Spring* (1962) drew spectacular attention to new problems created by society's increased ability to interfere with nature's processes.

The single fact of the existence of the automobile has had tremendous influence in making American nature everywhere more accessible; in 1960, there were fewer than a half-dozen places in the United States more than ten miles from a road.

The railroad and the automobile have created the "tourist trade," now a major source of income to a large segment of the population, which in turn has raised a whole new set of questions about land use. The presence of a hundred thousand campers, hunters, and fishermen, and sightseers in an area considerably changes one's concept of it as "nature." Since the National Park System alone handled eight million visitors in 1962, with prospects of increased attendance each year in the foreseeable future, the simple question of space, to say nothing of others more complicated, becomes a vital one.

On the other hand, whatever the triumphs of the "scientific" conservationists since Hetch Hetchy, the Romantic tradition of Bryant and Muir has by no means disappeared. (Muir himself, for that matter, was honored by a commemorative postage stamp in 1964.) The United States of the sixties is in the grip of a cult of nature as powerful as any that the nineteenth century produced. Americans are exhorted by travel clubs, recreation societies, nature-study leagues, tourist councils, fish-and-game clubs, and even by Presidential Advisory Committees to make love of nature a national policy. The *Conservation Yearbook* for 1962 listed (exclusive of all government agencies, national, state, and local) eighty-nine *national* and two hundred and twenty-two *private* organizations, ranging from the Central Ohio Angler's Club to the powerful National Wildlife Association, all concerned with the study and use of nature.

"The outdoors lies deep in the American tradition," writes *Outdoor Recreation*; for "our spiritual and physical well-being," says *Living Wilderness,* we must "strengthen our religious convictions by contact with the wilderness." "We must preserve those places," writes the Governor of Oregon, "where we can go for self-refreshment . . ., where creative and spiritual forces can be recharged and revitalized." A new religion of nature is in the making, established on principles and couched in language that William Cullen Bryant would have recognized—and some of which he could easily have used. Devotion to nature has been linked with a pervasive nostalgia for a fast-disappearing past that was presumably "close to nature" and therefore simpler, more virtuous, and somehow more American.

This reinvigorated Romanticism is exemplified in a new wave of nature writers, spiritual descendants of Burroughs and Muir who, though considerably more sophisticated, approach nature in essentially the same way. Such men as Adolph and Olaus Murie, Edwin Way Teale, Roger Peterson, Sigurd Olson, Joseph Wood Krutch, Hal Borland, Wallace Stegner, E. B. White (and such professionally-trained naturalists as the late Robert Marshall and Aldo Leopold) stand directly in the tradition that stems from Bryant and Thoreau. To them nature heals, teaches, guides, refreshes, gives moral solace, and trails divinity just as it did a century and a half ago. Contact with nature, wrote Robert Marshall, brings relief from "the terrible neural tensions of modern existence." "Man is whole," writes Supreme Court Justice William O. Douglas, "when he is in tune with the winds, the stars, and the hills." The intangibles of nature, writes Sigurd Olson (perhaps the most eloquent and thoughtful of the group) lie in "the opportunity of knowing what simplicity really means, the importance of the natural, the sense of oneness with the earth" —which might have come from Thoreau.

The clash of country and city values is a common theme in contemporary writing as it was in Emerson's day. Quotations from Wordsworth, Bryant, and Thoreau on the illnesses of urban life spring up in profusion in the nature magazines. The Wilderness Society's journal, *Living Wilderness,* is filled with references to the "noise and clutter" of city life and "the brutalizing pressures of spreading metropolitan civilization." Instead of surrendering to "the stress and strain of our urbanized, industrialized, mechanized civilization," writes Howard Zahniser in "Our World and Its Wildness," Americans ought to "seek instead that true understanding . . . drawn from an awareness of the great continuity of life on this earth." The Federal Housing Act of 1961, under its Open Space Land Program, has purchased park space within cities whenever possible, so that there may be, as John White of the Park Service wrote, "sequestered spots where man may get away from crowds to say with Wordsworth, 'Ne'er saw I, never felt, a calm so deep!' "

The new gospel of nature has been most clearly articulated in the so-called "wilderness movement," which represents a powerful countervailing force to the conservation-for-use school of thought that has dominated Federal and state policy over the past fifty years. The belief that nature exists only for man's use, however wise that use may be, wrote Rachel Carson in *Silent Spring,* is one "conceived in arrogance, born of the Neanderthal age of biology and philosophy, when it was supposed that nature exists for the convenience of man." The proponents of the wilderness movement do not regard man as the ultimate consumer. Their aim, as defined by the Wilderness Society (established in 1935), is to preserve the remaining relatively inaccessible areas of the country from further development, treating wilderness itself as a natural resource to be maintained as nearly as possible in its original primeval state. Unlike the park and recreational system, these wilderness areas are to be set apart from all but minimal use as places where, Bernard DeVoto once wrote, the visitor "may discover the simple experience of uncontaminated nature."

The movement has been marked by a strong undercurrent of mysticism reminiscent of Muir. Wilderness, writes Wallace Stegner, is an indefinable yet necessary ingredient in the spiritual life. Experience with nature primitive, unspoiled, free from human intervention, gives us

the chance to see ourselves single, separate, vertical and individual in the world, part of the environment of trees and rocks and soil, brother to the other animals, part of the natural world and competent to belong in it.

In the presence of wildness, says Sigurd Olson, carrying with it "that intangible sense of remoteness and solitude," people may "gain perspective and a sense of oneness with mountains, forests, and waters [*that*] enriches their lives."

Beginning in 1924 with the establishment of a portion of Gila National Park as wilderness area, the wilderness movement has gained wide support among wild-life associations and the general public. The National Park Service by 1957 had already designated fourteen million acres of land as wilderness or primitive areas. That year Senator Hubert Humphrey of Minnesota introduced a bill to establish a National Wilderness Preservation System, composed of public lands which still retained their primitive environment, to be kept "unimpaired for future use and enjoyment as wilderness." The bill's public reception illustrated what A. W. Smith, president of the National Parks Association, called "a basic shift of deep-seated attitudes toward nature, not conquest, but empathy, appreciation, enjoyment."

Subsequent discussions of this Wilderness Bill evoked in Congress some of the most thickly sentimental oratory of the past hundred years. Senator Frank Church of Idaho felt that these preserves would provide for "all those who find, in high and lonely places, a refreshment of spirit and life's closest communion with God." Senator Wayne Morse of Oregon thought the system would uplift campers, since "you cannot associate with the grandeur of this great heritage which God Almighty has given the American people and not come out of such a trip a better man or woman for having come that close to the spirit of the Creator." Secretary of the Interior Udall, a nature-writer of parts himself, believed that wilderness represents "a benchmark, a check of natural conditions against which they measure the soundness of values:"

In the wilderness is a standard of health, a yardstick of balance and order, essential to biologists, ecologists, and naturalists, as well as to the individual who needs a moment to stand vertical, free, alone, and to relearn what he honestly is.

The bill, which passed in 1964 (in company with a Land and Water Conservation Fund Act), includes more than nine million acres of National Forest Lands, principally in the West and Midwest; an additional five million acres in North Carolina and New Hampshire may be added later.

The beliefs which lie beneath the Wilderness Bill are

deeply ingrained in the American consciousness, as a study made at Glacier National Park in 1960 illustrated. A ranger interviewed three hundred and fifty visitors who made extended trips into the park's interior, with illuminating results. To some nature afforded "a temporary refuge" from "the stresses of life . . ., an important antidote which relieves or prevents stress through the healing powers of natural surroundings." Others experienced spiritual uplift in the mountains, reporting that "natural beauty . . . caused them to feel that there is a Supreme Being, a power beyond." Some described their pleasures at finding "the world of nature" opposed to "the artificialities of civilization;" others found aesthetic appeal in "the unspoiled beauty of Nature's grandeur." No doubt some of the less articulate merely wanted to go fishing, but the general consensus might well have been quoted directly from almost any nature poem or essay published in the nineteenth century.

The duality of the American attitude toward nature of course, is inherent. It has been clear in the American strain since the beginning. As the settlers saw it at Jamestown and Plymouth, the land is to be used; as the conservationists of Pinchot's time and after see it, it is to be used wisely. As the Romantic naturists of Bryant's generation saw it, the land is to be used for purposes beyond material profit and pleasure; as contemporary believers in the values of wilderness see it, these purposes transcend mere utilization with higher moral and spiritual compensations. So nothing has really changed. Nature is still to the American a function and a symbol, a fact and a value, a tool and an idea.

BIBLIOGRAPHICAL ACKNOWLEDGEMENTS

The most comprehensive treatment of the idea of nature in the American past is Hans Huth, *Nature and the American* (Berkeley, California, 1957). Stewart Udall's book, *The Quiet Crisis* (New York, 1963) is an excellent introduction to the topic, while John Ise, *Our National Park Policy* (Baltimore, 1961) is a critical history. Arthur E. Ekirch, Jr., *Man and Nature in America* (New York,

1963) is a sound and useful treatment, combining history-of-ideas technique with historical information. David Lowenthal has three articles which suggest a number of interesting avenues for exploration: "The American Image of Nature as Virtue," *Landscape* IX (Winter, 1959-60) 16-26; "Not Every Prospect Pleases," *ibid.*, XII (Winter, 1962-63) 19-23; and "Is Wilderness Paradise Enow?" *Columbia University Forum* VII (Spring, 1964) 34-44. Early attitudes toward nature are considered in Huth's book; Perry Miller's chapter VIII of *The New England Mind* (New York, 1939) is a brief analysis of the Puritan and nature. N. Bryllion Fagin, *William Bartram* (Baltimore, 1933) is the best study of the Quaker naturalist, whereas Ernest Earnest, *John and William Bartram* (Philadelphia, 1940) adds information on eighteenth-century natural science. Perry Miller's essay, "The Romantic Dilemma in American Nationalism and the Concept of Nature," *Harvard Theological Review* XLVIII (October, 1955) 239-53, is a key treatment of early romantic nature-writing. David Lowenthal's study, *George Perkins Marsh, Versatile Vermonter* (New York, 1958), and Marsh's own essay, "The Study of Nature," *Christian Examiner* CCXVII (January, 1860) 33-63, are the best sources of information about the ideas of this important figure. E. C. Oberholtzer, "The Chronicle of the Olmsteds," *Living Wilderness* XXIII (Spring, 1958) is a useful study of father and son. Charles Mason Dow, *Anthology and Bibliography of Niagara Falls* (Albany, 1921, 2 volumes) is a fascinating compilation of visitors' impressions over three hundred years.

There are a great number of studies of the conservation movement, of which some of the more useful are David C. Coyle, *Conservation: An American Story* (New Brunswick, 1957); Joseph King, *The Conservation Fight from Theodore Roosevelt to TVA* (Washington, 1959); A. F. Gustafson, H. Ries, C. H. Guise, and W. J. Hamilton, eds., *Conservation in the United States* (Ithaca, 1939); and Samuel P. Hays, *Conservation and the Gospel of Efficiency* (Cambridge, Mass., 1959). Gifford Pinchot's own *Breaking Ground* (New York, 1947) is of course primary material, and John Burroughs' estimate of Roosevelt, "President Roosevelt as Nature Lover and Observer," *Outlook* LXXXVI (July 13, 1907) 547-53, is an interesting interpretation. The nature-writers of the nineteenth century are treated in Norman Foerster, *Nature in American Literature* (New York, 1923); Philip M. Hicks, *The Development of the Natural History Essay in American Literature* (Philadelphia, 1924); Henry C. Tracy, *American Naturists* (New York, 1930); and in Francis W. Halsey, "The Rise of The Nature Writers," *Review of Reviews* XXVI (November, 1902) 567-71. The nature-study movement in education is treated in H. S. Good, *A History of American Education* (New York, 1963), with additional source material to be found in John Burroughs' "Nature Study," *Outlook* LXI (February 4, 1899) 326-28; and Henry S. Curtis, "Nature Study," *Educational Review* LXIII (April, 1922) 307-14. R. G. Lynch, "Conservation by and for the People," *Wisconsin Academy Review* XII (Spring, 1965) 30-33, provides a good statement of the conservation-for-use philosophy. Excellent sources of information on the contemporary back-to-nature wilderness movement are the files of such journals as *Living Wilderness, Outdoor Recreation, Audubon Magazine, The Natural Parks Magazine,* and any number of publications issued by the national and state park services. Especially good examples are: Robert Marshall, "The Problem of Wilderness," *Scientific Monthly* XXX (February, 1930) 141-48; Aldo Leopold, "Wilderness Values," *Living Wilderness* VII (March, 1942) 24-26; Sigurd Olson, "The Preservation of Wilderness," *ibid.*, XIII (Autumn, 1948) 1-4; Howard Zahniser, "Our World and its Wilderness," *ibid.*, XIX (Summer, 1954) 36-37; Robert McConnell Hatch, "Progress and Human Needs," *ibid.*, XXIV (Summer, 1959) 1-4, and Joseph Wood Krutch, "Man, Nature and the Universe," *Audubon Magazine* LXIV (May, 1962) 103-110. Sigurd Olson's superbly-written *The Lonely Land* (New York, 1961) is the best modern statement of this view of nature. *Life Magazine's* "Heirs of a Great Tradition," LI (Dec. 22, 1961) 103-110 is a review of contemporary nature writing and Wallace Stegner's "Whatever Happened to the Great Outdoors?" *Saturday Review,* (May 27, 1965) is a good contemporary estimate of the current issues. Ranger Daniel Henning's survey of Glacier visitors, "Evaluations of the Backcountry," is in *Living Wilderness* XXV (Autumn-Winter, 1960-61) 15-20.

VII

American Society
and the Idea of Equality

> By God! I will accept nothing which all cannot
> have their counterpart of on the same terms.
>
> —WALT WHITMAN

THOMAS JEFFERSON, who wrote the statement in the Declaration of Independence that "all men are created equal," never denied that there were individual differences among these men, nor have any political philosophers since. There are two ways of dealing with these variations among individuals in a free, democratic society. One is to equalize them by establishing limitations on the superior individual and furnishing protections for the less able. The other is to open the competition to all contestants, knowing that the differences among them will separate winners and losers. Actually, American society has done both. As John W. Gardner recently pointed out, if you say "All men are equal," the average American replies, "Of course." If you say "Let the best man win," he says, "Naturally." That these two points of view are in conflict seems not to matter; Americans have a deep emotional commitment to both. They believe that men are free and equal, and that freedom and equality are interconnected at the foundation of their unique way of life.

Jefferson's phrasing of the doctrine of human rights in the

Declaration eloquently stated this American conviction—and at the same time created an American dilemma. Those who signed the document apparently agreed that it was "a self-evident truth" that all men are created equal, and that in addition to life and property, men possessed the freedom to practice and enjoy that equality. Equality and liberty, the Declaration implied, are co-equal and co-existent. Abraham Lincoln re-stated the idea in slightly different terms, binding liberty and equality irretrievably together in his famous affirmation of faith in a nation "conceived in liberty and dedicated to the proposition that all men are created equal." From their beginnings Americans have considered liberty and equality as related, joined, interdependent.

Yet it is also clear that these two qualities are neither so compatible as Jefferson and Lincoln indicated, nor are they by themselves a sufficiently practical footing on which to construct a society. Liberty pre-supposes an open opportunity for an individual to develop his own interests and capacities to the fullest, with a minimum of interference. Equality assumes the existence of something or someone to which the individual is equal; it postulates always the restraining presence of others and of their liberties, and of standards set by others related to the public good. The attempt to construct and maintain a government based on men being both free and equal set up strains in the American system which have persisted from its inception to the present. To reduce these tensions by establishing a workable congruity between liberty and equality has never been, of course, exclusively an American problem. The French Revolution, which coupled *liberté* and *égalité* even more tightly than the American, created more questions than it provided answers. The British avoided the more difficult aspects of the issue by refining and circumscribing their definition of equality.

Americans since Jefferson's time have been fairly certain what he meant by liberty, and have managed rather successfully to define and realize it. They have never been quite certain what he meant by equality, nor have they been able to evolve a consistently acceptable concept of it to use as a social or political instrumentality. Jefferson himself spent a good deal of thought on the matter; there were those who did not understand it fully when he wrote the phrase in 1776, and those who disagreed with what they thought it might mean. John Randolph of Roanoke, for example, was quite definite, saying "I love liberty and I hate equality," a perfectly plausible position in the light of what he assumed Jefferson meant. What equality meant and how it was to be used once helped to cause a civil war. However, over a century and a half of discussion, Americans have agreed to assign certain values to the word *equality*. President Harry Truman's message to Congress in 1948, in which he established the Joint Congressional Committee on Civil Rights and the Commission on Civil Rights, stated these quite clearly:

We believe that all men are created equal and that they have the right to equal justice under law. . . . We believe that all men are entitled to equal opportunities for jobs, for homes, for good health, and for education. We believe that all men should have a voice in their government and that government should protect, not usurp, the rights of the people.

There are here four meanings of the term, all of them so commonly accepted in American life as hardly to need elucidation. In a political sense, the term is taken to mean that in making decisions in the state due weight and consideration will be given to the expression of the individual's will; that is, that each man has an equal right to express his judgment on issues affecting the government under which he lives. Legally, the term means that there shall be no special privileges given to any individual or class over another in the dispensation of justice; that is, that all men are entitled to equal treatment in the administration of the laws. Economically, the term means that each individual shall be offered similar opportunities for gaining and retaining property; that is, he should have equal circumstances for the acquisition of wealth. Socially, the term means that the individual must have equal opportunities for mental, moral, spiritual, and physical development; that is, that each shall have equal access to those agencies of society which allow him to develop his capacities and to satisfy his needs, without discrimination on any other basis than worth and ability. These meanings have developed at different times and at differing rates of acceleration over the span of American history. At any particular point in American history certain groups in society may have possessed either liberty or equality without the other, or both in differing degrees, or either or both in a particular region, or segment of society. The emphasis on the realization of equality in American life has varied widely with the times; definitions have developed slowly and planlessly.

During the first century of the nation's existence, the United States emphasized the attainment of political and legal equality, stressing the importance of the freedom to move and to advance oneself, to receive equal justice at bench and polling place. The need for this kind of equality rose out of the scramble for power in a new and open society, the levelling out of classes, the extension of equal chances to all through public education, widened suffrage, political opportunity. During the latter half of the nineteenth century the emphasis shifted toward economic equality, stressing the equality of each man's pursuit of wealth in a booming industrial society that offered great wealth to the winners of the *laissez-faire* race. In the twentieth century, there has been first a perceptible trend toward linking equality and security; that is, in considering individual citizens as being equally entitled to certain minimum social benefits under governmental guarantee. Second, there has been a massive reconsideration of the feasibility of distributing legal, political, social, and economic equality through the full range of American society, including within the term all those disadvantaged groups once prevented or discouraged from participating in equality's benefits.

How the American idea of equality, complete with its vaguenesses and inconsistencies, has moved from the Plymouth Pilgrims to the present day involves a process of historical development that is both complex and not entirely clear. The original colonists brought with them almost all their ideas of what the word *equal* meant, and found a few more meanings in their wilderness and revolutionary experience. The colonists were part and parcel, intellectually, of the Enlightenment, and they shared with their British and European contemporaries in the discussions that centered about the idea of equality in the seventeenth and eighteenth centuries. Calvin was no leveller, and his theology contained the elements of a strongly hierarchical system. Men were equal in moral incapacity and in their subjection to God's sovereignty, true, but there were few intimations of equality between the elect and the non-elect. The Calvinist never doubted that authority in state and society ought to be in the hands of those capable of exercising it best.

The American Puritan did not come to the new world looking for equality; he not only brought with him but he maintained all the distinctions of the British social system of the seventeenth century. (Laws forbidding ostentation in dress, for example, did not apply to magistrates or military officers and their wives.) He had no doctrinaire theories about civil or political equality, and for that matter he did not extend religious equality beyond his own faith—this was one reason the Puritans feared the levelling Quakers. "God Almightie," wrote John Winthrop,

in his most holy and wise providence hath soe disposed of the Condicioun of Mankinde, as in all times some must be rich, some poore, some highe and eminent in power and dignitie; others mean and in subieceion.

The Puritan Divinity Himself, as Woodbridge Riley once remarked, temperamentally rather resembled a Stuart king.

Nevertheless, the Puritan creed pointed also in another direction. Calvin denied the need for a clergy as mediators between man and God; he rejected much of the church's political hierarchy; he introduced elective methods into portions of church polity. Many of the implications of equality inherent in Calvin's creed were carried out by the radicals in Cromwell's Parliamentary Army, who hammered out during the revolution much of the apparatus of the modern democratic state. Roger Williams' bold experiment in Rhode Island was unusual; though no other colony followed him for a long time, Rhode Island did indicate the direction in which Calvin and the Reformation might lead once certain of its implications were followed.

The most powerful and immediate influence on American thinking about equality in the eighteenth century was of course John Locke, whose *Treatise on Civil Government* had immeasurable impact on political thought over the western world. Men are born, he wrote, "with an uncontrolled enjoyment of all the rights and privileges of the law of nature equally with any other man or number of men in the world." The idea of equality came to Locke as a corollary of his sensational theory of knowledge, later to be worked out in more detail by such men as David Hartley in England and Helvetius in France. When Locke explained that the mind at birth was an empty tablet, he implied that subsequent distinctions among men were the results of what experience wrote on that tablet. These differences and inequalities, were therefore not "natural," but artificial, products of experience rather than of nature. It did not seem inevitably God's will that one man should be superior to another, or thrive while another starved, but society's—and society could be changed.

Locke assumed (and so did Hobbes, who parted company with him from that point) that equality among men existed as part of that state of nature which preceded government, although it did not necessarily carry over without change into post-natural society. Locke's constitutions for the Carolinas did, after all, provide for a feudal social system and a hereditary nobility. But to accept Locke's assumption meant viewing the whole concept of equality from a new, secular angle, and raised difficult questions about the existence of inequalities based on individual differences.

Locke placed a new kind of doctrine, replete with explosive social and political implications, over against the accepted doctrine of the divine superiority of kings and the inherent privileges of certain classes over others. His belief that men were "by nature all equal, free, and independent" reverberated through the next century, in the language of the American Declaration of Independence, the French Declaration of the Rights of Man, and in every other revolutionary slogan, tract, and declaration produced by the Age of Revolutions. Rousseau's *Essay on Equality* (1755) added another dimension to the term. Equality, he explained, was a necessary pre-condition of a free and just government. There were in-equalities which had no remedies—age, health, strength, intelligence, even of wealth and power—but there existed in society certain moral and political inequalities which derived from "privileges which are enjoyed by some at the expense of others." These were remediable; the restraints and inequi-ties they imposed were amenable to reform.

Locke, Rousseau, and the Cromwellian tradition provided the theoretical foundations for the American idea of equality, but it also had already a firm practical basis in the American experience. The colonial settlement was far distant from England, Europe, and all the signs and distinctions of an aristocratic society. In a frontier society equality was a cold fact of life. The wilderness "stripped the garments of civiliza-tion" from a man, Frederick Jackson Turner wrote, and started him out all over again on an equal footing with his fellows. Indians, starvation, disease, and other hazards of frontier life killed an earl's son or a tinker's, a wise man or a fool, with equal objectivity. The lack of fixed social organiza-tion in the new country made it possible for a man to be free and equal in an actual and visible sense; furthermore, the mobility of frontier society allowed a man the chance to change his status rapidly, within fairly broad limits, if he did feel inferior to someone else. To survive in the isolated, self-dependent settlements that dotted the thin line of coast in the early days of settlement required men to work together, whatever their rank, condition, or merit, as John Smith made his men work at Jamestown. Thus Tocqueville observed, in his shrewd study of the American character, that "The soil of

America was opposed to a territorial aristocracy," and concluded that the equality forced on Americans by the conditions of their existence was the most compelling fact about the quality of their life.

The colonists had at least one thing in common, a desire for equality of opportunity, which was probably the strongest element in the American equalitarian tradition. Wealthy and successful Englishmen did not come to the colonies because they felt no need to better their condition; as historian Charles M. Andrews once wrote, "The colonists were not conservative, satisfied, and prosperous Englishmen." Those who came to the colonies were often those who were disadvantaged at home and stood to profit by the move; among them were farmers who wanted land, middle-class squires who hoped to become landed gentry, younger sons, unskilled workers, displaced laborers, searchers for religious tolerance, and so on. Among those who came were no doubt a majority who took the chance in order to improve their lot; in this they were all even and equal. Again Tocqueville put it concisely: "The happy and powerful do not go into exile, and there are no surer guarantees of equality among men than poverty and misfortune."

American society from the seventeenth century on displayed distinctive differences from, as well as similarities to, contemporary English society. Colonial society, like the English, was built on the recognition of certain stratifications which no one had reason to question or modify. Yet these strata were much broader and more vague than England's. Colonial society, like the home country's, possessed the whole range of criteria for class distinctions, of which property naturally was primary, and which included speech, education, dress and manners. But these criteria carried less weight than in England, and many of the signals of deference were conspicuously lacking in American society. British General Carleton, noting this, told his superiors in London, "It is impossible for the dignity of the throne and the peerage to be represented in the American forest." There was noticeably less doffing of caps, pulling of forelocks, and curtsying and bowing in the colonies. Few travellers failed to remark on the unusual fluidity of American class divisions, the result for the most part of the extraordinary breadth of economic opportunity an expanding society provided. A Philadelphian explained a great deal about the fact of equality of American society when he observed in 1776 that one-half the city was owned by men who wore leather aprons, and the other half by men whose fathers had.

By the middle years of the eighteenth century Americans, in common with the British and French, had evolved a fairly coherent body of opinion about the meanings and implications of the term *equality*. They knew that it did not mean perfect likeness, and that there were important differences among men; but it did mean that all men were alike in certain ways, and that their likenesses furnished tenable grounds for organizing a society on them. They agreed that all men were equally men—that is, that they possessed physical, mental, and spiritual qualities in common—and that they were all social beings who lived not in isolation but with each other. They assumed that all men owned a common relationship to God and to other men, and that they had common obligations arising from those relationships. They agreed also that all men possessed certain inalienable rights, derived from nature.

These things men held equally in fee simple in a state of nature, though when they organized themselves into society they agreed to suspend or to change some of them. It may be that "an equality among men" is a law of nature, John Wise explained (following Pufendorf) but that equality might need to be modified "for the sake of a civil state." The idea of distinctions appealed to the Enlightenment's sense of proportion and fitted neatly into the "Great Chain of Being" theory that provided God's pattern for a universal order. However, eighteenth-century philosophers stressed the fact that those necessary inequalities and distinctions imposed on individuals by society were, like a set of clothes, an artificial overlay. Underneath them all men were naturally equal, with the same faculties and potentialities. They might be unequal in many other ways (and they were very well aware of these ways) but they were all equal beneath, as men.

"Men in state of nature were equal," a contributor to *The New York Gazetteer* wrote in 1773. "Their actions were subject to no limitations but those which arose from the laws of God." When they enter civil society they "voluntarily give up a part of their natural rights, and bind themselves to the obedience of laws, calculated for the general good" by their social contract—but they cannot and do not surrender their natural equality of rights. Inequalities could be tolerated for the common good, by the need for order, peace, and stability, but never did they nullify the birthright equality of nature. Restrictions on equality might be necessary, but never natural. They had to be demonstrably justified, and most of all, imposed only by common consent. By this chain of reasoning the American revolutionaries made their demand for equality and its concomitant, liberty, into a theory of revolution. They translated the theory of equality as a natural right into a political principle, specifically applied to certain objectionable practices of Crown and Parliament. "All men are by nature equal and free," wrote James Wilson of Pennsylvania. "No one has a right to any authority over another without his consent." The next step was to apply this to taxes.

None of this meant that the eighteenth-century American believed there were no such people as leaders, or exceptional men who provided notable examples for others to follow. The fact that the origin of the American idea of equality lay in England was important, for the English never believed so strongly as Europeans in hereditary distinctions. While they accepted, as all contemporary societies did, the hereditary transmission of specific privileges, Englishmen also placed great store on individual distinction and accomplishment. If a man held place and power beyond his fellows, the British felt that somehow he ought to have done something to deserve it—won a battle, captured a ship, founded a colony, made a fortune. The practice of admitting particularly brilliant statesmen to Lords, or able young men to Commons, even if of doubtful background, indicated this. The English tradition tended to associate distinction with ability—not consistently, nor always practically, but to a greater degree than the Continental.

This feeling, for it was no more than that, proved particularly well adapted to the setting of the new English colonies. To gain positions of distinction in colonial society a man had to have at least some ability; it was possible for a mediocrity or a misfit to hold office and power, of course, but usually not for long in a frontier environment that continually tested and discarded men if they did not measure up. "All men are by nature equal," said Nathaniel Ames in his *Almanac*, "But differ greatly in the sequel." The quality of the American experience tended to reinforce the idea that some men were capable beyond their fellows. "The right to equality," wrote a Virginian in 1760, was most certainly one of "the original rights of men," but there were also among them "differences of capacity, disposition, and virtue" which led to the subordination of some to the guidance of others. American society during the revolutionary and Constitutional years instinctively recognized this, and its leadership usually went to men who were accustomed to have it and who by public consent deserved it.

Jefferson wrote the Declaration's statement about equality, and Continental Congress approved it, within the context of a peculiarly American kind of revolution. American revolutionary society had almost no privileged orders, ecclesiastical injustices, or invidious distinctions against which to revolt. Lacking these remnants of a feudal past, Americans (unlike the French) could more or less accept Jefferson's phrase without much argument, since the sweep of frontier experience and the temper of the British tradition tended to support it anyway. They felt no compulsion, as other revolutionaries did, to overturn a society that already tacitly recognized many of their claims for equality. The eighteenth-century American felt equal, and did not need to do much more than to affirm it.

Defining what equality meant after 1776 was important, but much more urgent was the problem of putting it into practice. The necessities of constructing a government in a disjointed postwar society required a somewhat different approach to the idea of equality than using it to justify a revolt. Revolution called for a theoretical definition of the term; government required an operative one. There was no room for error in the experiment that was the new American state, and plenty of reason to anticipate it. No people in history had ever been able successfully to establish a government based on the theory of equality the new United States had in mind, or anything resembling it, and the Founding Fathers were acutely aware of the lessons of history. There was no good reason, for that matter, for Americans to believe that they could succeed where others failed; indeed, to the European mind the attempt itself was sheer folly. Yet there stood Jefferson's phrase, embedded in the Declaration and implemented by the Constitution. It was a believable and quite inspirational rallying cry for a revolution, but exactly what did it mean, and whatever it meant, how did one use it as a practical rule for predicting and controlling political behavior?

Every prominent American gave some attention to this problem. Paine, who never had any doubts about the validity of Jefferson's axiom, accepted "the unity or equality of man" as "one of the greatest of all truths" and went on to lend his considerable revolutionary talents to the French. Joel Barlow, like Paine, had no reservations. "Equality of right is nature's plan," he wrote in his *Vision of Columbus* (1787) , "And following nature is the march of man." In his opinion, the fact "all men are equal in their rights," was so obviously true that he had "no conception how any man in his senses can entertain any other." There were many who agreed with Paine and Barlow, but others moved on the matter with less confidence.

Fisher Ames, who objected violently to Paine's "spurious falsehoods and perverted truths," thought equality the "pernicious doctrine" of demagogues. A believer in government by "the wise, the rich, and the good," Ames thought "equal rights" meant simply that "to whatever [*men*] have a right, it is as much to be protected and provided for as the right of any other persons in society." To preach otherwise "hastens the journey of the demagogue to power," probably meaning Thomas Jefferson. Franklin, a wiser man than either Ames or Paine, had an instinctive disregard for what he called "pensions and peerages" and could identify an empty head or a stuffed shirt at a hundred paces on the bench, in the military, or at Court. While he recognized, he once said, that "Time, Chance, and Industry" created distinctions among men, he also believed that all of them were fundamentally equal in "the important ends of civil society, and the personal securities of life and liberty."

The most thoughtful discussion of the meaning of equality was that which began in 1813 between Thomas Jefferson and John Adams, when, in political retirement, these two great exponents of differing philosophies corresponded at length about the doctrine and its implications. John Adams was willing to agree that equality was a "law of nature," but what did that mean? Nothing more than the fact that men "are all of the same species, and this is all that the equality of nature amounts to. . . . Nature has ordained that no two objects shall be alike, and no two perfectly equal." Equality most assuredly did not mean what some of its more extreme proponents said it did; "equal rank and equal property can never be inferred from it, any more than equal understanding, agility, vigor, or beauty. Equal laws are all that can ever be derived from human equality." On the contrary, Adams argued, the "Author of Nature" established among men "a physical inequality, an intellectual inequality, of the most serious kind." And society, in order to insure its leadership by those best qualified to lead, had "a right to establish any other inequalities it may judge necessary for its good." Inequality, wrote Adams,

is the ordinance of God Almighty, in the constitution of human nature, and wrought into the fabric of the universe. Philosophers and politicians may nibble and quibble, but they will never get rid of it. . . . It is a part of the natural history of man.

Neither Adams nor Madison (who essentially agreed with him) nor any of those who distrusted the doctrine of equality, had any idea of completely rejecting it. The present danger, from their point of view, lay in attempts of well-meaning idealists to build a government on it. No "society can pretend to establish a free government," Adams warned Jefferson, "without attention" to the need for an aristocracy—not the false aristocracy of Britain and Europe, but the true "natural aristocracy of virtue and talents" that existed "in every nation and in every party." A free and stable state must be governed by such men, lest it be easily taken over by "an aristocracy of land jobbers and stock jobbers" elevated to positions of authority by sheer money-power.

Jefferson, over the years since 1776, had already explored the meanings of the doctrine he wrote of in the Declaration, and by the time of his passage with Adams he had formed a relatively unified theory of equality. He believed it the birthright possession of every man, a gift of God and nature; it was a self-evident, natural right which society could neither award nor deny. This natural state guaranteed all men perfect equality of human privilege (life), political prerogative (liberty), and personal opportunity (the pursuit of happiness). However, Jefferson also recognized that men might be unequal in other respects, physical, intellectual, psychological, even moral. "I agree with you," he told Adams, "that there is a natural aristocracy among men. The grounds of this are virtue and talents. . . . There is an artificial aristocracy, founded upon wealth and birth, without either virtue or talents." Like Adams, Jefferson believed that the aim of government is to provide "for a pure selection of these natural *aristoi* into the offices of government." Unlike Adams, he trusted the wisdom of the majority to put them there; the people might occasionally err in their selection, but in the long run they would choose the right leaders. If one guarantees "to the citizens the free election and separation of the aristoi from the pseudo-aristoi . . ., they will elect the really good and wise. In some instances, wealth may corrupt, and birth blind them, but not in sufficient degree to endanger the society."

The philosopher of Jeffersonian political democracy, if one could be chosen, was most probably John Taylor of Caroline, Virginia, whose *Inquiry into the Principles and Policy of the Government of the United States* (1814) contained a lengthy, reasoned reply to the ideology of Federalism that John Adams represented. Whereas Adams began with the presumption that men were unequal in everything except biological status, Taylor began by assuming with Locke that equality is the natural state of all men and aristocracy unnatural. Aristocracy, claimed Taylor, arose from special privilege; once having been so created, it tended to maintain itself by the same means. Adams' theory that a "natural" aristocracy rested on knowledge, talent, and virtue was open to question. None of these qualities, Taylor reminded him, were transmissible to the next generation—but *wealth* was, which usually turned out to be the chief support of that aristocracy that Adams assumed was "natural."

What was the answer, then? Taylor stated it quite explicitly. The true doctrine of equality did not assert "equality of stature, strength, or understanding," nor that all men were equal in other than "moral rights and duties." It did mean, however, that in a free and open society that offered equal opportunity, a majority of its citizens could attain a level of talent and virtue sufficient to govern themselves without help from an aristocracy of any kind. The best men ought to govern, he agreed, but Taylor could not discover in contemporary society those admittedly superior men that Adams and the Federalists implied were there. Instead, he believed that the average man could reach a level of worth high enough to justify Jefferson's faith in his ability to choose the right governors. "Talents and virtue," he wrote, "are now so widely distributed, as to have rendered a monopoly of either, equivalent to that of antiquity, impracticable." In what was essentially a preview of Jacksonianism, Taylor made the common man equal in his superiority.

According to Alan Grimes, "to the extent that there was an underlying and unifying theme to the Jacksonian movement, it existed in an emphasis on equality." Certainly that is what Tocqueville observed most clearly in Jacksonian America. "The more I advanced in the study of American society," he wrote, "the more I perceived that this equality of condition is the fundamental fact from which all others seem to be derived, and the central point at which all my observations constantly terminated." The Jacksonians did not believe that men were equal in talents or capacities, or that they all ought to share equally in property. But they did believe, passionately, that men were equal by nature and equal in the possession of their natural rights. Jacksonianism, broadly construed, was a re-affirmation of the principles of the preamble of the Declaration, especially that portion dealing with the equal right to pursue happiness—for Jackson's was an energetically acquisitive age. "All men are placed under circumstances of *perfect* equality," wrote Francis Wayland in his popular textbook on *The Elements of Moral Science* (1835). "Each separate individual is created with precisely the *same right to use* the advantages which God has endowed him, as every other individual."

Almost every foreign observer who travelled in the United States during the period remarked on the pervasive influence of the idea of democratic equality on American life. Michel de Chevalier, who visited the United States in 1833, wrote that

In the United States the democratic spirit is infused into all the natural habits and all the customs of society; it besets and startles at every step the foreigner who, before landing in this country, had no suspicion to what a degree his every nerve and fiber had been steeped in aristocracy by a European education.

American manners confused the European most. Some objected to the American habit of carelessly blowing tobacco smoke about and to the frequent and aimless expectoration of tobacco juice. Others could not understand the lack of the usual marks of class distinction; Britisher John Fowler in 1831 was amazed to see American workmen walking the streets on Sunday wearing "sleek coats, glossy hats, watch-guards, and deerskin gloves!" American serving-people, foreign travellers almost unanimously agreed, did not know their places, but "entertain such notions of equality and independence," wrote one observer, "as fit them poorly for their station in life." However much American equality shocked and puzzled them, many such travellers nevertheless caught some glimpse of the powerful drive it imparted to American life. Captain Frederick Marryat, who with typical British hauteur disliked almost everything he saw in the United States, admitted in his *Diary in America* (1839) that with all its faults, "among the advantages of democracy the greatest is, perhaps, that *all start fair*; and the boy who holds the traveller's horse, as Van Buren is said to have done, may become President of the United States."

The Jacksonians asserted that all men were indeed possessed of equal rights—a number of them, some specific and some vague—and of the opportunities those rights provided. The Federalist program, they claimed, closed off those opportunities; thus Jacksonians opposed all the prerogatives of privilege —charters, monopolies, grants, legislative favoritism—which seemed to deny economic equality of opportunity. The Jeffersonians, primarily concerned with promoting political equality, devoted little organized attention to economics, but political equality to the Jacksonians was of small importance without some kind of economic equality, or of equal opportunity to strive for it.

The extension of the suffrage seemed to Jackson's men to have guaranteed political equality at the ballot-box. Now, wrote Orestes Brownson, the country "having passed through one phase of the revolution, passes on to another, and attempts the realization of *social* equality, so that the actual condition of men in society shall be in harmony with their acknowledged rights as citizens." For this reason Jackson's party favored a *laissez-faire*, freely-competitive economy as a means of promoting equality of access to property and wealth. The Adams-Jefferson concept of specially-qualified leadership had no place in Old Hickory's political system, which considered any aristocracy, "natural" or not, as undemocratic and possibly un-American. There was no need for a special group to mediate between the common man and the truth. The Jacksonians sought to equalize men in the enjoyment of their rights, and to give them an equal start in their pursuit of happiness.

The great proliferation of reforms that characterized the

period between 1820 and 1850 was directly linked to this Jacksonian effort to equalize opportunity. Tocqueville noted this, with his usual perspicacity, writing of the Americans that "for equality their passion is ardent, insatiable, invincible; they call for equality in freedom; and if they cannot obtain that, they will call for equality in slavery." The Jacksonians were eager to make sure that the great bursting of American prosperity was not restricted to a few haves, and that the have-nots had an equal chance to share in it. Thomas Skidmore's fiery pamphlet, *The Rights of Men to Property* (1829) saw the era as an economic feast, at which those

who have been the first to sit down to the table . . ., have disposed of the whole dinner, in such a manner as that nine-tenths of the beings that now people this globe, have not the wherewith to dine.

Equal rights for women, equal entry to public education, freedom for the slave, the right of labor to organize, the regulation of the conditions of labor, utopian communitarian experiments, and the rest of the reformist ferment of the times were all part of the Jacksonian's demands for complete equality of the conditions of advancement, for the final erasure of privileged inequalities from American society.

James Fenimore Cooper, as aggressively an American nationalist as ever existed, was one of those not fully attuned to the Jacksonian equalitarian mystique, and his comments on the contemporary concept of equality were by far the most penetrating of the period. Cooper was by temperament an aristocrat, the product of a landholding New York gentry; he was also a convinced democrat and a fierce partisan of the American way of life. His ideas and feelings pulled him both ways. Acutely conscious of the values of social order and tradition, Cooper was equally aware of the values of experimentation and progress. Jacksonian levelling was not for him; neither were the pseudo-aristocratic pretensions of the tie-wig Federalists or Calhoun's Greek-style slave state. Cooper spent a great deal of time and thought attempting to define and redefine exactly what the right kind of democratic equality should be, trying to make it workable and at the same time philosophically acceptable to a uniquely American society. *The American Democrat* (1838) was the most thorough treatment of the issue that occurred between the Jefferson-Adams correspondence and the Lincoln-Douglas debates.

Cooper made it clear first of all that a democrat could be an intelligent gentleman; equality meant neither reducing all men to the lowest level of mediocrity nor raising all men to the highest of superiority. He believed strongly in the virtues of a graded society, for "All that democracy means," he wrote

is as equal a participation in rights as is practicable, and to pretend that social equality is a condition of popular institutions, is to assume that the latter are destructive of civilization, for, as nothing is more self-evident than the possibility of raising all men to the highest standards of tastes and refinements, the alternative would be to reduce the entire community to the lowest.

Equality was strictly a matter of civil and political rights for all men (not women, children, criminals, or slaves) and no more than that. To Cooper it did not mean equality of talent, or property, or even of potential; the American political system, in fact, resting as it did on the elective process, explicitly recognized this, for "choice supposes a preference, and preference inequality of merit, or of fitness."

The key principle in Cooper's equalitarian theory was his concept of the "democratic gentleman," developed most fully in *The American Democrat*. Equality and democracy, he explained, were not exact categorical opposites. Absolute equality was as dangerous to democracy as complete aristocracy. The most practicable and desirable kind of equality lay between these two extremes, neither in a sterile, dead-level society, nor in those "privileged orders, entails, and distinctions . . ., devised permanently to separate men into castes." The democratically equal society was flexible, permitting movement up and down within justly established limits. It allowed men to become great by their own acts, or to fail by them; it imposed a system on society and allowed reasonable and realistic variations within it. The presence of differences in a democracy, based on the right principles of separation, did not seem to Cooper incompatible with the democratic ideal. What did threaten that ideal was the current Jacksonian notion, as he interpreted it, that "a democrat can be only one who seeks the level." "In a democracy," Cooper explained, "men are just as free to aim at the highest attainable places in society, as to obtain the largest fortunes;" it is this quest that produces the "democratic gentleman" who recognizes "the right of all to participate in power." What Cooper had in mind, in slightly different terms, was the Jeffersonian aristocracy of worth and Adams' natural aristocracy of talent. He hoped to define as clearly as one could and to re-establish the older equalitarian ideal as it might successfully operate in Jacksonian America.

In the expanding North and West, where laborer, farmer, trader, artisan, and capitalist found the Jacksonian philosophy a perfect fit, the contemporary rhetoric of equality rang bright and true. In the South, where all ideas had to be tested in reference to King Cotton and King Slavery, it had an ominous sound. The South could not afford to countenance for a moment the implications of either Jefferson's phrase or Jackson's interpretations of it. To admit the validity of any philosophy of equality based on natural rights or equal access to society's benefits raised too many dangerous questions, not only about Negroes, but about the political control of the South by a privileged minority of slaveholders and their allies.

John C. Calhoun of South Carolina set up a line of defenses. He began by asserting that men were not born as Jefferson claimed they were, either free or equal. They were instead "born subject, not only to parental authority, but to the laws and institutions of the country where born, and under whose protection they draw their first breath." Nature did not grant a man rights. He earned them, and society granted them to him when it was to society's advantage to do so. "It is a great and dangerous error," Calhoun wrote in obvious distaste for democracy, either Jeffersonian or Jacksonian, to suppose that all people are equally entitled to liberty. It is a reward to be earned, not a blessing to be gratuitously lavished on all alike . . .—a reward reserved for the intelligent, the patriotic, the virtuous, and deserving;—and not a boon to be bestowed on a people too ignorant, degraded, and vicious, to be capable either of appreciating or of enjoying it.

An individual's ability, according to Calhoun, determined his place in society—nothing else—and if one's abilities did not entitle him to a higher place than he occupied, he deserved none. Individuals, he wrote, "differ greatly from each other, in intelligence, sagacity, energy, perseverance, skill, habits of industry and economy, physical power, position and opportunity," and no doubt in other ways as well. Inequality of endowment naturally produced inequalities of condition as all men, driven by self-interest, attempted to better themselves. It was this urge to excel, to be unequal, that in Calhoun's opinion provided the motive power for the progressive advancement of the whole society. He explained this in an inspired image:

It is, indeed, this inequality of condition between the front and rear ranks, in the march of progress which gives so strong an impulse to the former to maintain their position, and to the latter to press forward into their files. This gives to progress its greatest impulse. To force the front rank back to the rear, or attempt to push forward the rear into line with the front, by the interposition of the government, would put an end to the impulse, and effectually arrest the march of progress.

The great complicating factor in all discussions of equality, as Calhoun perceived, was the existence in the United States, under constitutional protection, of the institution of slavery. Benjamin Franklin, as president of the Pennsylvania Antislavery Society, had long before pointed out the inconsistency of the Declaration's statement with the existence of a system which extended "freedom to only *part of the human race.*" If all men were created equal, and if they were entitled equally to all those things the Declaration, the Jeffersonians, and the Jacksonians said they were, slavery was a visible denial of the whole concept—unless certain conditions and terms were very carefully defined and delimited. The fact that slaves were Negroes was providentially convenient, for it always served to shift discussions of equality, when they touched on slavery, into the context of race.

The presence of the Negro slave and the Indian savage in the seventeenth and eighteenth centuries created special problems for Americans at the very beginnings. The early colonists were not well prepared to deal with racial diversity, and how to relate Indian and Negro to their society always puzzled them. Unlike the Spanish, who had long experience with darker peoples, the English had no racial minorities at home and little understanding of other cultures. Locke said that men were created equal in nature: contemporary anthropology assumed that all men were descended from the same act of creation by God, and therefore were literally created equal. If so, Negro slaves according to Locke's logic were created free, for "Creatures of the same species and rank . . ., born to all the same advantages of nature, and the use of the same faculties, should also be equal one amongst another without subordination or subjection."

Since the society for which Locke wrote contained very few Negroes and fewer Indians, American Lockeans faced a troublesome problem. Was his axiom true of them as well? Negroes and Indians were obviously different in color, and apparently different from white men in other ways as well. Yet Locke and the Bible (so some said) argued for the equality of all mankind. Dr. Benjamin Rush found in Genesis the "strongest argument that can be used in favor of the original and natural equality of all mankind," and was himself a strong antislavery proponent. Science seemed to support the Biblical view; the great Linnaeus' *Systema naturae* published in 1735 placed all races of men under the same classification.

Jefferson, who owned slaves, carefully explored the theory of equality as it concerned different races. His *Notes on Virginia* contained a long and somewhat inconclusive discussion of Negroes, in which he thought he recognized important differences in the physical, emotional, and intellectual makeup of white and Negro. But Jefferson was too much the scientist to generalize on less than sufficient information. He offered his opinions, he said, "with great diffidence," since "to our great reproach it must be said that though for a century and a half we have had under our eyes the races of black and red man, they have never been viewed by us as subjects of natural history." Any statement about the inferiority of the black race, he concluded, was "a suspicion only." On the other hand, most of his contemporaries were much less careful about drawing their conclusions.

Neither slavery nor its abolition were important issues in Jefferson's time. By 1830 the concentration of the Southern economy on cotton made the preservation of the system, in the South's opinion, an economic and social necessity. At the same time the temper and quality of the opposition to slavery changed when William Lloyd Garrison opened the era of militant abolitionism with his famous challenge of 1831 in *The Liberator*. The South had either to accept racial equality and give up slavery, or establish white racial superiority and retain it. To defend slavery it was essential to destroy the ideal of equality among the races of men, which the pro-slavery writers set out to do.

First, however, it was necessary to destroy Jefferson, for wherever the Southerner turned, that flashing phrase from the Declaration confronted him. The statement, wrote Chancellor Harper, was "exuberantly false and arborescently fallacious." Jefferson had a weakness for "strange eccentricities," explained novelist William Gilmore Simms, "quaint expressions, gleaming paradoxes, and sweeping assertions." His "nowhere accredited dogma," said J. H. Hammond, was nonsense, and Thomas Cooper of South Carolina agreed that it was "a great deal of nonsense. . . . Nothing can be more untrue; no human being ever was, none is, or will be born free." George Fitzhugh spoke of the Virginian as "the genius of innovation, the architect of ruin, the inaugurator of anarchy," and Professor Albert Bledsoe of the University of Virginia wrote an entire book, *Liberty and Slavery,* to prove him mistaken. Not all the attacks on him were Southern, for that matter—Senator Pettit of Indiana called Jefferson's phrase "a self-evident lie"—but by 1850 Jefferson and his Declaration were thoroughly discredited below Mason's and Dixon's line.

Opposing views of the equality clause of the Declaration were not new, of course, but differences between those of North and South were deeply intensified by the abolitionists' exploitation of the issue after 1830. The antislavery people made the nation conscious of the wide variance between equality in theory and practice simply by demanding for the slave that which the Declaration seemed to declare was the right of all men. Their interpretation of the phrase "all men are created equal" was literal and unequivocal. William H. Seward believed the American system "founded in the natural equality of *all* men, not alone *American* men, nor alone all *white* men, but men of every country, clime and complexion are equal, not made equal by human laws, but born equal." There were differences of opinion, however, among the abolitionists as to exactly what this equality of white and Negro involved. One group believed that it meant that "the men who are now slaves must be admitted to all the rights, privileges, and immunities, political, social, and religious, which belong to American citizens generally." Another view, apparently more widely accepted, interpreted the term *equality* to mean in this context that the Negro was "equally entitled to his life, liberty, and the fruit of his toil," and not necessarily immediate social and political equality. Whatever their differences, all abolitionists agreed with William Ellery Channing's conclusion that "the equality of nature makes slavery wrong."

Proslavery leaders replied either by categorically denying the equality clause of the Declaration, or by launching a counter-attack—that slavery was actually the only system that encouraged *true* equality. The Declaration was never intended to apply to the Negro, they argued; the preamble simply meant that the signers sanctioned no royal or aristocratic class in the new Republic. "The doctrine of equality contained in it refers to the Anglo-Saxon race," the Ohio Constitutional

Convention of 1850 resolved. "All (*White*) men are created equal," said the New York *Day Book*. William Gilmore Simms explained that since men were born unequal, and since their so-called inalienable rights were violated daily by laws passed for society's betterment and protection, enslaving the Negro for the benefit of society was hardly the infringement of a right to equality that he never had. The Richmond *Examiner* brushed the Declaration aside, since it was not part of the law of the Union and therefore inapplicable to slavery: "The Union was not founded upon the Red Republican principle of the equality of all men, but upon the common-sense principle that the negro is a negro, and the white man is his superior and lord, by nature and by the providence of God."

The doctrine meant "an equality among equals," or "equality among those whom the Almighty Creator himself has made equal," wrote J. H. Van Evrie, one of the most energetic of Northern apologists for slavery. This was a "sounder philosophy" on which to base a society, he continued, "than that of Thomas Jefferson and his friends of the French Revolutionary school." George Fitzhugh, in *Sociology for the South* (1854) and *Cannibals All!* (1857) proved to Southern satisfaction that men were unequal and that a stable and progressive society could not exist without recognizing it. The real strength of Southern society, said Robert Toombs of Georgia, was that it was built on "the perfect equality of the superior race, and the legal subordination of the inferior race." Alexander Stephens later made it clear that the solidity of the Confederacy rested on the fact that "its foundations are laid, its cornerstone rests, upon the great truth that the negro is not equal to the white man, that slavery, subordination to the superior race, is his natural and moral condition." The South by 1850 had fully accepted an updated feudalism that sounded as if Jefferson, the Declaration, and the natural rights philosophy had never really existed.

To prove the inherent racial inequality of the Negro the proslavery group enlisted the aid of science. To elude the Biblical argument over creation, Dr. Joseph Clark Nott of Alabama evolved a theory of multiple creation, suggesting that the Negro was the result of a separate act of creation by God, thus not equal to the white and designed by God for subordination. (Eventually anthropologists of the period postulated five separate acts of creation and five races.) This theory gained wide acceptance for its convenient explanation of how God meant the Negro to be inferior. The Richmond *Examiner* editorialized:

The negro race is the result of a different act of the Creator than that which originated the Caucasian, and is consequently beyond the scope of those abstract axioms of the white race, which declares that all men have equal rights.

Nott's book, *Two Lectures on the Natural History of the Caucasian and Negro Races* (1845) was an invaluable source of quotations for proslavery writers over the next half-century and more. Count Arthur Gobineau's *Essay on the Inequality of the Races,* which finally appeared in English in 1860, also proved useful, but Nott, one of Gobineau's American translators, had already spread most of his ideas. "The plain and inevitable deduction is this," Nott wrote in one of his many articles,

that the negro is a totally distinct and inferior animal and species of animal from the Caucasian; that the negro is the connecting link between man and the brute creation; that the negro is intended by nature for a similar dependence upon the Caucasian man, in which only the ox, the ass, and the horse fulfill the intent of their creation.

Nor was Nott alone in his deduction. Professor Louis Agassiz, Harvard's famed scientist, agreed with Nott's views in substance, arguing that since "the amalgamation of races" produced "a mongrel, nondescript type, deficient in physical and mental energy," the superior race must always remain dominant. Dr. Samuel G. Morton, Dr. John Bachman, George Combe the phrenologist, and dozens of popularizers, such as John Campbell's *Negro Mania, Being an Examination of the Falsely Assumed Equality of the Races,* (1851) helped to publicize Nott's theories. The Negro, by reason of his inequality, was a natural slave, wrote Dr. Samuel Cartwright of New Orleans, and talk of equality utter folly. (Dr. Cartwright also distinguished himself by identifying the serpent in Eden as a Negro in disguise.) "Comparative anatomy discloses, history tells," Cartwright continued, "chemistry proves, and the Bible reveals, that by a higher law than the union, the Constitution, or any other human enactments, the negro is a slave." John C. Hurd's *Law of Freedom and Bondage* (1858, 1862) set out to prove that the Negro's racial inferiority provided the soundest possible legal basis for making and keeping him a slave. The stamp of science on such ideas convinced many Americans, North and South, that whatever equality meant, it did not mean that the Negro was equal to the white man. The English traveller William Chambers by 1855 found that all over the United States, regardless of section, it was "a fixed notion . . . that the coloured is by nature a subordinate race."

One of the most thorough, and—because of the situation and the participants—the most important discussion of racial equality occurred during the debates between Abraham Lincoln and Stephen A. Douglas in 1858. Both men knew that this was a vital national issue in the Congressional campaign, one whose importance far transcended the senatorial contest in Illinois. Both faced it squarely. Douglas took the prevailing Southern view that the equality clause of the Declaration "had no reference to the negro, the savage Indian, the Fejee, the Malay, or any other inferior or degraded race." The signers of the document "referred to the white race alone, and not to the African, when they declared all men to have been created equal; they were speaking of British subjects on this continent being equal to British subjects born and residing in Great Britain." Douglas' answer was no doubt the popular one (he won the election) but it was far too late in the sweep of events to make this simplistic explanation satisfactory.

Abraham Lincoln was well aware of the deeper implications of the issue of racial equality, and he had a subtler and much clearer mind than Douglas'. Lincoln had already given the subject thought—"If one man says it [*the Declaration*] does not mean a negro," he once wrote, "why not another say it does not mean some other man?" Or, as he wrote Joshua Speed, following out Southern logic could mean that the Declaration might someday be amended to read, "All men are created equal except negroes and foreigners and Catholics." In 1857, at his address at Springfield, Illinois, he stated his position carefully. The framers of the Declaration, he said, meant to include all men in their declaration of human equality,

but they did not intend to declare all men equal in *all respects*. They did not mean to say that they were equal in color, size, intellect, moral developments, or social capacity. They defined with tolerable distinctness in what respects they did consider all men created equal—equal with certain inalienable rights, among which are life, liberty, and the pursuit of happiness. This they said, and this they meant. They did not mean to assert the obvious untruth that all were then enjoying that equality, nor yet that they were about to confer it immediately upon them. In fact, they had not power to confer such a boon. They meant simply to declare the right, so that the enforcement of it might follow as fast as circumstances should permit. They meant to set up a standard maxim for free society, which should be familiar to all, and revered by all; constantly looked to, and even though never perfectly attained, constantly approximated.

During the debates with Douglas he elaborated his position, saying of the Negro:

I agree with Judge Douglas that he is not my equal in many respects —certainly not in color, perhaps not in moral or intellectual endowment. But in the right to eat the bread, without the leave of anybody else, which his own hand earns, he is my equal and the equal of Judge Douglas, and the equal of every living man. . . . If the Negro is a man, why then my ancient faith teaches me that "all men are created equal," and that there can be no moral right in connection with one man's making a slave of another.

First, Lincoln separated the issue of equality from the confusing and confused argument from racial differences and tied it once more to the tradition of natural rights. Second, he established equality of opportunity and of civil position as integral parts of the argument; and last, he applied the standards of the American theory of equality specifically to slavery. At a time when very few people were thinking clearly about the issue nobody else stated its ramifications so thoroughly and precisely.

The Civil War settled a number of major political and social issues in American life, but it did not define the broader meanings of equality. After the war, when Americans had time to consider some of the implications of Darwinian biology, the discussion took a different direction. What Darwin had to say about the origins of the human species did not support the theory of multiple racial origins, nor did it appear to substantiate the Biblical account. The fact that in nature the fit survived seemed to indicate that *inequality* was a basic natural law. From the evolutionary point of view nature valued superiority more highly than equality; the strong and the weak were not equal, nor apparently had nature ever intended them to be. Theories and devices which made them so were clearly unnatural. Darwinian evidence demonstrated, wrote scientist Thomas Henry Huxley, "that men are not all equal under whatever aspect they are contemplated, and the assumption that they ought to be considered equal has no sort of *a priori* foundation."

The implications of the Darwinian-Spencerian school produced a group of writers in England and the United States who launched a thorough and well-executed attack on the doctrine of equality as their predecessors had conceived it. Their position was developed most completely in England, beginning with Sir Henry Maine's *Ancient Law* (1861), followed by Sir Erskine May's *History of Democracy* (1870), James Stephens' *Liberty, Equality, and Fraternity* (1873), and Maine's *Popular Government* (1885). Maine, especially, was popular in American intellectual circles; so too was Lord Acton, who attributed the failure of the French Revolution to "its theory of equality" and who considered the doctrine the most dangerous foe of democracy.

There was general agreement on the American side of the

Atlantic. In an era of savage economic competition, ardent nationalism, burgeoning wealth, and material expansion, these attacks from abroad on the idea of equality found a receptive audience. "The doctrine that all men are equal," William Graham Sumner wrote, "is being gradually dropped, for its inherent absurdity." An American millionaire was, Sumner believed, "the finest flower of a competitive society" —he was superior, he had the money to prove it, and no foolishness about equality. Abbott Lawrence Lowell's *Essays on Government* (1899) rejected "the exploded doctrine of the natural right" of equality, and Nicholas Murray Butler's *True and False Democracy* (1907) was even more explicit. To him "the cornerstone of democracy is natural inequality, its ideal the selection of the most fit."

Barrett Wendell, Professor of Literature at Harvard, explained that the doctrine of equality was alien to the Anglo-Saxon tradition, really derived from untrustworthy "philosophical vagaries of Eighteenth Century France." True Americans would not, he hoped, place confidence in ideas "borrowed from the cloud-spun theories of clever Frenchmen." "The idea of natural equality is one of the most pernicious delusions that has ever afflicted mankind," wrote Lathrop Stoddard, the most violent Darwinist of the period. "Nature knows no equality. The most cursory examination of natural phenomena reveals the presence of a Law of Inequality as universal and inflexible as the Law of Gravity." Stoddard went on to suggest, in his book, *The Revolt Against Civilization,* the organization of a new American political philosophy called Neo-Aristocracy, whose adherents could seize the ruling power of the country from "the vast host of the unadaptable, the incapable, the envious, and the discontented who presently possessed it."

What equality really meant, in the opinion of the Social Darwinists, was the equal right to compete, the equal opportunity to survive. True equality "sets each man on his feet," said Sumner, "and gives him leave to run," nothing more. "We cannot go outside of this alternative," he wrote, "liberty, inequality, survival of the fittest; not—liberty, equality, survival of the unfittest." The only definition of equality usable in contemporary society was that kind of equality which Justice Field, in the famous "Slaughterhouse" cases of 1872, called "the equality of right among citizens in the pursuit of the ordinary avocations of life."

Equality of opportunity, inequality of ability—one put the two together to obtain a picture of real life, wherein each strove to excel and the better man won. "God has intended the great to be great and the little to be little," said the great preacher Henry Ward Beecher, thereby granting Christian dispensation to Darwin and Spencer. Even liberal sociologist Lester Ward suggested that "equality of opportunity is the only means of determining the degree of merit" among individuals. It was a fact of life, the later nineteenth century decided, that society naturally structured itself on the lines of the individual's ability to survive. The old-fashioned concept of equality, applied under modern conditions, wrongly circumscribed the liberty of the fit to compete for survival.

As a result, beginning about 1880, the meaning of equality narrowed and particularized. Discussions of the term centered on the specific privileges it granted to the individual within the state—equality at law, the equal right to vote, equality of economic opportunity, equality of access to educational privileges, and so on. Whereas at an earlier time *equality* was a broadly conceived theory of democracy, it now became the sum total of certain allowable practices in political and economic society. As Arthur Twining Hadley of Yale observed, few of his generation would accept Jefferson's statement in the Declaration literally and generally any more; they were much more likely to conceive it in selective and functional terms of current practices, in contrast to the theoretical quality it possessed a century before.

There were answers to this, of course. Whatever the logic of the Social Darwinist view of life, there were many who refused to accept it and who thought the competitive game the Darwinists called life was rigged. The great issue in the struggles against monopoly in the years between 1880 and 1914 was the claim that this view of the world allowed great concentrations of economic power to cut off that same equality of opportunity their supporters talked about. "Muckraking" journalists, such as Ida Tarbell, Henry D. Lloyd, and Ray Stannard Baker, showed how the trusts shut off competition, while the third-party political platforms that dotted the period demanded laws to guarantee equality of opportunity for the little man and the little business. Henry George proposed his Single Tax to insure equal access to the fruits of the land; reformers offered variously-shaded schemes of socialism to counteract the stifling inequalities created by "Big Business." The eighties and nineties were angry decades, and J. H. Tucker, writing in *The Atlantic,* related "the organized discontent in the midst of us" directly to "the spirit of equality . . ., the demand for equal economic opportunity now paramount in our social and political discussions." It might be, some of the reformers admitted, that as the Spencerian claimed, men were not equal in nature. But if men were not actually equal in all things, in the interests of social justice they ought to be treated as if they were in certain important things.

Edward Bellamy's tractarian novel, *Equality* (1897), summarized the reformers' claims most completely. Published nine years after his tremendously successful *Looking Backward,* Bellamy's book was intended to supplement its predecessor's recommendations for social and economic reforms with a further exposition of the theory beneath them. His aim, he said, was to prove that "equality is the vital principle of democracy" and to outline an economic theory that would open up equal opportunities for everyone. "What is an equal right to life, but a right to the equal material basis for it?" asked his narrator.

The cornerstone of our state is economic equality, and is not that the obvious, necessary, and only adequate pledge of these three birthrights—life, liberty and happiness?

The new order of society, therefore, must begin with "equality of opportunity for the pursuit of happiness." All men should have an equal start in life's race—in clothing, shelter, food, health, education, and all those elements which affect the running of it. But of all opportunities the most important was economic—from this all other equalities flowed. Bellamy ended his book by proposing a kind of socialistic, anti-monopolistic state not markedly different from the one described in his earlier novel, but he made clear in the process the importance which he and his fellow-reformers placed on equality in economic life.

All this, from Sumner to Bellamy, applied to white Americans only. What they said most certainly had no influence on the position of the Negro in American society, which had changed very little in many respects since slavery days. Ironically, the Civil War had undermined the natural rights doctrine of equality by freeing the slave and making racial equality a matter of unavoidable controversy. The slavery system simply suppressed the issue either by dehumanizing the Negro or by declassing him. One could rationalize the Negro's position in prewar society by saying that the Negro was not a man, and thus not eligible for that equality granted all men under the Declaration—or one could eliminate him from equal participation in the benefits and rights of society by saying that as a slave he was not actually in that society. But freeing him from slavery changed all that. The Negro existed legally as a person, and something had to be done about him; if he were a free man, as the law said he was, the Declaration's statement must certainly be applied to him. The postwar generation would therefore have to prepare to receive him on equal terms.

The postwar generation, North and South alike, did no such thing. It solved its problem by adopting the pre-war Southern attitude toward the Negro and writing it into law. The Negro was inferior (nobody was quite sure why) and his inferiority was to be marked by his segregation; he was not equal, and he was not to be accorded equal treatment or equal rights. So the South lost the war, and won the argument over the Negro's position in society. So far as the Negro's equality was concerned, by 1890 the Civil War might not have been fought.

The belief that the Negro belonged to an inferior and unequal race went practically unquestioned throughout the nineteenth century and still today retains strong popular support. Articles in the major magazines through the nineties and after—among them such powerful liberal journals as *The North American Review, Harper's, Atlantic,* and *The Nation*—simply accepted this as fact. Books on the order of Charles Carroll's *The Negro a Beast* (1900), Robert Shufeldt's *The Negro: A Menace to Civilization* (1907), and perhaps the most vicious, Shufeldt's *America's Greatest Problem, The Negro* (1915) circulated freely, while the crude racist novels of Thomas Dixon (one of which became the movie, "Birth of A Nation") fixed the stereotype of the "black menace" firmly in the popular mind. The concept of the Negro's inherent inferiority, of course, aided substantially in justifying the increased amount of social segregation that came after 1880, for if the races were not equal, it was natural to keep them apart. Inequality was translated directly into segregation. By 1900 relatively complete separation of the races had been accomplished North and South, in the North by agreement, in the South by legislation.

The decision of the United States Supreme Court in *Plessy v. Ferguson* in 1896 set a social pattern for racial inequality that lasted until 1954. The "separate but equal" doctrines as applied to Negroes was already a half-century old (usually in schools) and segregation was legal in a majority of the states. Justice Henry Brown, writing the majority opinion of the Court in 1896, simply gave the practice national judicial sanction. The Louisiana statute under review, he wrote, had nothing to do with racial equality, but only with racial segregation. There was no reason to assume "that the enforced separation of the two races stamps the colored race with a badge of inferiority." However, if a feeling of racial inferiority did exist in American society, it did not fall within the authority of the law to attempt to eliminate it, for "legislation is powerless to eradicate racial instincts or to abolish distinctions based upon physical differences." Furthermore, he continued, "if one race be inferior to another socially, the Constitution of the United States cannot put them on the same plane."

Justice Harlan in his dissent argued that if the issue were not racial equality, it clearly *was* equality of civil rights. "Our Constitution is color blind," he wrote. "The law regards man as man, and takes no account of his surroundings or of his color when his civil rights as guaranteed by the supreme law of the land are involved." The whole doctrine of "separate but equal," Harlan maintained, was "a thin disguise" for imposing "servitude and degradation" on the Negro. Public opinion was undoubtedly on Justice Brown's side; Theodore Roosevelt invited Booker T. Washington to the White House amid a storm of criticism, but in so doing T. R. was far in advance of his time.

The common belief that the Negro was inferior and unequal, however, was absorbed into a larger theory of racial superiority ascribed to the white "Aryan," "Nordic," "Teutonic," or "Anglo-Saxon" civilization with which Americans identified themselves. Gobineau in France, Houston Chamberlain in England, Penka and Cuno in Germany, among others, postulated the existence of a higher, Teutonic type of man who belonged to a superior master race. For that matter, Josiah Nott's book, *The Types of Mankind,* written with G. R. Glidden in 1854 to prove the superiority of white over Negro, was still selling in its ninth edition in 1900. Chamberlain's *Foundations of the Nineteenth Century* (1879) was especially influential in identifying Aryans as Teutons, Teutons as Anglo-Saxons, and the English and Americans as their inheritors. (Chamberlain also proved Jesus to be little, if any, Jewish, and mostly Aryan.) The belief that there were superior and inferior races became allied with the idea of white supremacy, not merely over Negroes, but over all the colored and "non-Aryan" peoples of the world.

George E. Woodberry, Professor of Comparative Literature at Columbia University and a well-known literary critic, stated the matter squarely in his lectures at the Lowell Institute in 1905. "It belongs to a highly developed race," he said, "to become, in a true sense, aristocratic"—not democratically equal, but aristocratically superior. If racial equality were not true, so the reasoning ran, then human equality was not true either, and a government based on that doctrine not likely to be successful. Madison Grant's violently racist book, *The Passing of the Great Race* (1916), besides rehashing Gobineau and Chamberlain, put the issue of racial equality into an American setting by warning the country that "the great race" ("Nordic," a term he introduced) was in danger of burial under a flood of immigration of "lesser races," yellow, black, and non-Nordic white. Lothrop Stoddard's *Rising Tide of Color* (1920) underlined the same warning, and with Grant's books had much to do with the revision of the United States' immigration laws after 1917. The Naturalization Service for many years classified Mexicans, Chinese, Filipinos, Poles, and Hungarians as "races," while during the twenties and thirties the majority of federal legislation governing immigration was based on the assumption that immigrants of certain races or from certain nations were inherently inferior to others.

Much of it still is. The introduction of the quota system in 1921, which stemmed directly from such ideas of racial and national inequalities, has withstood all subsequent attempts to change it. The principle formed the basis for the National Origins Act of 1929 and the Immigration and Nationality Act of 1952, which Congress passed over President Truman's veto. President Kennedy's message to Congress in 1963 called for a complete revision of restrictive legislation based on national origins, but his death suspended efforts to that end. Kennedy, in a message published posthumously, termed the quota system a violation of "the spirit expressed in the Declaration of Independence that 'all men are created equal,'" but the laws still remain in force.

There were no real differences between the Nordic racist theories of 1900 and the Southern white supremacy doctrines of 1850. Both rested on the same prejudicial assumptions and depended for support on pseudo-scientific evidence, most of it discredited by reputable scientists. Not many laymen, however, listened to the anthropologists and biologists who spoke out against the popular concepts of racial inequalities; it was easier to believe Grant and Stoddard, just as it had been convenient to accept Nott and Cartwright. William G. Ripley's

Races of Europe utterly demolished the Nordic myth in 1899; so did Franz Boas' *Mind of Primitive Man* (1911). Archaeologist J. H. Breasted's work, among others, destroyed the concept of a purely Aryan-Nordic civilization. Very few Americans, however, seemed to be listening. South Carolina's Senator McLaurin and Massachusetts' Senator Hoar no doubt reflected the majority opinion when they agreed unctuously in the Senate during the nineties on "the divine right of the Caucasian to govern the inferior races" at home or abroad.

There was little doubt by the nineteen-twenties that public opinion judged Sumner and Darwin right, that the idea of equality in its eighteenth-century sense was outmoded, that attempts to apply it to the realities of modern life were misguided and possibly dangerous. "In the last few years," *The Scientific Monthly* concluded in 1924, "the doctrine of equality has been under attack and *inequality* given the sanction of natural law, ethnology, and science." "The First Law of Nature is inequality," editorialized the *Saturday Evening Post*. "Inequality is an essential part of the scheme of things." Professor F. H. Hankins of Smith College, writing in 1923 on "Individual Differences and Democratic Theory," spoke of the "inevitable inequality among men" which produced, whether one liked it or not, "rank in society, a consequence of the native powers handed down from one generation to the next . . ., determined by their organic inheritance." Edwin Grant Conklin, Professor of Biology at Princeton, summarized the prevailing scientific view of race in his McNair Lectures of 1920 at the University of North Carolina by saying that each race possessed certain identifiable traits. The white race was superior to others "in love of adventure, of discovery, of freedom within the limits of the social order," and the yellow race "in virility, conservatism, and reverence for obligations." While the red, brown, and black races had "characteristic virtues and defects," Conklin failed to list them, concluding that while "every race has contributed something of value to civilization, the white, yellow, and brown races lead, and probably in the order named."

President George Cutten of Colgate told the *New York*

Times in 1923 that Jefferson's phrase was "untrue to facts. It sounds well, but when we attempt to find anything in nature that accords with it, we are doomed to disappointment, for nature's inexorable law is *inequality*." Dr. Cutten then applied his conclusions to political theory, explaining that since "only a small proportion of people in our country, or any other, have sufficient mental ability to govern themselves," equality simply led to "confusion and anarchy." A "well-known capitalist," as the *Century Magazine* identified him, was bluntly eloquent about the same point. The ideal of equality, "borrowed from the French encyclopaedists and that madman Rousseau," was "unfitted to modern society." It was high time, he concluded, to remind the inferior and unequal of "the comfort and joy of knowing one's place," and it ought to be realized that "talk of equality is nonsense,"

ambition is folly; that greedy, discontented, pushing people are ill-bred; that those who can become rich do so; and those who cannot become rich do not do so by taking thought. Thinking will not make you equal to your betters, but it may make you wretched. The pygmy cannot stretch his stature by wishing.

The forthright sincerity of the *Century's* unnamed capitalist was echoed more subtly by the elitist "new Humanism" that swept across the intellectual horizon of the twenties and thirties. Expressed most clearly by Paul Elmer More, Irving Babbitt, Stuart P. Sherman, Ralph Adams Cram, and George Santayana, humanism updated the Federalistic theme of Adams and Ames, explaining the virtues of a class-structured society which placed power in the hands of a superior natural aristocracy of talent, taste, and restraint. More, who of the group developed the most comprehensive social theory, had something of the Calvinist in him; he found mass human nature weak, vacillating, untrustworthy, in need of some kind of aristocracy to lead it. A believer in what he called "an outspoken class consciousness," More adamantly opposed the levelling reforms of the era's progressives and social reformers. "We need to be . . . guided by the discriminations of reason," he wrote in *Aristocracy and Justice* (1915), "to control our equalitarian relaxation . . . by a stricter idea of the distinctions of value." Cram called equality a "mere myth" —progress always came from "the supreme leadership of the few, seers, prophets, captains of men, and so it will always be." Equalitarianism, critic T. S. Eliot wrote with weary contempt, is simply incompatible "with that which makes life worth living." Irving Babbitt spoke out for class distinctions as More had hoped others would. Babbitt's *Democracy and Leadership* (1924) proposed a kind of Adams-like aristocracy that would guide democracy without destroying it. Jefferson's concept of a wise majority he considered a "pernicious conceit;" there would always be leaders, and the only way to save twentieth-century democracy from its equalitarian errors was to recognize "some form of the aristocratic principle." The idea of equality was a legacy from Locke and Rousseau (especially the latter, whom he passionately hated) and quite irrelevant to the facts of modern life.

Babbitt's attack on equalitarianism was direct and incisive, but the most thorough contemporary critique of the concept was that of Arthur Twining Hadley, economist-president of Yale, who chose "The Conflict Between Liberty and Equality" as the topic of his West Memorial Lectures at Stanford University in 1924. Hadley did not argue that Jefferson's phrase was wrong; he considered it right and proper in its application to eighteenth-century conditions. Since the revolutionary generation needed "a convenient phrase for justifying acts of armed resistance to England," the Declaration furnished it. Actually, Hadley believed, the system founded on the Declaration seemed to work; the doctrine of equality it stated helped to form the foundation for a stable, prosperous, and democratic government. However, over the next hundred years, Hadley explained, American society changed and its needs changed. Those theories so eloquently stated in 1776 no longer fitted the requirements of life in 1876, and as time passed they seemed to be increasingly incompatible. In twentieth-century society, Hadley believed, you cannot have both liberty and equality. If you choose liberty, you create inequalities; if you choose perfect equality, you infringe on the liberty of some to provide equality for others. This was especially true in the economic sector of society, where competition automatically created inequality. (Herbert Hoover later put it concisely, "No economic equality can survive the working of biological inequality.") Liberty is dynamic, equality static; liberty motivates itself, equality needs enforcement. This to Hadley was the great issue of his time—which should the United States choose?

The choice was not so clear, perhaps, as Hadley saw it, for as it happened Americans never made it. Instead they compromised it, as they are prone to do with apparently inescapable alternatives. Thomas Carver, another prominent economist, in the same year as Hadley's Stanford speech, pointed a way out. There were, he said, at least two kinds of equality possible; both (though seemingly antithetical) could successfully operate in American society at the same time. First, there was equality of opportunity to improve one's condition, to rise in the world, to gain more wealth, to develop one's talents. Americans loved this and believed in it. Second, Carver explained, there was an equality of actual *condition* (that the reformers had long demanded) which could be attained by social regulations such as equal pay for equal work, fair and minimum wages, laws of health and education and morality, and so on. Americans believed in this kind of equality too, as they had always believed in fair play and aid for the underdog. One could compete to produce inequality; one could also be guaranteed a kind of across-the-board equality at the same time. One could follow both Sumner and Ward, Spencer and Jefferson, and somehow make it work. What Carver explained was, in effect, what the American himself had already unconsciously worked out. This concept of a double equality, of a blending into social and economic unity of mutually conflicting principles, continues still to dominate American thinking about the matter.

There is substantial agreement on all levels of American society that men are not equal, certainly not in talent or ability. John Dewey and Robert A. Taft, standing at opposite ends of the political spectrum, agreed on this in the 1930's, Dewey explaining that a belief in equality did not mean "equality of natural endowments," Taft that men are always unequal in "mental power, character, and energy." There is also virtually unanimous agreement that all men are equal before the law, with the right to the same justice as others; that all men are politically equal, with the right of universal suffrage; that all men must have equality of opportunity, with the right to exploit one's endowments to their natural limits. It is assumed that legal and political equality are accomplished facts (except in portions of the South and Southwest) which leaves the third kind of equality—opportunity—as the variety most frequently at stake in contemporary America.

What exactly does equality in this sense mean in modern life? Broadly, it generally is taken to mean equality of access to the normal rewards of American society, an absence of obstructions in the way of anyone's reasonable chance for a decent living and a meaningful life. Equality, writes Chairman John A. Hannah of the Civil Rights Commission, is "an absence of artificial or arbitrary barriers to man's spiritual, mental, and political development." Or as President John Kennedy wrote in 1962, "I do not mean to say that all men are equal in their ability, character, or motivation. I do say that every American should be given a fair chance to develop all the talents he may have." Senator Barry Goldwater, whose political philosophy lies far to the right from that of the late President, said almost exactly the same thing while campaigning in 1964:

When the Declaration declares that "all men are created equal" it doesn't mean that their accomplishments, skills, achievements, or ambitions are equal. No, on these levels, there is no equality. There is only equality of opportunity.

The traditional analogy employed in discussions of equality of opportunity in modern American life has been that of a Darwinian race in which all are entitled to an equal start but in which there must be winners and losers in an unequal finish. "All start fair," wrote commentator Douglas MacLeane in 1921,

but however fairly contested, life's race is to the swift and life's battle to the strong. Free competition is bound to manifest inequality of gifts. Given equal opportunity, but not equal natural advantage, and the weak necessarily go to the wall.

Herbert Hoover, speaking at Kings' Mountain in 1930, explained the idea thus:

We train the runners, through free and universal education, we strive to give them an equal start, our government is the umpire of fairness. The winner is he who shows the most conscientious training, the greatest ability, the strongest character.

Senator Robert Taft, writing in 1939 as the voice of responsible conservatism, defined equality of opportunity as the provision for all of a free public education and legislation guaranteeing "a minimum living." After that, each was on his own:

The American way of life certainly does not guarantee equality in mental power or in character or in energy. It has only guaranteed that a man who had the necessary qualities might rise in public life and acquire a greater influence, a greater fame, a greater power, than his fellows.

If we "recognize the existence of unequal abilities," said industrialist Benjamin Fairless later, "we must recognize the need for unequal rewards." All that equality of opportunity means in today's world, according to conservative Felix Morley, is "opportunity for every talented, energetic, and law-abiding individual to forge ahead."

By emphasizing equality of opportunity—an equal start in the race—over those other kinds of equality possible in modern society, twentieth-century America has been able to absorb the Darwinian-Spencerian ethic into the stream of traditional, natural-rights equalitarian thinking. If nature rewards the swift and strong, those who are neither cannot complain if they have an equal chance to disclose their shortcomings. The distinctive American blend of frontier experience and individualism, long before Darwin, convinced the American of the values of open competition. Allowing the individual freedom to make best use of his talents is an old American tradition, underlying a powerful belief in the validity of competitive performance. Equality of opportunity to compete is a necessary condition for it.

The deep, almost religious interest of the American in competitive sports has been a major factor in conditioning the public to an acceptance of this concept of equality; it is not accidental that the normal American way of presenting the idea is almost always in terms of an athletic contest. This kind of equality, furthermore, has proved to be the most believable and workable kind, consistent with the realities of modern life. One can live with the idea that men are unequal in talents, and at the same time claim for each man an equal chance to use them. To conceive of equality in this manner allows each individual the liberty to compete or not to compete as he wishes, in responding to the equal opportunities presented to him.

Yet the matter of equal opportunity today is not so simple as the popular interpretations of it make it seem. For equality means something more than fair competition among unequals, as theologian Reinhold Niebuhr has explained. It means also that there are to be no invidious distinctions nor prejudicial discriminations in treatment among individuals, whatever their inequalities of talent. "It is not that all men are created equal," he writes, "but the statement is a symbol of the fact that all men are to be treated equally, within the terms of the gradations of function which every healthy society uses for its organization." By thus extending the idea of equality beyond competitive theory into actual social terms, Niebuhr brings equality of opportunity into a civil and economic context, as recent civil rights and fair economic practices legislation has done. Nor is it, however easily the phrase rolls off the pen, a simple task to furnish everyone that "equal start in the race." The start may be equal; sometimes other conditions of the race are not. To provide an equal chance for all, without favoring those who are in the best position to take advantage of it, is not easy in contemporary society. A New York Puerto Rican, a Texas Mexican, or a Mississippi Negro, for example, are obviously not in positions to make the most of those opportunities which society presumably presents equally to all Americans. To suppose otherwise is sheer nonsense. There are and long have been powerful elements in American society dedicated to narrowing or eliminating exactly such equal opportunities to certain racial, national, and economic groups, and they have been relatively successful at it. Whatever the acceptance of the idea of equality within the American credo, it still remains the substance of things hoped for, certainly not accomplished. While the majority of Americans may agree that men are unequal, those inequalities often may rest on color or language or religious faith, rather than on differences of ability or potential.

As a result, the most important trend in recent American life has been the attempt to attain in it a greater equality of actual condition, involving a rejection of the "contest" image customarily used to explain what equality means. The analogy is not wholly relevant to the social realities of modern life, some feel, because it postulates certain conditions which do not exist. If the ideal of equality is to provide to all the essential conditions for full individual development, then such matters as substandard housing, inadequate education, malnutrition, and unemployment bear close relation to any discussion of equality in today's society. Society can provide an equal start for the well-nourished and well-educated, and the ignorant and hungry—but the race is utterly unequal and the winners are determined before it starts. The order of finish in the Darwinian race may not always be a true index to the talents of the contestants.

"Equality of opportunity is not an adequate goal for the social order," *The Christian Century* editorialized in 1932. "Our traditional ideal has been fair competition for a limited number of prizes, and the time has come when that concept of society does not meet the moral demands." It is better to strive to create "equality of *condition,* of the needs of life," wrote sociologist E. H. Goss in 1936, than "to satisfy the competitive urge and reward the few." Why should some, others ask, by virtue of being blessed at birth with superior mental or physical equipment, or fortunate enough to have been raised in a superior environment, be entitled to greater chances for reward? People are born into very different circumstances with very different heredities and equipped with very unequal gifts—ought a man to be penalized in the so-called "equal" race for rewards by being stupid or unhealthy, or colored or poor?

The point that the modern critic of equality makes is simply that there are certain inequalities which are undeserved discriminations and which quite possibly deserve redress. Granting that great inequalities exist among men, might it not be socially desirable to provide compensating opportunities for those of unequal abilities? One of the primary objectives of the government since *The Christian Century's* editorial (and also one opposed by many) has been the attempt to establish greater equality of *condition* as an essential requirement for greater equality of *opportunity*—ranging from the Federal Social Security Act itself through fair housing, fair employment, educational aid, slum clearance, and health and insurance legislation.

This concept of equality has developed in large part out of the conditions of contemporary mass society. The ultimate aim of equality of condition is to provide in equal quantity for the mass all those things once possessed only by the elite. The kind of life lived by the few, complete with its values, rights, norms, privileges, and culture, is thus to be extended throughout society on an equal basis. The extension of equality in this sense is a distinguishing characteristic of twentieth-century life, made possible by mass production and mass consumption, through which it may—hopefully—be made real. Where all the good things of life may be made to exist in profusion, everyone may expect to participate equally in their consumption. That perceptive observer of American life, Alexis de Tocqueville, noted the beginnings of this trend long ago. Remarking on the fierce equalitarianism of Jackson's time, he thought he saw a reason for it in the fact that whereas "once none but the wealthy had watches," now in America "everybody has one in his pocket." The first signs of what appeared in the twentieth century as the so-called "revolution of rising expectations," another name for equality of condition, lay there.

The most important effect of this has been the recent extension of the idea of equality of opportunity, and of condition, to the American Negro. That it is recent is attested to by the fact that until the establishment of the Civil Rights Commission in 1948 there seemed to be little public discussion of the issue. In 1936 it was possible for Professor William Russell of Columbia, for example, to write an entire book, *Liberty and Equality in America,* without once mentioning the Negro American. When philosopher T. V. Smith, then a member of Congress, and Senator Robert A. Taft of Ohio engaged in a radio debate on current issues, later published in 1939 as *Foundations of Democracy,* the portions of the discussion concerning equality made no mention of the Negro. Nor was it until 1938, in *Missouri ex rel Gaines v. Canada,* that a major case involving Negro equality reached the Supreme Court.

The Second World War, of course, and the postwar surge toward independence of the colored peoples of Africa and Asia, were great catalytic factors in precipitating the issue. The United States after 1941 suddenly became aware of the international and interracial implications of Jefferson's simple phrase, and equally aware of the irony involved in fighting a war against a racist philosophy abroad while practicing something resembling it at home. America's image of herself as the champion of the democratic way of life did not square with the disturbing realities of racial prejudice and inequality. The single most powerful domestic issue of the past decade as a result has been the Negroes' demand for full equality, in the full sense of the term. No issue since the Civil War has so tested the theory and practice of equality in American life.

Inescapably, the discussion of Negro equality is still entangled with racist thought, for the principle of inequality has traditionally been associated with racial inferiority. Segregation always implies inequality—this has been the drift of the Supreme Court's interpretations since 1938—and however unacceptable the racist concept of superiority remains to scientists, it is still closely linked with inequality and segregation in the popular mind. Anthropologists almost unanimously agree that mankind displays "psychic unity," meaning that all individuals, basically, behave the same way in similar situations, whatever their race. Differences of behavior among races, scientists have concluded, are results of cultural conditioning rather than of inherent superiorities or inferiorities peculiar to any race. No reputable tests have shown one race to be unequal to another in innate mental capacity; differences of intelligence appear instead to show differences of educational opportunity rather than of inherent mental characteristics. A UNESCO group of seventeen scientists concluded in August, 1964, for example, that

Neither in the field of hereditary potentialities concerning the overall intelligence and the capacity for cultural development, nor in that of physical traits, is there any justification for the concept of "inferior" and "superior" races. The peoples of the world today appear to possess equal biological potentialities for attaining any civilization level.

A great deal of the contemporary opposition to Negro equality is deeply rooted in a belief in white racial superiority, notwithstanding the conclusions of science. The Citizens' Councils of the Southern states apparently hold substantially the same beliefs today concerning racial inequalities as the proslavery writers held in the early nineteenth century. The Reverend Carey Daniels' book, *God the Original Segregationist*, which sold more than a million copies its first year, is little more than a refurbishing of the Biblical proslavery arguments of the eighteen-fifties. Tom P. Brady of Mississippi, in his *Black Monday* (1954) published as a protest against the Supreme Court's decision in *Brown v. Board of Education,* simply restated the old multiple-creation theory first put forward in 1845, postulating the creation of three separate races, white, yellow, and black, of which the black, "like the modern lizard, evolved not." The Negro, according to Brady, has "an inherent deficiency in mental ability, a psychological and temperamental inadequacy that requires his separation from white society and limits severely his participation in its rights and processes." Professor Henry Garrett and his pupil Dr. Audrey Shuey, on the basis of certain tests, have similarly concluded that there are definite differences in Negro and white intelligence. However, among scientists, Drs. Garrett and Shuey seem to be virtually alone in this; Dr. Shuey's study in fact has been unequivocally rejected by a panel of scientists as "unsupported by any substantial scientific evidence."

Nevertheless, it is certain that whatever the scientific evidence presented, or whatever Biblical interpretations one may choose, a very large number of Americans, North and South, feel that the Negro race is inherently inferior and therefore not to be treated as equals in certain areas of American life. If, as publisher David Lawrence of *U. S. News and World Report* explains, "God has created men of different colors, just as he created birds of different colors," and everyone knows that "birds of a feather flock together," there are many like him who assume that this justifies the existence of inequalities based on race.

How differently ideas of racial differences can operate within the same framework of reference can be illustrated by the example of two Southern reactions to the Supreme Court decisions of 1954. R. Carter Pittman of Alabama, in a speech to the State Bar Association reminiscent of the Southern anti-Jefferson diatribes of a century before, claimed that the Virginian, in his exposition of the ideal of equality, "defaced" the truth by "perverting" it into "a powerful appeal to the simple-minded peasants." The Jeffersonian philosophy of equality, he continued, was forced on a helpless South "by carpet-bag doctors of pseudo-science" who were soon "run out" so that Alabama could recapture the original purity of its slaveholding society. The Jeffersonian concept, in Pittman's view, was later reinforced by "the alien equality philosophy of Karl Marx" which today thrives nowhere "except in four Communist countries and within a secret chamber of a strange Supreme Court of the United States." Yet over against the mindless racism of Pittman one may set the statement made not long after by novelist William Faulkner, a thoughtful and sensitive observer and interpreter of the South, caught like his homeland in the struggle between ancient wrongs and new beliefs. "To live in the world of 1955," he wrote, "and be against equality of race or color is like living in Alaska and being against the snow. To stand against equality on grounds of race and color can invite a situation in which the whole white and/or free world as we know it can disappear."

It is Faulkner, with quiet and moving eloquence, who has perhaps summarized best how the American of our time—despite the invective of the racist and the cynicism of the elitist—would define that phrase coined in Philadelphia almost two centuries ago:

There is no such thing as equality *per se,* but equality *to*—to equal right and opportunity to make the best use one can of one's life within one's capacity and capability, without fear of injustice or oppression or threat of violence.

If this is what twentieth-century America believes, and strives to realize, one feels that Thomas Jefferson would have approved.

BIBLIOGRAPHICAL ACKNOWLEDGEMENTS

Anyone who wishes to write on the subject of equality in America must acknowledge indebtedness to T. V. Smith, whose *American Philosophy of Equality* (Chicago, 1927) is a seminal book in the field; his debate with Robert A. Taft, published as *Foundations of Democracy* (New York, 1939) provides insight into the views of both men. Another classic treatment is Henry Alonzo Myers, *Are Men Equal?* (New York, 1945) which though written from a doctrinaire point of view, is thoughtful and stimulating. Sanford A.

Lakoff, *Equality in Political Philosophy* (Cambridge, Mass., 1964) is an excellent general source of historical information; George L. Abernethy, *The Idea of Equality* (Richmond, 1959) is a useful anthology of selections with running commentaries. Clinton Rossiter, *Seedtime of the Republic* (New York, 1952) is the best source of information on the colonial and eighteenth-century American view of equality; Ralph Barton Perry, *Puritanism and Democracy* (New York, 1944) is equally useful for the Puritan's view. Alan P. Grimes, *American Political Thought* (New York, 1955) contains a superb brief treatment of Jacksonian equality, while his *Equality in America: Religion, Race and the Urban Majority* (New York, 1964) is an excellent consideration of the concept in its modern setting. E. L. Godkin, in *Unforeseen Tendencies of Democracy* (New York, 1898) has a penetrating chapter on equality in the nineteenth century, while Abbott Lawrence Lowell, *Essays on Government* (New York, 1889) and Nicholas Murray Butler, *True and False Democracy* (New York, 1907) are illustrative contemporary treatments. Among dozens of other essays on the topic, most useful are John Tucker, "The Goal of Equality," *Atlantic* CXII (October, 1913) 480-90; Carrol D. Wright, "Have We Equality of Opportunity?" *Forum* XIX (May, 1895) 301-12; and Henry C. Merwin, "The American Notion of Equality," *Atlantic* LXXX (September, 1897) 354-63; Thomas Henry Huxley's article, "On the Natural Inequality of Man," *Nineteenth Century* CXLV (January, 1890) 1-13, is a good example of the Huxleian influence on American thinking. Charles C. Alexander, "Prophet of Racism, Madison Grant," *Phylon* XXIII (Spring, 1962) 73-90, is a useful essay on Grant; however, Grant's and Stoddard's books are still easily available in many libraries. William Stanton, *The Leopard's Spots: Scientific Attitudes Toward Race in America 1815-1859* (Chicago, 1960) ; and Thomas Gossett, *Race: The History of an American Idea* (Dallas, 1964) are definitive studies of racism and equality. Jacques Barzun, *Race: A Study in Modern Superstition* (New York, 1937) is an excellent general book, and Oscar Handlin, *Race and Nationality in American Life* (Boston, 1957) is the best historical study of racism's impact on American social ideas. Robert E. Cushman, *Civil Liberties in the United States* (Ithaca, 1956) has a chapter on the legal aspects of racial discrimination, while Leo Pfeffer, *The Liberties of an American* (New York, 1956) reviews the court decisions relating to Negro equality. The proslavery argument against equality is reviewed in Russel B. Nye, *Fettered Freedom* (East Lansing, 1964) .

Recent discussions of equality are varied and prolific. John W. Gardner, *Excellence: Can We Be Equal and Excellent Too?* (New York, 1961) is a thoughtful discussion of the problem of equality and mediocrity; see also Claude M. Fuess, "The Retreat from

Excellence," *Saturday Review* XLIII (March 26, 1960) 21-3. The issue of equality of opportunity and what it means is treated in such articles as Herbert Spiegelberg, "A Defense of Human Equality," *Philosophical Review* LIII (March, 1944) 101-24; Benjamin Fairless, "Quality versus Equality," *Vital Speeches* XXIV (September, 1958) 759-62; George X. Biddle, "The Curse of Outworn Ideals," *Century* XCIX (March, 1920) 717-20; George B. Cutten, "Nature's Inexorable Law," *New York Times,* July 1, 1923; F. H. Hankins, "Individual Differences and Democratic Theory," *Political Science Quarterly* XXXVIII (September, 1923) 388-412; see also Thomas Hewes, *Equality of Opportunity* (Pittsfield, Mass., 1959). Arthur Twining Hadley's Stanford lectures were published as *The Conflict Between Liberty and Equality* (New York, 1925); his Oxford lectures, following parallel ideas, appeared as *Undercurrents in American Politics* (New Haven, 1927). In this connection, Thomas N. Carver's essay "Economic Equality," *Quarterly Journal of Economics* XXXIX (May, 1925), 473-7, is pertinent. Robert Taft's *A Republican Program* (New York, 1939), and Herbert Hoover's *Challenge to Liberty* (New York, 1934) present their views of equality of opportunity. A thoughtful contemporary essay by a brilliant theologian is Reinhold Niebuhr's "Liberty and Equality," *Yale Review* XLVII (September, 1957) 1-14. Contemporary studies of race are not hard to find. Claude E. Stipe, "Race and Culture," *Journal of the American Scientific Affiliation* XVI (June, 1964) 36-43, is an excellent summary of the various modern theories of racial equality. Tom P. Brady, *Black Monday* (Winona, Mississippi, 1954) is a prime example of the Southern extremist point of view; R. C. Pittman's speech of July 16, 1954, reprinted in *Vital Speeches* XX (October, 1954) 754-61, is another. William Faulkner's statement, "To Claim Freedom is Not Enough," appeared in *The Christian Century,* November 30, 1955.

Index

Clark, Champ, 200
Clark, George Rogers, 228
Clark, John Bates: critic of *laissez-faire*, 136-137
Clark, John M., 144-145, 149
Clark, Joseph: task of the individual, 252
Clay, Henry: neo-mercantilism of, 123
Clayton Act, 144
Cleveland, Grover: veto of drought aid, 132; on critics of *laissez-faire*, 135
Cleveland, Harland: the U.S. and the U.N., 98
Colden Cadwallader, 263
Cole, Thomas, 268, 274-275
Colonies: divisive factors in, 54-55; uniting factors, 55-56
Colonists, American: building new society, 3; common heritage, 7; belief in progress, 8
Columbus, Christopher: on beauty of America, 256; interest in reports of gold, 257
Combe, George, 330
Commission on National Goals, 167-168
Committee to Defend America by Aiding the Allies, 93, 177
Committee for Economic Development, 155
Commons, John R., 139, 145
Communications: advances in intercolonial, 55-56; developments in, 72
Competitive principle, 105, 107-109; origins of, 109; depression and revised thinking on, 149
Comte, Auguste: mentioned, 21; and social science, 22-23
Condorcet, Marie: on progress, 2; on perfectibility of man, 4; mentioned, 3
Conklin, Edwin Grant: McNair Lectures, 341
Conservation Yearbook (1962), 298
Constitution, 46, 113; a nationalizing force, 64
Constitution, 65
Constitutional Convention, 49-50
Continental Congress, 54, 59, 169
Conwell, Russell: individual opportunity, 230
Cooley, Charles Horton: effects of Spencerian struggle on society, 142; mentioned, 246, 247

Coolidge, Archibald: America as a world power, 85
Coolidge, Calvin, 90
Cooper, James Fenimore: quoted, 19; nature in works of, 273; thoughts on democratic equality, 322-324
Cooper, Thomas, 327
Cornwallis' surrender, 7
Corwin, Edward S.: quoted, 133
Cotton, T. G.: on progress, 25
Council of Economic Advisers, 156
Council of nations: suggested by Wilkie, 95
Coxe, Tench: asylum theme, 180
Cram, Ralph Adams, 342, 343
Crane, Stephen, 29
Creation, Multiple: Nott's theory of, 329-330
Crèvecoeur, St. Jean de (John Hector St. John): assimilative process, 56-57; mentioned, 51, 263
Croly, Herbert: on American optimism, 1; possibility of ideal democratic society, 28; *Promise of American Life*, 144; constructive individualism, 236-237; principle of 20th century individualism, 240; factor of association, 246; mentioned, 228
Cromwellian revolution, 47
Curti, Merle, 180
Cutten, George: inequality natural law, 341-342

Dana, Charles A.: defends *laissez-faire* philosophy, 135
Dana, Richard Henry: on Wordsworth, 268
Daniels, Carey, 351
Darwin, Charles: mentioned, 21; change in human thought about itself, 219-220
Darwinian explanation of life and *laissez-faire*, 129
Darwinian hypotheses: and progress, 20
Darwinian theory: equated with progress, 21-22; made compatible with Christianity, 22; in Spencerian economics, 130, 131; and equality of the races, 333
Daughters of the American Revolution, 79
Davenport, Russell: "team" concept, 250
Dawson, William Leon, 284

Index

Index

MacDonald, William: favors isolationism, 82

Machine Age: impact of, 218

Machines and progress of mankind, 13-14

Mackay, Charles: on the American, 47

MacLeane, Douglas: equality Darwinian, 346

MacLeish, Archibald: on preamble to Declaration, 167; postwar disillusion, 201; *The Land of the Free*, 244

MacNeice, Louis, 243

Madison, James, 317

Mahan, Alfred Thayer: independent nationality, 81; mentioned, 198

Maine, Henry, 333

Manifest destiny, 197

Mann, Horace: on the common school, 15; individualistic in education, 224-225

Marsh, George Perkins: on advances in scientific knowledge, 17-18; answer to superabundance myth, 281-282

Marsh, James: on discovery of truth, 215

Marshall, Alfred: economics of, 145-146

Marshall, John: biography of Washington, 69

Marshall, Robert: on contact with nature, 299

Marryat, Frederick: quoted *ix;* on basic equality in America, 321

Martineau, Harriet: visit to America, 12

Mason, George: on geographical isolation of America, 183

Massachusetts: mass public education, 15

Mather, Cotton, 51, 109, 259-260

Mather, Increase: *Remarkable Providences*, 189

Mathews, F. Schuyler, 284

Mathews, William: self-reliant individualism, 231

May, Erskine, 333

Mayo, A. D.: divine intervention, 190

Maxey, Chief Justice (Pennsylvania), 246

McClintock, Samuel: providence and Revolutionary victory, 190

McClure, William: America destined to pre-eminence, 68

McGuffey, William H.: sense of mission in Reader, 173

McKenna, Hinky-Dink, 231

Mead, Margaret: the contemporary world, 40

Melville, Herman: quoted, 164; insufficiency of self, 216

Mercantilism, 111-112

Mercenaries: use of, 44

Merriam, Charles E.: on progressive political philosophy, 27

Merriam, William: on 1900 census, 29

Mexican War, 198

Migration, internal, 71-72

Military caste: lack of, in America, 46

Military Order of the Loyal Legion, 79

Mill, John Stuart: economic philosophy, 124-125, 126-127, 129

Miller, A. C.: sick economy, 147

Mills, Robert: quoted, 67-68

Mineral Lands Act, 291

Mirabeau, Honoré G. V. R., 112

Mission, American sense of: search for national purpose, 164-165; historical necessity, 165-167; out of people at large, 167-168; constancy of, 168; American democracy a model, 168-172; toward millennium of liberty, 172-177; versus concept of example, 177-179; serve as refuge, 179-181; American sense of difference, 181-185; Americans divinely chosen, 185-189; divine guidance in national affairs, 189-191; new theories of nationalism, 191-192; Puritans and divine design, 192-193; native-born and national purpose, 193-194; shift of ideals, 194-195; national purpose, 19th century, 195-197; manifest destiny, 197-201; First World War, 201; national purpose, 20th century, 202-206

Missouri ex rel Gaines v. Canada, 350

Mitchell, Samuel, 263

Mitchell, Wesley C., 145

Moley, Raymond: inevitable participation in international affairs, 94

Monroe, James, 184

Monroe Doctrine, 184

Moore, Tom: opinion of U.S., 50

Index